It's Saturday Morning!

CELEBRATING THE GOLDEN ERA OF CARTOONS

1960s – 1990s

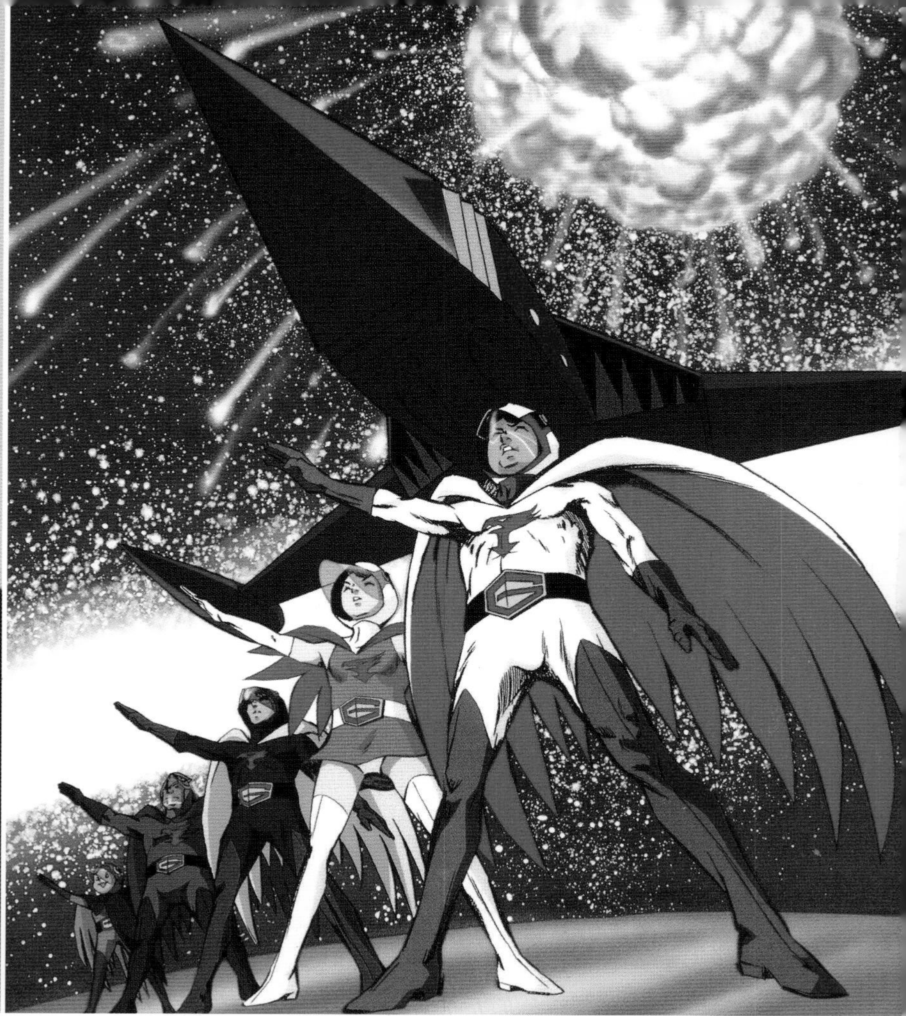

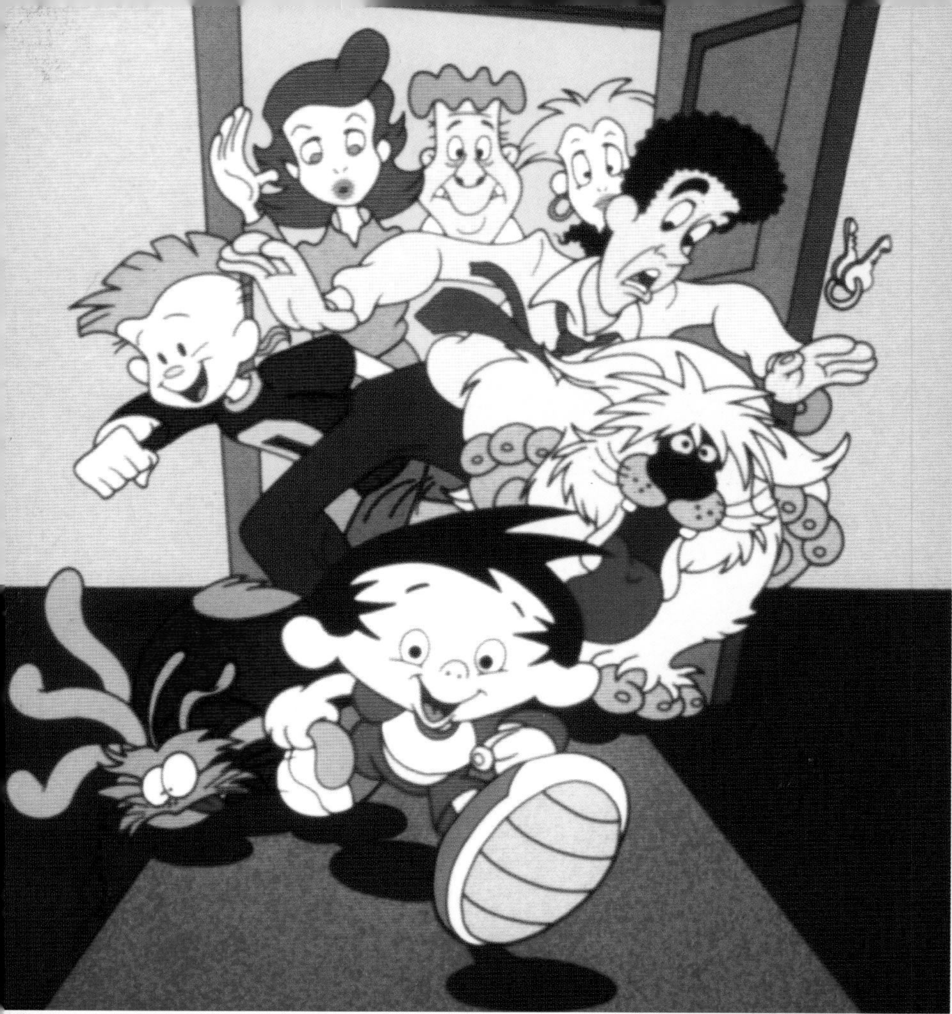

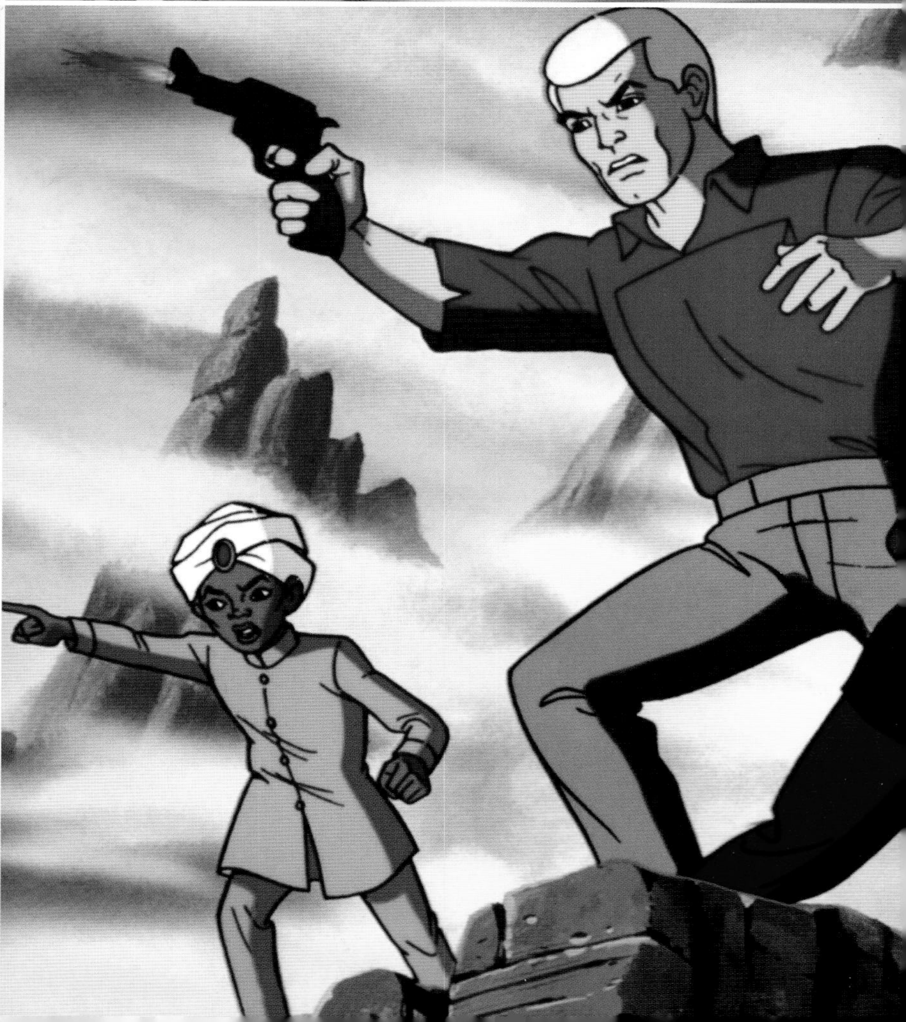

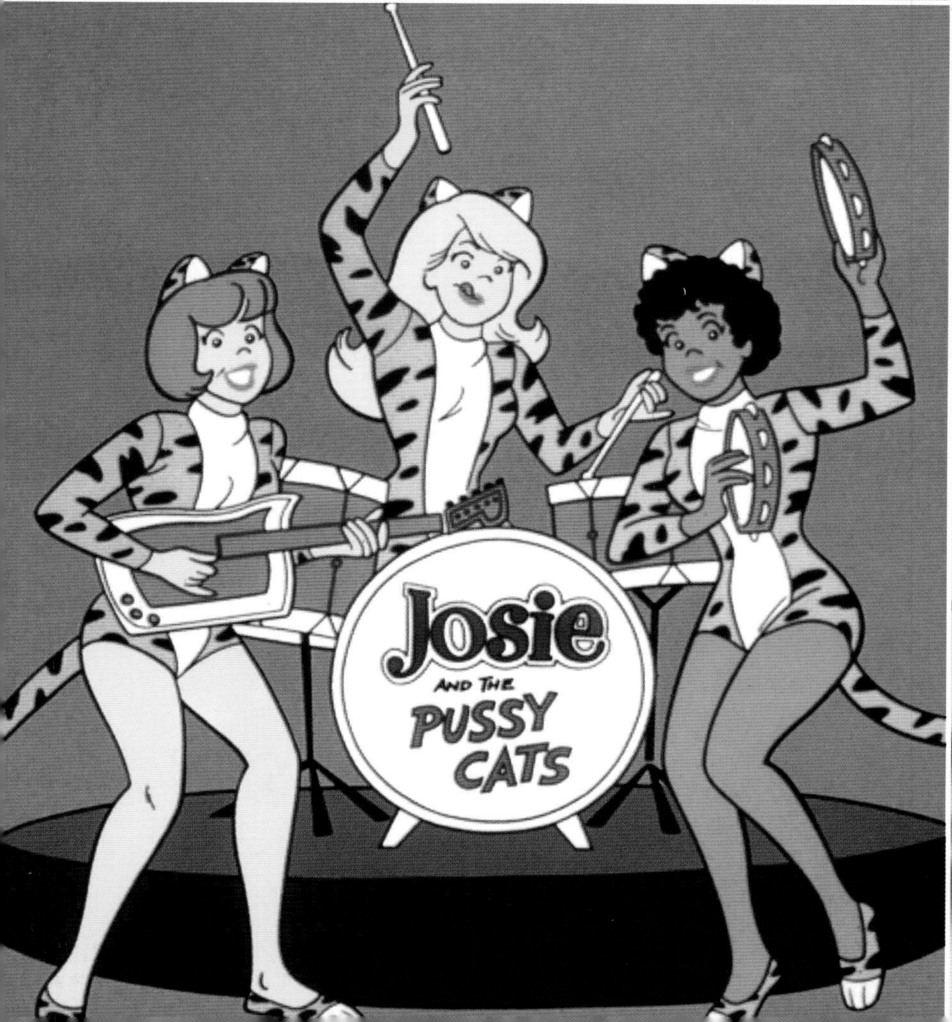
Josie
AND THE
PUSSY
CATS

It's Saturday Morning!

CELEBRATING THE GOLDEN ERA OF CARTOONS

1960s – 1990s

Joe Garner and Michael Ashley

Foreword by Howie Mandel

Brimming with creative inspiration, how-to projects, and useful information to enrich your everyday life, Quarto Knows is a favorite destination for those pursuing their interests and passions. Visit our site and dig deeper with our books into your area of interest: Quarto Creates, Quarto Cooks, Quarto Homes, Quarto Lives, Quarto Drives, Quarto Explores, Quarto Gifts, or Quarto Kids.

© 2018 Quarto Publishing Group USA Inc.
Text © 2018 Joe Garner and Michael Ashley

Published in 2018 by becker&mayer! books, an imprint of The Quarto Group,
11120 NE 33rd Place, Suite 201, Bellevue, WA 98004 USA.

www.QuartoKnows.com

becker&mayer! books titles are also available at discount for retail, wholesale, promotional, and bulk purchase. For details, contact the Special Sales Manager by email at specialsales@quarto.com or by mail at The Quarto Group, Attn: Special Sales Manager, 100 Cummings Center Suite 265D, Beverly, MA 01915 USA.

21 22 23 24 25   6 5 4 3 2

ISBN: 978-0-7603-6294-5

Library of Congress Cataloging-in-Publication Data available upon request.

Design: Sam Dawson
Design Assistance: Katie Benezra and Megan Sugiyama
TV icon illustrations: Russ Gray
Editorial: Delia Greve
Production: Tom Miller
Image research: David Perkins

Printed, manufactured, and assembled in Singapore, 05/21.

Every effort has been made to track down the copyright holders and primary sources of the images. If you believe there is an omission or incorrect citation please contact becker&mayer! at QuartoKnows.com so that we may update for later editions.

306414

Joe Garner Dedication

To all the animators, writers, directors, and actors who made
Saturday mornings so magical.

Michael Ashley Dedication

To my brother Kevin. Watching Saturday morning cartoons
with you were my golden years.

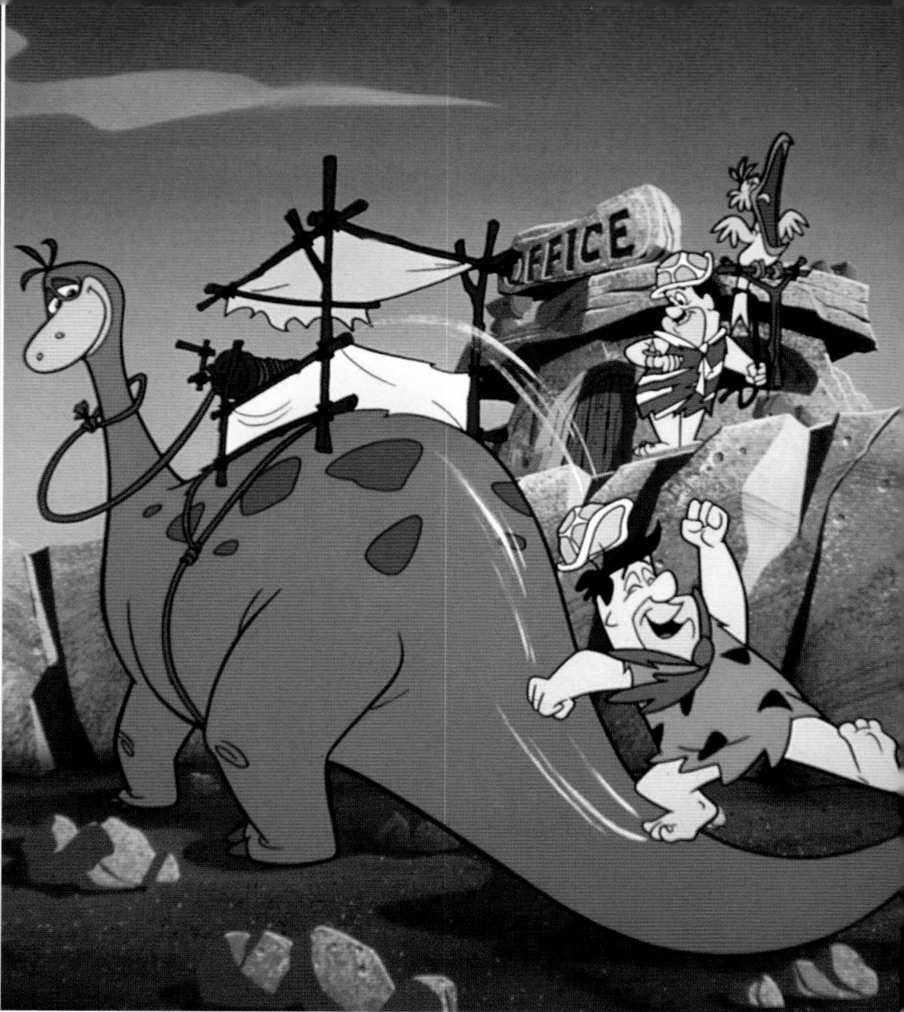
OFFICE
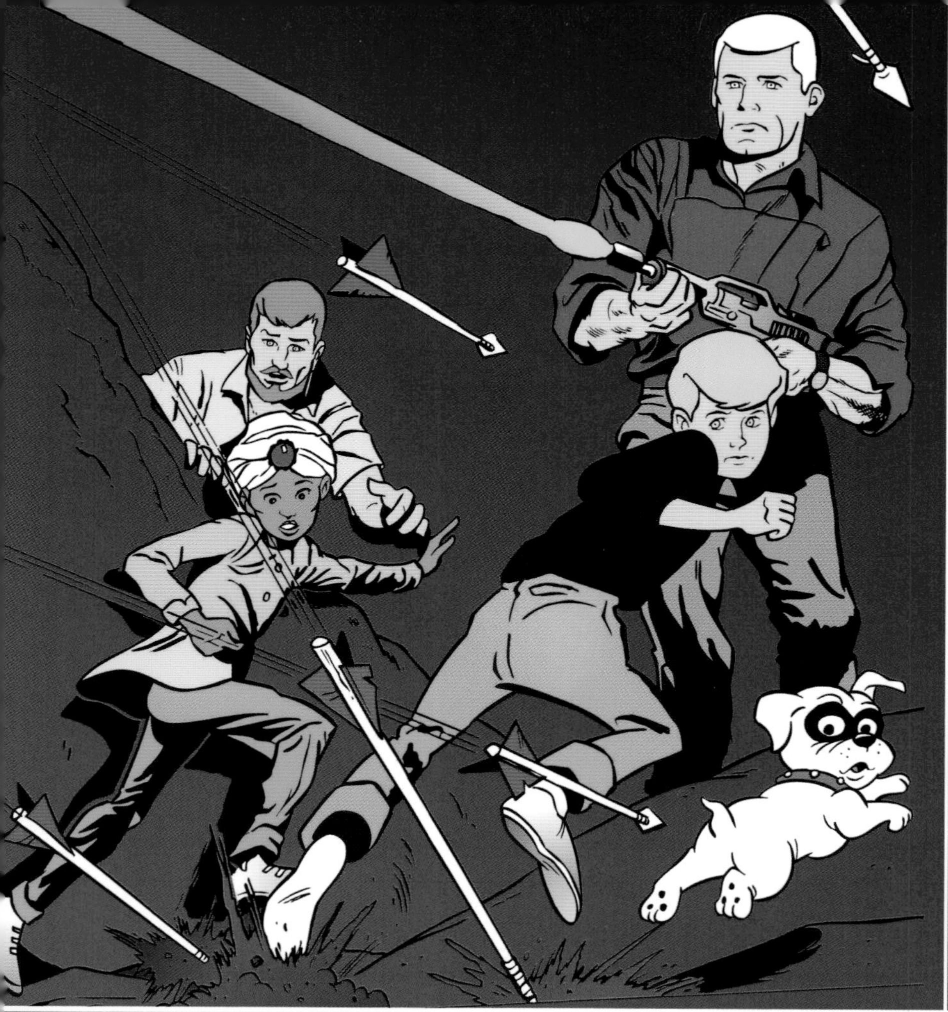
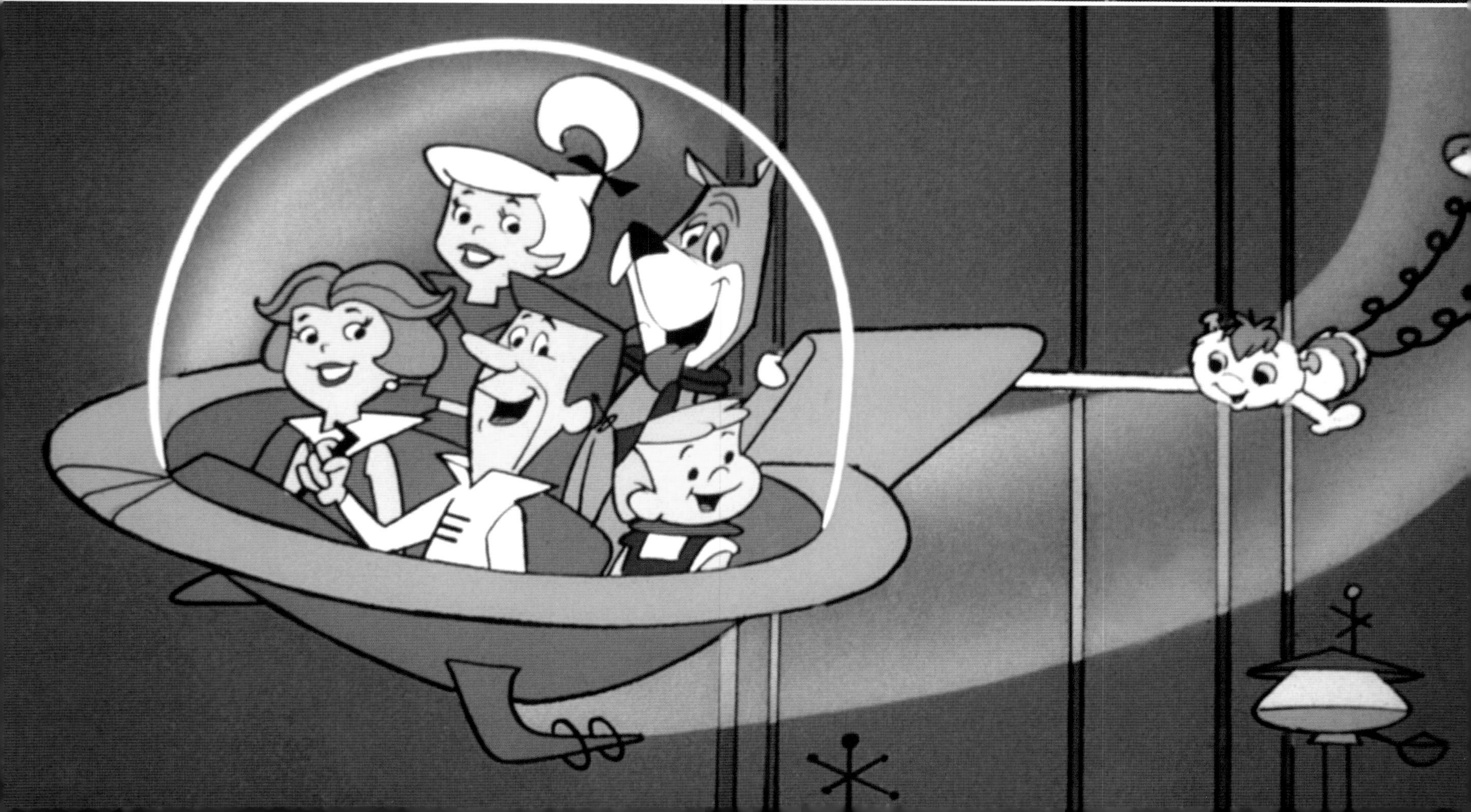

Contents

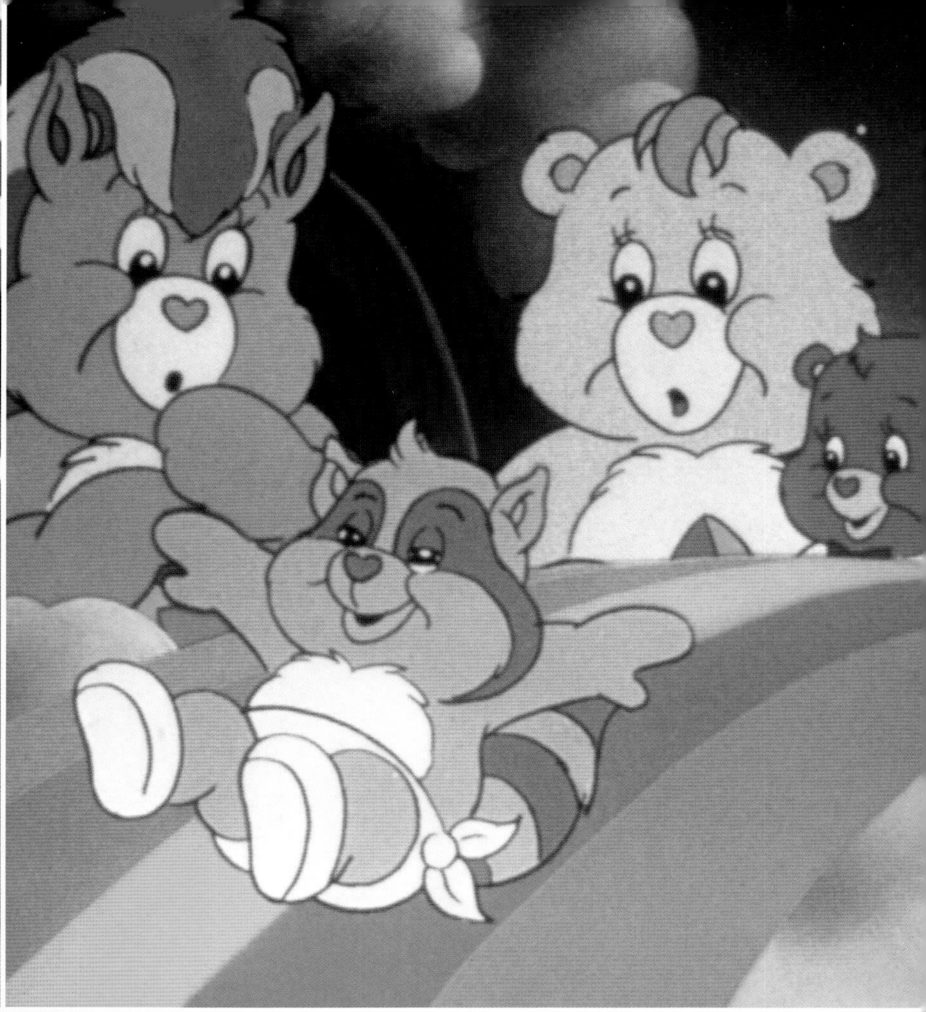
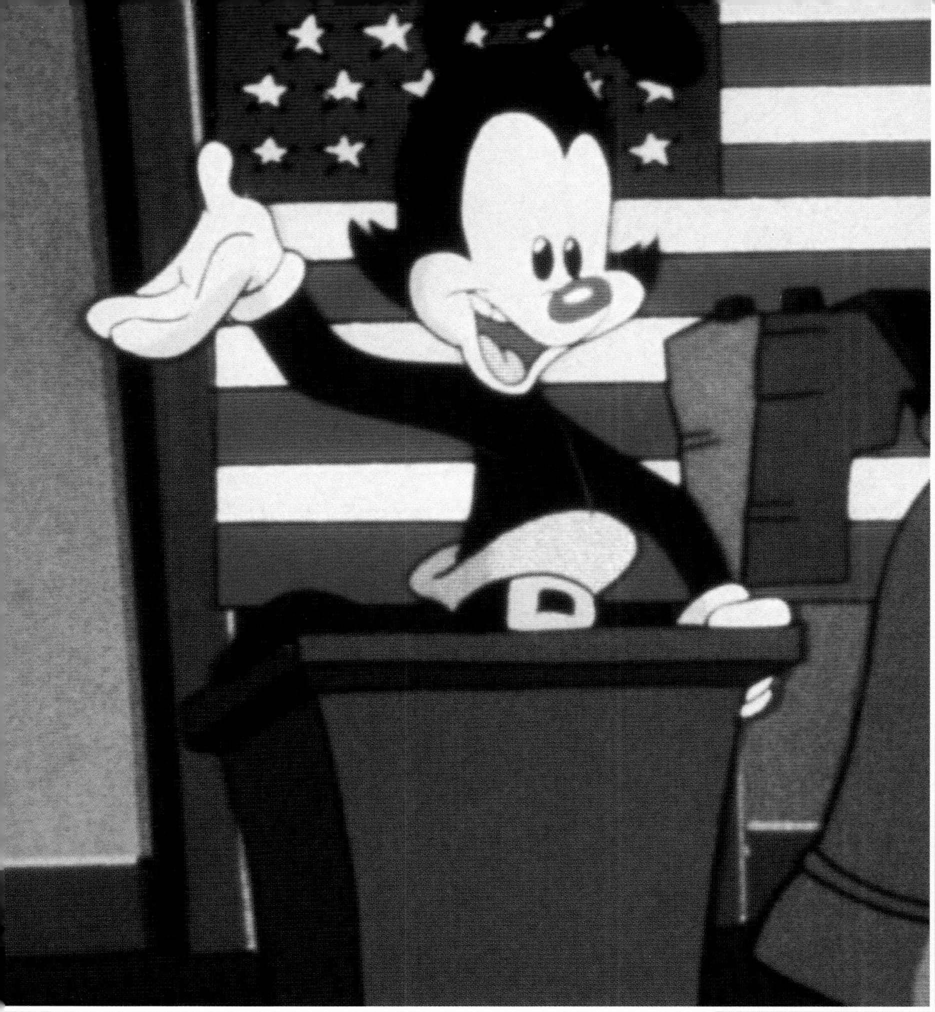
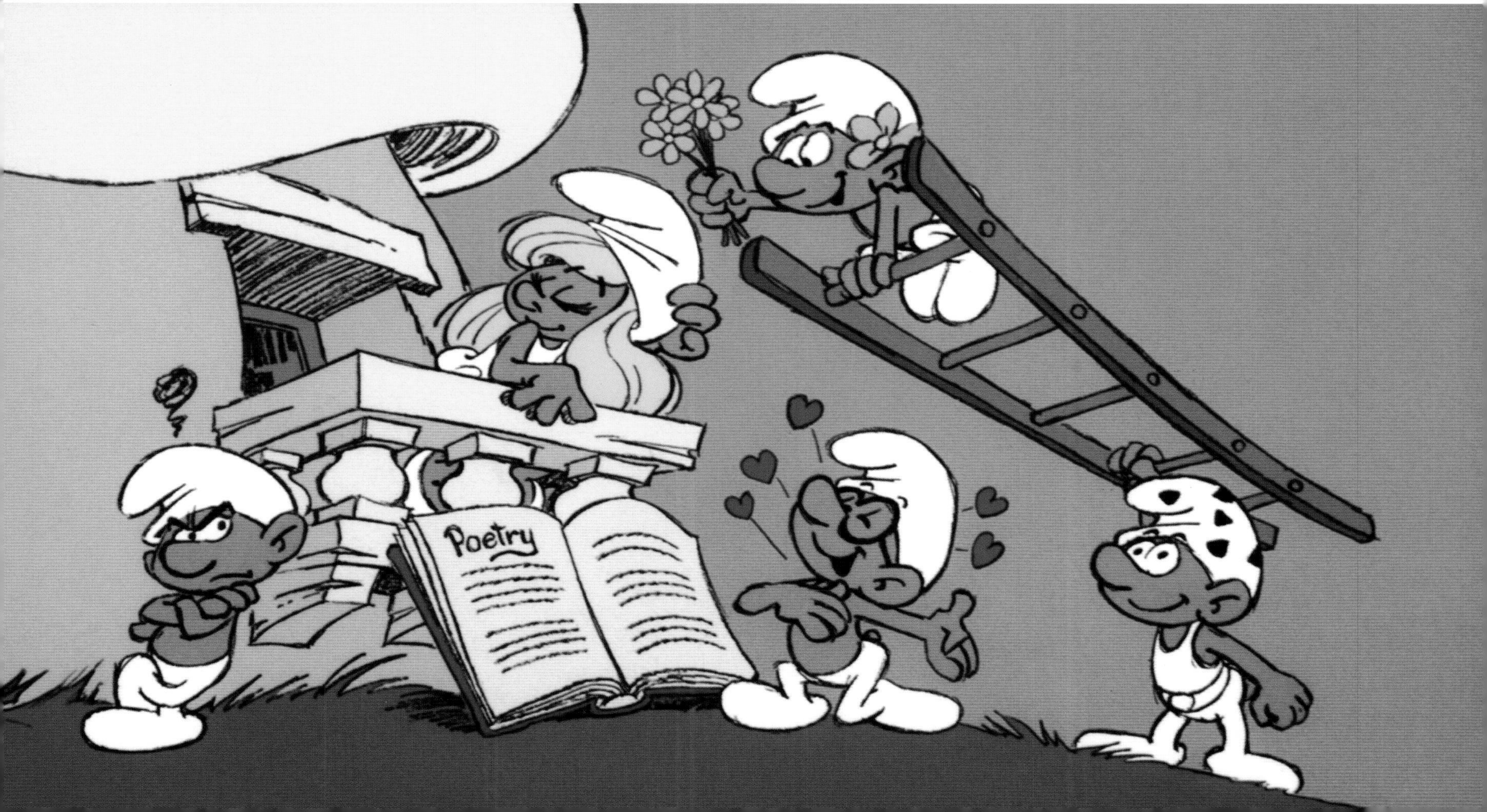
Poetry

You Could Take an Anvil to the Head, Fall Off a Cliff—How Great is That?!

By Howie Mandel

I love silliness. Silly transcends any language, culture, age, or gender. If it's silly, if it's goofy, if it's funny—it's escapism. Whether it be *Bobby's World* or my stand-up routines. I tell people if you want to get away from whatever you need to get away from for a couple of hours, come see me live. That same escapism is what I felt sitting in front of the TV watching Saturday morning cartoons.

I grew up in the 1950s before doctors diagnosed kids with ADHD but I'm sure I would have qualified. I couldn't sit still in class. I didn't finish my GED. Yet every Saturday morning I would get up earlier than the cartoons began, turn on the television, and watch the test pattern until they started. I wanted to be there for the first little blip of anything entertaining.

The shows I watched as a kid were so dynamic and expansive. They became worlds unto themselves. Looking around as a child, your living room felt drab, *boring*. Then you flipped on the set and Saturday morning cartoons roared to life. Funny, bursting with sound and color, they offered musical rainbows of imagination. When they were on, you just melted into your TV. You wanted so badly to be in that imaginary world. Everything there was exciting and limitless. What an amazing place! You could fall off a cliff and not get hurt.

The Warner Bros. Cartoons were my favorites. They were the ones that really influenced me. I especially loved *Bugs Bunny* and *Wile E. Coyote*. I enjoyed physical, silly comedy. Featuring slapstick and musical numbers, they were loud and physical rather than story-based. I grew up in an era in which cartoons were my introduction to comedy and show business, whereas somebody a couple generations back may have gravitated toward vaudeville.

Voice legend Frank Welker is the person who brought me into cartoons and who would eventually become a close friend. My stand-up routine led me to a show called *Laugh Trax* where we first met and performed live together. That's also where I met Jim Staahl and Jim Fisher, co-creators of *Bobby's World*. Frank was the one who said, "You should do voices!" He recommended me for the voice of Gizmo in *Gremlins*, which led me to voice the characters of Animal, Bunsen, and Skeeter on *Muppet Babies*. He also introduced me to an industry very different from anything else I had ever done.

Working in animation can be collaborative, but also insular. I found it utterly different from my preconceptions growing up.

I often found myself in a little booth with a

ABOVE: Howie Mandel poses with the animated Bobby from *Bobby's World*.

good fortune to meet the legendary Jim Henson, an icon on par with giants like Hanna and Barbera. But just as soon as I met him, he said, "Okay, let's go." After that, I was sent into my own little room, the childhood equivalent of a "time-out." Dark and quiet, here you sat on a stool in a corner. You couldn't talk to your friends. You weren't allowed to chew gum. You couldn't even make noises—apart from what they were paying you to say.

Still, from being there, reciting those scripted lines, emitting those noises, you wind up unleashing the zaniest, craziest, most colorful world for other people to escape to. That's the real adult magic.

Kids, on the other hand, experience a different kind of magic growing up. As children, everything seems to be imbued with wonder—or at least drama. Every little occurrence feels so huge. It's no wonder cartoons seem to magnify daily life to outlandish proportions. But then again, that's what make them so great.

ABOVE: In addition to being the creator of *Bobby's World*, Howie Mandel voiced Baby Animal and Baby Skeeter on Jim Henson's *Muppet Babies*.

person on the other side of the glass, asking me, "Can you try that take again?" So much for musical rainbows of imagination.

Such disparity between what you imagine something to be and what it actually turns out to be has always fascinated me. For instance, I had the

This is exactly what I tried to evoke with *Bobby's World*. The biggest problems in my childhood often involved something an adult might consider trivial—like not wanting to go to visit somebody. Whenever I was told I had to go visit so-and-so, my imagination

soared. *What is it going be like? Smell like? Look like?* Cartoons are the perfect medium to act out such ponderings because of their ability to dramatize our imaginations. What might begin as something mundane grows and grows in front of our eyes to become something fantastic.

Ultimately, experiences such as these demonstrate cartoons' unique appeal. With cartoons, there is nothing we can't do. That's the feeling I had on the outside looking in as a kid, as well as from the inside looking out as an adult. I especially experienced this with *Bobby's World*. For instance, I might say something to my collaborators like, "Wouldn't it be funny if Bobby is just sitting there, and out of boredom, the house turns into a rocket ship and blasts into outer space?"

Instead of looking at me like I was nuts, people would nod and say, "Okay, yes. Let's write that down." An adventure would start. But then the adventure itself would morph! It would become a musical. Not only that, but for no apparent reason, BJ Thomas would suddenly appear live, singing a song. The point is, there are no rules with cartoons. That's their beauty. That's why animation exploded into primetime, expanding to encompass dedicated networks.

Once upon a time, cartoons were thought of as strictly a Saturday morning thing. Not anymore. Folks realized just how far this medium could go. Nowadays, there is so much animation it can make you feel like a kid in a candy store every day. But there's also a downside to this new model of having all the cartoons we could ever want on tap.

Saturday morning cartoons were the last remaining bastion of our culture, the last real experience shared by everyone. I can't imagine anybody my age that didn't partake in Saturday morning cartoon-watching. That's just what we did. We may have watched different cartoons; we may have laughed at different things, liked different things, were turned off by different things, but we were all there on Saturday mornings. There isn't anything in existence now that unites us like those could. There isn't one thing that grabs everybody, even of a certain age. Not one.

The fact that Saturday morning cartoons don't exist anymore is sad. Ask any kid today, "Do you watch Saturday morning cartoons?" and they'll look at you funny. "What do you mean?" They'll say. "Of course, I do. I also watch them on Monday, Tuesday, and Wednesday."

It's great to be a kid in a candy store. Who doesn't want that? But it's only possible to really appreciate what you had when it's gone—when you're an adult looking back at all that magic, remembering a special time when Saturday was *reserved* for cartoons.

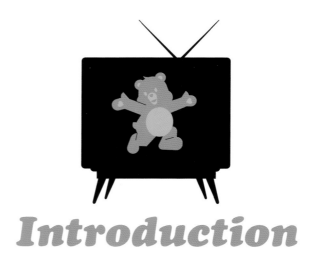

Introduction

It might as well have been called Kidsday. Outside, snowflakes are falling. Inside, you are toasty warm beneath your *Scooby-Doo* patterned comforter. As the first rays of sunlight danced across your window pane, your eyes flicked open with one all-consuming thought: *It's Saturday morning!* You scramble down your bunk bed, throwing the covers off your little brother. Unlike a school day, he doesn't need prodding to get going. The two of you tiptoe past your parent's closed door all the way to the kitchen to gorge on sugary cereal: Cap'n Crunch, Lucky Charms, Cocoa Puffs, and Cookie Crisp. Milk splashes onto the linoleum floor and countertops—endearing little remains for your hardworking parents snoozing 'til noon.

You don't have time to worry about such messes. *The Smurfs* are calling. You have an appointment with them. Pronto. Then it's off to see *Disney's Adventures of the Gummi Bears*, *Muppet Babies*, and *Alvin and the Chipmunks*. Come to think of it, you have quite a packed morning. It's time to get going. You grab your brother's hand, rushing toward

what promises to be yet another amazing Saturday morning of childhood bliss.

Whether you grew up in the '60s, '70s, '80s, or even the early '90s, Saturday mornings promised unbridled joy. Weekdays could drag you down with chores, school, and teachers who never stopped assigning homework. Saturday morning was Kidsday, even if it only lasted for a few hours. Coast-to-coast, televisions throughout America offered an incredible form of alchemy. Seated on your couch or on the floor gazing up at the screen, you had an opportunity to turn boredom into adventure—tedium into laughter. Excitement reigned supreme and you were there to soak it all up. During these golden moments, you were no longer just a little boy or girl ruled by bedtimes and report cards. You were a green teenage turtle with nunchucks, rising from the sewer to take on the evil Foot Clan army. You were Josie, the rockin' lead singer of an all-girl band, thwarting international intrigue.

Long before the segmenting of television programming into niche cable channels, streaming

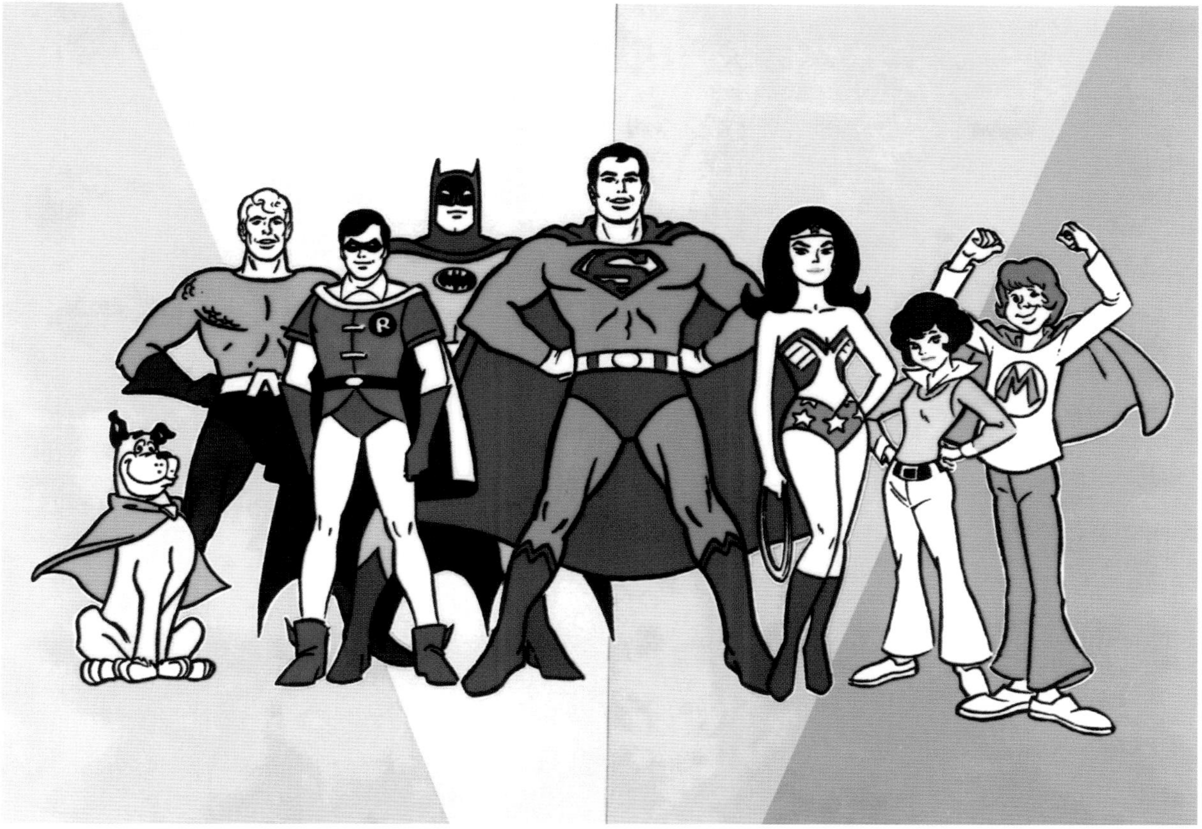

TOP: *Super Friends* debuted in 1973 and ran for over a decade.

shows, or the personalization of media via YouTube preferences, American networks broadcast cartoons to mass audiences, creating a collective societal experience that no longer exists today. Saturday morning cartoons united children across the country. They all knew the same programs, the same characters. They could recite the same theme songs: *Flintstones, meet the Flintstones. They're the modern Stone Age family*. Story arcs seeped into playtime. Children reenacted scenes of He-Man battling Skeletor on the playground or speculated what might happen next on *Tarzan, Lord of the Jungle*.

From *Jonny Quest* and *Super Friends* to *Darkwing Duck*, the Saturday morning lineup offered wonders and marvels. Whether or not children recognized all of the underlying moral messages, cartoons exerted an undeniable influence. Series after series shaped their dreams and imagination.

Similar to how jazz grew extemporaneously from New Orleans nightclubs or how blues swam out of the Deep South bayous, Saturday morning cartoons developed as an American art form, honed by cultural and economic factors. Decade by decade, the changing milieu impacted the stories told. President John F. Kennedy's commitment to landing on the moon by the end of the 1960s intensified interest in science-fiction shows, such as *The Jetsons* and *Space Ghost*. Meanwhile, live-action and animated programs based on pop songs and groups, such as the *The Archie Show*, caught fire with audiences swept up in the musical revolution. In the 1970s, the powerhouse animation

ABOVE: Smurfette plays coy with a fellow Smurf.

studio Hanna-Barbera combined teen bands and mystery solving with shows like *Scooby-Doo, Where Are You!* and *Josie and the Pussycats.* The emphasis on education expressed through humor was evident in programs such as *Fat Albert and the Cosby Kids* and *Schoolhouse Rock!* Though many characters in '80s series began life as toys, like in *G.I. Joe: A Real American Hero, Care Bears,* and *He-Man,* the creators instilled their narratives with life lessons. By the time the '90s rolled around, cartooning had grown up; shows had become more self-conscious. *Darkwing Duck* spoofed vigilante cape crusader fare and spy fiction conventions, while *Tiny Toon Adventures, Animaniacs,* and *Pinky and the Brain* possessed a "meta sensibility," often breaking the fourth wall and skewering pop culture with knowing jokes aimed at kids and adults alike.

It's Saturday Morning! presents the most groundbreaking and beloved cartoons, decade by decade. Though it was no easy task narrowing which shows to include from the wealth of programming that was broadcast over four decades, the shows were selected based on specific criteria—the first being popularity. How long did a series stay on the air? What were its ratings? Did it receive many awards? For instance, not only did *The Smurfs* win multiple Daytime Emmys, it ran for nearly the entirety of the 1980s. The second criterion was its cultural impact. Did the show resonate beyond just its Saturday morning time slot? While certain shows lasted only a year or two—such as *Space Ghost*—the program had a significant impact on the cultural zeitgeist. A third criterion taken into account was whether the series broke new ground in either animation or content, such as *Pee-wee's Playhouse.*

Each selected and profiled show has a story—how it came to be, its characters and plot, as well as its legacy within pop culture. Through interviews with creators, producers, writers, and/or voice actors, we'll take a peek behind the various series' origins and the creative intentions while also reminiscing about why we loved these shows and the effect they had on childhoods.

Children's author Maurice Sendak once wrote, "The magic of childhood is the strangeness of childhood—the uniqueness that makes us see things that other people don't see." Similar to a glowing spark, each of our childhoods shines

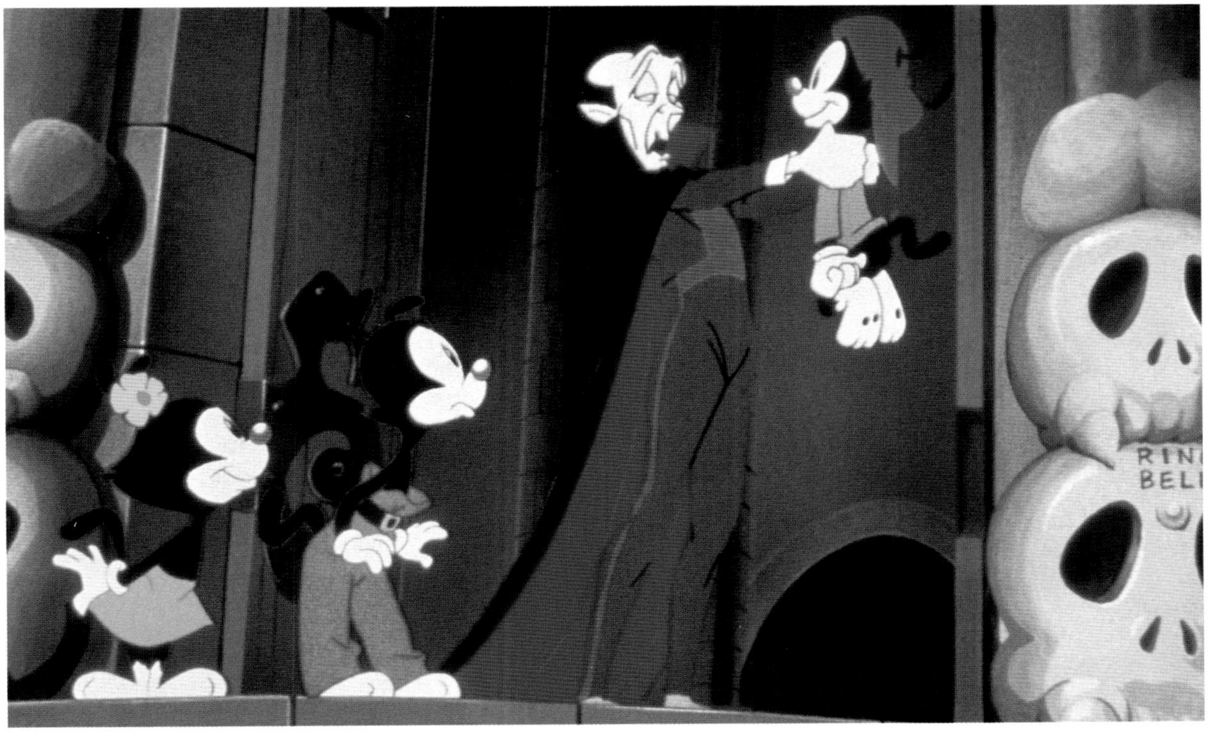

TOP: Dot and Yakko watch as Wakko confronts Dracula.

brightly for a brief moment, then is gone. As this book evidences, one common thread running through each cartoon series is its inventive weirdness—the way it mirrored the strangeness of childhood. No wonder so many shows featured unusual realms, peculiar characters, funny names, and odd ways of speaking. We, the authors of this book, like many of you reading, are the products of these shows. Though a generation apart—Joe Garner in the 1960s and Michael Ashley in the 1980s—we both grew up in the Midwest (Garner in Illinois and Ashley in Missouri), participating in the weekly Saturday morning ritual. Both of us credit Saturday morning cartoons with shaping our love of stories and our futures as writers. Not only did we watch the shows, we played alongside with the toys, inventing our own imaginative adventures.

With streaming and on demand, today's children never have to suffer through endless commercial breaks, waiting until their program finally comes back on. As adults, we attempt to remind ourselves of these shows by finding old clips on YouTube. We might feel happy to reunite with these spectacles from our youth, but it cannot transport us back to that milk-stained sofa, immersed in a world of superpowers and grumpy cats devouring lasagna.

Of course, we cannot return to a simpler time, one with fewer dietary restrictions, but we hope these pages allow you to recall the sublime mornings when running out of Golden Crisps was your biggest concern. We share in those moments—rehashing old memories, reliving the stories that made us who we are, and imagining something even greater waiting around the corner. This is for all the kids who never stopped dreaming.

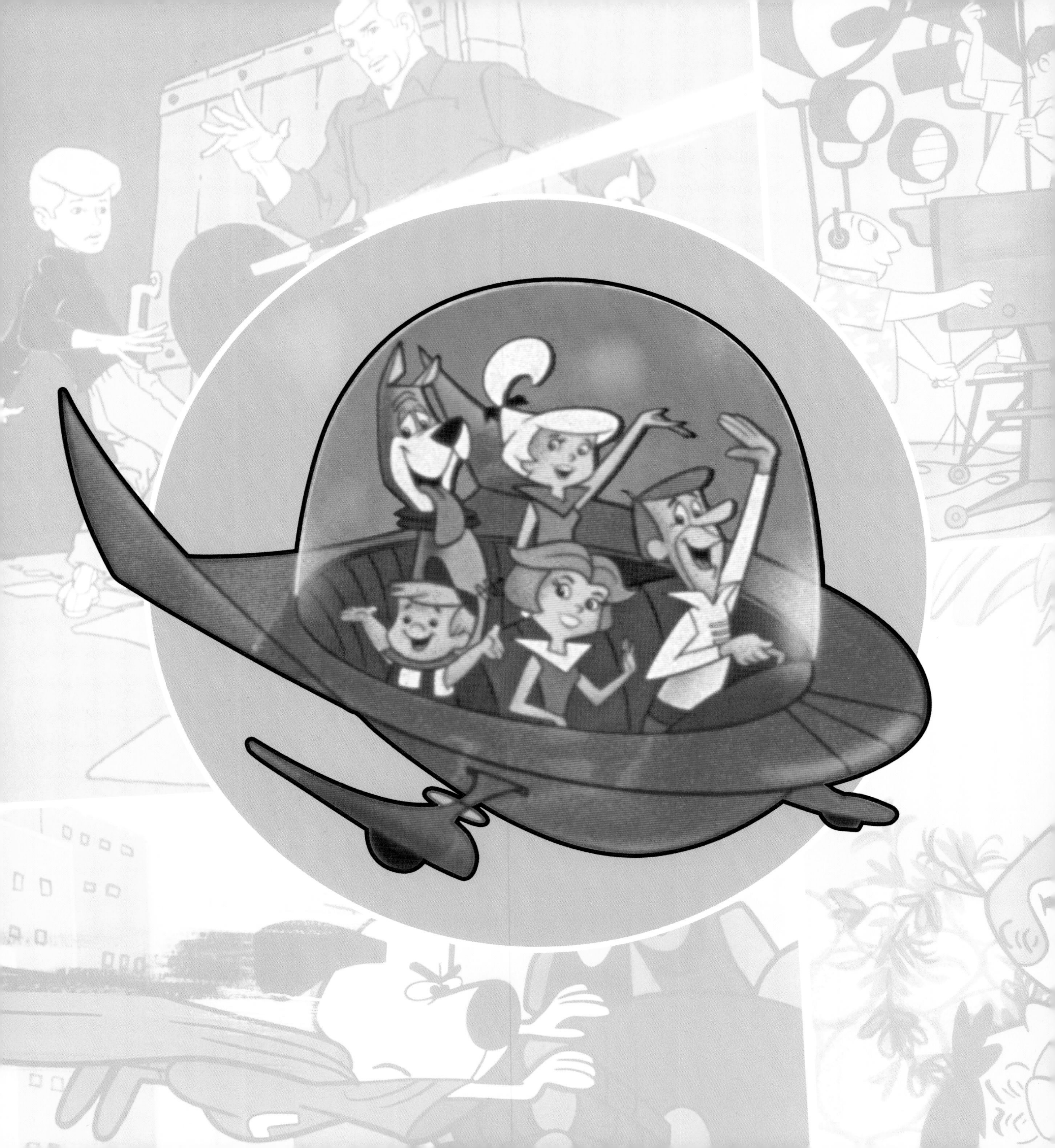

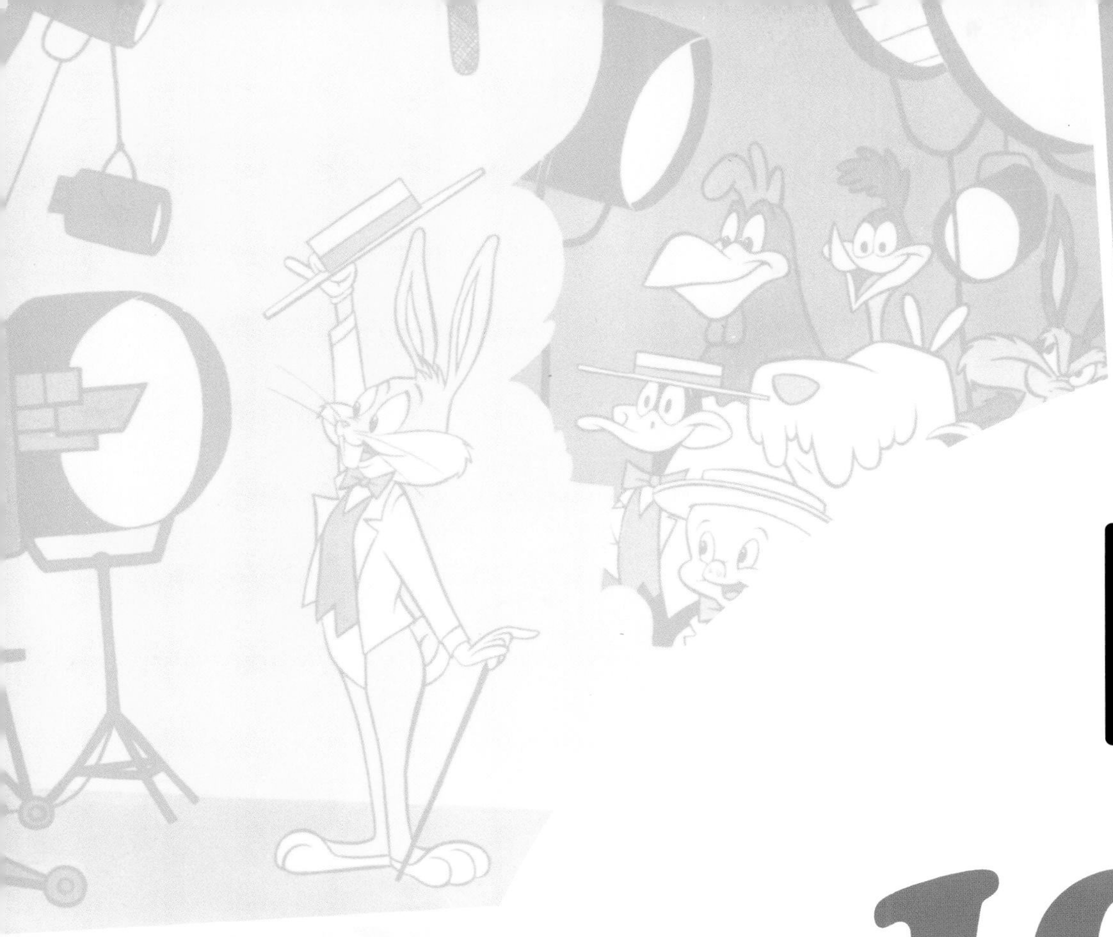

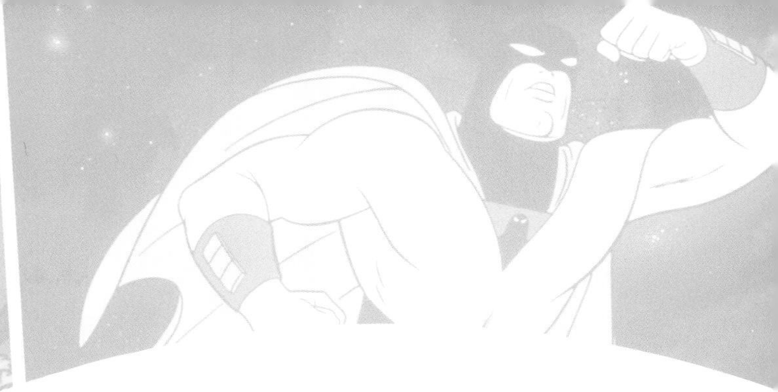

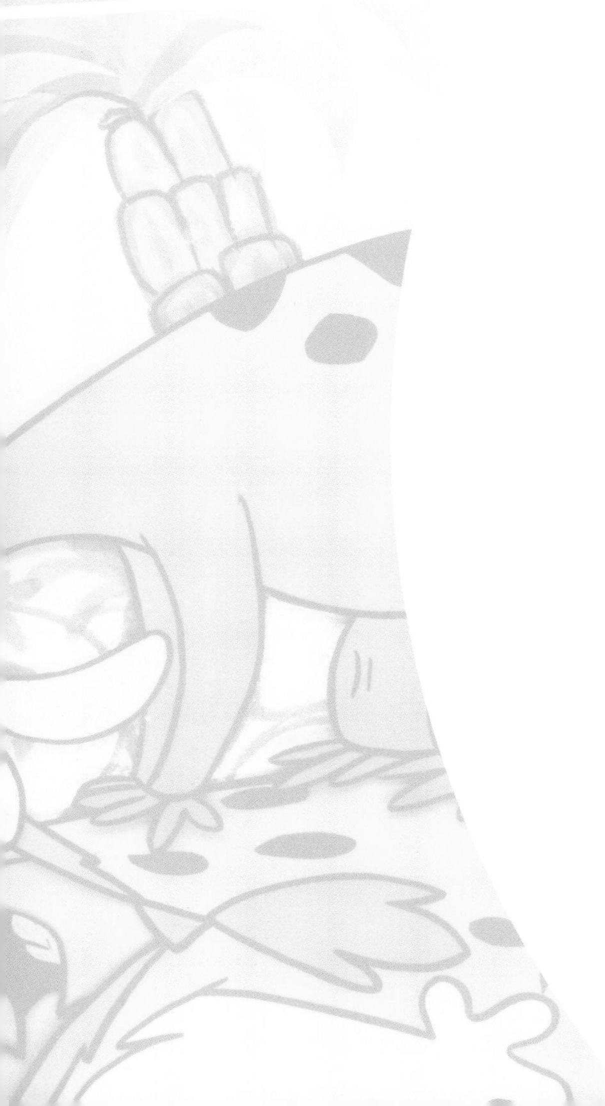

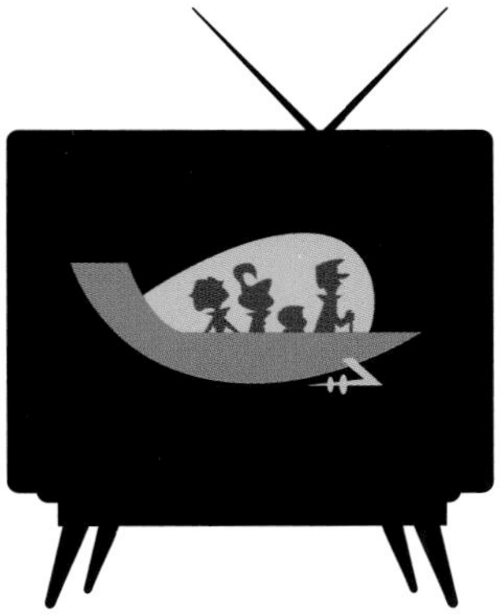

1960s

Some of the best known and beloved Saturday morning cartoons, such as *The Flintstones*, *The Jetsons*, and *The Bugs Bunny Show,* emerged in the flower power decade of unprecedented change. Featuring clever writing and pioneering animation techniques, these soon-to-be-classics would set the stage for future animated series to come.

OPPOSITE: The Jetsons Family in their aerocar. *The Jetsons* cartoon ran on various networks for almost twenty years.

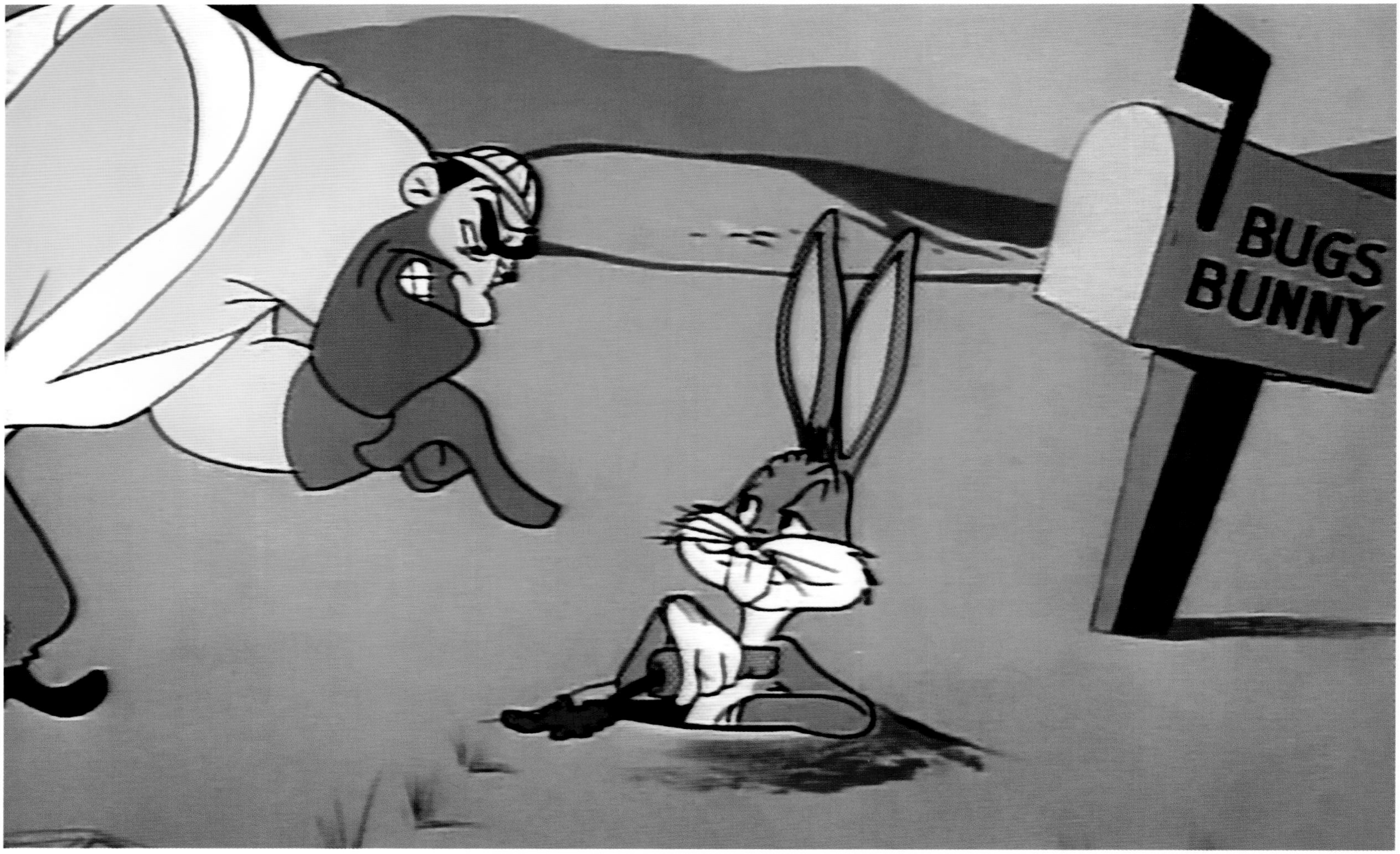
BUGS
BUNNY

YEARS ON AIR

1960–68

NETWORK

ABC

NUMBER OF EPISODES

52

CHARACTERS AND VOICE ACTORS

Bugs Bunny/Daffy Duck/Porky Pig/Tweety Bird/Sylvester the Cat/Yosemite Sam/Foghorn Leghorn/Marvin the Martian/Pepé Le Pew/Speedy Gonzales/Wile E. Coyote/Road Runner/Tasmanian Devil: Mel Blanc
Granny: June Foray

The Bugs Bunny Show

When it comes to Saturday mornings, no character—not even Mickey Mouse—can rival the success of the white-gloved, wisecracking rabbit Bugs Bunny. The carrot-munching cottontail with the mash-up Brooklyn-Bronx dialect ushered in and then dominated the golden era of Saturday morning cartoons. But the "wascally wabbit" made his showbiz debut long before the invention of television as a goofy antagonist for Porky Pig in the 1938 Warner Bros. animated short, *Porky's Hare Hunt*. Although he was an unnamed character in the piece, the film proved pivotal to his cinematic development.

Joseph Benson 'Bugsy' Hardaway served as the storyboard artist and codirector for *Porky's Hare Hunt*. A fellow employee labeled his early sketch of the rabbit "Bugs's Bunny" and the name stuck. Between 1945 and 1964, nearly every animation director at the Warner Bros. cartoon studio worked with Bugs, most famously Chuck Jones, Friz Freleng, and Robert McKimson. "They were divided among us because we made about twelve a year," says Freleng. "I did four or five, Chuck did five, Bob did three. Because, if one person did all of Bugs Bunny, we wouldn't have time to do anything else. So I would do five Bugs Bunnys and maybe four Tweetys or some Daffy Ducks, and a couple of other characters. Altogether, we were doing thirty cartoons a year."

Each of these various directors contributed to Bugs's evolving look and personality. As Freleng explains: "So, they were all Bugs Bunny. [But] I can tell the difference between mine and the other animators. It's like looking at someone's handwriting and yours. You can tell the difference." To this end, Jones gave Bugs triangular eyes, flexible eyebrows, and developed Bugs's suave, intellectual attitude. "Chuck was very sophisticated in his approach to Bugs," Freleng recalls. "Chuck was a reader, and it crept into his cartoons. He was using clever dialogue for gags. And I think that some of his lines were a little above the head of the audience, especially a kid audience."

BUGS BUNNY TV
6/1/61
WHITES WHITE
GRAY TORQ1
FL.1
CREAM1
SHAD. YEL1
LT BL. GRAY1
WH.
BLK
CREAM1
YEL OR.1
PINK1
BLK
WH
GRAY TORQ1
CREAM1
CREAM1
WH.
GRAY TORQ
LT BL GRAY1
YEL OR1
TO LT BL GRAY 3
TRACE OVERLAPPING BLACKS IN "D"
INKER
"MEDIUM" INK LINES
WARNER BROS. PICTURES INC. ©
sent this one to Leslie

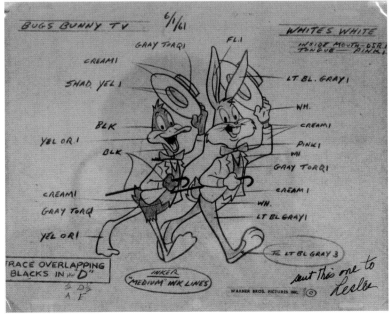

OPPOSITE: Bugs Bunny greets confrontation with his characteristic nonchalance.

TOP: Animator Chuck Jones, with his most famous creation, Bugs Bunny. Jones is responsible for other iconic characters such as Wile E. Coyote, Road Runner, and Daffy Duck. Jones also created the animated film and Peabody Award-winning special *Dr. Seuss's How the Grinch Stole Christmas*.

BOTTOM: Coloring instructions for Bugs Bunny and Daffy Duck as they sing the show's theme song: "This Is It."

It was also in Jones's 1941 animated short, *Elmer's Pet Rabbit*, that the character was first called "Bugs Bunny" on-screen.

Freleng's version of Bugs took Bugs's intelligence even farther, emphasizing the character's cunning personality. Freleng's Bugs is the one who destroys dippy Elmer Fudd's robot, helps police apprehend gangsters Rocky and Mugsy, and wages a running battle through history against Yosemite Sam. "I used the action, or the personality of the character, but I didn't let him talk too much," explains Freleng. "The more human Bugs Bunny acts, the funnier it is. Because Bugs is really not a rabbit. He is an abstraction. He has long ears and a tail, and we're establishing him as a rabbit, but he's like a human." Meanwhile, McKimson's Bugs appears as the bowlegged, physically aggressive bunny who violently square-dances with two hillbillies bent on humiliating him for thwarting their hunting trips in *Hillbilly Hare*. Using what would become characteristic Merrie Melodies slapstick, Bugs pulls their ears and pokes their eyes before leading them off a cliff.

While these directors honed Bugs's look and attitude, radio comedian Mel Blanc supplied his trademark voice. It was clear to Blanc the impudent rabbit needed an equally tough accent: either Brooklyn or the Bronx. Blanc chose a combination of both. Nuances in his voice-over work were further influenced by the 1934 film, *It Happened One Night*. Freleng particularly liked the scene in which Clark Gable chomps a carrot while talking with Claudette Colbert. Blanc mimicked this by eating carrots while performing, munching and spitting them out as he recited lines. And his talent went far beyond eating while talking. He went on to voice most of the supporting cast, earning him the title of "Man of a Thousand Voices." In a 1981 interview with David Letterman, Blanc acknowledged his versatility, explaining that "they show me a picture of the character, and then they show me a storyboard,

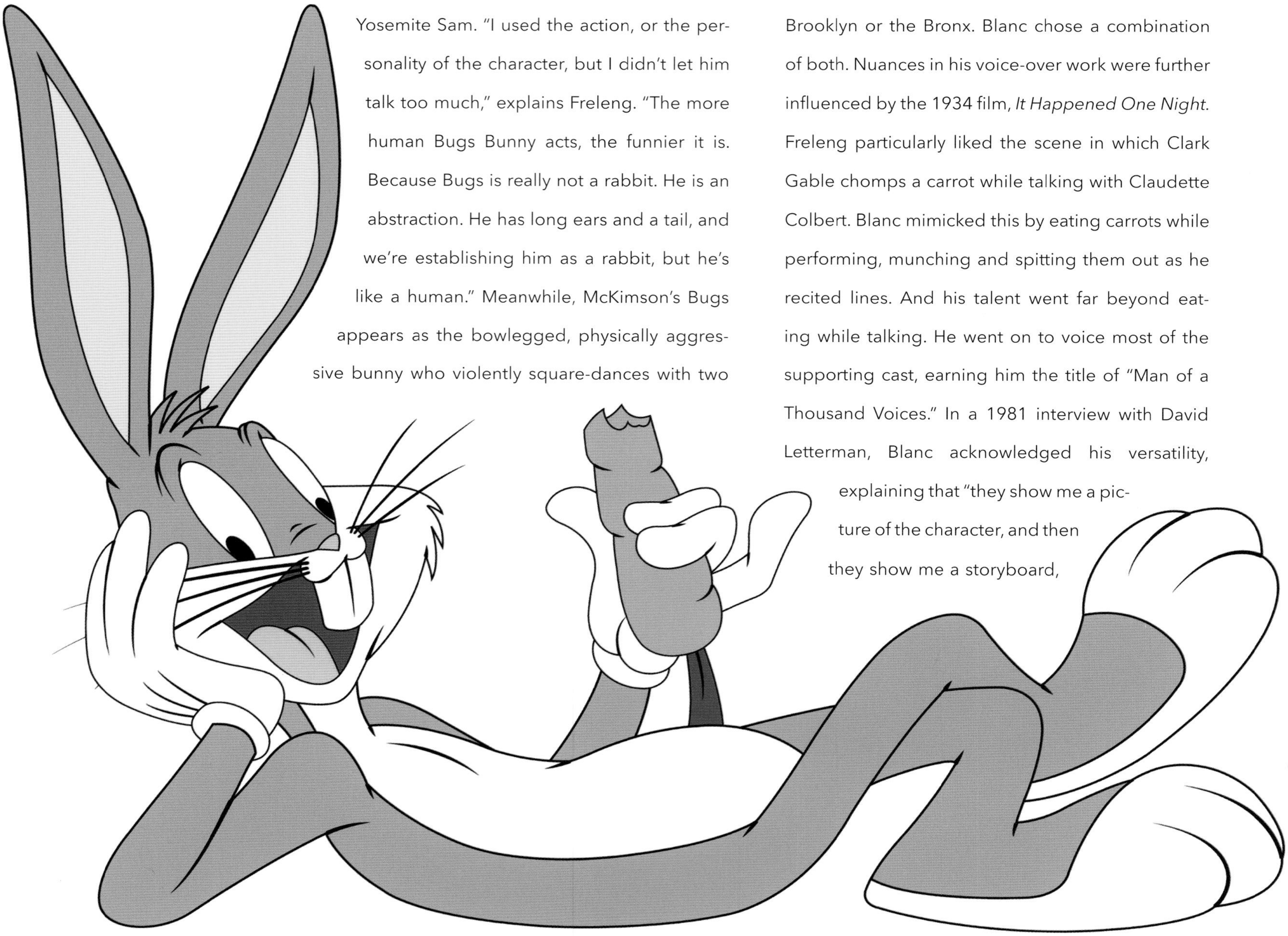

which shows what the character is going to do in the cartoon. From this I have to create the voice."

With the help of Blanc and other top creative talent, the pre-1948 Warner Bros. theatrical cartoons began airing on individual television stations around the country via syndication. By 1960, *The Bugs Bunny Show* debuted as a prime-time half-hour program on ABC. After two seasons, the network moved it to Saturday mornings with sponsorship by General Foods. Each episode opened with a curtain raise revealing a spotlighted stage onto which Bugs and Daffy Duck entered, singing the show's rousing theme song, "This Is It" by Jerry Livingston and Mack David. Operating under the premise that Bugs and his cohorts were filming a variety show before a TV audience, a procession of characters would then march across the stage, including Tweety Bird, Speedy Gonzales, Hippety Hopper, Yosemite Sam, Sylvester the Cat, Elmer Fudd, Pepé Le Pew, the Road Runner, Wile E. Coyote, Marvin the Martian, the Tasmanian Devil, and the blustery Foghorn Leghorn. Afterward, Bugs would participate in all kinds of comic misadventures with his zany pals in comic shorts.

In 1968, CBS took over the series, coupling it with the popular *The Road Runner Show* to create *The Bugs Bunny/Road Runner Hour* combining sequences from both to link the seven cartoons featured in each episode. In 1971, *The Road Runner Show* moved to ABC, and a reconstituted half-hour *Bugs Bunny Show* aired on CBS, featuring reedited groupings of the cartoons. The show continued on ABC and CBS for the next thirty years with a variety

ABOVE: Animation director Tex Avery wrote the script for the short, "A Wild Hare," which included Bug's most famous line, "What's up, Doc?"

"What's Up, Doc?"

Director Tex Avery is credited with providing Bugs Bunny with his trademarked expression. Avery wrote it into the script for the short, *"A Wild Hare"*. Because Avery had heard it often where he grew up in Texas, he didn't think much of the phrase when he included it. However, the "What's up, Doc?" scene generated such a huge audience reaction it became Bugs's most famous line.

OPPOSITE: Bugs Bunny in his classic pose with carrot in hand.

BOTTOM: Bugs Bunny charmed a number of female rabbits over the course of the show's run.

Sam
Tweety
Road Runner
Sylvester
Wile
Daffy Duck
Speedy Gonzales
RESERVED
Bugs Bunny

LEFT: The cast of *The Bugs Bunny Show*. Bugs Bunny (center), (top row left to right): Foghorn Leghorn, Yosemite Sam, Tweety, (second row left to right): Pepé Le Pew, Road Runner, Sylvester, (bottom row left to right): Wile E. Coyote, Daffy Duck, Speedy Gonzales.

RIGHT: Actor Mel Blanc, the voice of Bugs Bunny, Daffy Duck, Porky Pig, and many others, during a recording session in the 1950s.

of pairings, including Road Runner, Sylvester and Tweety, and other Looney Tunes characters. In 2000, Warner Bros. offered the Looney Tunes and Merrie Melodies film library to Cartoon Network, a corporate cousin owned by Time Warner. As a result, *The Bugs Bunny Show* ended its run of four decades—one of the longest in the history of network television.

Bugs Bunny remains one of the most beloved cartoon characters of all time and has been featured on nearly every conceivable type of merchandising, from Pez dispensers to snow globes. Besides serving as the mascot for Warner Bros., he helped recruit American troops to fight in World War II via cartoons showing him squaring off against tyrants Adolf Hitler, Francisco Franco, and Benito Mussolini. According to the *Guinness Book of World Records*, Bugs holds the record for appearing in more films (short and feature length) than any other animated character. In 2002, *TV Guide* named him the number one greatest cartoon character of all time.

To what does Freleng attribute the longevity of Bugs and his animated cohorts? "Because we made them personalities. They weren't just drawings moving around. We created our own characters, and we created a strong personality for each of them. Bugs Bunny had his own unique personality." Writing in the first person as Bugs, Looney Tunes writer Bob Clampett expounds on Bugs's one-of-a-kind personality: "Some people call me cocky and brash, but actually I am just self-assured. I'm nonchalant, imperturbable, contemplative. . . . . When momentarily I appear to be cornered or in dire danger and I scream, don't be *consoined*—it's actually a big put-on. Let's face it, Doc. I've read the script and I already know how it turns out."

Slinky

What walks down stairs, alone or in pairs
And makes a slinkety sound?
A spring, a spring, a marvelous thing!
Everyone knows it's Slinky.

Did you know the Slinky was invented by accident? Mechanical engineer Richard James was trying to designs springs that could keep sensitive ship equipment from shifting at sea in 1943. One day, he inadvertently knocked his samples off a shelf. To his amazement, they "walked" instead of falling. Ever since, millions of Slinkys have walked out of stores, becoming one of the most popular American toys of all time.

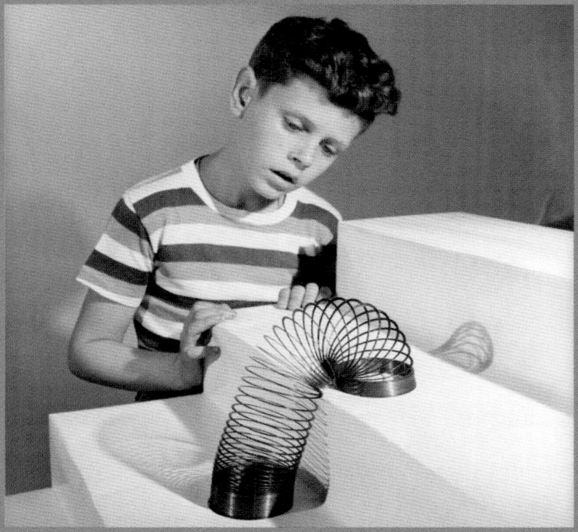

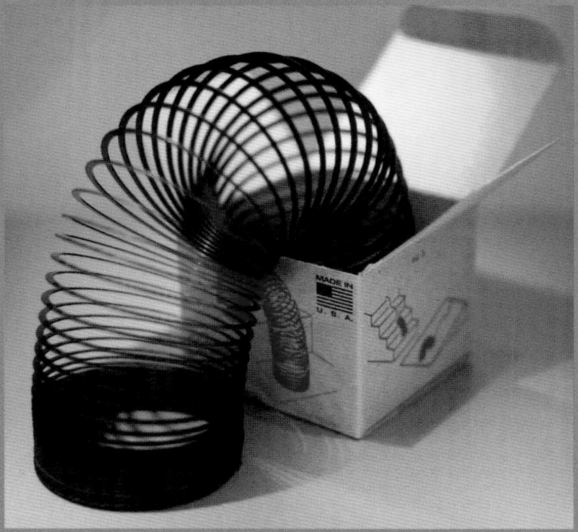
MADE IN
U.S.A.

LEFT: Watching Slinky going down steps was one of the most popular activities to do with the toy.

RIGHT: "It's Slinky, it's Slinky, it's fun, it's a wonderful toy!" One of the most iconic toys of the 1960s.

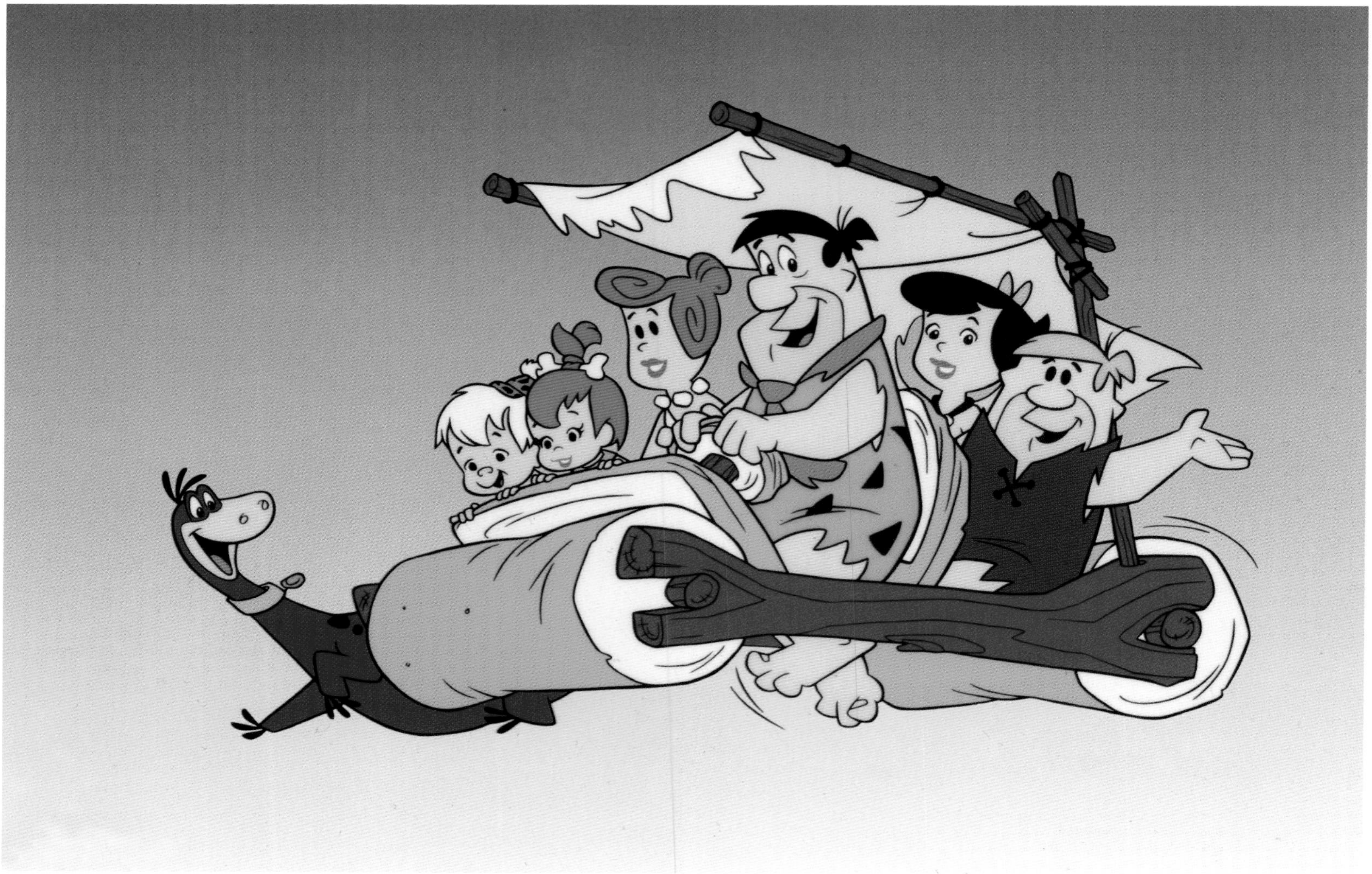

YEARS ON AIR

1960–1966, 1967–1970

NETWORK

ABC, NBC

NUMBER OF EPISODES

166

CHARACTERS AND VOICE ACTORS

Fred: Alan Reed
Wilma & Pebbles: Jean Vander Pyl
Barney & Dino: Mel Blanc
Betty: June Foray (Pilot, 1959)
Bea Benaderet (1960–1964)
Gerry Johnson (1964–1966)

The Flintstones

Flintstones. Meet the Flintstones.

They're the modern Stone Age family.

From the town of Bedrock, they're a page right out of history.

TV Guide ranks *The Flintstones* as the second greatest TV cartoon of all time, right behind *The Simpsons*. This "modern Stone Age family" from Bedrock was prime time's first animated series, debuting thirty years before the wacky working-class clan from Springfield. But before the prehistoric sitcom premiered, the notion of adults sitting in front of their sets to watch cartoons seemed improbable. That is until up-and-coming producers Bill Hanna and Joe Barbera discovered that adults accounted for

40 percent of the audience for the *The Huckleberry Hound Show*, a popular series about an easy-going blue hound dog with a southern drawl.

The producing duo astutely realized that the right blend of satire, slapstick, and well-crafted characters could possess universal appeal, transcending age demographics. Pursuing their new goal of an adult-oriented, prime-time cartoon, they brainstormed all kinds of characters, from pilgrims to hillbillies to Romans and Native Americans before ultimately landing on cavemen. Hanna and Barbera pitched their idea to dozens of prospective sponsors, as well as networks, even acting out scenes

from their storyboards. While NBC and CBS passed on their idea, the perpetually third-place network ABC took a chance on the Paleolithic comedy, airing the first episode on Friday, September 30, 1960, at 7:30 p.m. Sponsors included Winston cigarettes, Alka-Seltzer, One-A-Day vitamins, and Post cereals.

Audiences, both young and old, quickly fell in love with *The Flintstones* but critics took aim. The *New York Times* called the series "an inked disaster" and the *Baltimore Sun* declared it "not a very good [comedy] inhabited by unpleasantly uncouth people." Meanwhile, TV critic Jay Fredericks claimed he "was solemnly assured by a local television official

OPPOSITE: The Flintstone characters with their open air, self powered car: (left to right) Dino, Bamm-Bamm, Pebbles, Wilma, Fred, Betty, and Barney.

ABOVE: Actors Mel Blanc as Barney Rubble, Bea Benadaret as Betty Rubble, Alan Reed as Fred Flintstone, and Jean Vander Pyl, Wilma Flintstone, 1960-1966.

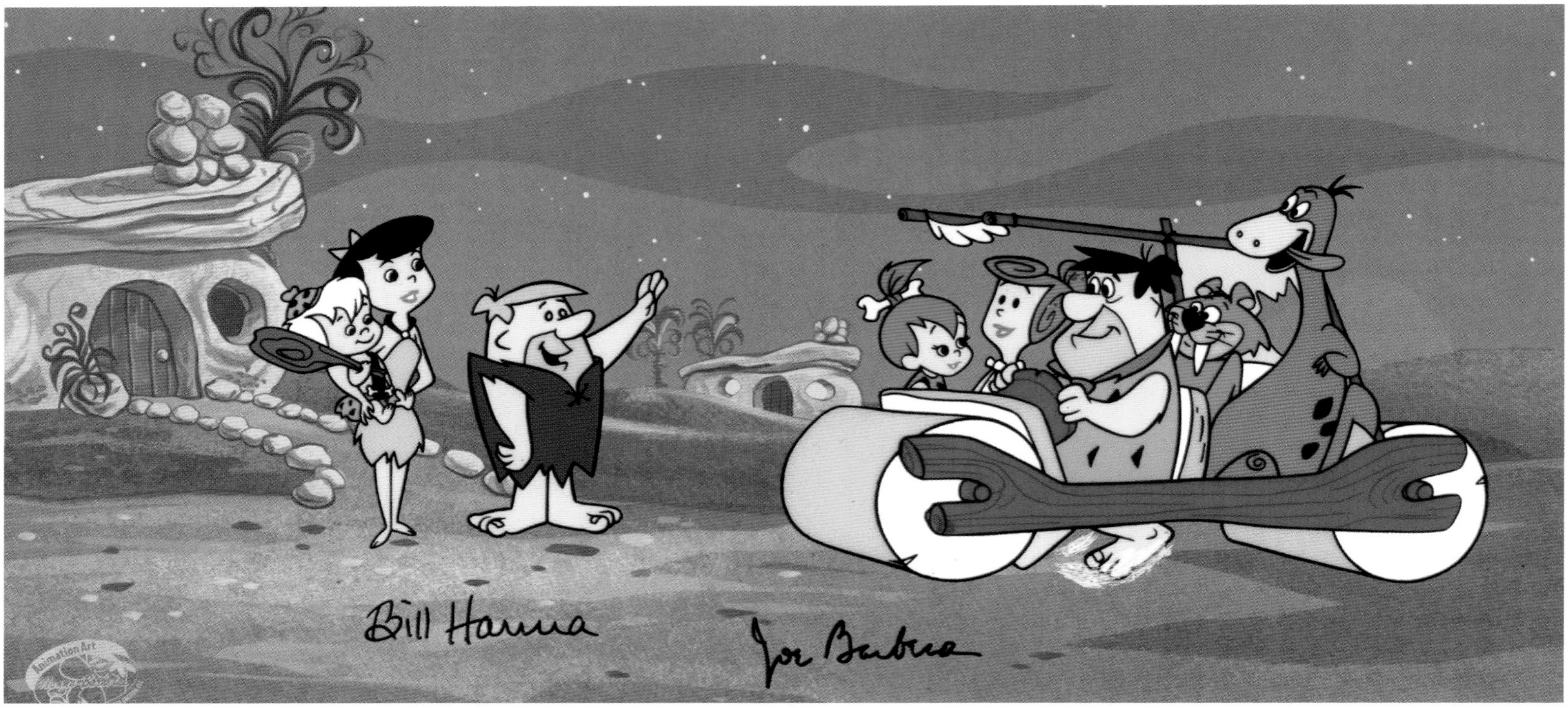
Bill Hanna
Joe Barbera

TOP: The Rubbles wave to their neighbors in this animation cel signed by Bill Hanna and Joe Barbera.

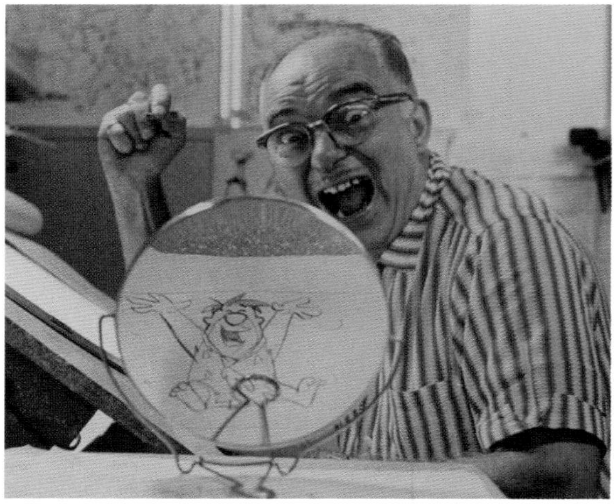

RIGHT: Animator Carlo Vinci uses a mirror to draw facial expressions for Fred Flintstone.

a couple of months ago that *The Flintstones* would be (a) hilarious and (b) THE show of the season. It is neither. The whole series is weak." Despite critical barbs, *The Flintstones* became a genuine hit, finishing the season at number 18 in the Nielsen ratings.

One theory as to why audiences immediately accepted the show was that the characters closely mirrored those from the popular 1950s sitcom, *The Honeymooners*, starring Jackie Gleason. Bill Hanna once remarked, "I personally thought *The Honeymooners* was the funniest half-hour on television." Similar to Gleason's blustery Ralph Kramden, Fred Flintstone is overweight, overbearing, and continually plotting hare-brained ideas. Ralph drove a bus; Fred operated a bronto-crane. His better half, levelheaded Wilma, spoke with a sharp tongue like Alice Kramden. Neighbors Barney and Betty Rubble acted as best friends and comic foils, resembling *The Honeymooners* predecessors, Ed and Trixie Norton. Both loyal wives and homemakers spent much of their time keeping their husbands in line.

Ed Benedict, one of the original *Flintstones* designers, recalled the process of creating the look for both of these cave-dwelling couples. "When I was told the studio was coming out with these new characters set in the Stone Age, I sketched up some characters carrying clubs and wearing long beards. Joe [Barbera] didn't like that much, so I straightened them up, took off the beards and made them look more neat and clean-cut. I was also told they had a pet, so a dinosaur seemed appropriate, and that's how Dino came about."

Though the series premise placed them in prehistoric times, the Flintstones and Rubbles were just average Stone Age, middle-class, blue-collar folks. The sometimes affable, other times irascible Fred toiled at the Bedrock Quarry & Gravel Company, hounded by his demanding boss, Mr. Slate. But when quittin' time rolled around, he and his pal Barney pursued off-hour amusements such as bowling, shooting pool, or cavorting with fellow club members at the Loyal Order of Water Buffaloes. Most episodes centered on the pair becoming entangled in one of Fred's outlandish schemes that inevitably backfired, landing them in hot water with their wives. Now and then, the show's writers reversed the roles, placing Wilma and Betty in a predicament that eventually put them at odds with their husbands. And like traditional sitcoms, episodes usually ended with Fred and Barney redeeming themselves, reminding the women why they love them.

To further relate to traditional sitcom viewers, the writers provided all of our contemporary conveniences to the Bedrock denizens, with Stone Age twists, of course. A ram's horn acted as telephone. Characters drove skin-topped convertibles with their bare feet providing the locomotion. Dinosaurs and other prehistoric beasts supplied the power to operate vacuum cleaners, moving cranes, and

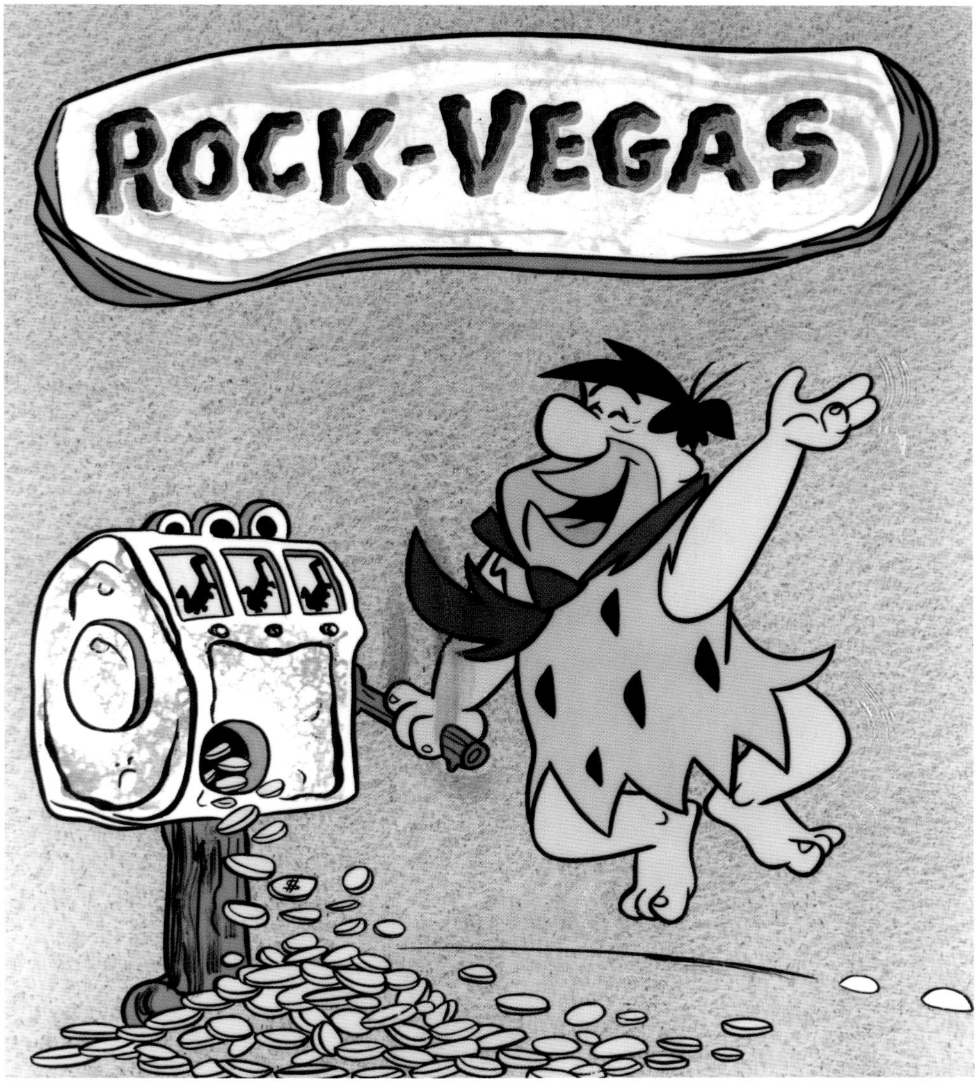
ROCK-VEGAS

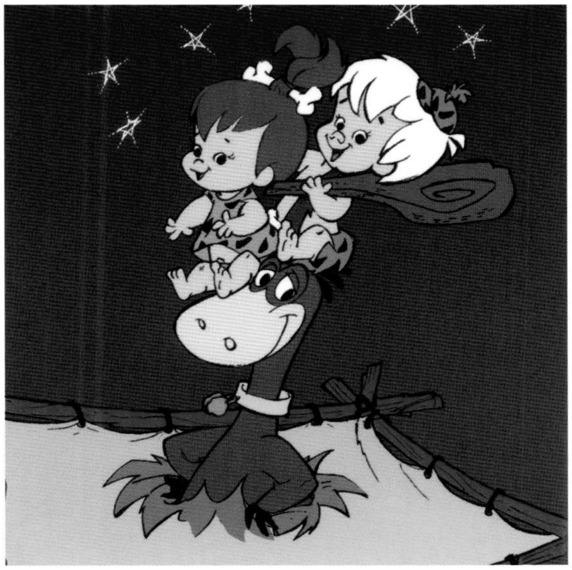

TOP: References to "stone" and "rock" were frequently added to names of objects and places as a play on the show's prehistoric theme.

BOTTOM: Fred and Wilma's daughter Pebbles and Barney and Betty's son Bamm-Bamm get a lift from Dino.

BOTTOM: The Flintstones and the Rubbles made a pop-culture impression well beyond the ten years the show was on the air.

in-sink food disposal units. A running gag also featured beleaguered creatures commenting directly to the audience how overworked or underappreciated they felt in their jobs.

While clever plotting and humorous takes on prehistoric archetypes kept the fun going, by the third season, the producers needed a new element to keep the series fresh. They decided Fred and Wilma should have a child named Pebbles. In an interview with *Emmy TV Legends*, Barbera revealed he originally intended the child be a boy until he spoke with the Ideal Toy Company. "One day, I received a call from the guy in charge of *Flintstones* merchandising. He said, 'Hey, I hear you're having a baby on the show.' I said, 'Yeah.' He said, 'Is it a boy or a girl?' 'What else, a boy. A chip off the old rock.' He says, 'That's too bad. If it was a girl, we could've made a hell of a deal.' I said, 'It's is a girl.'" They sold three million Pebbles dolls within the first couple of months.

Capitalizing on baby fever to entice more fans, the Rubbles became parents in season four when they adopted a toddler left on their doorstep. They named him Bamm-Bamm because of his incredible strength and his tendency to repeatedly slam his big wooden club—or people—into the ground while yelling, "Bam, bam . . . bam, bam!" Even with the popularity of its growing family, *The Flintstones*

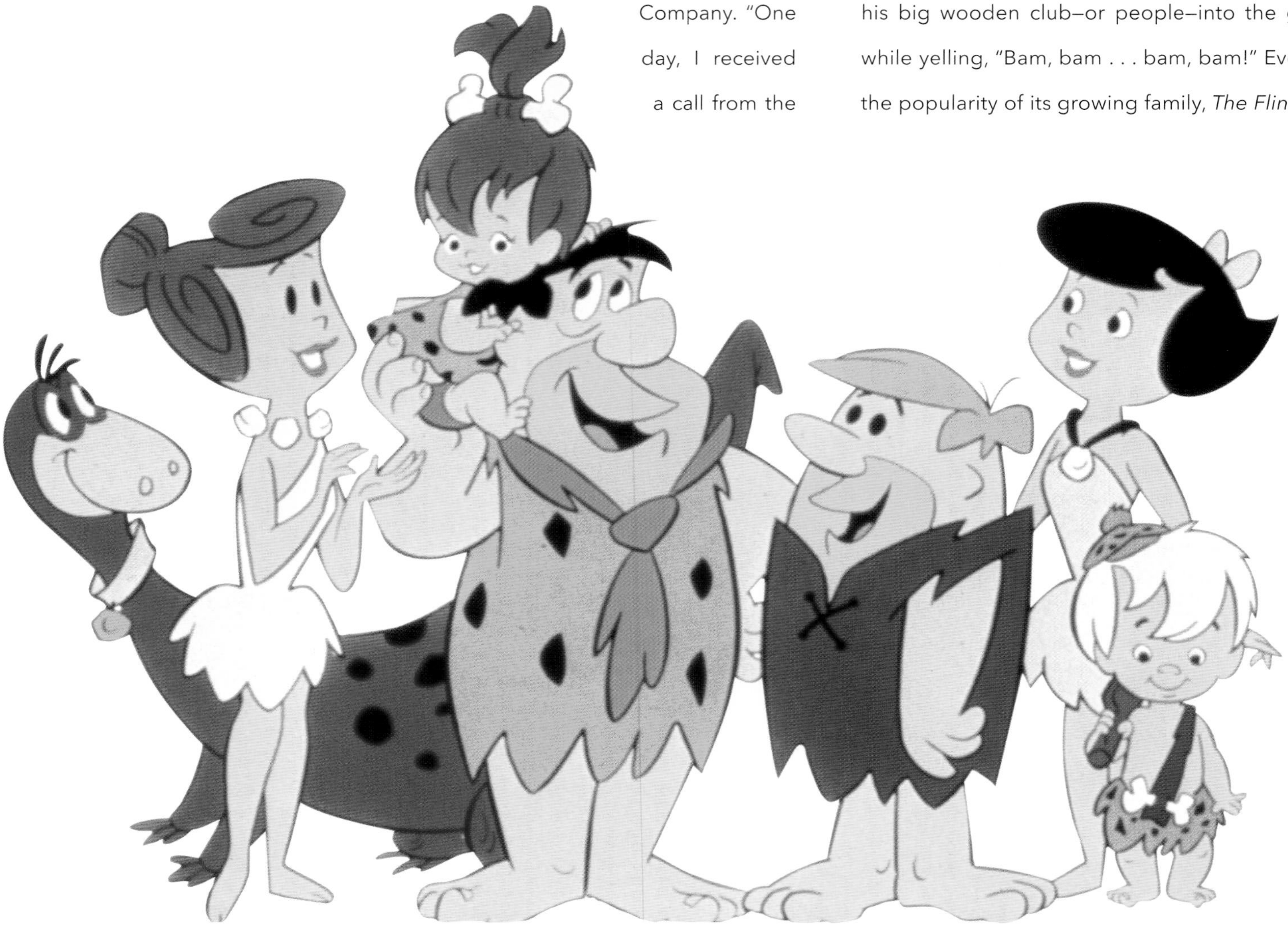

concluded in 1966 after six seasons. Reruns of the series then found a new audience as part of NBC's Saturday morning lineup from 1967 to 1970. The original program may have run its course, but *The Flintstones* launched a number of spin-offs. In addition to two live-action films, there were a number of TV series, including 1971's *The Pebbles and Bamm-Bamm Show*, *The Flintstone Comedy Hour* the following year, *The New Fred and Barney Show* in 1979, *The Flintstones Comedy Show* in 1980, *The Flintstone Kids* in 1986, and *Cave Kids* in 1996.

The offshoots, adaptations, and merchandising generated from *The Flintstones* supplemented fans' enduring adoration of the show. For decades, Fred, Wilma, Barney, and Betty (not to mention their offspring) have been licensed for countless products, such as breakfast cereals, children's vitamins, games, books, theme parks, and action figures. *The Flintstones* became an instant classic, not simply because the creators fashioned an alternate bedrock suburbia satirizing modern life, but because the characters were well-crafted and genuinely funny. Though Fred may have been inspired by Ralph Kramden, he paid forward this classic archetype, influencing future dads in sitcom history, including Homer Simpson and Peter Griffin. Possessing the distinction of being the longest-running animated show prior to *The Simpsons*, Hanna-Barbera's gamble paid off handsomely. It's no wonder the duo sang "Yabba Dabba Doo" all the way to the bank.

ABOVE: Actor Alan Reed with character Fred Flintstone.

The Birth of a Catchphrase

Fred Flintstone's iconic "Yabba Dabba Doo!" was the brainchild of voice actor Alan Reed. Reed remembered how his mother used to say, "A little dab'll do ya" (which was the advertising tagline for the hair-care product Brylcreem). Recalling the line during a recording session, Alan said, "'Hey, Joe, where it says yahoo, can I say Yabba Dabba Doo?' Barbera said, 'Yes.'" And a classic catchphrase was born.

The Jetsons

YEARS ON AIR

ABC (1962–1963)
CBS (1964–65, and 1969–71)
NBC (1965–67, 1971–76, 1979–81
and 1982–83)

NETWORK

ABC, NBC, CBS

NUMBER OF EPISODES

24 Original

CHARACTERS AND VOICE ACTORS

George: George O'Hanlon
Jane: Penny Singleton
Judy: Janet Waldo
Elroy: Daws Butler
Astro: Don Messick
Rosie: Jean Vander Pyl
Cosmo G. Spacely: Mel Blanc
Mr Cogswell: Daws Butler

In the early 1960s, the promise and wonderment of the Space Race captivated Americans. Bill Hanna and Joe Barbera, creators of *The Flintstones*, were equally inspired. If a modern Stone Age family could make it big, why not a futuristic one? On September 23, 1962, seven months after astronaut John Glenn made his historical Earth orbit, *The Jetsons* blasted off on the ABC Television Network. Composed by Hoyt Curtin, the musical director for the Hanna-Barbera animation studio, the catchy theme song introduced viewers to the space-age family. *Meet George Jetson . . . his boy, Elroy . . . daughter Judy . . . Jane, his wife . . .*

As the music played, viewers got a peek into their ultra-modern lifestyle, complete with flying cars, jet packs, moving sidewalks, and robot maids. But the series was not just futuristic in the world of the show; *The Jetsons* was ABC's first series to broadcast in color. Also, just as *The Flintstones* was modeled after *The Honeymooners*, another popular 1950s TV sitcom *Blondie* was the prototype for *The Jetsons*—so much so that Penny Singleton, who played Blondie, provided the voice of wife and homemaker, Jane Jetson. Other similarities to *The Flintstones* abound. Just like Fred, George suffered from an overbearing boss. Voiced by Mel Blanc,

Cosmo G. Spacely was the greedy, egomaniacal president and owner of Spacely Space Sprockets. Though George worked just one hour a day, two days a week, he regularly received Spacely's wrath. "JETSON!!!" Spacely would yell into the videophone, threatening to fire George for the slightest offense.

A couple years prior to *The Jetson*'s debut, Hanna and Barbera had learned the importance of grounding a period cartoon from their success with *The Flintstones*. Both cartoons presented life from opposite historical periods, but they contained recognizable aspects from the present. Even so, the creators gave *The Jetsons*' writers and designers free rein to create their high-tech setting. Animator Jerry Eisenberg noted, "We weren't bound by any particular rules. I remember when we were developing the series, designer Tony Benedict brought in a book one day. The title of it was *1975 and the changes to come*. Thirteen years in the future. It was an interesting book because it showed predictions of what there would be in 1975, new ideas, new appliances, whatever."

Heralding visions for tomorrow, the show's designers created cutting-edge locales, transportation modes, and gizmos. They constructed Orbit City in which homes and businesses perched high above the ground on adjustable columns. George Jetson commuted to work in an aerocar that resembled a flying saucer with a transparent bubble top that converted to a briefcase upon arrival. Daily life was assisted by numerous electronic, labor-saving

OPPOSITE: The Jetsons family: (left to right) Rosie, Elroy, George, Jane, Astro, and Judy.

ABOVE LEFT: Jane and robot maid Rosie watch soap operas while their chores are done by space age devices.

ABOVE RIGHT: (clockwise from top left) Penny Singleton, the voice of Jane Jetson; George O'Hanlon, the voice of George Jetson; Daws Butler, the voice of Elroy Jetson; Don Messick, the voice of Astro; Janet Waldo, the voice of Judy Jetson.

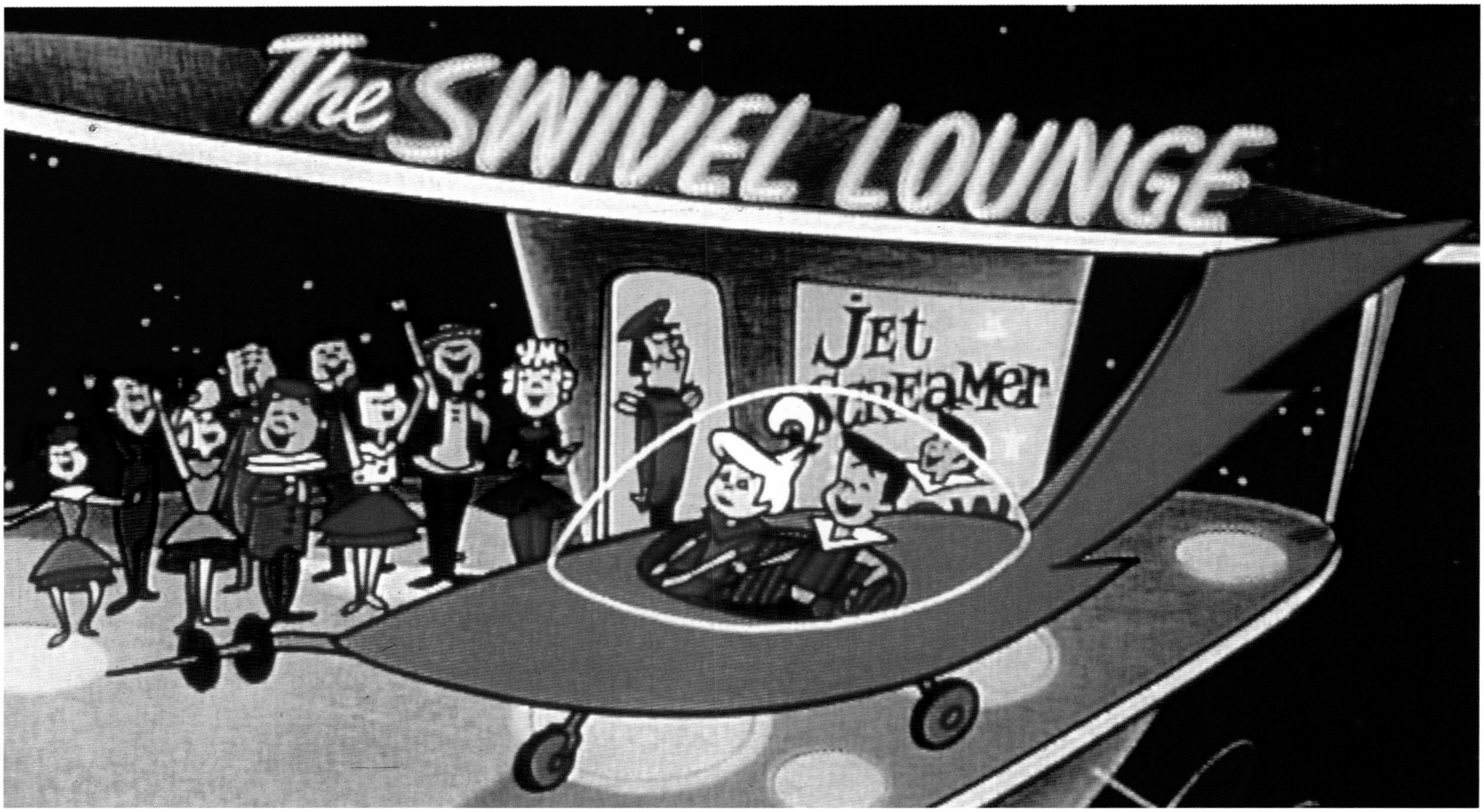
The SWIVEL LOUNGE
Jet

ABOVE: Judy Jeston wins a contest to meet her celebrity crush Jet Screamer in the episode "A Date with Jet Screamer."

devices, including a food replicator, flying pods, and watches with videoconferencing capabilities.

Yet, despite the futuristic setting, the writers grounded their stories on basic family themes. One popular episode involved teenage Judy Jetson's crush on the ultimate pop idol of 2062, Jet Screamer, where she enters a songwriting contest for the chance to win a date with the space-age heartthrob. Like many fathers of daughters in the '60s, George is dubious of rock 'n' roll and hoped to foil Judy's chances. He replaced her original song with her younger brother Elroy's secret code, "Eep, Opp, Ork, Ah Ah." But the crazy lyrics actually become the winning entry, so George tags along to try to stop the date.

Actor George O'Hanlon, who auditioned for the original part of Fred Flintstone, voiced this space-age patriarch of the Jetson clan. "George Jetson is a very average man," said O'Hanlon. "He has trouble with his boss, he has problems with his kids, and so on. The only difference is that he lives in the next century." And who can forget George's wife, Jane? Her shrewd character was perfectly encapsulated in the introductory scene: George offers her a few bills, and she takes his entire wallet instead. A member of the Galaxy Women Historical Society, Jane was also a fan of Leonardo De Venus and shopped at Mooning Dales.

Similar to their parents, the Jetson children behaved much like kids from the 1960s, even if they were blessed with the latest technologies. Judy, the sixteen-year-old daughter, attended Orbit High School and engaged in timeless teenage activities like gossiping on the telephone and shopping with friends. However, the animators invented many cool gadgets for her, such as controllable zero-gravity switches that allowed for dancing in midair, and a floating robotic diary named Didi, voiced by the sultry actress Brenda Vaccaro. Elroy, her six-and-a-half-year-old brother, went to Little Dipper School and happened to be exceptionally smart in all space sciences.

The Jetsons also had pets, including their beloved yet dimwitted Great Dane, Astro. As a sign of how household pets may one day evolve, Astro possessed a fundamental grasp of the English language. Derived from the sound of a barking dog's "Ruff, ruff," Don Messick, who voiced Astro, had the idea to replace the first letter of any word with an R. "I love you, George" became "I ruv roo, Reorge." One of the most memorable gags involved George giving Astro a walk on a gravity-suspended treadmill. A cat suddenly stumbles in front of Astro and the dog takes off after it. The treadmill's speed becomes too fast for George and he gets caught in it. His plea for his wife's help became a familiar catchphrase from the show: "Jane! Stop this crazy thing!"

Another popular member of the Jetson household was their humanoid robotic maid, Rosie. Actress Jean Vander Pyl, who also voiced Fred Flintstone's long-suffering wife, Wilma, supplied Rosie's vocals. In the first episode of the series, "Rosie the Robot," we discovered Rosie was an older model, yet the

ABOVE: Astro chases puppy love in a passing aerocar—right off the end of the family's walking strip.

A FUTURISTIC CONVENIENCE, STRAIGHT OUT OF THE PAST

After the flying cars landed, the Jetsons and fellow Orbit City citizens traversed between home and work on moving walkways. It was an invention not of the future but from centuries past. Inventor Alfred Speer patented moving walkways in 1871, though it would take nearly a century for them to be put in use. The first moving walkway was installed at Dallas' Love Field in 1958.

whole family came to love her. In "Rosie's Boyfriend," Rosie fell for Mac, the robot assistant of Henry Orbit, the apartment supervisor of Skypad Apartments where the Jetsons lived. Although Rosie was fond of Mac, Rosie was clearly the more intelligent robot and often scolded him for his childish behavior.

Though Rosie and other secondary cast members, like Spacely's arch-competitor Mr. Cogswell of Cogswell's Cosmic Cogs Company, rounded out an amusing show with a great premise, the original series only lasted one season. Most TV experts

TOP: Mealtime made easy with Jane's computerized, automated kitchen.

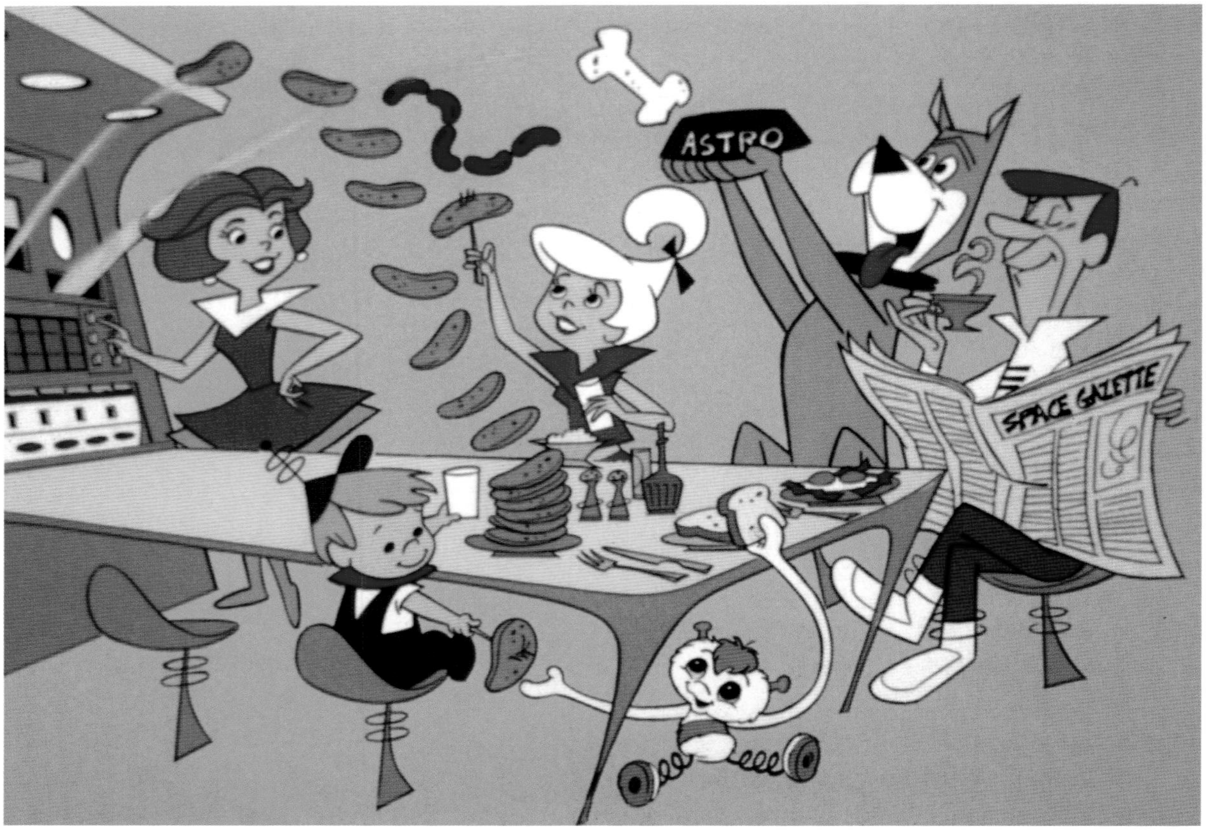
ASTRO
SPACE GAZETTE

speculate the cancellation was due in large part to it being produced and broadcast in color. In 1962, less than 3 percent of US households owned a color television set. Even then, only those viewers in Detroit, Chicago, San Francisco, and Los Angeles could see the show in color as these were served by ABC-owned and operated stations. Consequently, the *Jetsons'* bright and shiny future appeared dull and unengaging in black-and-white to most of the viewing populace.

Following its cancellation on ABC, the program would spend the next two decades on Saturday mornings, with subsequent runs on CBS (1964–65 and 1969–71) and NBC (1965–67, 1971–76, 1979–81 and 1982–83). From 1985 to 1987, new episodes of *The Jetsons* were produced for syndication. In 1990, *Jetsons: The Movie* debuted, serving as the series finale to the television show.

For those who experienced this era of Saturday morning cartoons, *The Jetsons* is indelibly affixed in their memories. Danny Graydon, author of *The Jetsons: The Official Guide to the Cartoon Classic*, aptly sums up the show's enduring popularity: "It coincided with this period of American history when there was a renewed hope—the beginning of the '60s, sort of pre-Vietnam, when Kennedy was in power. So there was something very attractive about the nuclear family with good honest values thriving well into the future. I think that chimed with the zeitgeist of the American culture of the time." Who knew the future could be so out of this world funny—or so much fun?

Battleship Board Game

"You sunk my battleship!" was the signature phrase shouted in the iconic commercial introducing this highly popular board game. A high stakes battle of wits, this pastime involved strategy and a bit of luck and actually began as a pencil-and-paper game dating back to World War I, well before Milton Bradley released the plastic board game in 1967.

Since then, the Battleship board game has sold more than 100 million copies and was one of the first games to make the leap to computers when it was produced for the Z80 Compucolor system in 1979.

1 2 3 4 5 6 7
A B C D E F G H I J

AGES 7 & up
2 Players
BATTLESHIP
THE CLASSIC NAVAL COMBAT GAME
MB

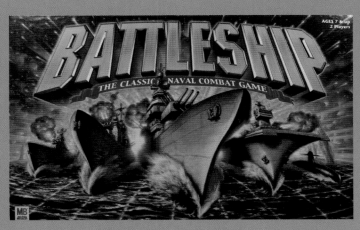

ABOVE: Each Battleship player has a five-piece fleet: an aircraft carrier, cruiser, destroyer, submarine, and battleship. Once each player arranges the ships on a grid of squares, the other player attempts to "sink" their opponent's ships by calling out the squares where they believe the enemy ships are hiding. White pegs represent misses and red pegs indicate hits.

YEARS ON AIR

1964-1965

NETWORK

ABC

NUMBER OF EPISODES

26

CHARACTERS AND VOICE ACTORS

Jonny Quest: Tim Matheson
Race Bannon: Mike Road
Bandit: Don Messick
Hadji: Danny Bravo
Dr. Benton C. Quest: John Stephenson

Jonny Quest

A throwback to the radio dramas of the 1930s and 40s, *Jonny Quest* became network television's first-ever animated adventure series. Hanna-Barbera studios asked cartoonist and designer Doug Wildey to reimagine the action-adventure genre for a cartoon. At the time, Wildey was renowned for his success with his graphic novel *Rio,* as well as hundreds of stories he produced about the old west for Marvel, DC, and Dell. In order to really bring the story to life, Barbera also suggested Wildey look to his favorite James Bond film, *Dr. No,* for ideas—which inspired the villainess character of Dr. Zin and the show's overall quasi-spy tone. Drawing further on heroic

characters, such as *Doc Savage, Tom Swift,* and *Jack Armstrong—the All-American Boy,* Wildey created a hit show around a preteen protagonist solving action-packed, fast-paced mysteries.

Intelligent and brave, eleven-year-old Jonny easily won the love and respect of audiences as being the coolest kid ever. Voiced by actor Tim Matheson, Jonny experienced the same trials and tribulations as his young viewers. He was no fan of school. He would rather battle mummies or fight off giant condors than attend classes. The only difference was that he actually got to do it, thanks to his father, sophisticated world-renowned scientist and explorer Dr. Benton Quest, investigator of unusual phenomena for the US government.

The Quests' compound was located at the tip of the Florida peninsula at Palm Key, but missions took them around the globe to confront formidable foes. One of these excursions resulted in meeting Hadji Singh, a streetwise eleven-year-old Kolkata orphan who became Jonny's adopted brother after saving Dr. Quest from a knife attack. Always clad in his bejeweled turban and Nehru jacket, and possessing mystical powers, Hadji became Jonny's best friend. "I wanted a clear difference between these two kids who were roughly the same age, a different perspective and lifestyle to spice things up," says Wildey. "I wanted to use a minority character other than the typical black kid from the ghetto, which so many others had used in comic strips and comic books. There were objections to the character but there are always objections about everything when you are doing an animated series."

The *Jonny Quest* entourage was rounded out with characters such as Race Bannon, special agent, bodyguard, and pilot, who served as a tutor and caregiver for Jonny and Hadji. An expert in firearms and hand-to-hand combat, he was voiced by actor Mike Road (*Fantastic Four*) and physically modeled after 1950s film star Jeff Chandler with his chiseled good looks and gray-white hair. His name came from two comic strips Wildey never did sell: one concerned an American race-car driver named Stretch Bannon, and the other told the tales of a Race Dunhill, a world-traveling writer.

Animals also played a significant part in the show, especially Bandit, Jonny's loyal dog. Though fans were fond of him, he was not Wildey's first choice for a creature companion. "I never liked the dog," admitted Wildey, who would have preferred a small white cheetah or monkey. "There are a lot of story possibilities for a monkey and it can do things realistically that a dog could never do. But they wanted a dog for some reason, maybe merchandising. They used the dog for comic relief and it was easier for some of the artists to draw funny dog stuff."

The Saga of Chip Ballou was actually the show's initial working title. Wildey wanted the titled character's name to imply the theme of the series: adventure. "I picked the name Quest out of the Los Angeles phone book because it just sounded

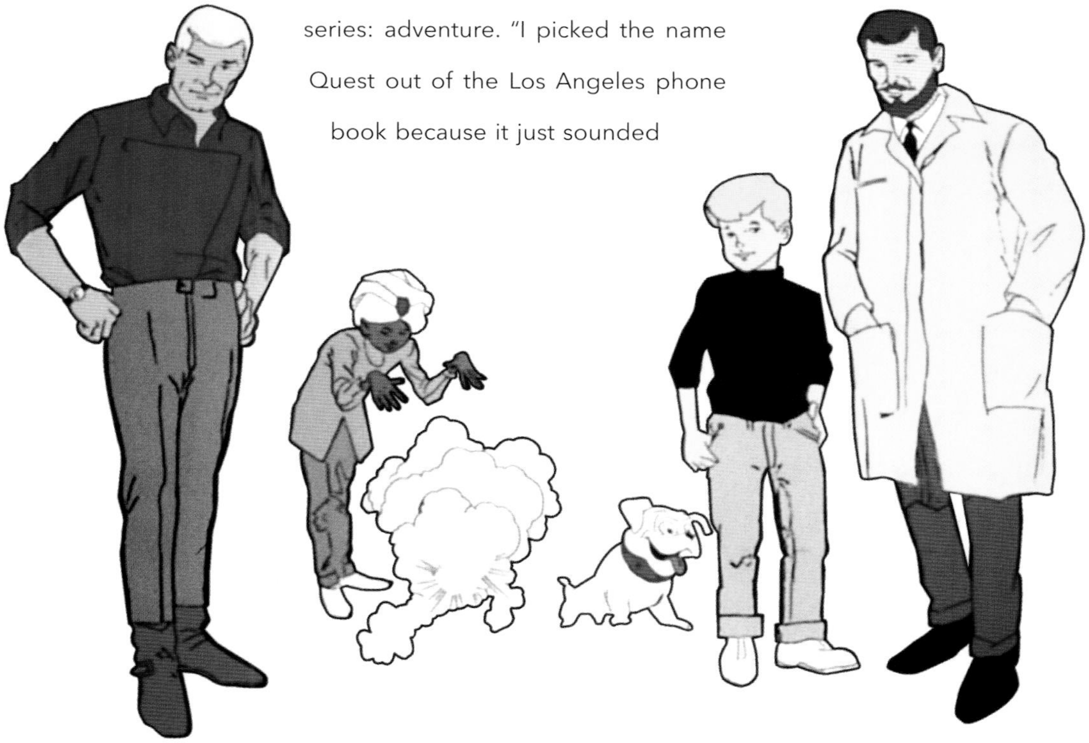

OPPOSITE: (left to right) Hadji, Race Bannon, Jonny Quest, and Dr. Benton Quest spring into action.

BOTTOM: Hadji demonstrates his mystic powers for Jonny, Race, and Dr. Quest.

good to me," remembers Wildey. "It was Joe Barbera who came up with the name 'Jonny' without the 'h' so his name is really 'Jonathan'. I liked that. The letters just seemed right."

Beyond Jonny's cool name, the whole series was aimed at boys and girls excited by a daring lad thrust into exotic locales and futuristic scenarios. Reflecting the mid '60s hipness with its funky big-band jazz theme song and stylish danger by way of Ian Fleming, *Jonny Quest* had a more serious tone than its cartoon counterparts. As comics historian Daniel Herman observed, "The look of *Jonny Quest* was unlike any other cartoon television show of the time, with its colorful backgrounds, and its focus on the characters with their jet packs, hydrofoils, and lasers."

With so much of the series' emphasis on futuristic gadgets, it may be surprising to learn Wildey didn't share many of the same tastes as his audience. "I do not like science fiction," Wildey acknowledged. "I was constantly reading magazines, like *Scientific American*, *National Geographic*, *Popular Mechanics*, and *Science Digest* to get ideas and to extrapolate what might realistically exist in the next ten years because we figured the series might last that long, even if just in reruns. That's how we came up with some of those things, like lasers, and it ended up making the series timeless rather than tied to that particular time period."

Wildey's thorough research resulted in episodes like "The Robot Spy," in which the sinister Dr. Zin plots to steal Dr. Quest's experimental ray gun and sends a spider-like robot to his lab. The robotic arachnid is nearly unstoppable as it tears through the compound with top-secret information. That is, until a well-placed shot to its eye results in a horrific explosion. An image of Dr. Zin is transmitted through the damaged eye, with the villain vowing he and Dr. Quest will surely meet again. Wildey's personal favorite episode, however, was "Shadow of the Condor." One of the reasons Wildey wrote it was because fellow artist Warren Tufts was a huge airplane fanatic and was working on the series at the time. In the episode, Race experiences engine trouble, forcing him to set the jet down on a small airstrip located high up in the Andes. There the Quests meet a World War I German ace, Baron Heinrich Von Freulich, who flew with the famous Condor Squadron. The baron has a collection of vintage planes and tricks Race into an air battle. Race's guns are empty, forcing him to outmaneuver the baron and hope for the best.

Suspenseful episodes such as these, as well as other stories featuring invisible monsters and so-called lizard men, captured the imaginations of children hungry for heroes with brawn and brain, but the show lasted just one season. Reruns were broadcast Saturday mornings on CBS from 1967 to 1970, then on NBC from 1971 to 1972. Like Hanna-Barbera's other sci-fi program, *The Jetsons*, *Jonny Quest* was one of the few series to have aired on each of the Big Three television networks.

In spite of being so short-lived, the program's popularity spawned *Jonny Quest*–themed merchandise and promotional items. PF Flyers sneakers offered a code ring with a magnifying lens, signal

flasher, and a secret compartment. There were board games, coloring books, card games, puzzle sets, and paint-by-number kits. As every child knows, the thrill of watching television is imagining yourself as the character on-screen. And there was nothing more far-out than slipping into Jonny Quest's world for thirty minutes on Saturdays. Just as soon as you did, you were in for the adventure of your young life.

OPPOSITE TOP AND BOTTOM: Race Bannon and Jonny fight off the powerful lizard men in the show's debut episode "The Mystery of the Lizard Men."

ABOVE: Hadji stops a knife, saving Jonny and Race.

YEARS ON AIR

1964–1973

NETWORK

NBC, CBS

NUMBER OF EPISODES

124 (Original episodes)

CHARACTERS AND VOICE ACTORS

Underdog: Wally Cox
Sweet Polly Purebred: Norma Macmillan
Simon Bar Sinister/Riff Raff/ Batty Man: George S. Irving

Underdog

There's no need to fear! Underdog is here!

Of all the strident cries from TV's anthropomorphic superanimals, none rang with more familiarity to young cape-wearing boomers of the '60s than that of Underdog, the champion of champions. While not the first furry or four-legged cartoon crime fighter, the rhyming Dog of Steel was the most powerful of all, dominating Saturday morning airwaves for an astonishing nine years.

Of course, *Underdog*'s creators didn't generate the popular pooch for strictly artistic purposes. He was made to sell sugary breakfast cereal. As the saying goes, "necessity is the mother of invention," and in 1959, account executives at Dancer Fitzgerald Sample, a top New York ad agency, desperately needed a new cartoon for one of their biggest clients, General Mills, purveyor of kid-craving breakfast

cereals like Trix and Cocoa Puffs. Account executive W. Watts "Buck" Biggers teamed with the agency's creative director and copywriter Chet Stover, marketing expert Tread Covington, and top artist Joe Harris to pull off their mission. Although Harris had just invented Trix's trademark floppy-eared "silly rabbit" that year, he and the group were stuck when it came to ideas. Nothing seemed right. The fact they were competing for a time slot against Jay Ward and Bill Scott, who created *Rocky & Bullwinkle,* only added to their stress.

Then one morning the team experienced a breakthrough. Stover recounted watching George Reeves, star of *The Adventures of Superman* on *I Love Lucy* the night before. Eureka! The team now had their hook: they would develop a show about a caped crusader. Despite this epiphany, the Dancer Fitzgerald Sample ad guys still felt outgunned by the talents at Ward and Scott. In fact, Biggers recalls

saying to Stover, "We're going to be the underdog." At this moment, the notion of a beagle-turned-superhero was born.

Soon after, Biggers and his partners left their ad agency to form their own animation production company, Total TeleVision (TTV), with the purpose of generating cartoon characters urging kids to buy General Mills cereals. TTV successfully created several shows to accomplish this aim, including *King Leonardo and His Short Subjects*, which followed the bungling king of Bongo Congo, and *Tennessee Tuxedo and His Tales*, the misadventures of a penguin named Tennessee Tuxedo and his best friend Chumley the walrus, escapees from the zoo. However, *Underdog* became the true breakout hit upon its 1964 premiere on NBC.

A spoof on superhero melodramas, each *Underdog* episode began with George S. Irving, the gruff-voiced Broadway character actor who

OPPOSITE: America's first animated canine crime fighter with his perpetual damsel in distress, intrepid TV reporter Sweet Polly Purebred.

ABOVE LEFT: In addition to Earth-based enemies, Underdog grappled with enemies from other worlds.

ABOVE RIGHT: Underdog had many super powers: X-ray vision, supersonic flight, physical invulnerability, and yes, even super breath.

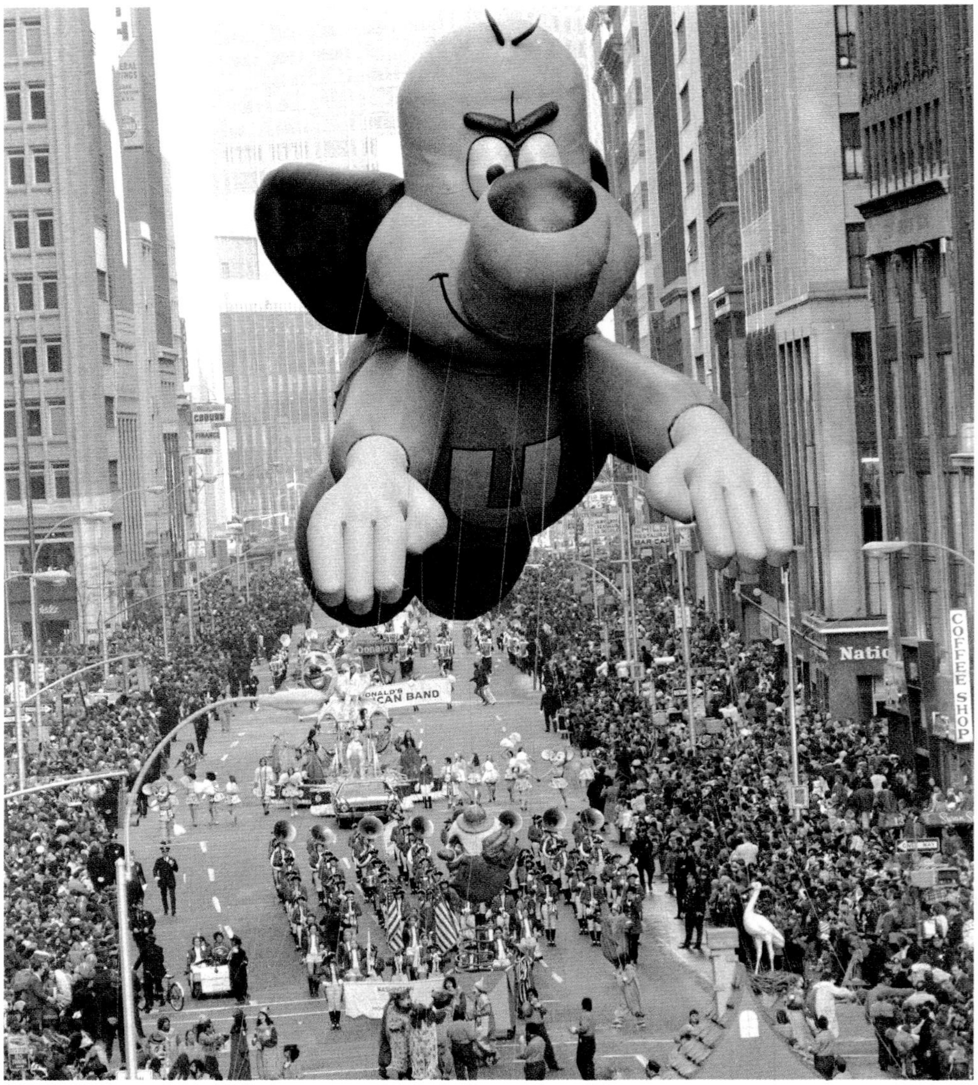
COFFEE SHOP

ABOVE: Underdog first flew over the famed Macy's Thanksgiving Day Parade in 1965. He was retired in 1984.

set the scene and narrated as needed. Drawing upon Superman's reliable secret-identity formula, Underdog maintained dual personas throughout the show. When not saving the world from evil, he assumed the alter ego of a "humble and lovable" bespectacled beagle known as Shoeshine Boy. Comedy actor Wally Cox provided the voices for both identities. Cox, one of TV's all-time great milquetoasts, initially achieved stardom by portraying a bookish high school science teacher in the 1950s series, *Mr. Peepers*. "His voice was well known to a lot of people," recalled Biggers, "making his sheepish everyman the perfect choice."

Throughout the series nothing galvanized Shoeshine Boy's superhero transformation quicker than pleas from the show's version of Lois Lane, TV reporter Sweet Polly Purebred, played by voice actress Norma MacMillan (also the voice of Casper the Friendly Ghost and Gumby.) Whenever in peril, Polly would sing, "Oh where, oh where has my Underdog gone? Oh where, oh where can he be?" Hearing her, Shoeshine Boy would rush to the scene of the crime, then dart into the nearest telephone booth. Here he would activate his superpowers in an explosive burst with such force he usually destroyed the booth before emerging in a clearly too-large red jumpsuit with a white *U* across the front. "When Polly's in trouble I am not slow," Underdog would proclaim. "It's hip-hip-hip and away I go!"

Silliness clearly pervaded the show with its Superman spoofs, but Underdog did possess powers he used to face off against the bad guys. Not only was he stronger and faster than any living dog or human, he had X-ray vision and ultrasonic hearing. He could also fly fast and shatter glass with the sound of his devastating roar. Underdog's super canine powers came from the super energy pills stored in his ring, monogrammed with a *U*. (Years later, Underdog's pill-popping became a delicate issue for NBC, which insisted the scenes be edited out of episodes.) No matter the source of his powers, these abilities serviced Underdog in his quest to fight off an array of villains, such as Fearo the Ferocious, Overcat, Riff Raff, and his primary nemesis, Simon Bar Sinister—the mad scientist who always uttered "Simon says . . ." just as he was about to execute one of his criminal misdeeds.

In addition to taking on Earth-based enemies, Underdog grappled with enemies from other worlds, such as the Marbleheads from planet Granite in the episode "The Marbleheads" or the aliens from the episode "Zot." No matter the adversary or situation Underdog found himself in, the episodes typically unfolded as four-part serials with other cartoons, including *Go Go Gophers* and *The Hunter* occupying the middle spots. A recurring element then concluded each show. Similar to Superman, a crowd of bystanders would look up and shout: "Look in the sky! It's a bird! It's a plane!" Then a confused little old lady would say: "It's a frog!" Another onlooker would respond dubiously, "A frog?" Finally, Underdog, speaking to the audience and not watching where he was flying, would say, "Not plane, nor bird, nor even frog, it's just little old me." At this point he would smash into something and say, "Heh-heh-heh. Underdog."

This amusing manner of superhero parody bestowed Underdog with well . . . underdog status. Perhaps little was to be expected from a canine dressed up in a cape in order to peddle breakfast cereal. Yet *Underdog* ended up with surprising popularity. The Biggers and company's brainchild managed to outperform most other cartoons from the 1960s, lasting three seasons and producing over one hundred episodes. After wrapping its run on NBC in 1967, the show then moved to CBS where it aired until 1973.

ABOVE: Each episode concluded with Underdog, speaking to the audience—not watching where he was flying—saying, "Not plane, nor bird, nor even frog, it's just little old me." At which point he would smash into something and say, "Heh-heh-heh. Underdog."

While on air and even after it left television, *Underdog* became a part of the popular culture lexicon. Introduced in 1965, a giant Underdog balloon floated down New York's 34th Street as part of the Macy's Thanksgiving Day Parade until it was retired in 1985. Publishers, including Charlton, Gold Key, Spotlight, and Harvey put out a slew of *Underdog* comic books. The lovable rhyming mutt even got his own Little Golden Book, *Underdog and the Disappearing Ice Cream*. Underdog appeared in a 2005 commercial for the Visa Check Card and starred in a 2007 live-action film, loosely based on the animated series. In addition, *TV Guide* ranked him as one of the "50 Greatest Cartoon Characters of All Time." Not bad for an underdog, right? Or as he might say, "I am a hero who never fails; I cannot be bothered with such details."

The Archie Show

YEARS ON AIR

1968–1969

NETWORK

CBS

NUMBER OF EPISODES

17

CHARACTERS AND VOICE ACTORS

Archie Andrews/Hot Dog/
Mr. Weatherbee/Pop Tate/
Mr. Lodge/Coach Kleats:
Dallas McKennon
Betty Cooper/Veronica Lodge/
Miss Grundy/Big Ethel:
Jane Webb
Reggie Mantle: John Erwin
Jughead: Howard Morris

For the typical preteen Saturday morning viewer, the kids from Riverdale High—Archie, Veronica, Betty, Reggie, and Jughead—seemed like just the kind of cool clique you hoped you could hang with when you became a teenager. They even had their own rock band! But the cool characters comprising *The Archie Show* were actually created long before rock'n'roll even existed. In 1939, publisher John L. Goldwater, along with partners Louis Silberkleit and Maurice Coyne, launched the comic book publishing company, MLJ Magazines. Goldwater aspired for

the success of the *Superman* comics, and believed a character based on a normal, everyday guy could be just as winning. Inspired by the popularity of the *Andy Hardy* movies that starred the top box-office attraction of the day, Mickey Rooney, Goldwater's fledgling company began publishing about just such a character: the one and only Archie Andrews.

Archie represented the all-American teenage boy. Kids liked his goofball personality and parents appreciated his good-natured charm. In addition to navigating the travails of adolescence, Archie

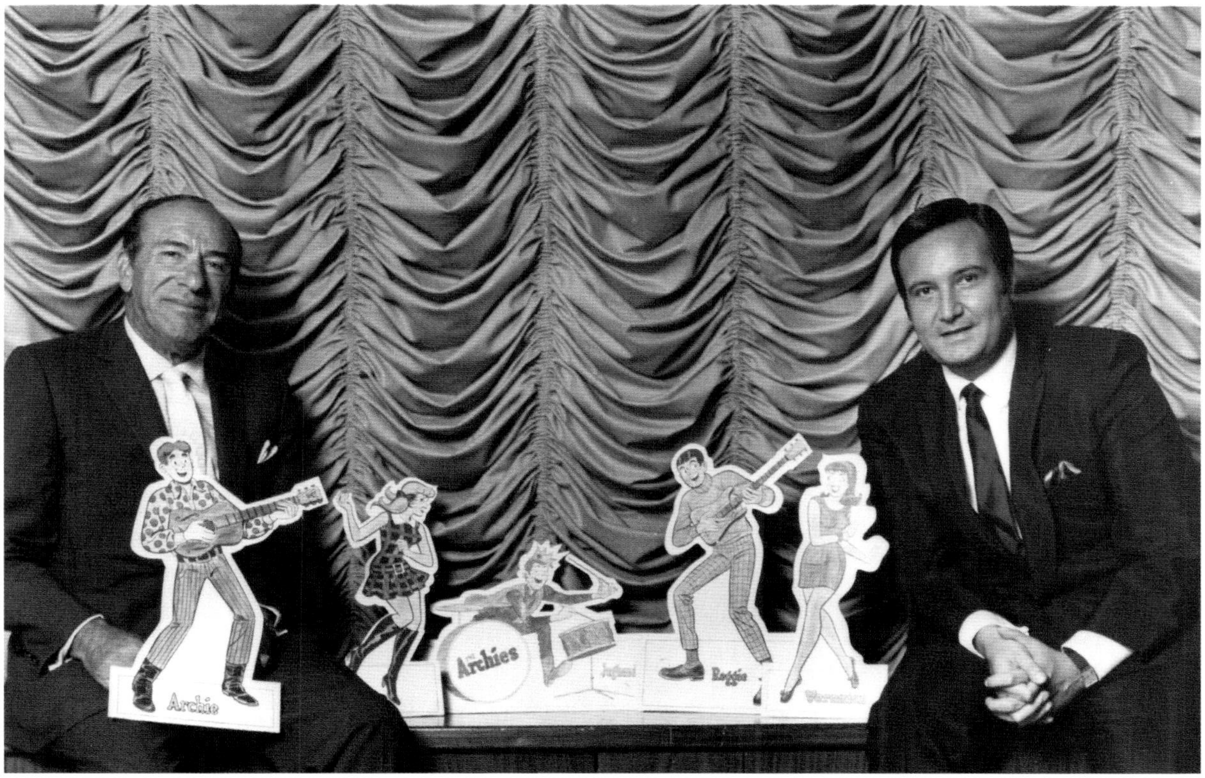
Archie
Archies

OPPOSITE: The stars of *The Archie Show* (left to right) Jughead Jones, Veronica Lodge, Archie Andrews, Betty Cooper, and Reggie Mantle.

TOP: Producer Don Kirshner (right) poses with carboard cutouts of the cartoon pop group "The Archies," circa 1968.

continually faced a vexing conundrum most males would die to grapple with, something that made the comics and the eventual series irresistible: a good old-fashioned love triangle. According to Goldwater, "I dreamed up the carrot-topped, freckle-faced character as a hapless 'everyman' teenager perpetually torn between two loves: one blonde and one dark." A cast of pals also surrounded Archie, styled after actual kids Goldwater met while hitchhiking through the Midwest during the Depression. Collaborating with artist Bob Montana and writer Vic Bloom, Goldwater placed Archie and friends in idyllic Riverdale where Archie played sports, navigated romantic entanglements, and puttered around in his Model T jalopy.

These wholesome stories, focusing on teenage intrigue, caught the attention of Filmation Associates, an animation and live-action production company responsible for such adaptations as *The New Adventures of Superman*, *Aquaman*, and *The Hardy Boys*. Filmation liked the idea of bringing Archie to Saturday mornings and took on the task of animating the Riverdale gang into *The Archie Show*. "We did a ton of superhero shows, and by '68 it was obvious there were just too many of those types of shows around," said producer Lou Scheimer. "So we got the rights to Archie Comics, and it was interesting because it was the first of the non-superhero comic books that was brought to television, and it was an extraordinarily successful show."

Modeled on the live-action series, *The Monkees*, which had debuted two years prior, Filmation designed much of the program around pop music. Each episode included two eight-minute stories separated by three short segments. The first short

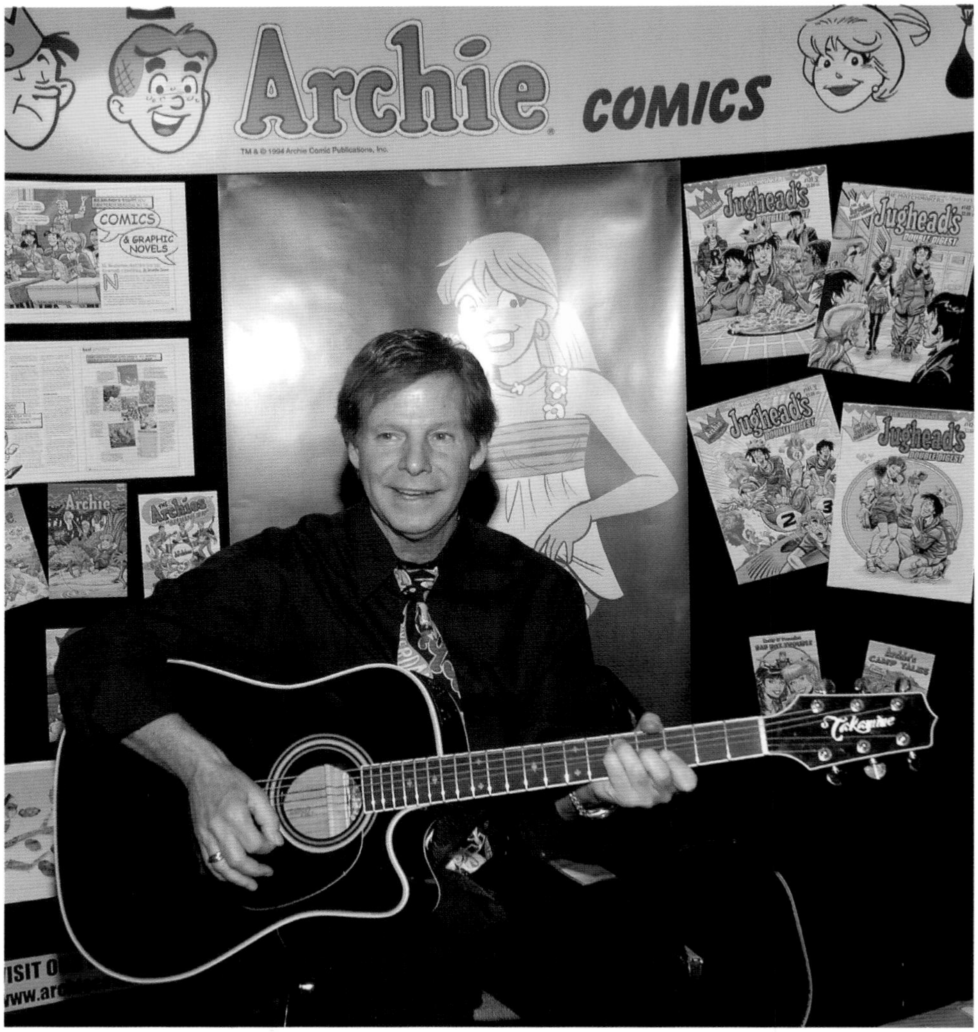
Archie
COMICS

ABOVE: Singer Ron Dante, real-life lead singer of The Archies (Sugar, Sugar) attends New York Comic Con at the Jacob Javits Center, April 18, 2008.

segment was "The Dance of the Week," which featured one or more of the cast teaching the audience a new dance step. "The Song of the Week" was the next segment and was performed by the Archies, a fictional band featuring sessions musicians Ron Dante (lead singer) and Toni Wine (duet and backing vocals). The third segment offered a short joke followed by the second Archie story. In 1969, the Archies scored a real-life no. 1 hit single with their bubblegum song, "Sugar, Sugar," written by Jeff Barry and Andy Kim. Selling over six million copies, *Billboard* Hot 100 ranked it number one song of the year, the first and only time an animated fictional band clinched the award.

Undoubtedly, Filmation's quasi-musical animated series connected with audiences. Soon, millions of kids were eagerly following Archie's misadventures. They ate up the delicious awkwardness of Archie bouncing like a ping-pong ball between his girlfriends, the sweet, attractive blonde Betty Cooper, and the beautiful, rich, spoiled brunette Veronica Lodge. Likewise, Archie's rivalry with the handsome yet conceited Reggie Mantle spiced up story lines. Reggie's penchant for selfish schemes and deceitful tricks never ceased to put him at odds with Archie. Unfortunately for Reggie, his shenanigans always seemed to backfire on him. "Jughead" Jones (real name: Forsythe Pendleton Jones III) rounded out the gang, providing comic relief. A nonconformist who liked nothing more than eating everything in sight, Jughead was known for wearing his signature whoopee cap and being quite lazy. He was also fiercely loyal to his best pal, Archie. A host of beloved secondary characters populated Riverdale, including teacher Miss Grundy, Coach Kleats, principal Mr. Weatherbee, jock Big Moose, the school's self-described genius Dilton Doily, and Pops, owner of the gang's favorite hangout, Pop's Chok'lit Shoppe.

In 1969, due to the show's popularity, Filmation decided to revamp *The Archie Show* after just seventeen episodes. The show was reimagined into *The Archie Comedy Hour* with all-new material, including Filmation's newest animated star, Sabrina the Teenage Witch. The new format contained two

Sabrina segments, one at the start of the show and one at the end, with a new "Funhouse" joke in the middle, loosely based on the sketch comedy hit, *Laugh-In*. Other segments included Sabrina's Magic Trick and Dilton Doily's Inventions, followed by an Archies music segment.

Archie was a huge hit in comic books and animation throughout his various iterations, but it wasn't until 2016 that the Riverdale gang succeeded in becoming a live-action series. Several years prior, Goldwater's son, Jon Goldwater, took over his late father's company—now named Archie Comics—and repositioned the franchise to be more current and fresh. As part of the reboot, he teamed with Warner Bros. to bring a reimagined Archie to The CW Network. Dispensing with the innocence of the earlier material, the dramatic series *Riverdale* is angst-infused, featuring the gang discovering the darkness and dangers behind their town's wholesome facade.

Before the Saturday morning cartoon, the *Archie Andrews* radio program aired from 1943 to 1953. The fact that teens in the twenty-first century still gravitate to the amusing tales of the gang is a testament to Archie's timelessness and continuing pop cultural relevance. Not only did *The Archie Show* offer lots of fun and laughs while producing hit music, it set the stage for future musical-based Saturday morning cartoons, like *Jem* and *Josie and the Pussycats*. Clearly, Goldwater's hunch paid off: audiences have and continue to love themselves some Archie Andrews, America's all-American teenage boy.

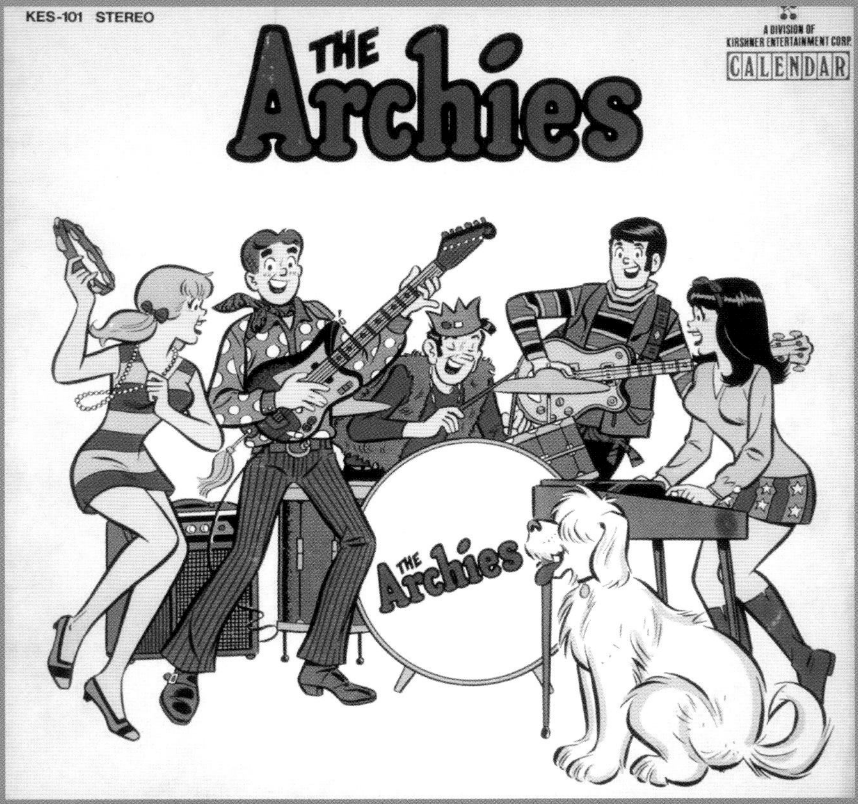
KES-101 STEREO
THE Archies
A DIVISION OF KIRSHNER ENTERTAINMENT CORP.
CALENDAR
THE Archies

ABOVE: The Archies was the first-ever animated band to release an album.

The Archies

Riverdale's favorite band, The Archies, was an eclectic grouping of instruments . . . each played by a character. There was even a four-legged conductor to boot!

Archie – lead guitar

Reggie – bass guitar

Jughead – drums

Hot Dog (Jughead's dog) – conductor

Betty – tambourine

Veronica – organ

Alpha-Bits Cereal

"My mommy says I'm healthy; my teacher says I'm wise; I owe it all to Alpha-Bits, the cereal surprise!"

In the 1960s, Post cereal advertised their latest offering as the "new extra healthy, sugar-sparkled oat cereal." The company used postman Loveable Truly as the cereal's mascot, voiced by insult comic Jack E. Leonard. Over the years, other mascots have included the Alpha-Bit Wizard and the Alpha, a computer that makes bits. And who can forget the cereal's other memorable taglines such as, "Tastiest cereal you've ever met—it's just like eating up the alphabet!" and "They're A-B-C-Delicious!"

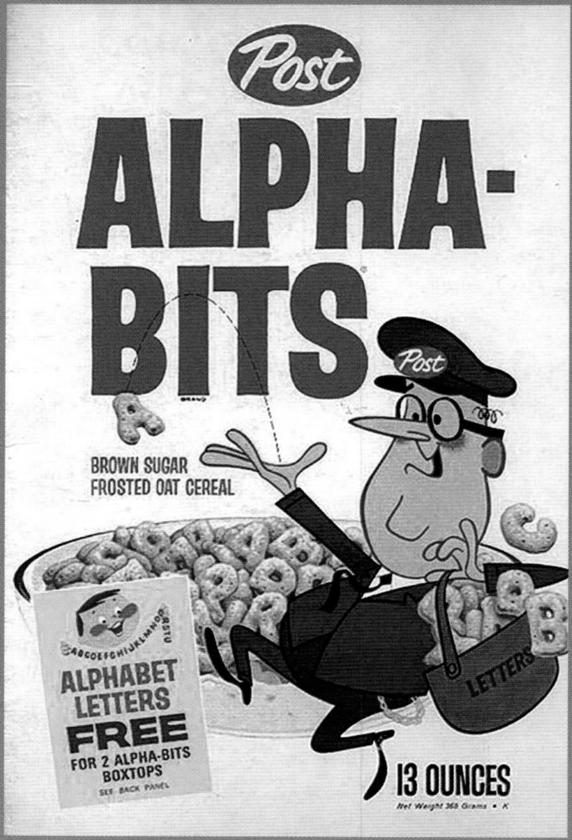
Post
ALPHA-BITS
Post
BROWN SUGAR
FROSTED OAT CEREAL
ALPHABET
LETTERS
FREE
FOR 2 ALPHA-BITS
BOXTOPS
SEE BACK PANEL
LETTERS
13 OUNCES

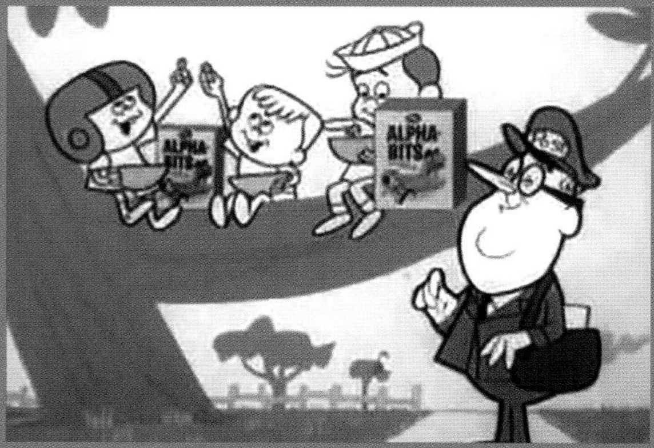

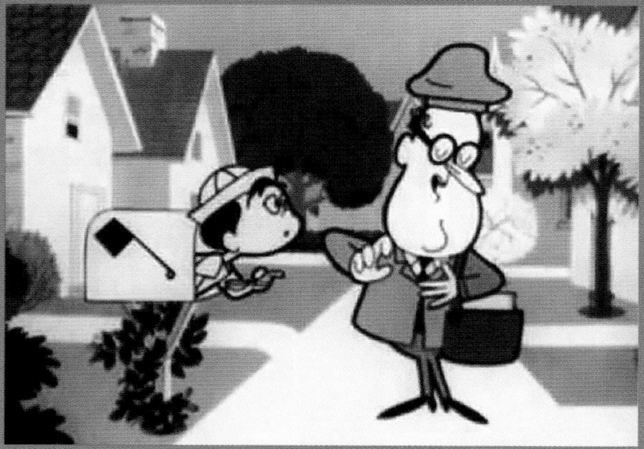

ABOVE: Postman Truly on the box and in the 1960's commercial for Alpha-Bits..

Space Ghost

The imaginative tales of Space Ghost, the mighty interstellar cop, hailing from Ghost Planet, glued kids to their television sets on Saturday mornings. The show helped launch the popularity of superhero cartoons in the 1960s. Prior to this show, the animated superhero genre mostly focused on the cartoony animal variety: Underdog, Mighty Mouse, and Adam Ant. *Space Ghost*, debuting in 1966 on CBS, became an instant hit, ushering in a wave of "human-like" super guys.

Much of *Space Ghost*'s popularity may be attributed to Hanna-Barbera designer and idea man, Alex Toth, whose credits include *Super Friends*, *Sealab 2020*, *The Herculoids,* and *Birdman*. Toth came to animation from the comic book world, having done a stint at DC Comics. Skilled at designing

YEARS ON AIR

1966–1968

NETWORK

CBS

NUMBER OF EPISODES

20

CHARACTERS AND VOICE ACTORS

Space Ghost: Gary Owens
Todd: John David Carson
Jan: Ginny Tyler
Jace: Tim Matheson
Blip: Don Messick

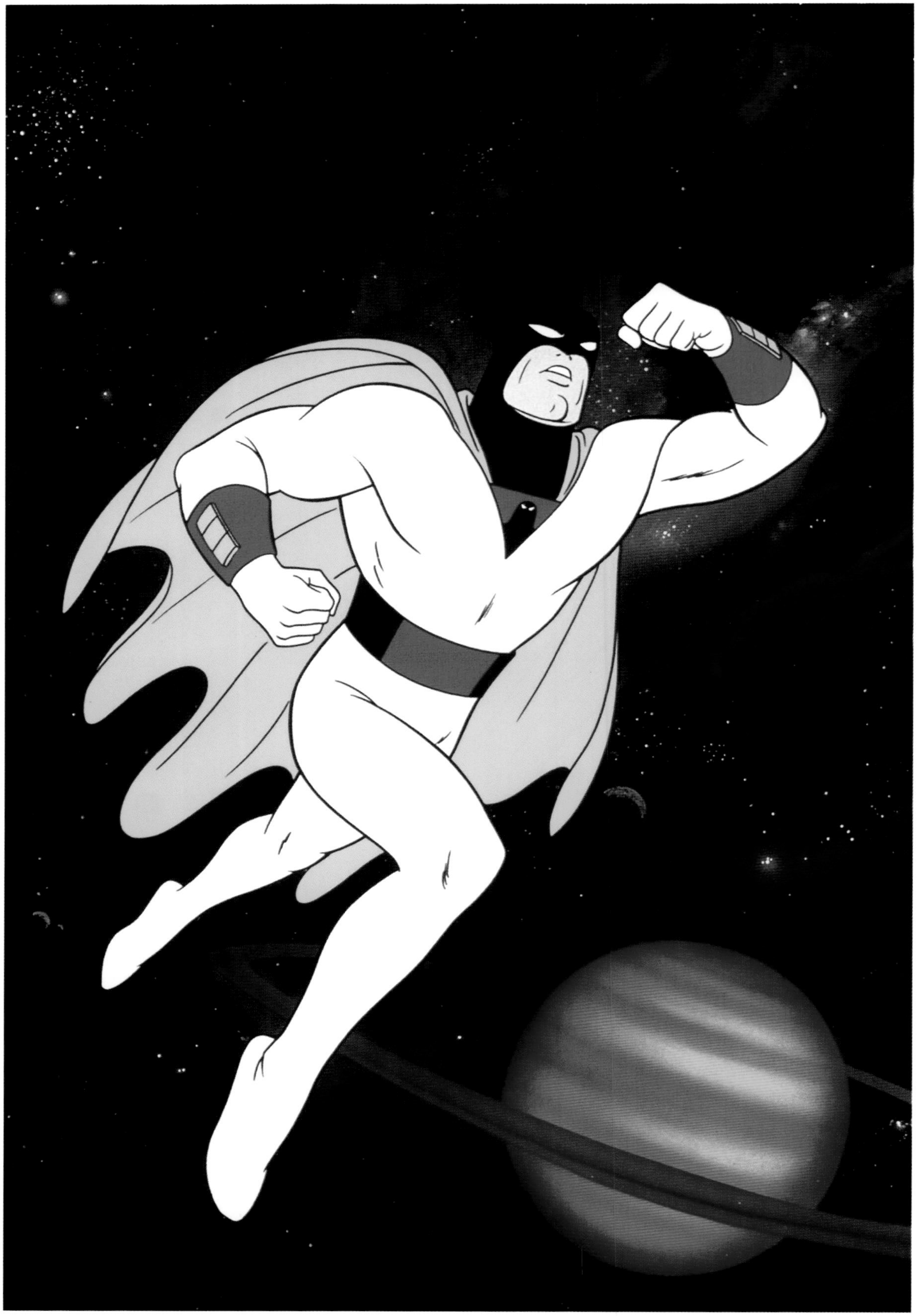

realistic-looking characters, Toth had worked on Hanna-Barbera's action-adventure series *Jonny Quest* prior to taking the role of layout artist on *Space Ghost*.

Considerable credit, however, was also due to the inspired direction of then CBS VP in charge of Saturday morning programming, Fred Silverman. Silverman had recently inherited a slate of reruns, *Heckle and Jeckle*, *Tom and Jerry*, and *Tennessee Tuxedo*, and with them a considerable challenge. Research showed Silverman his "kidvid" viewers tended to abandon animal character cartoons after reaching a certain age. Young males were especially hard to reach and would turn off TV sets in favor of other boyhood activities. But based on the success of *Jonny Quest*, Silverman knew he could reach his coveted demographic if the show was done right. Thus he turned to the animation factory to find his perfect formula.

Intent on bringing the excitement of comic books to Saturday morning television, Silverman united with Toth at a

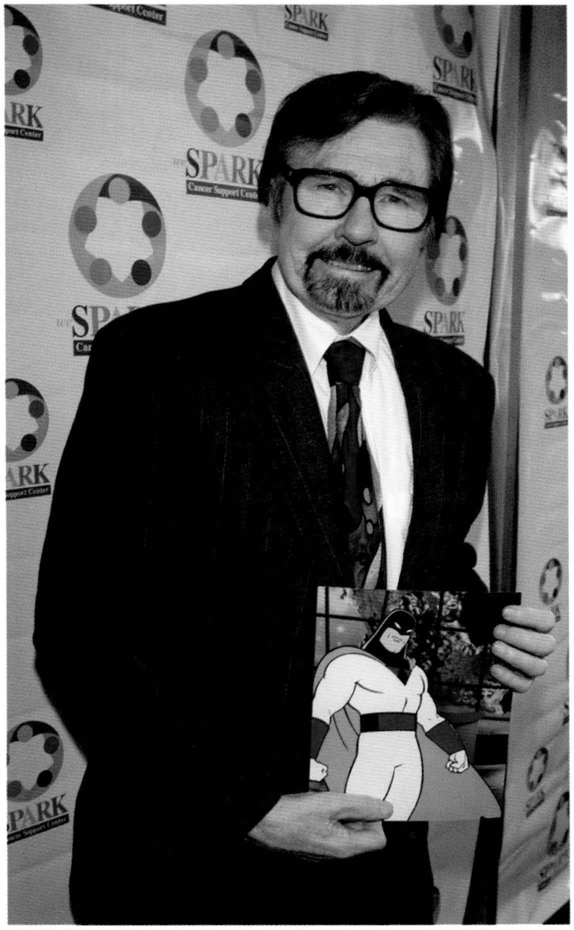
SPARK
Cancer Support Center

PREVIOUS: Main characters (left to right): Space Ghost, Blip the monkey, Jan, and Jace, 1966-68.

OPPOSITE: Inspired by Batman in design, Space Ghost was the first intergalactic superhero.

TOP: Actor Gary Owens, the voice of Space Ghost, 2005.

meeting with Hanna-Barbera to iron out the show's particulars. "Freddie Silverman came in banging around all kinds of ideas," Toth recalls. "We had locked down on *Space Ghost,* but the question of the costume was still up in the air. So there we were on Monday morning in Joe [Barbera]'s office, and in walks Freddie Silverman with this *Life* magazine in his hands and on the cover is Adam West and the kid, Burt Ward, as Batman and Robin. He throws the magazine down on Joe's desk and says, 'That's the look I want. I want that Batman look.' I said, 'Well, he's supposed to be Space Ghost. He should be white; you know?' And Silverman says, 'I want that Batman look.' So finally, Space Ghost wound up with that black cowl over his head."

Still, Toth worried about Space Ghost's look and felt determined to get it just right. "I didn't want that diaphanous, squirrelly cape that he wound up with, which looked like ectoplasm, but that's what they wanted," Toth lamented. He also didn't like how the black cowl looked superimposed against the darkness of space and decided to create a thick halo of light around Space Ghost's figure so he would stand out against the dark background. The juxtaposition of light and dark proved important; after all, Space Ghost earned his name not by being a specter haunting the stars, but based on the fact he could make himself invisible.

Once Space Ghost's look was settled, it was crucial to nail down his abilities. In essence, Space Ghost was an interstellar policeman who protected the cosmos from evildoers. Although he easily traversed the galaxy in his Phantom Cruiser, the caped guardian of the cosmos also needed to possess an arsenal of superpowers. He could fly, teleport, and envelop himself in an invisible, impenetrable forcefield just by pressing the "inviso" button on his belt. If that weren't enough, the power bands on his wrists were capable of releasing a devastating assortment of beams to freeze, shock, or blast the bad guys.

In addition to Space Ghost's superpowers, much of his heroic resonance was attributable to the booming baritone voice of actor Gary Owens, known for voicing of *The Green Hornet*. Owens, who also once nurtured ambitions of being a cartoonist while living in his native South Dakota, had transitioned to being a top-rated disc jockey on Los Angeles radio

BOTTOM: Space Ghost was also unique for his teen sidekicks, Jace and Jan.

station KFWB by 1965. Perhaps best known as the over-the-top announcer for the NBC sketch comedy series, *Laugh-In*, Owens provided the voice for a similarly commanding animated character, Roger Ramjet, the year before in the eponymous series. "We auditioned half of Hollywood," recalled Joe Barbera in an interview. "But Gary was perfect from the start."

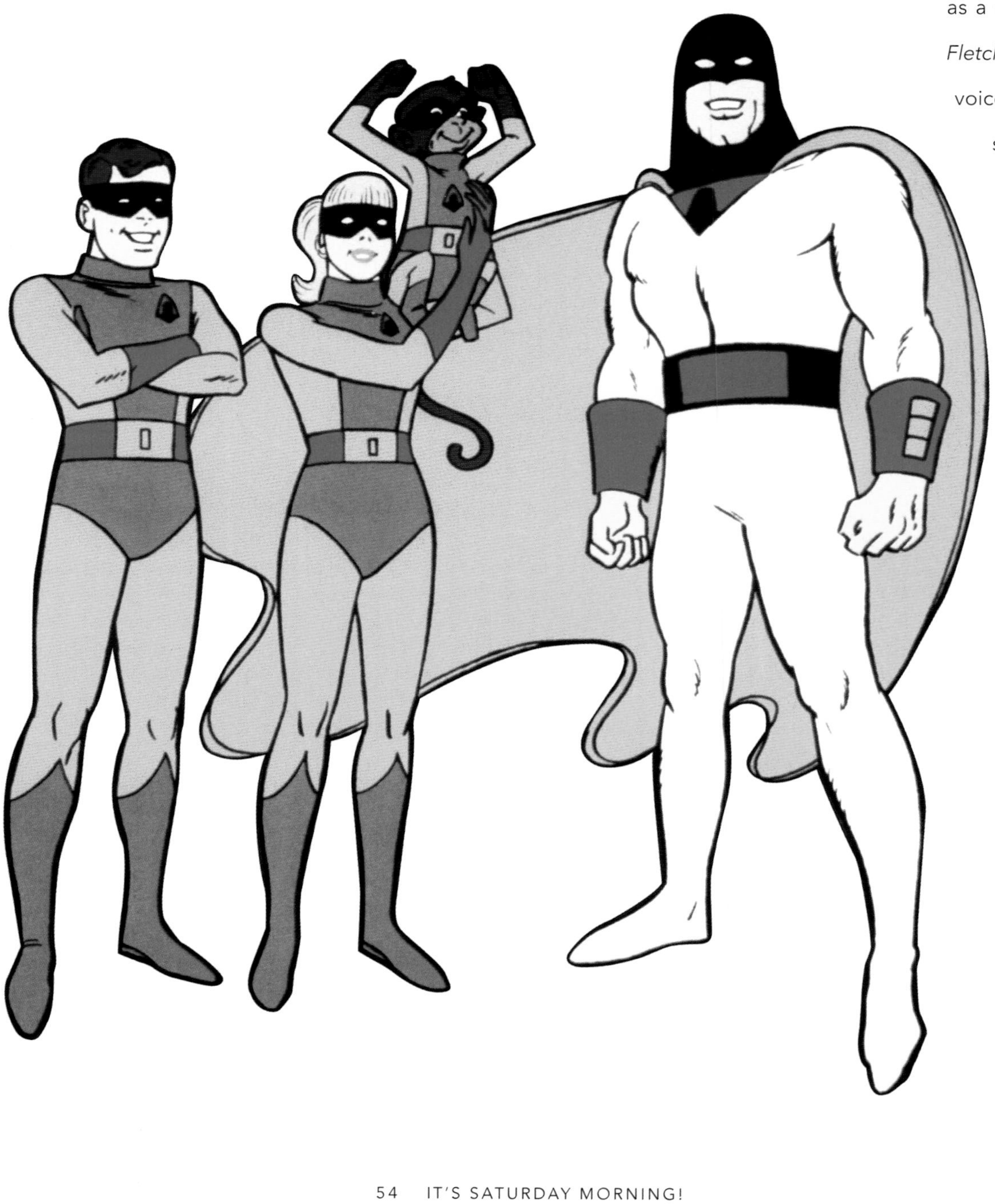

True to the superhero formula, Space Ghost didn't save the world by himself. Sporting face masks and jet packs, teenage twins Jace and Jan backed up Space Ghost, along with their monkey Blip (who also wore a face mask). The voice of Jan was provided by veteran voice actor Ginny Tyler, who previously supplied voices in *Mister Ed* and *Fantastic Four*. And before Tim Matheson would go on to enjoy a career as a movie star in such films as *Animal House* and *Fletch*, he voiced Jace. Meanwhile, Hanna-Barbera voice-over workhorse, Don Messick provided all the sounds of their pet monkey as well as the voices of the series' supporting characters and villains. From week to week, Space Ghost and his allies protected the universe from evildoers such as an insectoid alien named Zorak, a cat-like alien named Brak, and a rogue robot and creature king named Metallus.

Clocking in at an average runtime of just seven minutes per episode, *Space Ghost* raced along at two episodes per week, fighting off memorable villains and dispensing justice at warp speed. In fact, many fans attribute the show's success to the excitement of each installment's quick story line and resolution. Each pithy episode packed in action and adventure.

Despite the fact that Space Ghost remained a cipher, with little known about him other than his perseverance in fighting off arch supervillains, he was the show's biggest draw. However, after

two seasons, CBS ended the series. It may have continued its successful run if not for the pressure of the new antiviolence guidelines imposed on the network's Standards and Practices. This crackdown permeated Saturday morning programming and *Space Ghost* was the initiative's first casualty. The series was relegated to off-network reruns throughout the 1970s. In 1981, a series combining forty-two episodes (the original twenty with twenty-two new ones) broadcast on NBC under the title *Space Stars*. In the 1990s, *Space Ghost* resurfaced as a parody of superhero tropes decades after its initial airing.

The character of Space Ghost appeared in a surreal late-night talk show, *Space Ghost Coast to Coast*, on Cartoon Network and Adult Swim.

The series' legacy bears little relevance to its longevity. In spite of the fact only a mere twenty episodes aired over the course of two seasons, it birthed a generation of devoted fans. Like a few other Saturday morning cartoons, Space Ghost was the right character for the time, and the show struck a special chord with young viewers. No matter how much they've grown up, they'll always remember their hero's clarion cry, "Spaaaaaaace Ghost!"

ABOVE: Disintegration rays shooting from Space Ghost's Power Bands blast the oncoming asteroid.

ABOVE: William Hanna and Joseph Barbera with the theme park characters of (left to right) Huckleberry Hound, Scooby-Doo, Yogi Bear, and Fred Flintstone.

Hanna-Barbera Productions

"That's what keeps me going: dreaming, inventing,

then hoping and dreaming some more

in order to keep dreaming."

~Joseph Barbera

Beginning in the late 1950s and continuing through the 1980s, the team of William Hanna and Joseph Barbera produced the majority of cartoons appearing on the three major networks.

Is it any wonder TV's *60 Minutes* once referred to Hanna-Barbera as "the General Motors of animation"? At one point, the company produced nearly two-thirds of all Saturday morning cartoons.

They were the minds behind gems such as *The Huckleberry Hound Show, The Flintstones, The Yogi Bear Show, The Jetsons, Scooby-Doo, Josie and the Pussycats, Hong Kong Phooey, The World's Greatest Super Friends,* and *The Smurfs.*

ABOVE: William Hanna and Joseph Barbera, in their office, going over the script for the debut of *The Flintstones*, circa 1960.

Did you know?

- Hanna and Barbera first began working together at Metro-Goldwyn-Mayer in the 1930s.
- Hanna's name appears first because he won a coin toss the two had when titling their company.
- William Hanna voiced Tom's screams in *Tom and Jerry*.
- The duo won seven Academy Awards® and eight Emmy® Awards.

- There is a star dedicated to them on the Hollywood Walk of Fame.
- Hanna-Barbera generated several iconic pop-culture phrases, including *Yabba-Dabba-Doo!*, *Smarter than the average bear*, and *Wonder Twin powers, activate!*

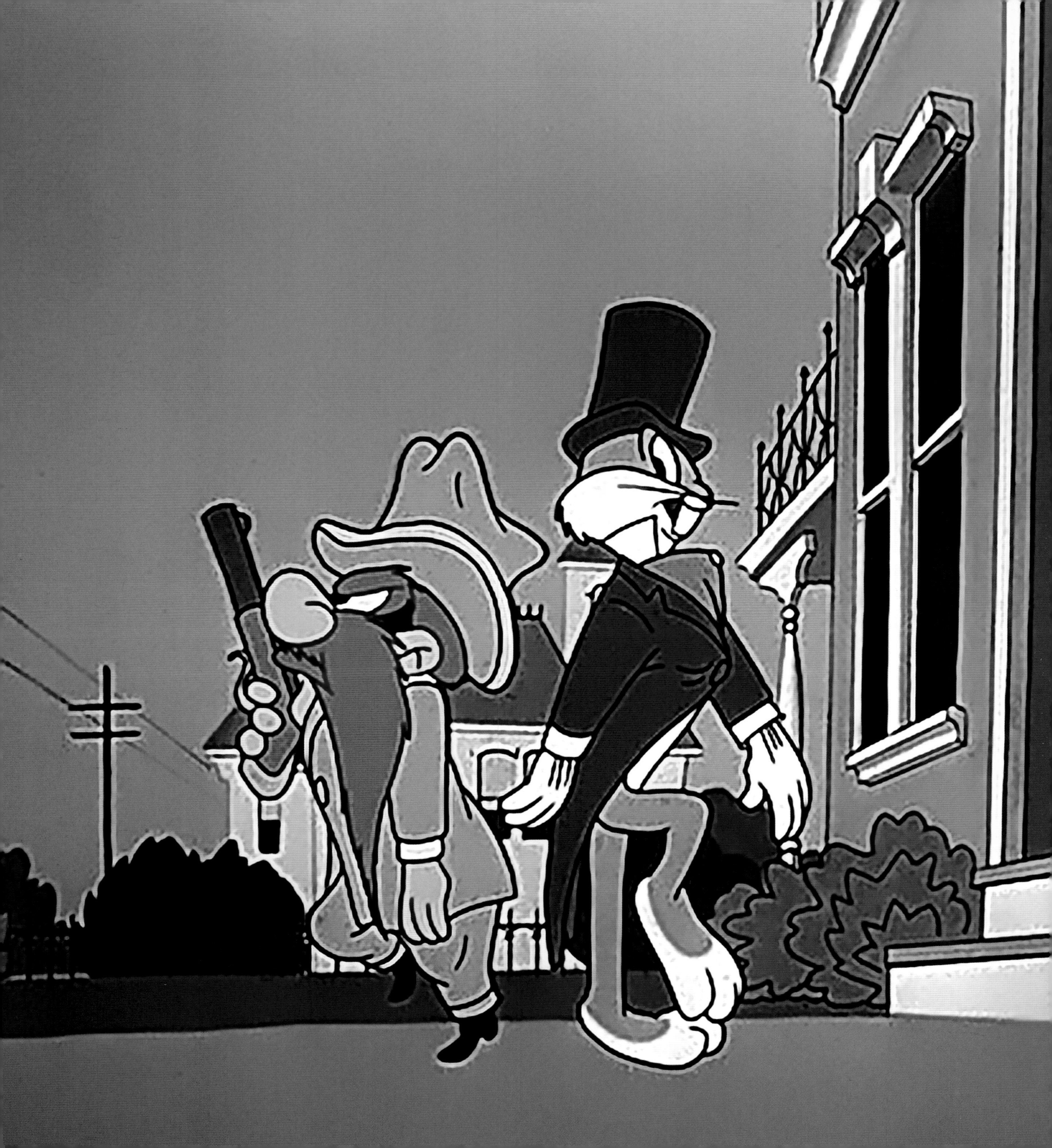

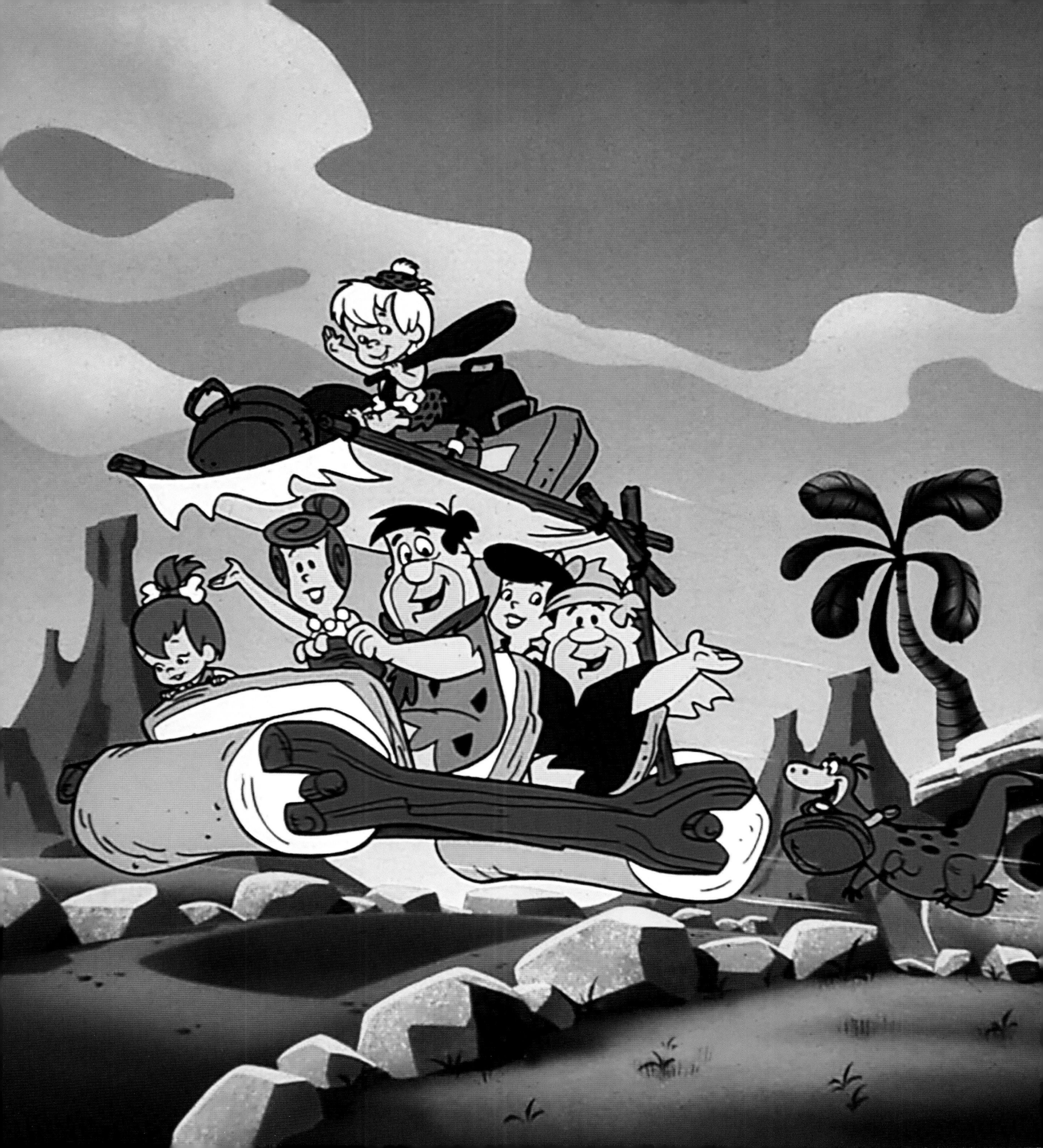

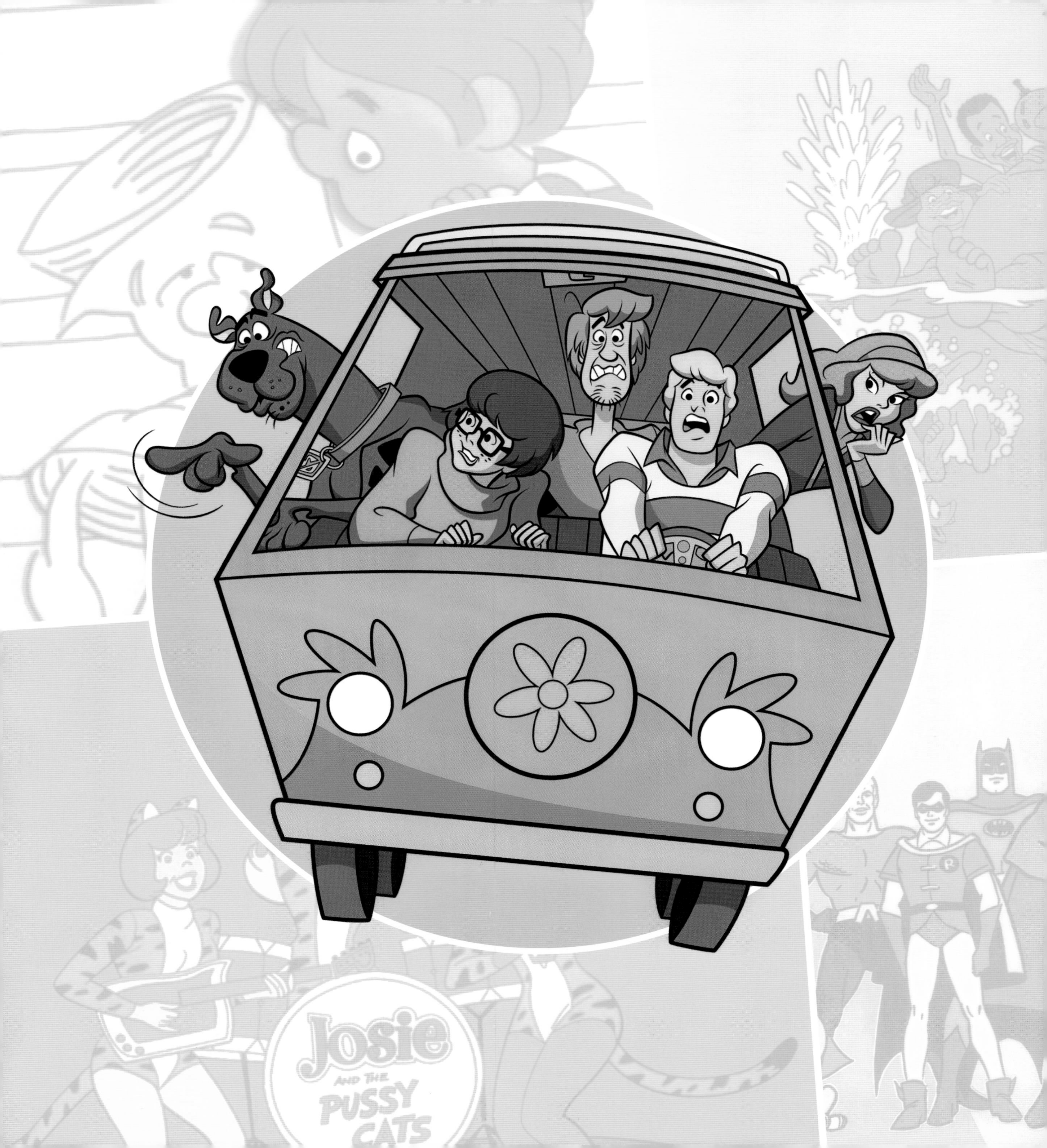
Josie
AND THE
PUSSY
CATS

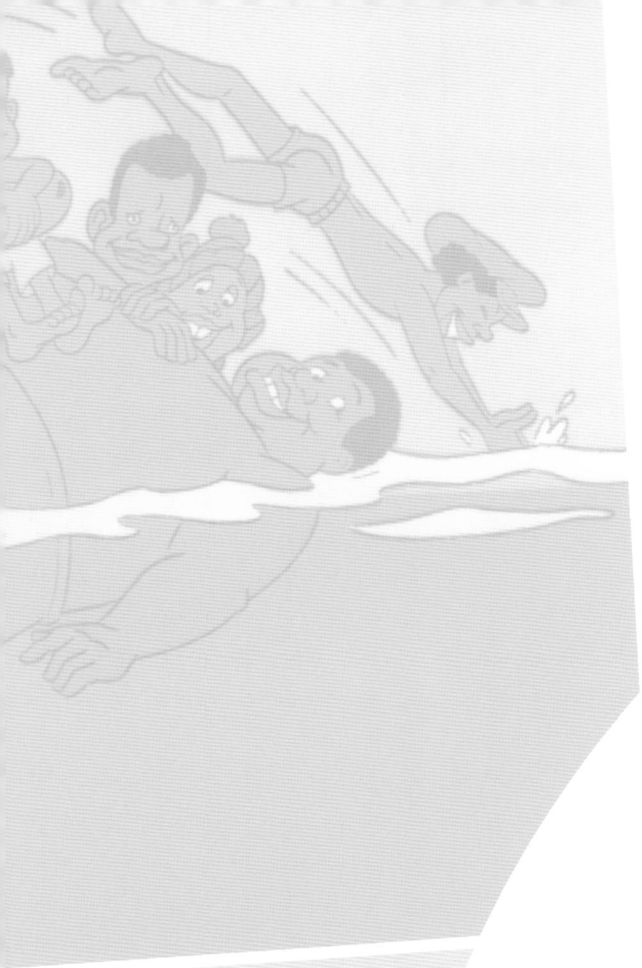

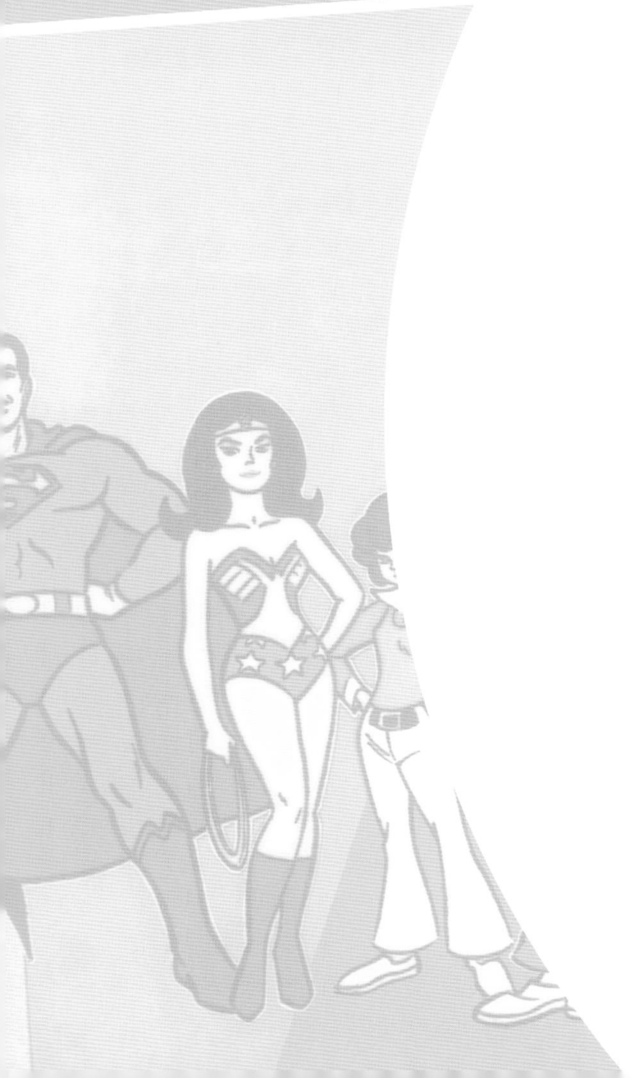

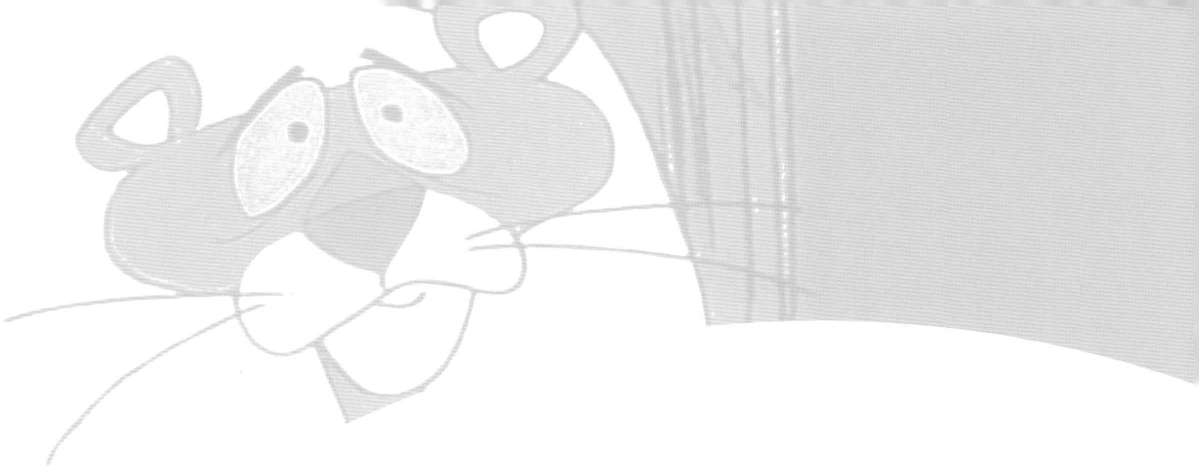

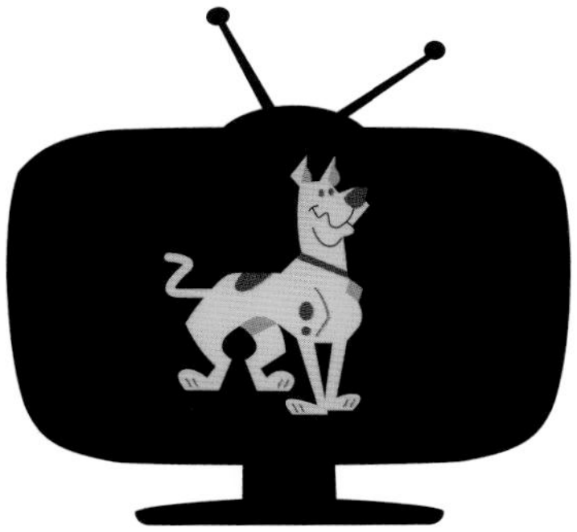

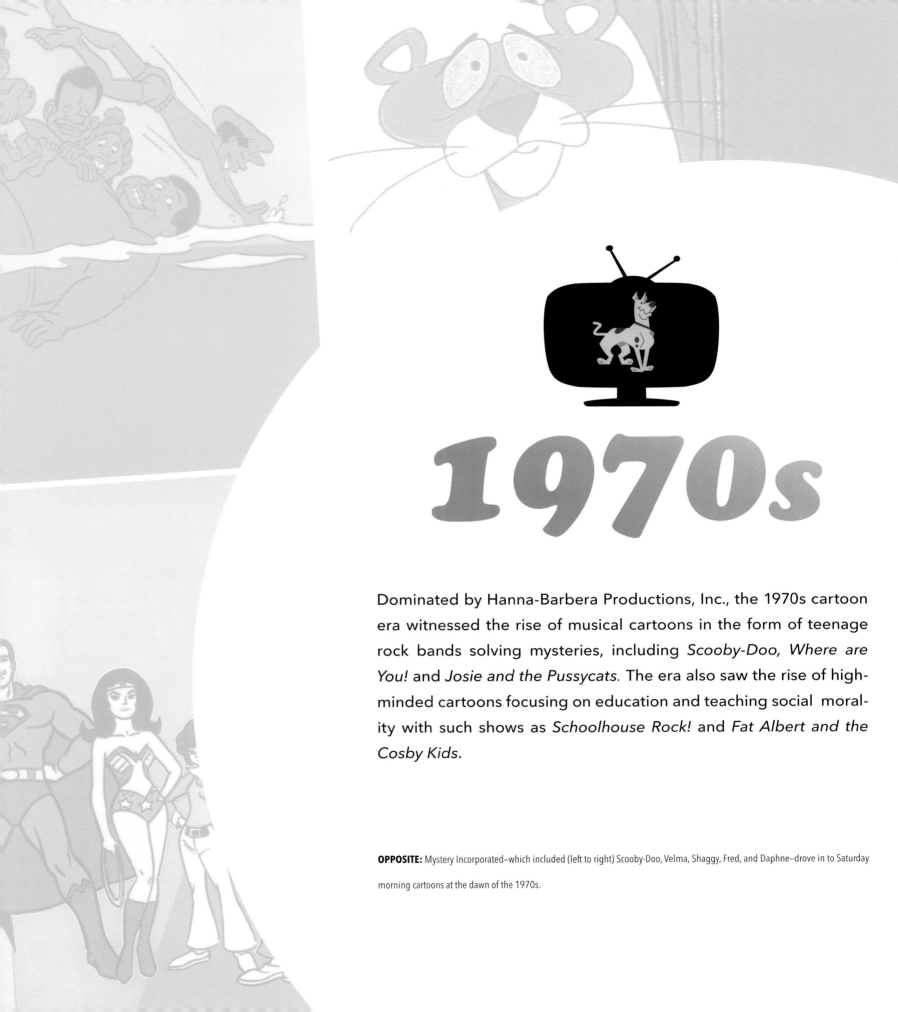

1970s

Dominated by Hanna-Barbera Productions, Inc., the 1970s cartoon era witnessed the rise of musical cartoons in the form of teenage rock bands solving mysteries, including *Scooby-Doo, Where are You!* and *Josie and the Pussycats.* The era also saw the rise of high-minded cartoons focusing on education and teaching social morality with such shows as *Schoolhouse Rock!* and *Fat Albert and the Cosby Kids*.

OPPOSITE: Mystery Incorporated—which included (left to right) Scooby-Doo, Velma, Shaggy, Fred, and Daphne—drove in to Saturday morning cartoons at the dawn of the 1970s.

The Pink Panther Show

YEARS ON AIR

1969-1979

NETWORK

NBC, ABC

NUMBER OF EPISODES

124

CHARACTERS AND VOICE ACTORS

Pink Panther: Rich Little ("Sink Pink" and "Pink Ice")
Announcer: Marvin Miller
Charlie the Ant: John Byner
The Inspector/Sergeant
Deux-Deux: Pat Harrington Jr.
Misterjaw: Arte Johnson

Possessing the urbane manners of an English gentleman coupled with fur the hue of cotton candy, the Pink Panther debuted in the Blake Edwards film of the same title in 1963. He began as a mere twinkle in French detective Jacque Clouseau's eye—or, more accurately, a diamond with a flaw in its center resembling a pink panther. Designed by Isadore "Friz" Freleng and layout artist Hawley Pratt (collaborators who brought the world Speedy Gonzales as well as Sylvester and Tweety), the Pink Panther also appeared via animation form in the movie's opening and closing credits.

"The reception was magnificent," said Freleng's production partner David H. DePatie in a 2010 interview with cartoonist Charles Brubaker. "We took the picture out to preview at Village Theater in Westwood, and when the titles came on, people got up, and they were jumping around and screaming and yelling, and at the end of the title sequence, they had to turn off the projector and turn on the house lights because people were just going really crazy about it. So it came off with a very, very good start."

In fact, audiences liked the lanky feline with long whiskers so much that the movie's distributor,

United Artists, hired Freleng and DePatie to produce theatrical cartoons based on the character, in the vein of Walt Disney's *Steamboat Willie*. Backed by the now famous sax riffs of renowned composer Henry Mancini, these shorts captured children's hearts. The 1964s *Pink Phink* became the first cartoon series to win an Academy Award for Animated Short Film. "You have to remember that at this time in the animation business the cartoons were theatrical cartoons," explained DePatie. "The theater owners ran a cartoon and a newsreel with the feature picture so that was the format. I was able to get a

very large contract from United Artists that surprised me at the time. We got a contract for 156 six-minute theatrical shorts. So we were in business and moving right along,"

Five years later, *The Pink Panther Show* debuted on NBC in 1969. The program generally unfolded as a series of two shorts starring the Panther and one starring the Inspector (modeled after the bumbling Clouseau). So-called "Bumper Sequences" placed the Inspector and Panther together, with Marvin Miller, an off-camera narrator, speaking to the Panther. Typical stories involved the cunning Panther

OPPOSITE: The Panther presses the flesh in the episode "Jet Pink."

ABOVE: Henry Mancini, composer of *The Pink Panther* theme, poses with the character.

BOTTOM: Pink Panther lounges beside a TV presenting *The Pink Panther Show.*

OPPOSITE TOP: The Pink Panther up to his typical hijinks in this frame from the *All New Pink Panther Show.*

OPPOSITE BOTTOM: Image from *The Pink Panther Show.*

outwitting his opponents with sophistication, such as in the episode "Dial P for Pink" in which the Panther foils every attempt by a safecracker to explode his way into a safe by returning each of the thief's devices to him with smooth aplomb just before they explode so the thief takes the blast instead.

As this episode's pantomime style demonstrates, what made *The Pink Panther Show* so unusual was its ability to convey great subtlety and humor with so little dialogue. In their book, *Encyclopedia of Cartoon Superstars*, authors John Kawley and Jim Korkis examine the Panther's quiet genius. "Born from a movie title sequence, and featuring no voice, he is perhaps the only cartoon character based on elegance and 'style.'"

Kawley and Korkis go on to compare the Panther to Felix the Cat, another classically animated personality originating in the silent film era and capable of powerfully emoting through body language. "He is almost always himself, silent, dignified, and attempting

to remain cool . . . No humans ever seem perplexed at this Panther, who is the only intelligent anthropomorphic animal in his cartoon universe." Like Buster Keaton and Charlie Chaplin, the feline's live-action antecedents, the Panther demonstrated what's possible through the magic of non verbal expression, although Rich Little did supply the Panther's voice in two shorts, *Sink Pink* and *Pink Ice.*

In addition to the Panther's draw as the program's centerpiece, other offshoots enlarged the show's universe. The sister series, including *The Ant and the Aardvark*, *Tijuana Toads*, *Hoot Kloot*, as well as *Misterjaw,* were also produced for broadcast and film release by United Artists. DePatie credits head writer John Dunn as the creative force behind these and the Panther narratives, which rounded out the show. "I worked

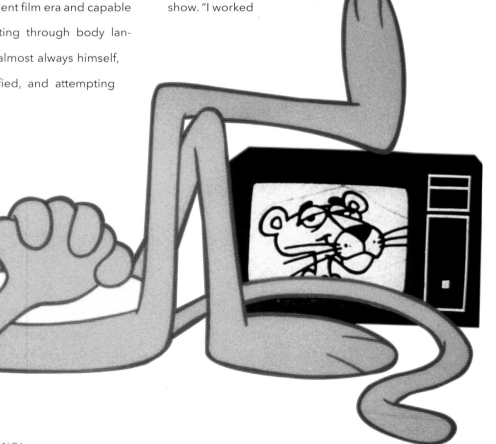

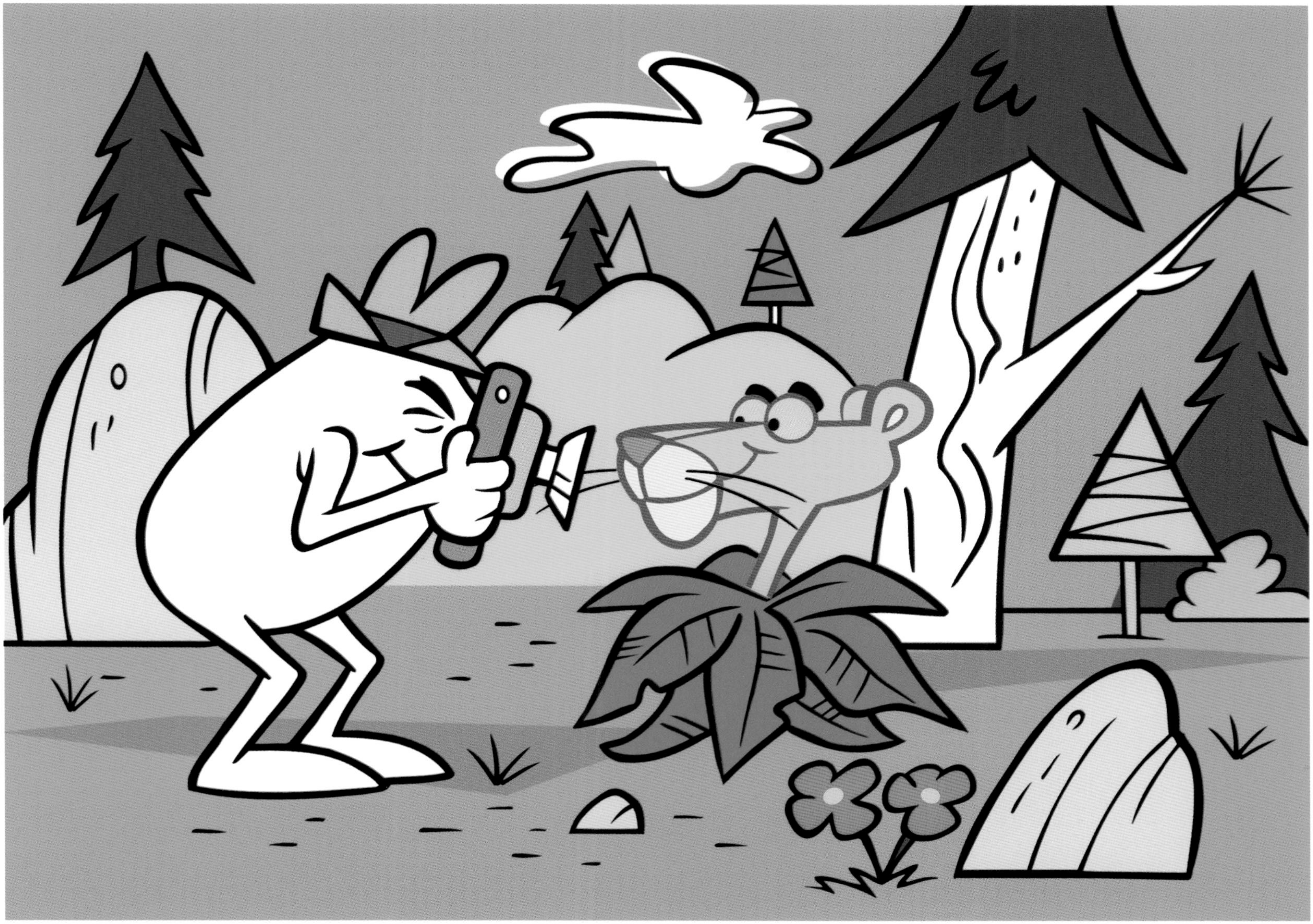

very close with John Dunn and he probably was the best creative mind, storywise, that I had ever worked with. He was responsible for the success of *The Pink Panther* and it was one of his original ideas that we keep the Panther as a pantomime character."

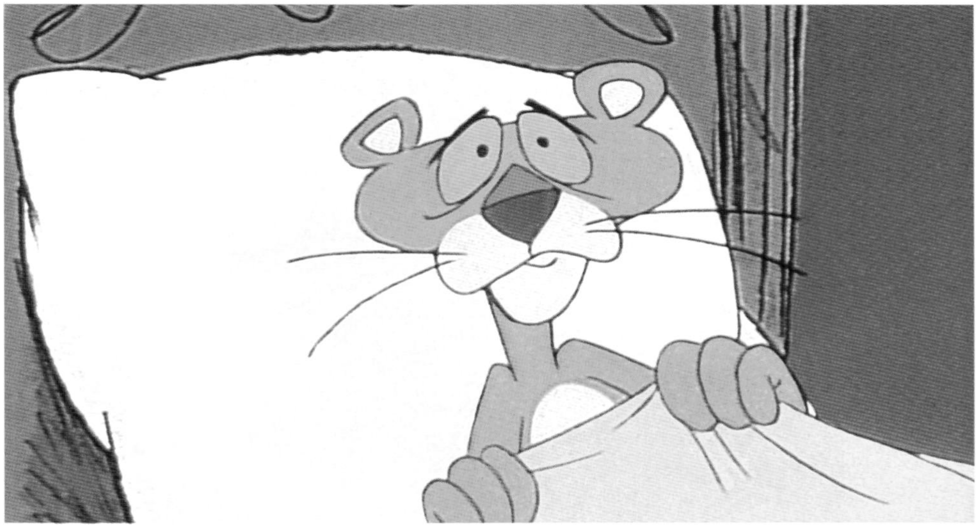

With the combined creative talents of Dunn, Freleng, DePatie, and their venerable cartoon directors, Hawley Pratt, Sid Marcus, Gerry Chiniquy, and others, the show lasted nine years on NBC before moving to ABC in 1978 where it was retitled *The*

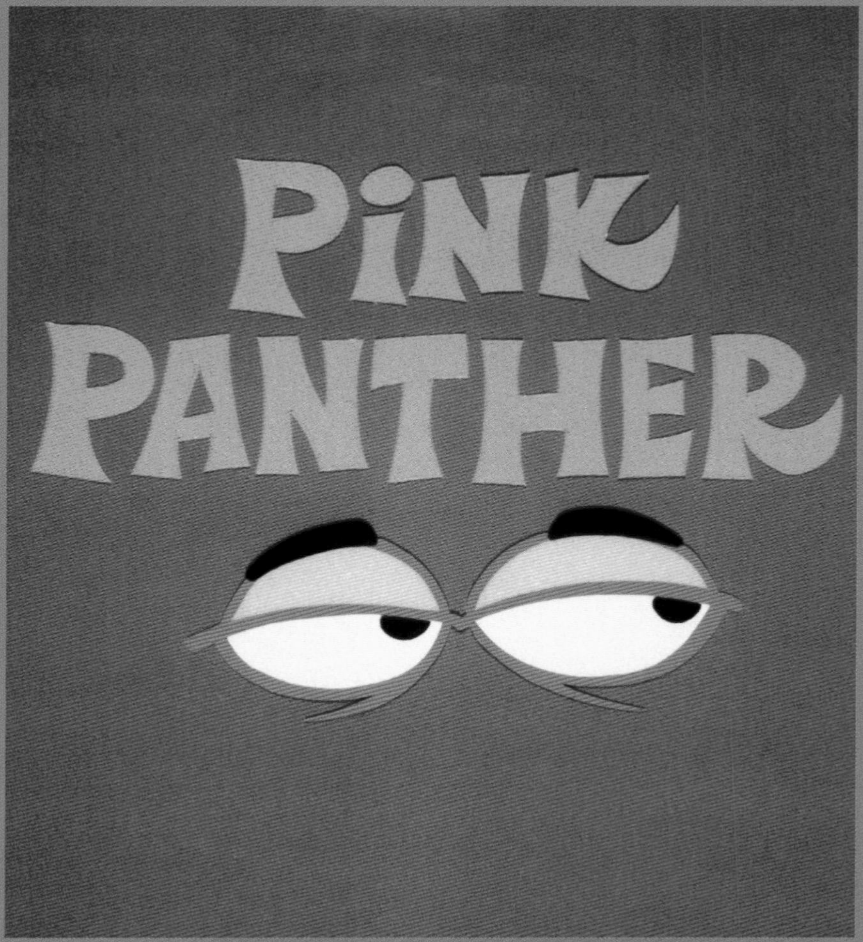
PINK PANTHER

ABOVE: A promotional image for *The Pink Panther Show* cartoon.

The Pink Panther Remains Silent

With the exception of a couple experimental shorts, the Pink Panther never officially speaks. There is good reason for this, according to designer Friz Freleng: "We tried several voices with him, but nothing ever worked. Actually, since he was originally created for a main title and didn't speak, there wasn't any reason for him to ever speak.

All New Pink Panther Show. Over its eleven-year life span on various networks, the series went by a variety of names, such as *The Pink Panther Meets the Ant and the Aardvark* (1970–1971), *The Pink Panther and Friends* (1974–1976), and this tongue twister: *The Pink Panther Laugh and a Half Hour and a Half Show* (1976–1977).

No matter its title, *The Pink Panther* made a profound impact on Saturday morning viewers and popular culture at large. In addition to comics based on the character and a string of later specials, such as *Olym-Pinks* (1980) and *Pink at First Sight* (1981), the NBC Saturday morning reboot *Pink Panther and Sons* starred the Panther as a dad of two talking sons. In 1993, *The Pink Panther* returned in cartoon form again, this time as a coproduction of MGM, Mirisch-Geoffrey-DePatie-Freleng, and United Artists. Lasting two seasons, it holds the distinction as the only series in which the Panther talks (other than the few lines in the two previously mentioned shorts).

It's no wonder the Pink Panther has appeared in numerous TV reiterations. He's also been appropriated for all manner of ad campaigns, such as Nike's Mercurial Vapor IV football boots and Sweet'N Low artificial sweetener. The character's name was even used as a slogan in the 1970s by various LGBT rights activist organizations. Clearly, Freleng, Pratt, and DePatie had tapped into something special and enduring with their pink creation. Alongside other major cartoon icons like Bugs Bunny, Mickey Mouse, and Tom and Jerry, the Pink Panther deepened the animated canon. Before there was Heathcliff, before there was Garfield exhibiting cat-titude, the Pink Panther slinked in—silently. Exuding grace and charm, this cool cat brought Saturday mornings to a new level of refinement that still remains unmatched.

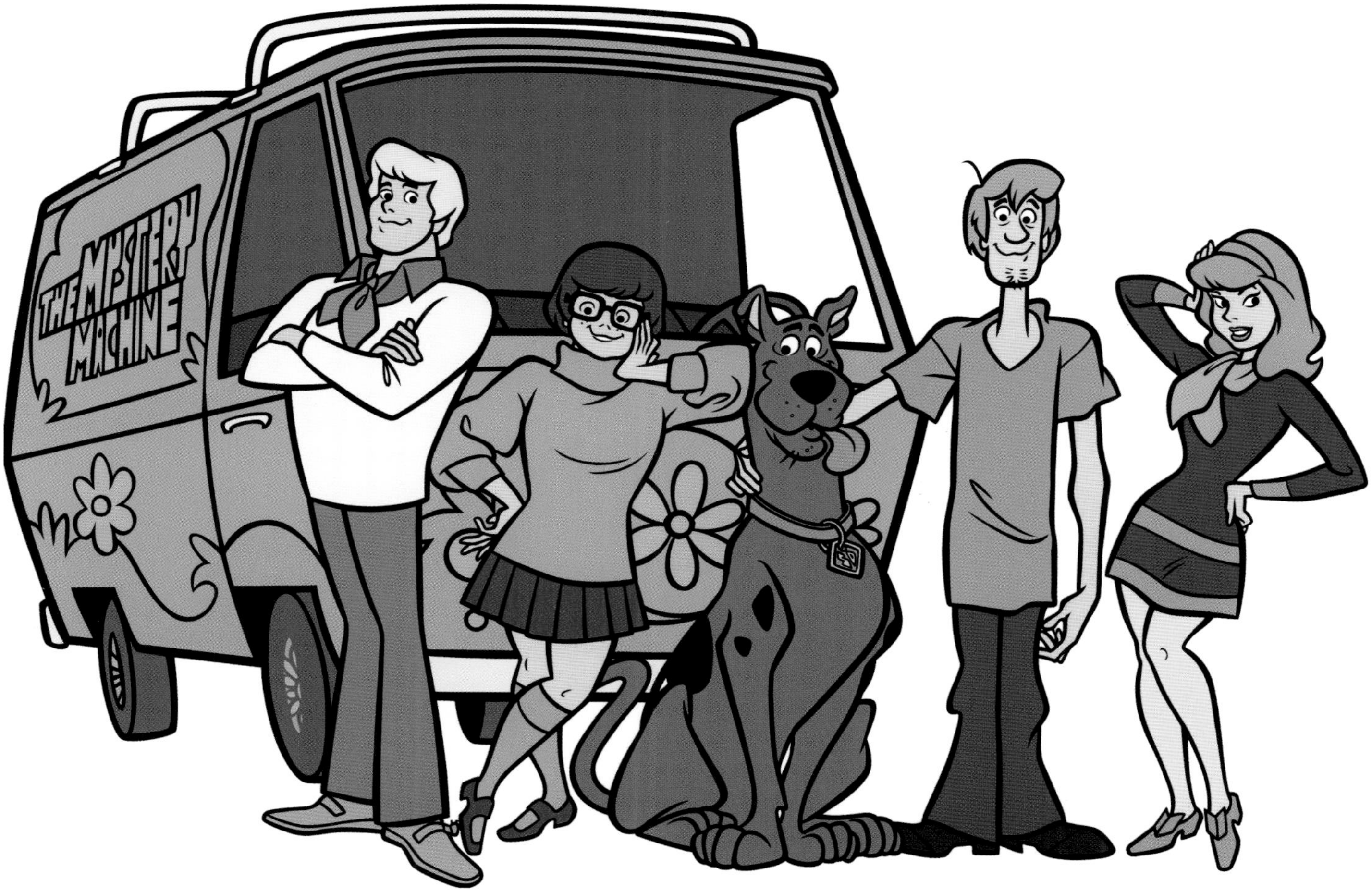
THE MYSTERY MACHINE

Scooby-Doo, Where Are You!

"I had always thought that kids in a haunted house would be a big hit, played for laughs in animation," said CBS Daytime Programming Executive Fred Silverman in an interview with the Television Academy Foundation. "And [I] developed a show with Hanna-Barbera. And there was a dog in there, but the dog was in the background; it was much more serious . . . And [CBS President] Frank Stanton said, 'We can't put that on the air, that's just too frightening. I booked a red-eye and I couldn't sleep. I'm listening to music, and as we're landing, Frank Sinatra comes on, and I hear him say, '*Scooby-do-be-do*.' It's at that point, I said, 'That's it, we'll call it, *Scooby-Doo*.'"

Influenced by the 1950s program *The Many Loves of Dobie Gillis*, featuring the beatnik Maynard G. Krebs as inspiration for Shaggy, and *The Archie Show* for its emphasis on a gang dynamic, Silverman spearheaded the Hanna-Barbera series, utilizing Ruby-Spears Productions. Writers Joe Ruby and Ken Spears established the show around a group of four teens and their Great Dane. The group fought crimes while cruising in their Mystery Machine van. According to Norman Rockwell Museum's

YEARS ON AIR

1969–1970 (original)

NETWORK

CBS

NUMBER OF EPISODES

41

CHARACTERS AND VOICE ACTORS

Scooby-Doo: Don Messick
Norville "Shaggy" Rogers: Casey Kasem
Fred Jones: Frank Welker
Daphne Blake: Stefanianna Christopherson/Heather North (various seasons)
Velma Dinkley: Nicole Jaffe/Emanuela Fallini (various seasons)

PREVIOUS: (left to right) Fred, Velma, Scooby-Doo, Shaggy, and Daphne with the Mystery Machine.

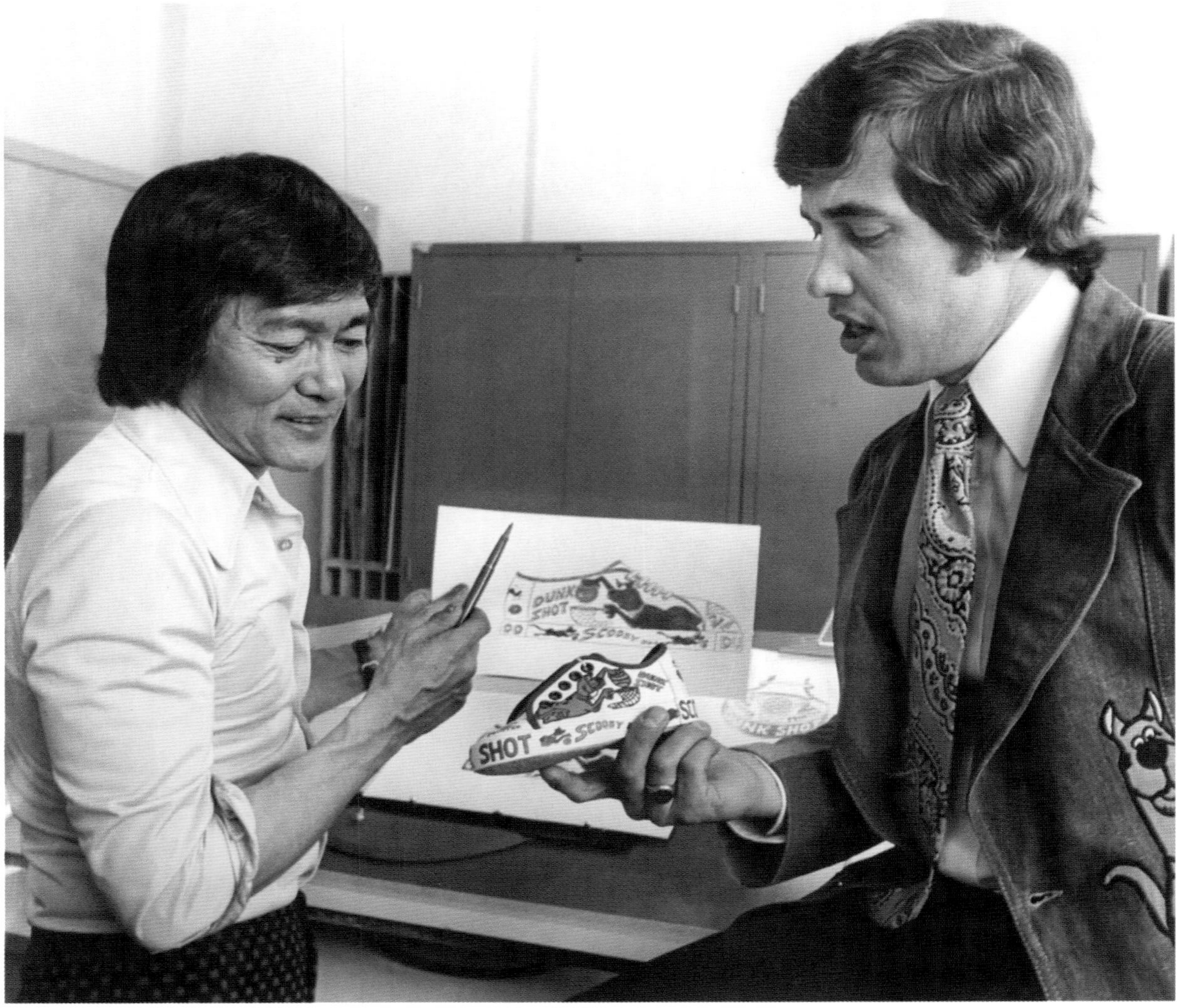
DUNK SHOT
SCOOBY
SHOT

TOP: Iwao Takamoto (left), the animation artist who designed Scooby-Doo, with Gary Johnson (right), the North America Operations of Hanna-Barbera Enterprises, review a design concept for Scooby-Doo tennis shoe, circa 1976.

OPPOSITE TOP: Velma loses her glasses at an inopportune time–one of the many recurring bits in *Scooby-Doo, Where Are You!*

OPPOSITE BOTTOM: Scooby and the gang celebrate Christmas in true Scooby-Doo fashion by solving the mystery of a dangerous snowman, from *What's New, Scooby-Doo!*, 2002.

Illustration History, "With CBS executives wary of the recent outcry against violence on television, they proposed that Hanna-Barbera include some comic relief to lighten the tone of the cartoon. According to Hanna-Barbera's layout and character designer Bob Singer, Barbera suggested that laughs could be provided by the canine, since Jonny Quest's pet dog, Bandit, was so popular in the earlier series."

Originally titled, *Who's S-s-scared,* Scooby assumed the lead role with his artistic design supplied by veteran animator Iwao Takamoto, who also designed the Jetson's dog, Astro. The network ultimately changed the show's title to stave off concerns of frightening children. Although Scooby was the comic relief and a chicken at heart, he still managed to rise to the occasion when the chips were down. Meanwhile, his four human counterparts possessed archetypal personalities. Shaggy Rogers, Scooby's sloppy owner and closest pal, shared Scooby's cowardly demeanor and laid-back attitude. Dashing and bold, the orange-ascot wearing Fred Jones led the group with a healthy dose of supernatural skepticism. Frumpy and bespectacled Velma Dinkley supplied the smarts, usually solving

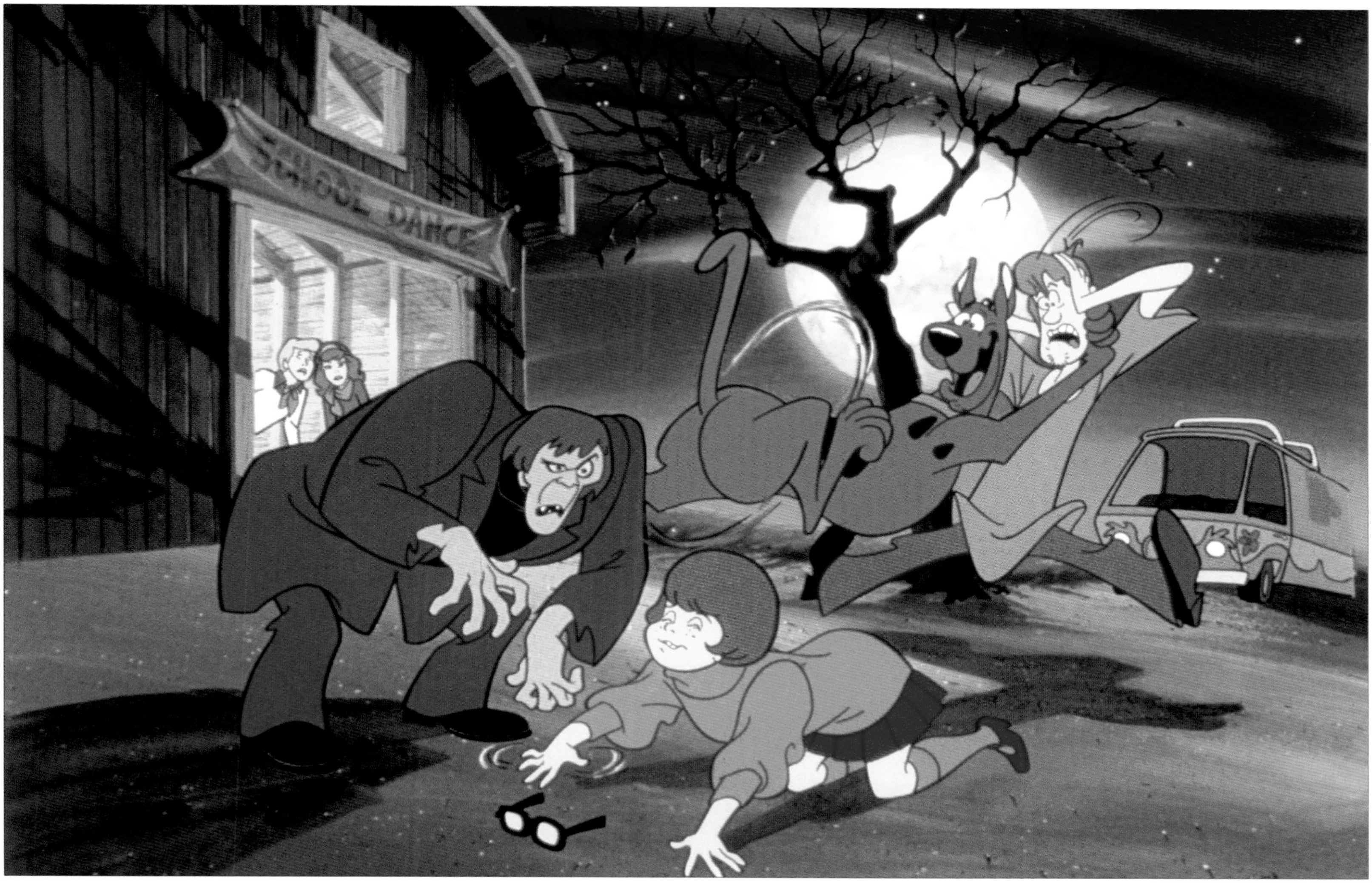
SCHOOL DANCE

the mystery. Her female counterpart, Daphne, was the show's bombshell, suffering from a tendency to stumble into one predicament after another, often requiring rescue.

This cast of five constituted Mystery Incorporated (or Mystery Inc.), an amateur organization of friends devoted to stamping out crime. Episodes typically involved the gang's plans of attending a teenage function derailed due to a Mystery Machine malfunction, such as a flat tire, positioning them nearby some sketchy location. The gang would then choose to investigate their surroundings, determine

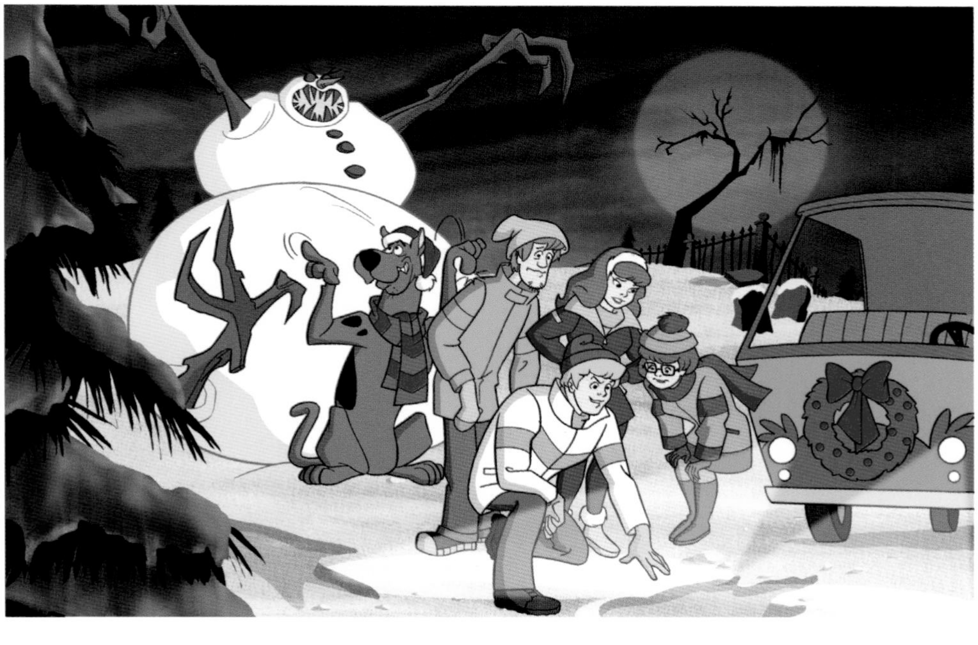

BOTTOM: Introduced in 1979, the puppy Scrappy-Doo was full of courage despite his size.

their locale suffered from some sort of monster infestation, and puzzle out the riddle. The first season's "Which Witch Is Which" was indicative of the usual scrape the gang would face. Traveling home from a fishing trip, the pals encounter a witch and a zombie who had been terrorizing a nearby swamp. Using deductive reasoning, as well as a good old-fashioned trip wire, our heroes manage to corner and unmask the villains. The zombie and witch turned out to be Zeke and Zeb, robbers who sunk their loot in the swamp and had been "haunting" it ever since as they tried to recover their stash.

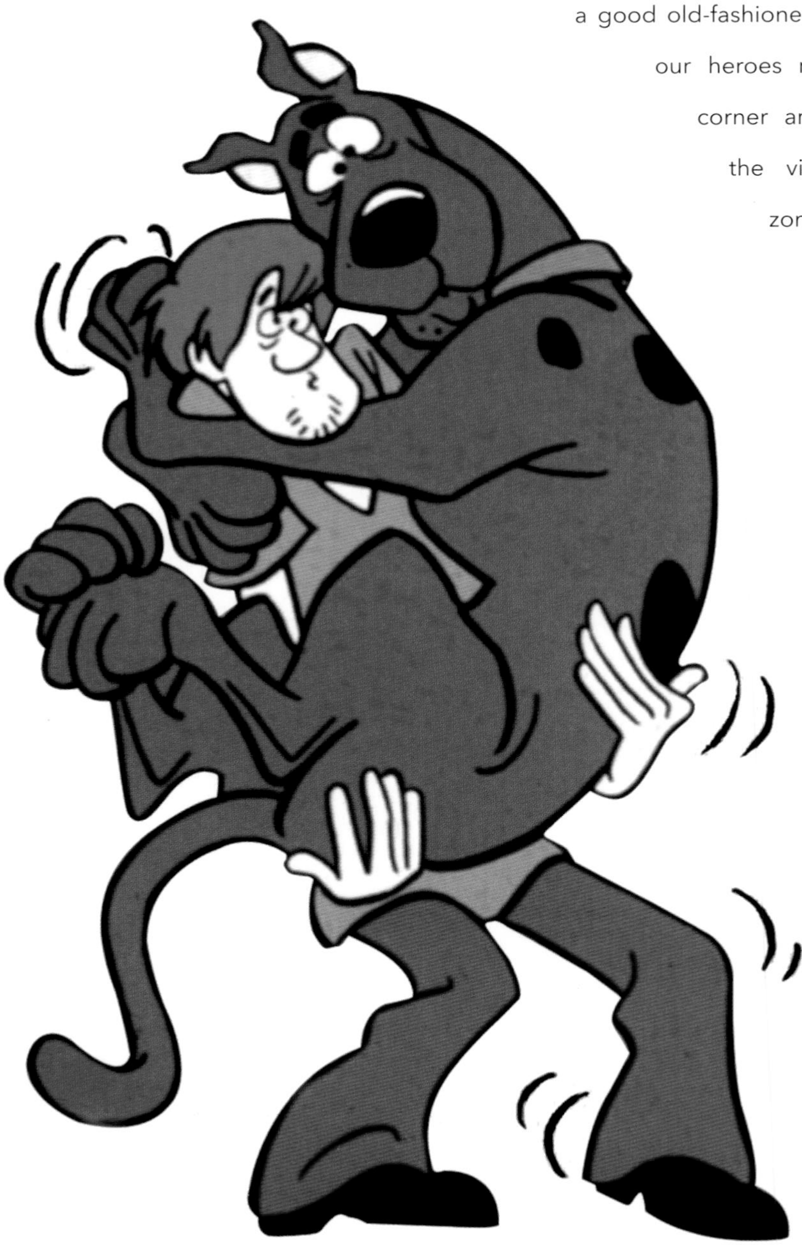

The clean and simple wrap-up of "Which Witch is Which" perfectly exemplifies the show's hallmark ending. No matter how gnarly the spooky hellion is first made out to be, inevitably, the gang uncovers his/her identity to be some sort of nefarious human in disguise. According to *Illustration History,* "As Joe Ruby and Ken Spears's original treatment notes, 'A logical ending always caps our stories, as the Mystery's five solve the most baffling tales of the unknown ever told!!'—meaning the bad guys could always be explained." In fact, this trope became so well-known, the following phrase, "And I'd have gotten away with it too, if it weren't for those meddling kids," gained huge prominence. It was even featured in the 1992 movie, *Wayne's World*. Garth (Dana Carvey) interrupts the dénouement and breaks the fourth wall by suggesting they do the "Scooby-Doo ending."

Scooby-Doo, Where Are You! had much more success beyond its Saturday time slot than just a few quotable lines or being referenced in popular movies. The original series, which lasted two years, spawned numerous follow-up and spin-off series—such as *The Scooby-Doo Dynomutt Hour*

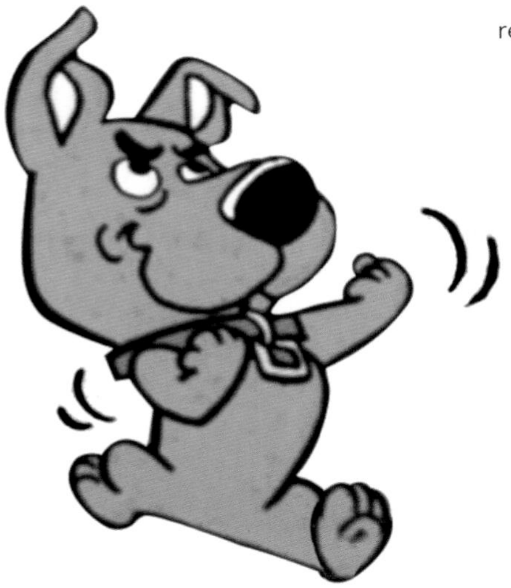

(1976–1978), *Scooby's Laff-A Lympics* (1977–1988), *Scooby-Doo and Scrappy-Doo* (1979–2010), *A Pup Named Scooby-Doo* (1988–1991), and *What's New, Scooby-Doo?* (2002–2006). For a while, the two-time Emmy®-nominated original series held the Guinness award for "most episodes of a cartoon series." (The following year, in 2005, *The Simpsons* regained the throne.) In addition to live-action feature film reboots in the 2000s, *Scooby-Doo* also expanded its entertainment pantheon into numerous video games, comics, breakfast cereals, Scooby Snack dog treats, and even world-tour stage plays.

In order to understand why *Scooby-Doo, Where Are You!* remains one of the most enduring and popular cartoons, we need look no further than what happened in February, 1971 on the other side of the world. After the BBC canceled the program, dozens of Scottish children rushed to the network headquarters demanding they bring it back. Originating at a crossroads in American life, when hippie culture gave way to the so-called "Me" decade, *Scooby-Doo, Where are You!* straddled conventions: grooviness mixed with the supernatural. Discussing its absurdness and timelessness in an interview with the Archive of American Television, producer Joseph Barbera said he always wished he had set an episode at Woodstock just so he could show the gang confronting zombies. "*Scooby-Doo* turned out to be the sleeper of all time," explained Barbera. Ultimately, just like the show's plotlines, the mystery of *Scooby-Doo*'s popularity turns out to be really quite simple after all: it's outstanding fun.

ABOVE: When faced with a new monster or mystery, Scooby-Doo and the Mystery Inc. gang had their favorite sayings.

Catchphrases Galore!

Just as the show had a formula, each Mystery team member also had their own trademark saying:

Shaggy: Zoinks!

Velma: Jinkies!

Daphne/Velma: What would you do for a Scooby snack?

Scooby: Ruh-roh-Raggy!

Fred: Looks like we've got another mystery on our hands.

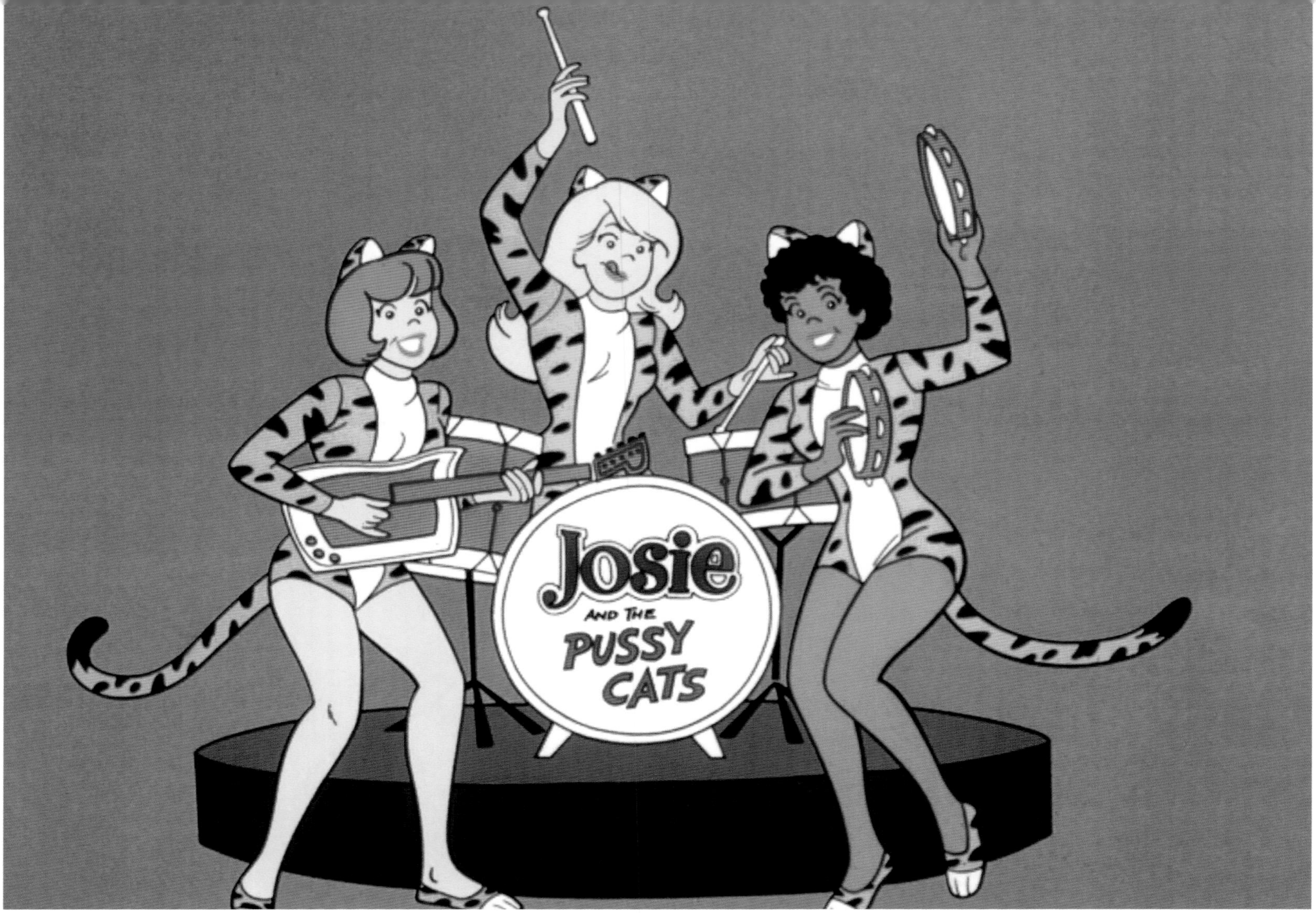
Josie
AND THE
PUSSY
CATS

YEARS ON AIR

1970–1971

NETWORK

CBS

NUMBER OF EPISODES

16

CHARACTERS AND VOICE ACTORS

Josie: Janet Waldo
Valerie: Barbara Pariot
Melody: Jackie Joseph
Alexander Cabot III: Casey Kasem
Alan: Jerry Dexter
Alexandra Cabot: Sherry Alberoni
Sebastian: Don Messick

Josie and the Pussycats

A little bit *The Archie Show*, a little bit *Scooby-Doo, Where are You!*, a little bit rock 'n' roll, Josie and the Pussycats split their time between jamming out as a plucky female trio and thwarting international plots for world domination. Clad in leopard-print leotards and sporting "long tails and ears for hats" as noted in the theme song, the teenage girls leaped off the *Archie* comics pages and onto CBS's early '70s lineup. According to Norman Rockwell Museum's Illustration History, they were part of Hanna-Barbera's plan "to recycle the idea of mystery-solving meddling kids."

Beginning with its suggestive title and the girls' skimpy outfits, *Josie and the Pussycats* differentiated itself from its animated forebears by offering a bit of sexy cheekiness, rare for a kids' show. Look no further than the song "Voodoo" from the episode, "A Greenthumb Is Not a Goldfinger." *I'm gonna do some voodoo on you baby/You can run, it doesn't matter anyhow/I'm bound to get you now.*

On the other hand, *Josie and the Pussycats* offered more than just innuendo or bubblegum pop to a generation a few years removed from the Civil Rights Movement. In fact, the character of Valerie can claim the distinction of being the first African American protagonist on an animated TV series. "As I look at it in retrospect, I do think it was ground-breaking," recalls Sue Steward, one of the musical group's real-life songwriters. "It was the first [cartoon] presenting women as the lead characters, as the crime fighters . . . they weren't anybody's angels! They did their own thing."

To this end, the *Josie and the Pussycats* cast offered a nuanced and playful version of girl power. Voiced by Janet Waldo—also known as the voice of Judy Jetson—the red headed guitarist Josie led the group. "Josie was a contemporary teenager, much more so than Archie," explained Dan DeCarlo in a 2000 interview with Mike Curtis for *The Comics Journal.* "She was an intelligent kid, she had goals, and wanted to succeed in life." The late *Archies* cartoonist and *Josie and the Pussycats* creator based Josie's original comic character on his wife, whom he met in Belgium during World War II. DeCarlo explained that he penned her voice using the same melodious tone his wife used whenever speaking. "Especially when she's talking to me or you or somebody else in the family. She gets very musical with her voice."

The show's second billing went to Valerie, the brains of the group who played the tambourine. Melody, on the other hand, functioned as the stereotypical dumb blonde whose earlobes wiggled

whenever danger lurked. The female who stole the show, however, was Alexandra Cabot, the original mean girl with the streaked ponytail resembling a skunk. Twin sister to Alexander Cabot III and the group's manager, Alexandra remained forever convinced she should be the star and possess Alan, Josie's man. Presumably modeled after Veronica from *The Archie Show*, Alexandra could be regularly

OPPOSITE: The three rockers–(left to right) Josie, Melody, and Valerie–with their iconic look of "long tails and ears for hats."

ABOVE: Alexandra Cabot once again getting the short end of the stick.

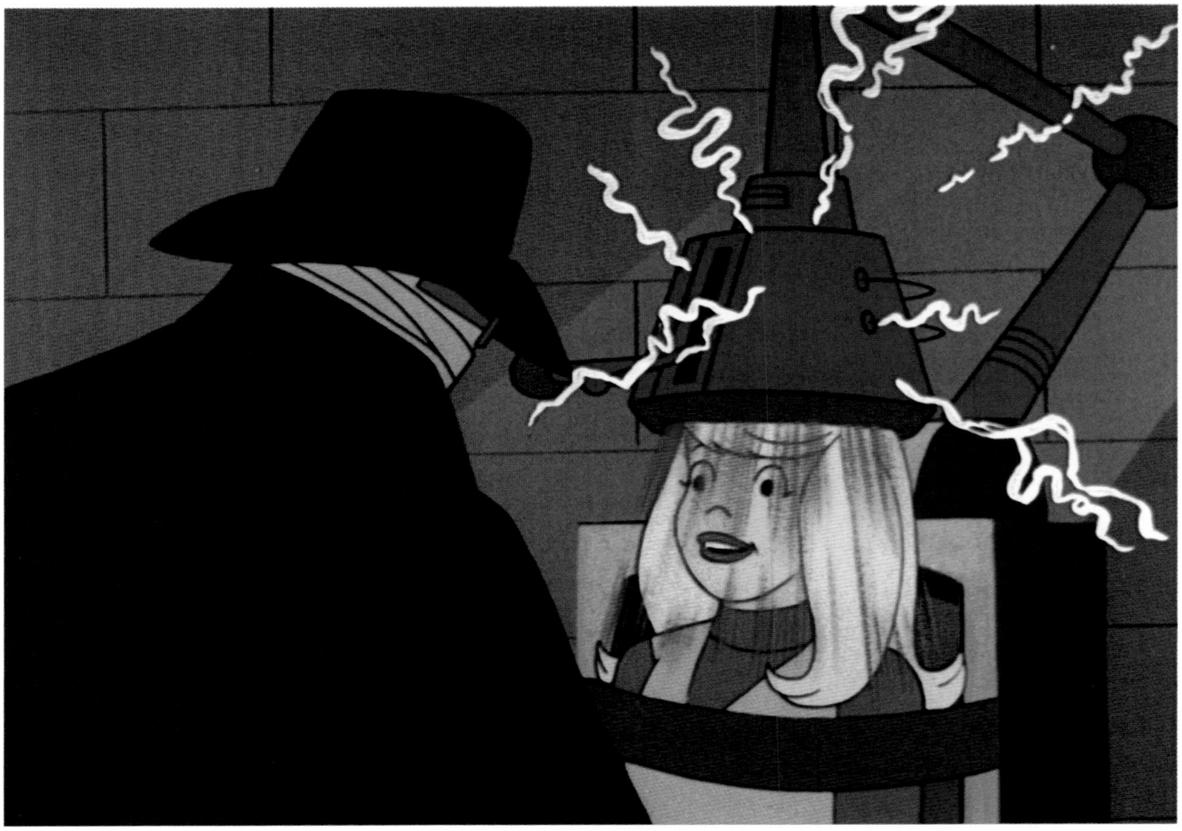

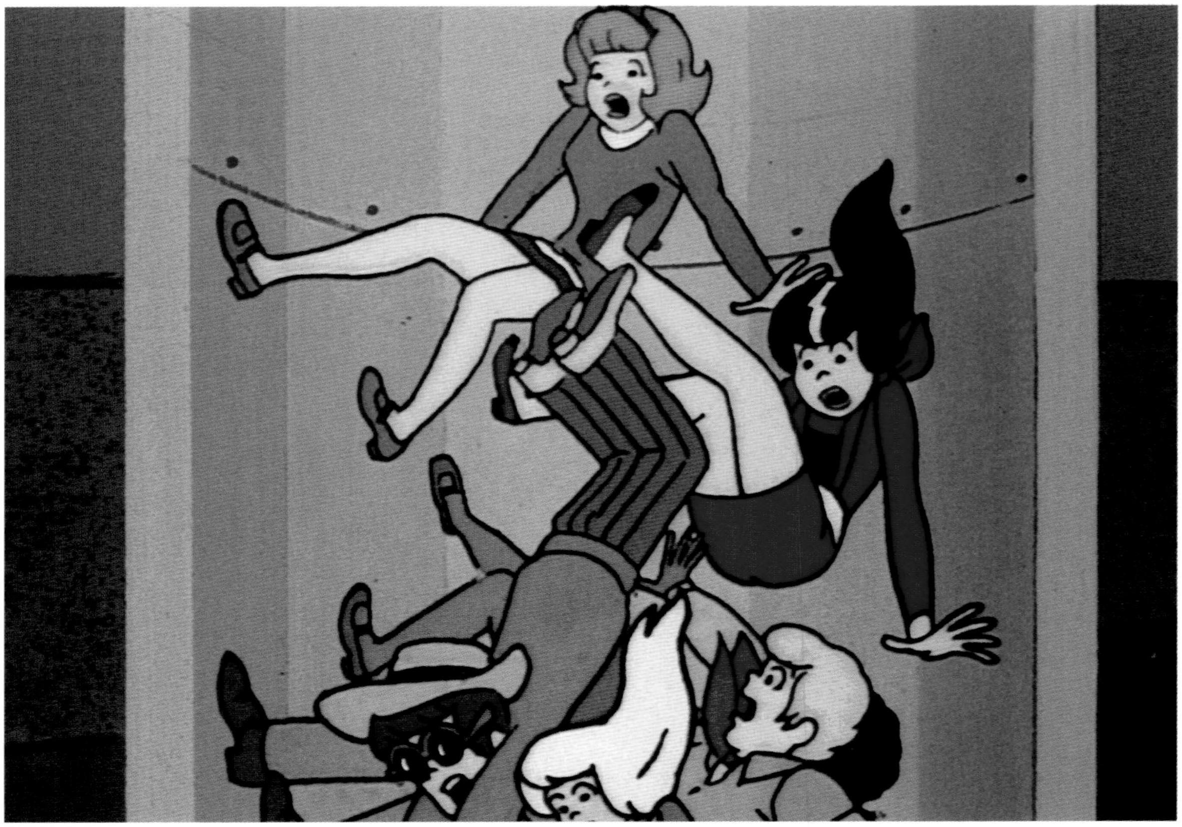

counted on to embroil the group in all kinds of crazy adventures due to her jealous antics.

From week to week, the band globe-trotted to exotic locales, performing gigs and recording songs while tangling with archvillains. In "Chile Today, Hot Tamale" the girls faced down a deranged south-of-the-border bugman called the "Scorpion" after he slipped nuclear capsules into Melody's bass drum. They also tussled with Dr. Strangemoon, a mad scientist bent on launching missile strikes against the planet in "Strangemoon Over Miami." Whenever the show's tension rose toward the climax, death-defying chase sequences ensued as the Pussycats' latest musical number kicked in.

When it came to developing this signature Pussycat sound, the creators took their mission seriously. In order to satisfy Hanna-Barbera's aspirations for a girl group capable of unseating *The Archies*' hold on bubblegum hits, they contacted the songwriter/producer team of La La Productions, Danny Janssen

and Bobby Young. Young was the lead singer of the Lettermen and Janssen had composed *The Partridge Family* theme song. "(Since) we catered to kids," Janssen explained, "they asked us whether or not we would do the music for Josie and The Pussycats." After recruiting a team of songwriters, including Austin Roberts, Bobby Hart, and Steward, the creative team arranged for an extensive talent search throughout the country for the right females to embody the trio in real life. After interviewing over five hundred applicants, they cast Cathy Douglas as Josie, Patrice Holloway as Valerie, and Cheryl Ladd

as Melody. The actual band went on to a release a pop album through Capitol Records in 1970 with a Motown-influenced sound.

Despite such strenuous preparations, the eponymous album didn't sell many copies, and in 1971, the first iteration of the show also ended. A spin-off series, entitled *Josie and the Pussycats in Outer Space*, debuted a year later and lasted for a season. The premise? Once again, Alexandra, the instigator, gums up the works for the band by shoving Josie out of the way at a photo shoot aboard a space rocket. Her maneuver accidentally causes their ship to take off, propelling

OPPOSITE TOP: Melody faces the invisible Mr. X in the episode "X Marks the Spot."

OPPOSITE BOTTOM: Josie and the gang take a fall in the episode "The Jumpin' Jupiter Affair."

ABOVE: The live-action Josie and the Pussycats (left to right): Cheryl Ladd, the voice of Melody, Cathy Douglas, the voice of Josie, and Patrice Holloway, the voice of Valerie, circa 1970.

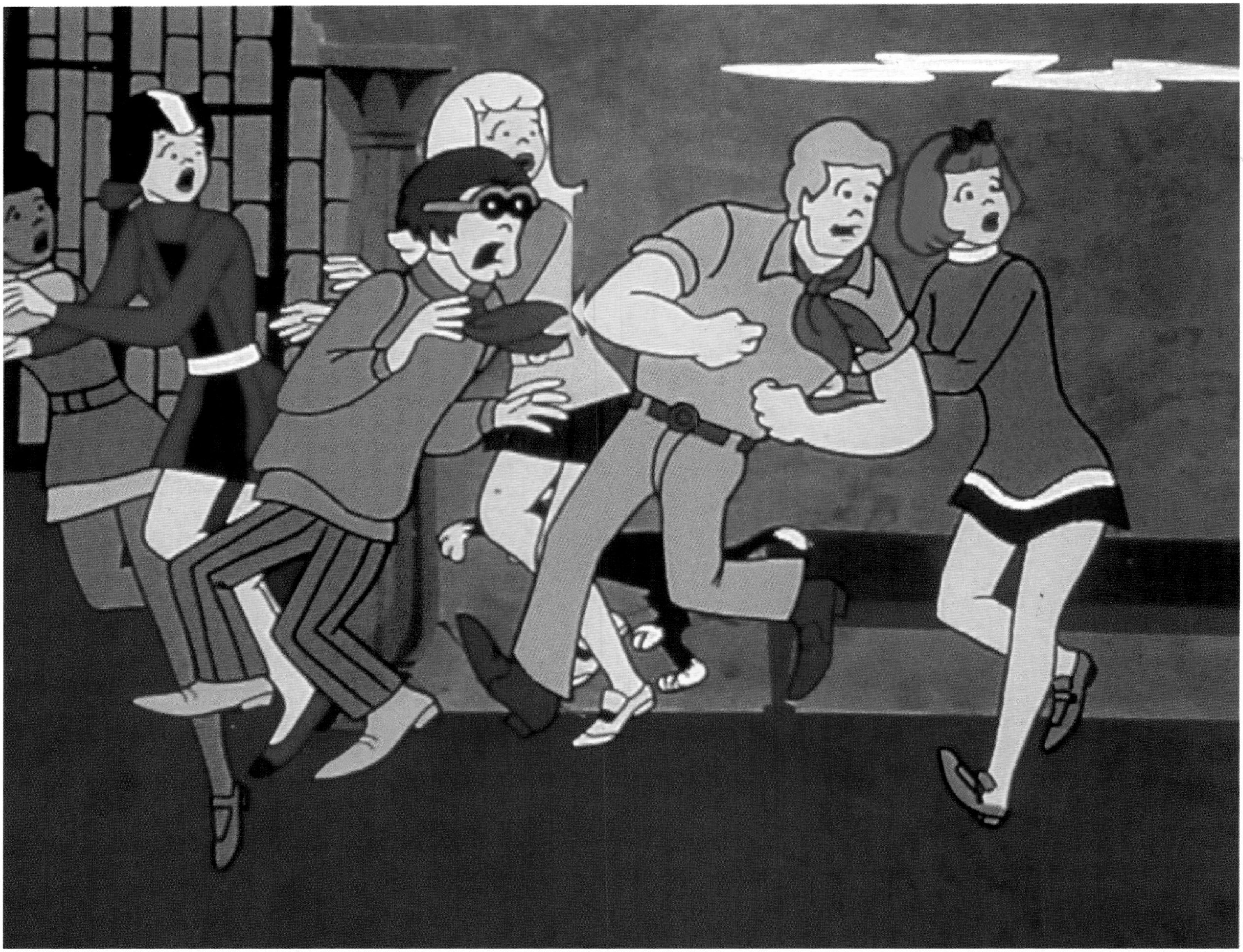

ABOVE: When the group travels to Bombay, they stumble onto a sinister plot in the episode "The Secret Six Secret."

the gang to outer space for a new series of interstellar adventures involving aliens and space pirates.

The original *Josie and the Pussycats* only lasted a brief time, but it gained such fan notoriety it never entirely went away. In addition to reappearing in a guest spot for the 1973 The *New Scooby-Doo Movies*, the franchise rebooted as a live-action film in 2001, starring Rachel Leigh Cook, Tara Reid, and Rosario Dawson. The show was precursor to the 1980s Saturday morning cartoon *Jem*, and recently the girls have also joined up with Archie and friends in CW's *Riverdale* (2017). Though strong, butt-kicking female ensembles have become more of the norm in recent years, it's easy to forget so many of them owe much to *Josie and the Pussycats*, the original gang of rockin' heroines.

The Theme Song Lyrics

Sing along with the crime-fighting girl band
with the lyrics to the theme song:

Josie and the Pussycats

Long tails and ears for hats

Guitars and sharps and flats

Neat, sweet, a groovy song

You're invited, come along.

Hurry, Hurry

See ya all in Persia

Or maybe France

We could be in India

Or perchance

Be with us in Bangkok

Make no difference

Everywhere the action's at

We're involved in this or that

Come on along now

Josie and the Pussycats

No time for purrs and pats

Won't run when they hear scat

They're where the plot begins.

Come on and watch the good guys win

Josie and the Pussycats

Josie and the Pussycats.

ABOVE: The cast of *Josie and the Pussycats* animated show: (top to bottom) Sebastian, Alexander, Alan, Alexandra, Josie, Valerie, and Melody.

Lite-Brite

Lite-Brite, making things with light
What a sight, making things with Lite-Brite!

Featuring multicolored pegs and a lighting panel, this toy inspired generations of would-be artists to create their own illuminated masterpieces. Ever since designer Joseph M. Burck of Marvin Glass & Associates invented Lite-Brite in the late '60s, it has remained a fixture in the world of toys, featuring merchandising tie-ins with Mr. Potato Head, *Scooby-Doo*, and, yes—Mr. T.

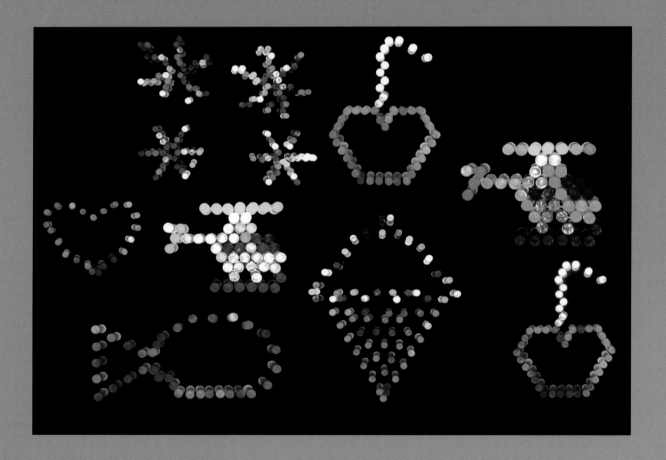

ABOVE: Compilation of Lite-Brite designs.

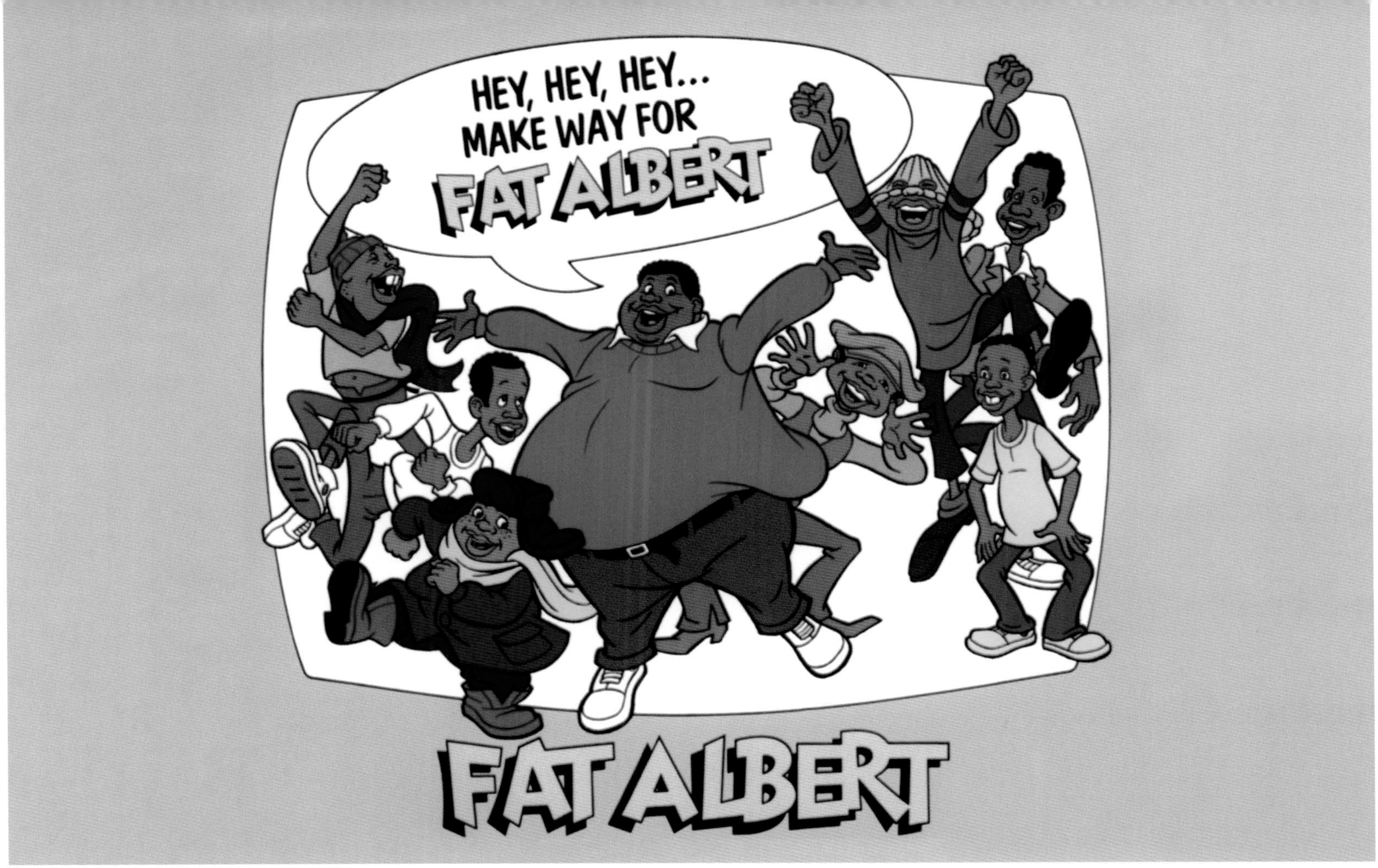
HEY, HEY, HEY...
MAKE WAY FOR
FAT ALBERT
FAT ALBERT

Fat Albert and the Cosby Kids

Hey, Hey, Hey, It's Fat Albert!

Bill Cosby first introduced the character Fat Albert with his signature line on the 1967 comedy album, *Revenge*. He told the story of an obese boy who scared the bejesus out of the other kids in his Philadelphia neighborhood by jumping on top of them in a game called "Buck Buck." As with much of Cosby's comedy, as well as other breakout African American comedians such as Richard Pryor and Chris Rock, the humorous narrative exposed the harsher realities of growing up in America as a person of color.

"I saw [Fat Albert] as a black, who's been rejected as a human being," said Cosby in a June 2013 *New York Times ArtsBeat Blog*. "In the eyes of some—capital letters—people, this color causes an insanity in their minds . . . I'm specifying where I lived and who I am, to these people. It is not idealized at all." Cosby's frustrations concerning racism influenced his routine, and later his Saturday morning cartoon, exposing first adults, then kids, to life's harsher realities with his characteristic playfulness. The inner-city setting, the quirky characters, and the difficult situations the characters faced all offered

YEARS ON AIR

1972-1985

NETWORK

CBS, Syndication

NUMBER OF EPISODES

110

CHARACTERS AND VOICE ACTORS

Fat Albert/James "Mushmouth" Mush/William "Bill" Cosby: Bill Cosby
"Dumb" Donald Parker: Lou Scheimer
Rudy Davis: Eric Suter
"Weird" Harold Simmons: Gerald Edwards
Russell Cosby/Bucky Miller: Jan Crawford

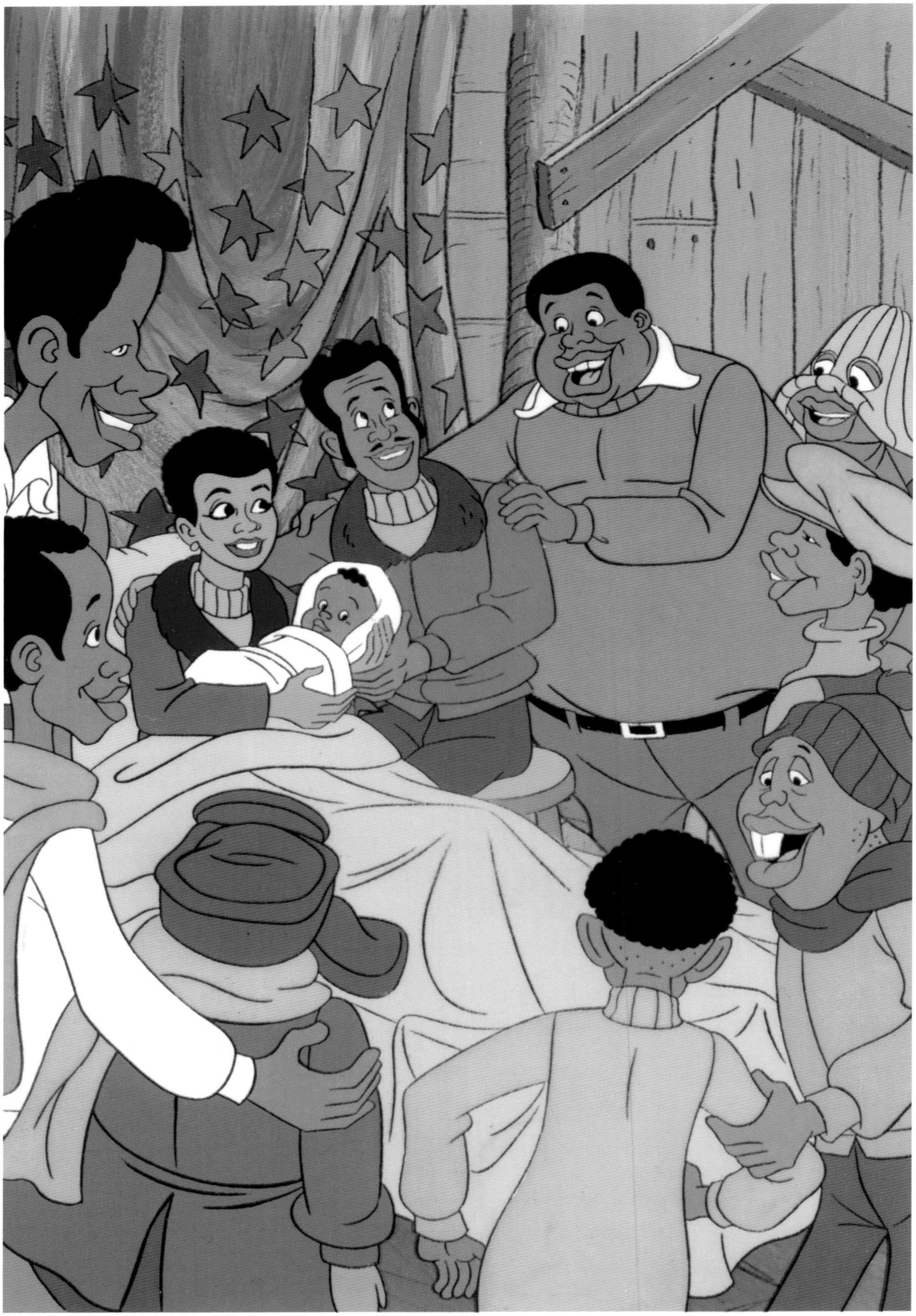

teachable lessons—as well a way to have a constructive conversation about differences.

An emphasis on positive social values, combined with Cosby's trademark humor, underpinned his 1969 prime-time special, *Hey, Hey, Hey, It's Fat Albert*, which later debuted as a CBS Saturday morning cartoon in 1972, backed by Filmation Associates. "There was this hullabaloo about values not being apparent in children's programming, especially on commercial networks," said Lou Scheimer, head of Filmation Associates, in *Classic TV*'s *Fat Albert and the Cosby Kids* by L. Wayne Hicks. "We decided to present a show that had those built-in values. The network was responsive."

With CBS onboard, the series placed Fat Albert and his pals, better known as the Junkyard Gang, in situations or moral dilemmas mirroring challenges commonly faced by kids—bullying, hygiene issues, stage fright, peer pressure, racism, drug and alcohol temptations, and boy/girl relationships.

Other recurring program tropes included the gang watching *The Brown Hornet,* a show within the show. Fat Albert and friends would race to the barely functioning TV set within their clubhouse to catch this series whenever the latest installment aired. Featuring a caped and masked superhero parody of *The Green Hornet*, the black superhero patrolled intergalactic space for evildoers with his assistant Stinger and robot sidekick Tweeterbell. Similar to the rest of the cartoon, this diversion offered more opportunities for lessons and helped guide the gang through whatever problems they were facing. A live-action commentary featuring Cosby accompanied each episode, and the show's ending featured the gang singing a song about the lessons they learned.

Fat Albert and the Cosby Kids has been likened to Aesop's Fables, with characters puzzling out life's head-scratchers. Integral

to the show's capacity to reach and teach children was the show's ability to bring to life idiosyncratic individuals. Fat Albert occupied the nucleus of the group of course, an unusual choice for a lead given his girth. "Overweight people, back in the '20s, '30s and '40s, on the Broadway stage and in movies, they immediately became the funny person, the clown," said Cosby in the *ArtsBeat Blog*. "The person you could make fun of, the person who made fun of himself. But these characters were invented because I wanted to change, break the stereotypes. I changed Albert, making him the leader and giving him the intelligence."

Albert, in turn, shepherded a group of oddballs and misfits reminiscent of the type of kids Cosby grew up with, including his own brother, Russell, the smallest gang member, who liked to make snide remarks. There was Weird Harold,

PREVIOUS: Hey Hey Hey! It's Fat Albert and the Junkyard Gang.

OPPOSITE: Fat Albert and friends in the Christmas special *Silent Knights*, 1977.

BOTTOM: Members of the Fat Albert and the Junkyard Gang: (left to right) Bill, Fat Albert, Russell, and Dumb Donald.

BOTTOM: The rest of the Fat Albert and the Junkyard Gang: (left to right) Rudy, Bucky, Weird Harold, and Mushmouth.

who was tall, but extremely clumsy; Mushmouth, who had a speech impediment; Dumb Donald, who didn't make the best decisions thus was called dumb; Rudy, the good-looking one, who was cocky and a bit vain; and Bill, who was Russell's older brother and acted as a voice of reason.

Unlike most other cartoons in this time period, the series stood out for featuring an all-black cast. Still, in his interview with *Classic TV*, show writer Larry DiTillio said he believes it is a mistake to constrict the show's value to its racial component. "*Fat Albert* wasn't specifically about being black—none of Cosby's shows before or since has been—but race wasn't overlooked. The characters, minor and major, were all black. But the program wasn't written for black children. It was written to reach everyone."

Producing a show celebrating inclusivity propelled *Fat Albert and the Cosby Kids* away from niche programing geared to discrete audiences. Instead, the cartoon broke color barriers. Spanning eight seasons into the mid-1980s, it received an Emmy®

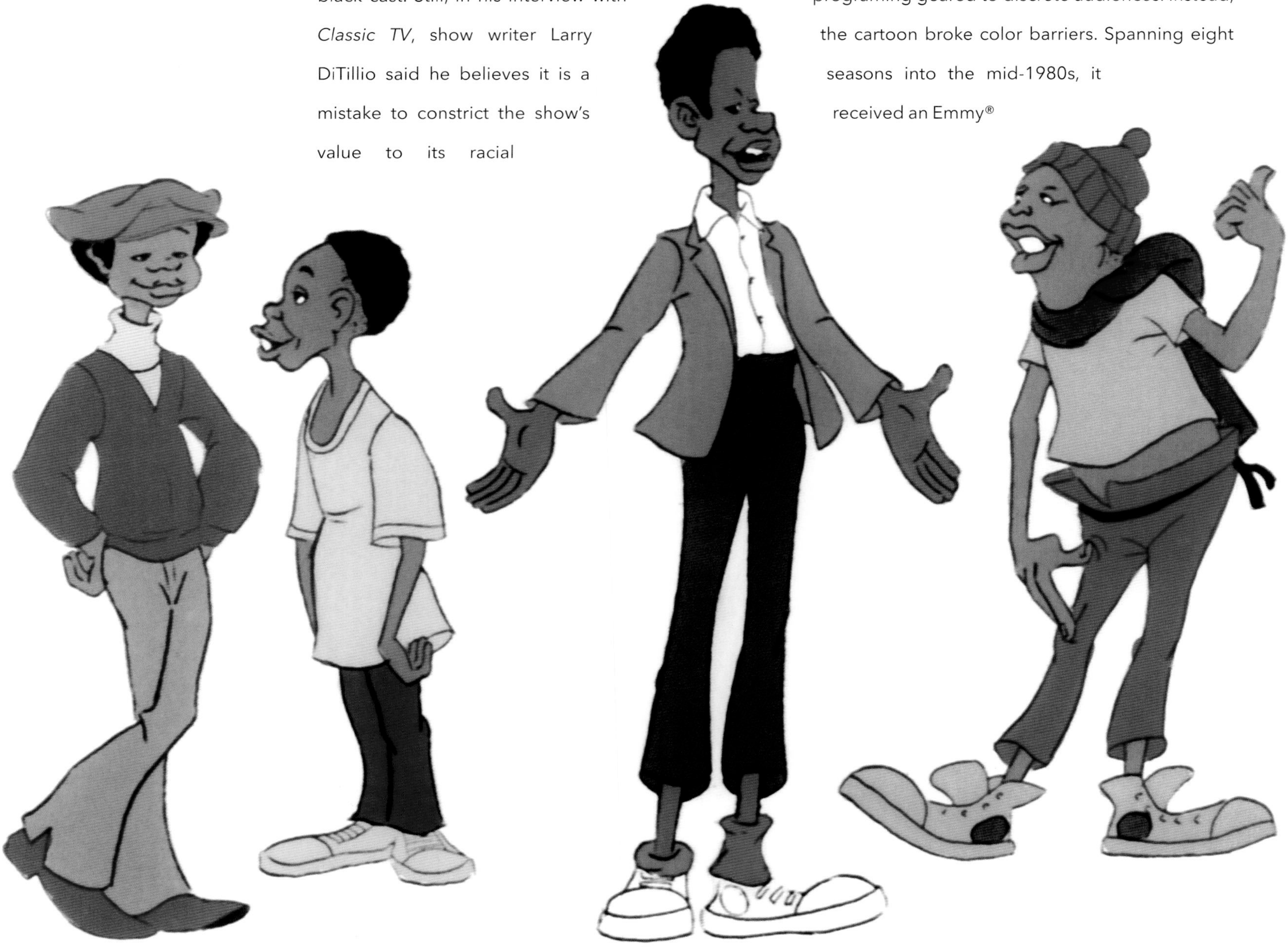

nomination two years after airing and in 1993, *TV Guide* named it as one of the "Best Cartoon Series of the 1970s." Spin-offs of *Fat Albert and the Cosby Kids* included *The Fat Albert Halloween Special* and the *Fat Albert Christmas Special* (both in 1977) as well as *The Fat Albert Easter Special*. The beloved series spawned lunch boxes, board games, books, and record albums. In 2004, Kenan Thompson played Fat Albert in the live action version of the movie.

Judging by the show's decades-spanning run, its awards and popularity, the creative team achieved their goal of establishing an uplifting show for everyone. Beyond its remarkable wit and sensitivity, it spoke to the universal problems people of all ages and races face. In 2013, National Public Radio interviewed historian Pamela Thomas, cofounder of the traveling show *Funky Turns 40: Black Character Exhibition,* about the program's influence. "Their stories were like your stories; their experiences were like your experience," said Thomas. "Bill Cosby's cartoon was so ground breaking, it just dealt with so many issues. . . . You don't realize it when you're watching it that you're getting all of these messages in a form that children can understand." *Fat Albert and the Cosby Kids* taught us that no matter where you start or what you look like, you matter as a human being—something every kid deserved to know.

ABOVE: Rudy gets a little help from his friends to face his fears.

Fat Albert Gets Real

Never shy about presenting real-world issues, a particularly hard-hitting episode, "Gang Wars," presented the dangers of inner-city life. In the episode, Fernando, a young Latino boy, who desired to one day become a famous comedian, pays the ultimate price. The only character to be killed on-screen, Fernando died as a result of gang violence.

The following day, Fat Albert gave a speech to his friends about their fallen buddy: "This was supposed to be a funny speech by a funny person, a guy who liked to make people laugh. But instead, here I am crying. His name was Fernando and he was killed last night trying to stop a gang war. Fernando used to joke that he wouldn't forget us when he became famous. All he wanted was a chance to grow, but a bullet took away that chance. Well, maybe he won't become world famous, but he'll always be famous to his friends. That's why we're naming this the Fernando Garcia Park."

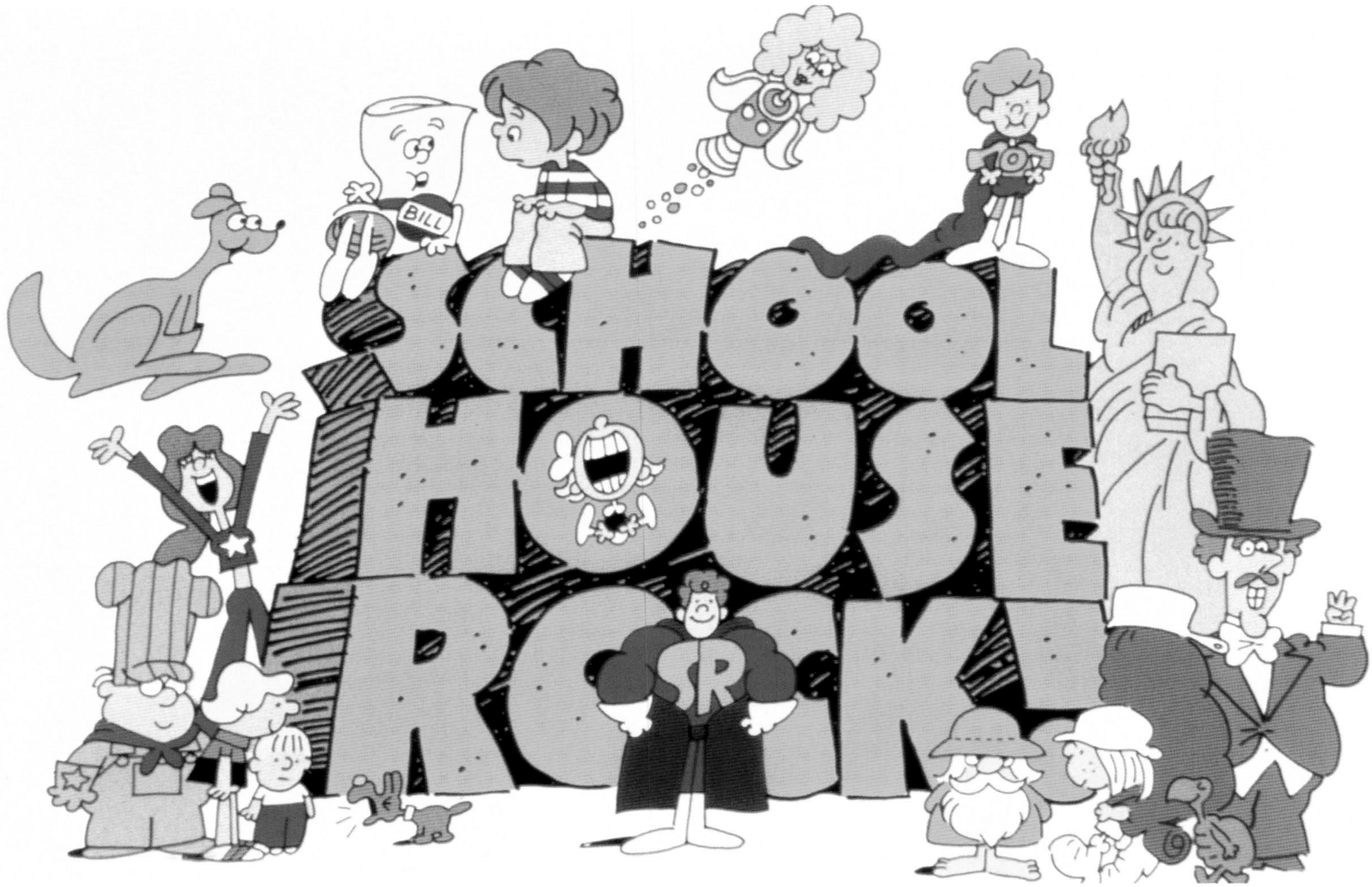
SCHOOL HOUSE ROCK!
BILL
SR

YEARS ON AIR

1973–1985

NETWORK

ABC

NUMBER OF EPISODES

64

CHARACTERS AND VOICE ACTORS

Vocals: Bob Dorough/ Jack Sheldon/Lynn Ahrens/ Val Hawk/Bob Kaliban/ Vicki Deney/Nancy Reed/ Grady Tate/Essra Mohawk/ Barry Carl/Blossom Dearie

Schoolhouse Rock!

Conjunction Junction, what's your function?

Hooking up words and phrases and clauses.

I'm just a bill.

Yes, I'm only a bill.

And I'm sitting here on Capitol Hill.

Well, it's a long, long journey to the capital city

It's a long, long wait

While I'm sitting in committee, but I know I'll be a law someday.

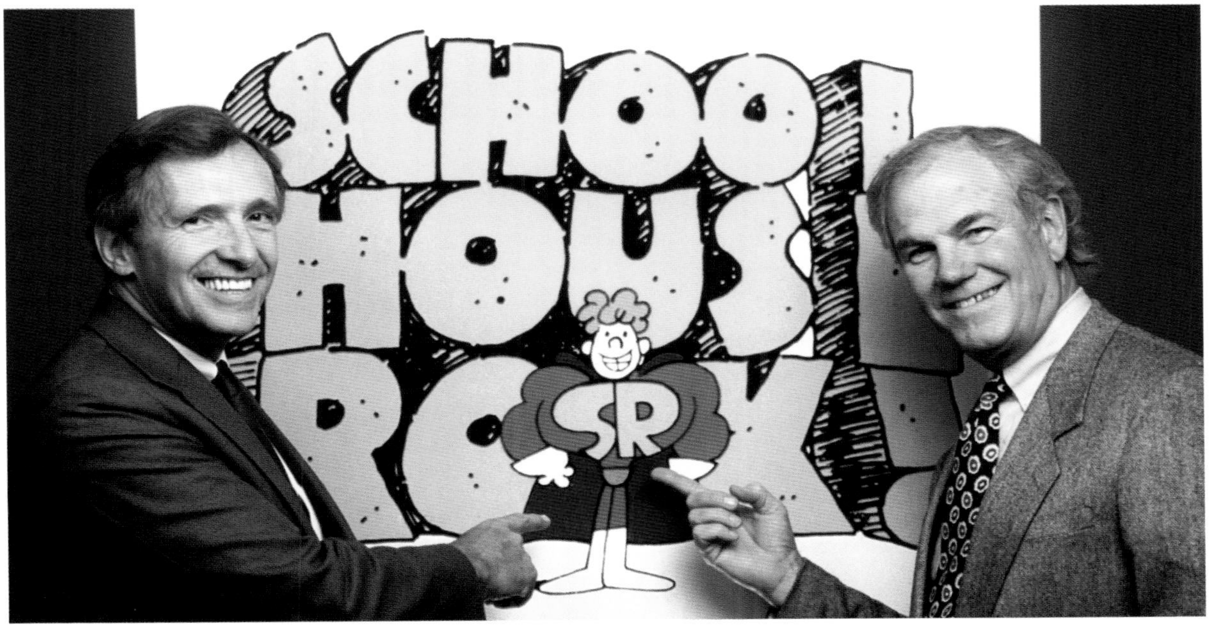
SR

OPPOSITE: This iconic illustration depicts many of the series' most famous educational segments.

TOP: *Schoolhouse Rock!* composer Bob Dorough (left) poses with singer Jack Sheldon (right), 1994.

Children growing up in the 1970s and 1980s knew the words to these classic songs. Even better, as they hummed along with the cartoons, they absorbed their meaning, fulfilling adman David McCall's vision. Of Madison Avenue's McCaffrey & McCall, McCall had an epiphany for a cool show using pop ditties to make school lessons stick. "His son, Davey Jr., had been having a lot of trouble with multiplication tables in school," explains cocreator/producer/songwriter George Newall. "But Dave noticed . . . the kid was singing the lyrics to every rock 'n' roll hit of the day. What if we produced an educational phonograph record of the multiplication tables set to rock music? Great idea."

Schoolhouse Rock! expanded from its initial concept of math lessons set to music to cover diverse topics such as grammar, history, and science. Served up as bite-sized knowledge nuggets during commercial breaks, the segments fulfilled 1970s Saturday morning programming constraints requiring a modicum of educational content. From the outset, McCall and company appealed to children's playful sensibility and intelligence instead of beating kids over the head with lessons. To this end, they brought on unique talents, like jazz bebop wizard Bob Dorough. "I was excited, but cautious," explains Dorough. "I thought the idea was a bit puerile, but then McCall added a line that shook my timbers. He said, 'But don't write down to the children.'"

Dorough didn't disappoint the creative team with his first stab at what soon became "Multiplication Rock" numbers, vindicating their faith in the project. "When Bob came back with 'Three Is a Magic Number,' we were astonished. He had put the three times tables into a context, based on the role of three in mathematics, religion, and even furniture-making," said Newall. More animated songs followed, incorporating elements of folk rock, funk, and country, leading ABC to snatch up the series in 1973 with McCaffrey & McCall producing.

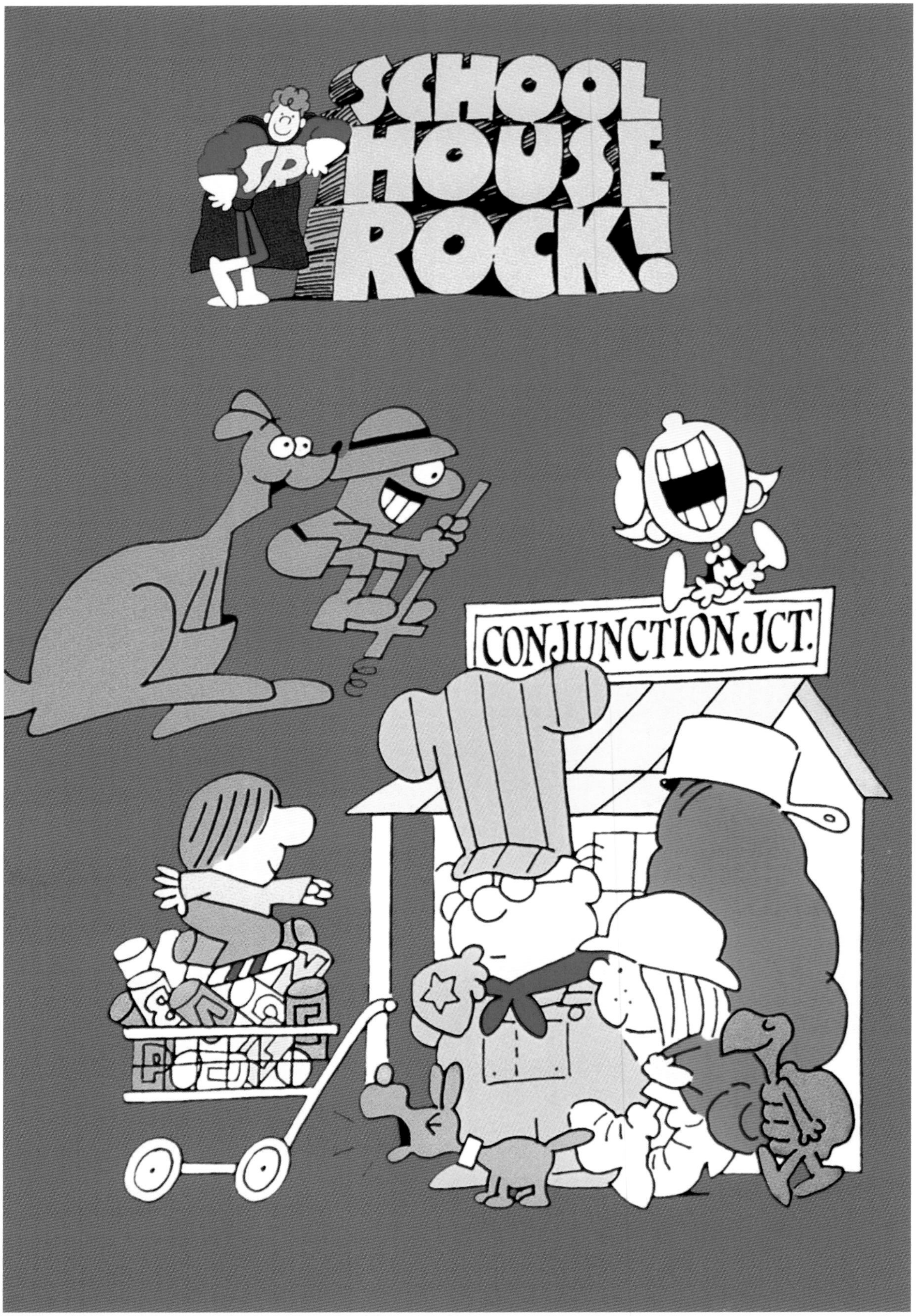
SCHOOL HOUSE ROCK!
CONJUNCTION JCT.

An educational consultant vetted each written segment before animators hand-painted each cel. In addition to Dorough, other musical exemplars brought their brilliance to produce outstanding segments. Blossom Dearie, a supper-club jazz singer who once played with Miles Davis, gloriously serenaded "Figure Eight" as ice-skaters sliced through a school girl's thought-bubble imagination. Acclaimed songwriter Essra Mohawk, who came up in the '60s performing with Frank Zappa and the Grateful Dead, sang "Interjections!," "Mother Necessity," and "Sufferin' Till Suffrage," promoting women's voting rights.

Not all of the performers were so well-known when they contributed to *Schoolhouse Rock!,* however. Long before she won the Tony Award for the musical *Ragtime* in 1998, lyricist Lynn Ahrens worked as a secretary for McCaffrey & McCall. "One day one of the producers of *Schoolhouse Rock!,* George Newall, passed by and casually asked me if I'd like to try writing a song," said Ahrens. Ahrens went on to compose and sing "The Preamble," which described the principles of the Constitution.

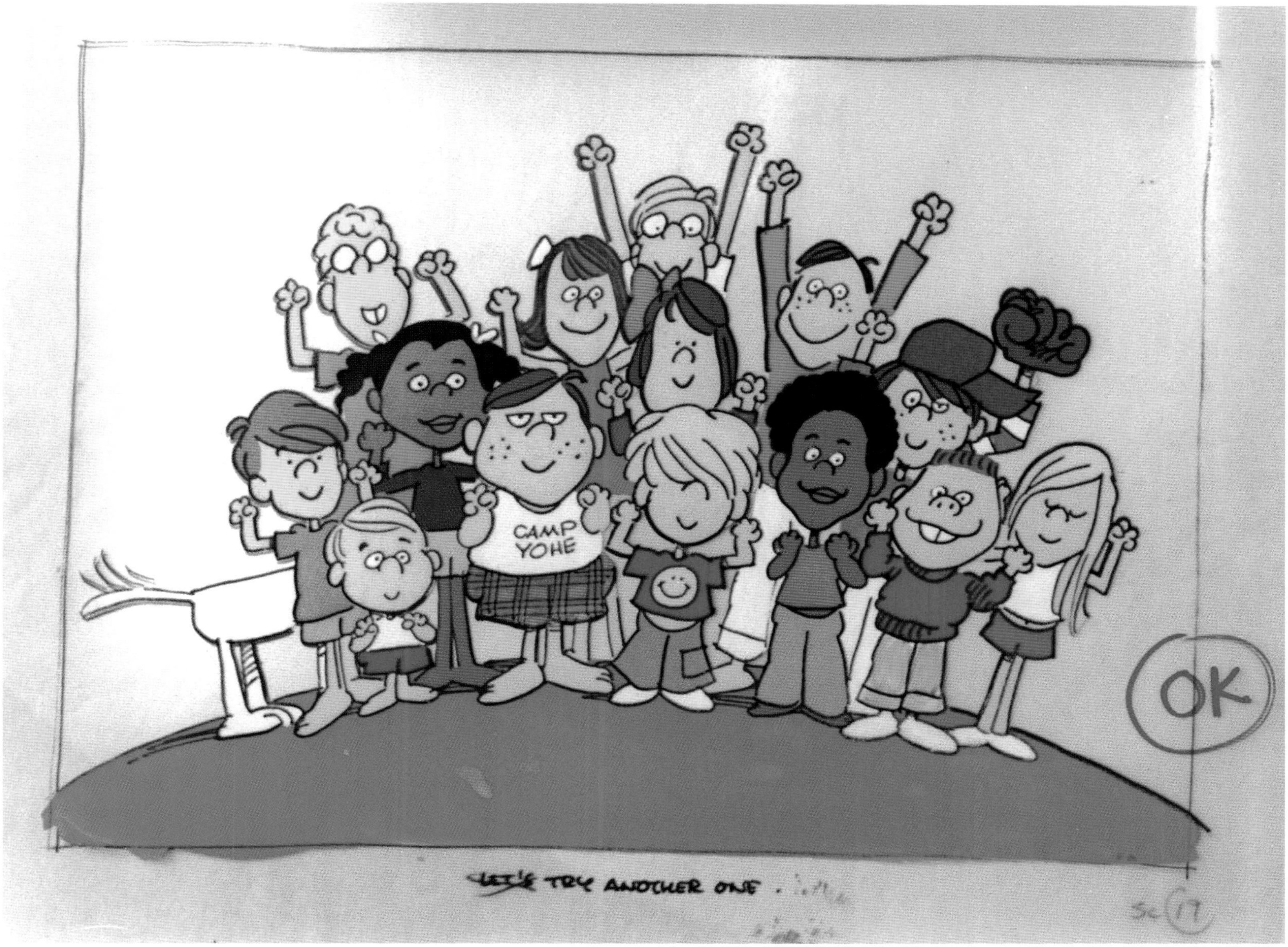
CAMP
YOHE
OK
LET'S TRY ANOTHER ONE

More songs by Ahern would soon follow, including "A Noun is a Person, Place, or Thing," in which she elucidated the ways nouns appear in our everyday usage:

Well, every person you know
And every place that you can go
And anything that you can show
You know they're nouns.

With the help of ace performers such as Ahrens, as well as Jack Sheldon, a trumpeter and singer who served as Merv Griffin's sidekick on the *Merv Griffin Show*, the dense educational material came alive. Sheldon lent his voice to "I'm Just a Bill," one of the most popular *Schoolhouse Rock!* numbers. On its face, the song's material could have suffered from being dry and technical. After all, its premise centered on the process of a congressional bill becoming a law. However, in the hands of jazz pianist

OPPOSITE: Artwork from one of the show's most famous songs, "Conjunction Junction."

ABOVE: A painted production cel from the "Let's Try Another One" segment.

TOP: This illustration from the musical segment "Them Not So Dry Bones" accompanied the song lyrics: *Shin bone connected to the knee bone (That means the tibia connects to the patella)* . . .

BOTTOM: Painted production cel from "I'm Just a Bill," one of the series' most famous segments.

Dave Frishberg, with animation supplied by Phil Kimmelman and Associates, the segment caught fire. In it, the title character, a depressed scroll of paper, struggles through a legislative maze, illustrating the quagmire nature of American politics. A similarly arcane topic, the human nervous system became fascinating in "Telegraph Line," equating the body's signals to telegram commands.

> *There's a telegram for you, sir.*
> *Better read it on the spot.*
> *It says your hand is near a stove*
> *That's very, very hot.*

Incorporating smart writing with clever imagery and verse, McCaffrey & McCall's invention did exactly what it set out to do. From the get-go, children loved *Schoolhouse Rock!* As a result, it lasted

twelve seasons. Critics adored it too, showering the series with four Emmy® Awards throughout the '70s and '80s. It also didn't hurt that the US bicentennial occurred in 1976, three years into production. *Schoolhouse Rock!* used the occasion to unfurl patriotic fare, such as "Fireworks," about celebrating Independence Day, and "The Shot Heard Around the World," offering a play-by-play of the war for independence.

Replacing conformity and blandness with hipness and humor, backed by jazzy, funky music, *Schoolhouse Rock!* sailed into pop-culture notoriety. After going off the air in the mid '80s, it returned the next decade as *Money Rock,* offering segments on the budget deficit and stock exchange. In 1996, a musical adaptation, entitled *Schoolhouse Rock Live!* began performing in various cities, continuing to this day. The 2000s witnessed *Earth Rock*, covering climate change and carbon footprints. Related parodies and spoofs have surfaced as popular culture references on shows, such as *The Simpsons*, *Family Guy*, and *Jimmy Kimmel Live!* In addition to a Museum of Television & Radio retrospective in 1995 commemorating the show, various artists have covered the music, including Blind Melon, Moby, the Lemonheads, and Buffalo Tom.

The fact that *Schoolhouse Rock!* continues to reemerge in various forms throughout politics, music, and entertainment is a testament to its execution and scope of purpose. A less authentic production devoid of humor and style might have died out long ago, forgotten in the annals of cartoon history. Instead, the show and concept continues to win over young hearts and minds, inspiring kids to question and think. Or as the show's intro states:

As your body grows bigger
your mind grows flowers.
It's great to learn . . . 'Cause knowledge is power.

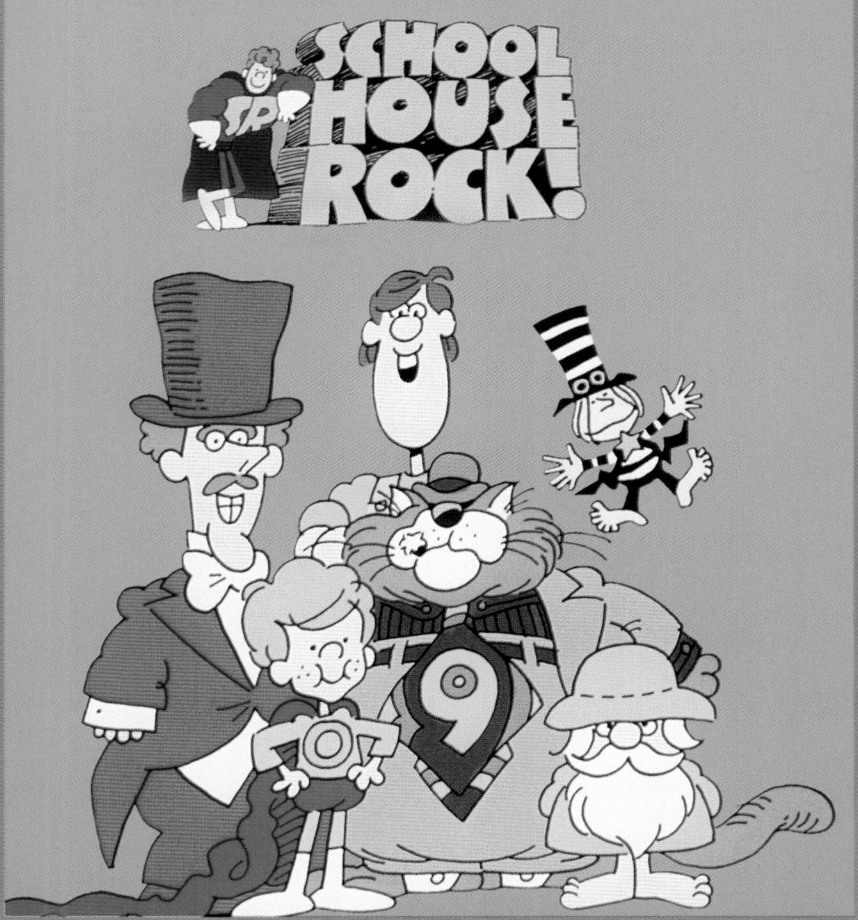
SCHOOL HOUSE ROCK!
SR
9

ABOVE: Artwork featuring beloved characters from the *Schoolhouse Rock!* program.

Three Is a Magic Number

Premiering in the pilot *Schoolhouse Rock!* episode and written/sung by Bob Dorough, this song proved to be one of the most popular hits from the series and has been covered by multiple performers including Blind Melon, Elizabeth Mitchell, and Embrace.

Three is a magic number
Yes, it is, it's a magic number
Somewhere in that ancient mystic trinity
You get three as a magic number
The past and the present and the future
The faith and hope and charity
The heart and the brain and the body
Give you three as a magic number.

Life Cereal

"Let's get Mikey!" "Yeah! He won't eat it. He hates everything."

"He likes it! Hey, Mikey!"

It might not have been as hard as you would imagine for Little Mikey to try a spoonful of Life. After all, the commercial featured Little Mikey's (whose real name was John Gilchrest) real-life brothers prodding him to try the cereal. (One of whom was actually named Michael; the other's name was Tommy.)

As everyone knows, Little Mikey, who hates everything, ended up enjoying what he tasted. The recipient of the 1974 Clio Award, this spot ran for more than twelve years and was ranked the number ten commercial of all time by *TV Guide*.

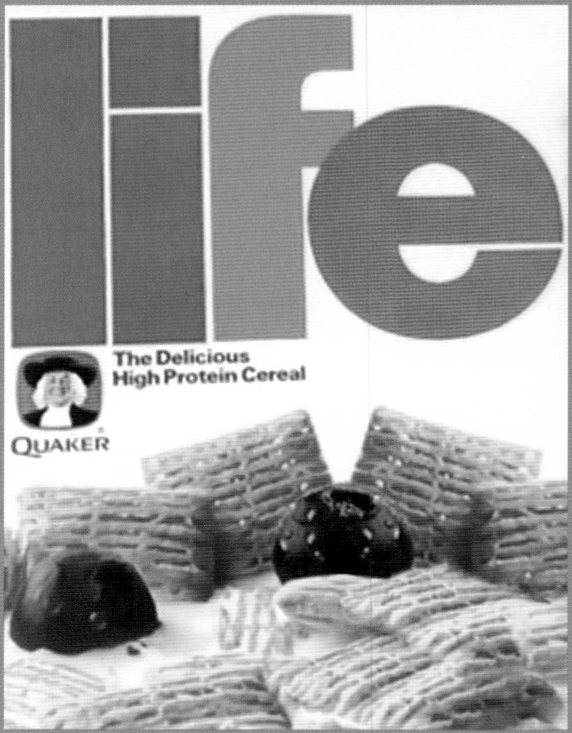
life
The Delicious
High Protein Cereal
QUAKER

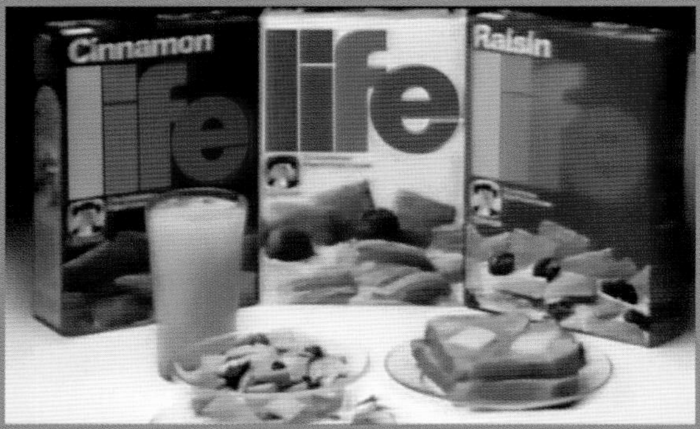
Cinnamon
life
life
Raisin

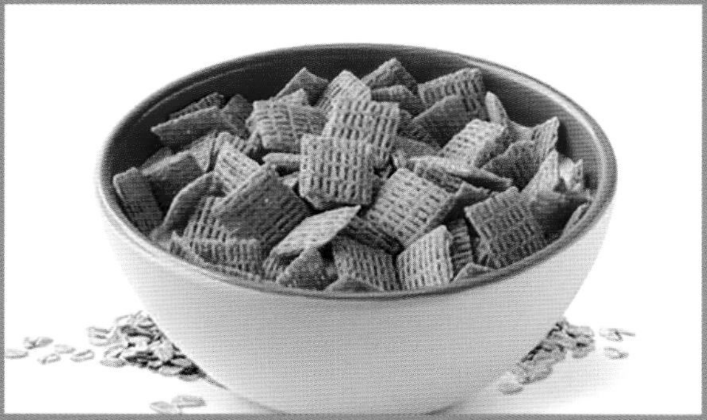

ABOVE: Life cereal came in three flavors, original, cinnamon, and raisin.

Super Friends

"To fight injustice. To right that which is wrong. And to serve all mankind!" This was *Super Friends'* stated mission. Headquartered inside the Hall of Justice, the most powerful superheroes ever assembled would team up to protect the innocent and thwart evil. The ensemble of ensembles, *Super Friends*, didn't dither with focusing on one caped crusader. Like the show's source material, DC Comics' *Justice League of America*, it brought audiences a bevy of the most recognizable crime fighters and defenders, including Superman, Batman and Robin, Wonder Woman, and Aquaman. The program also established new characters: teenagers Wendy and Marvin and their pet, Wonder Dog. Though these additions didn't possess much in the way of super powers, they helped youngsters self-identify with them as "hero-apprentices."

In addition to character modifications from the comics, the series toned down darker elements and brutality to accommodate the network's content guidelines. "Superheroes had fallen out of favor with networks as the 1970s began," according to David A. Roach in *The Superhero Book: The Ultimate Encyclopedia of Comic Book Icons and Hollywood*

YEARS ON AIR

1973–1986
(various titles/iterations)

NETWORK

ABC

NUMBER OF EPISODES

109

CHARACTERS AND VOICE ACTORS

Superman: Danny Dark
Batman: Olan Soule
Robin: Casey Kasem
Wonder Woman: Shannon Farnon
Aquaman: Norman Alden
Wendy: Sherry Alberoni
Marvin: Frank Welker
Narrator: Ted Knight

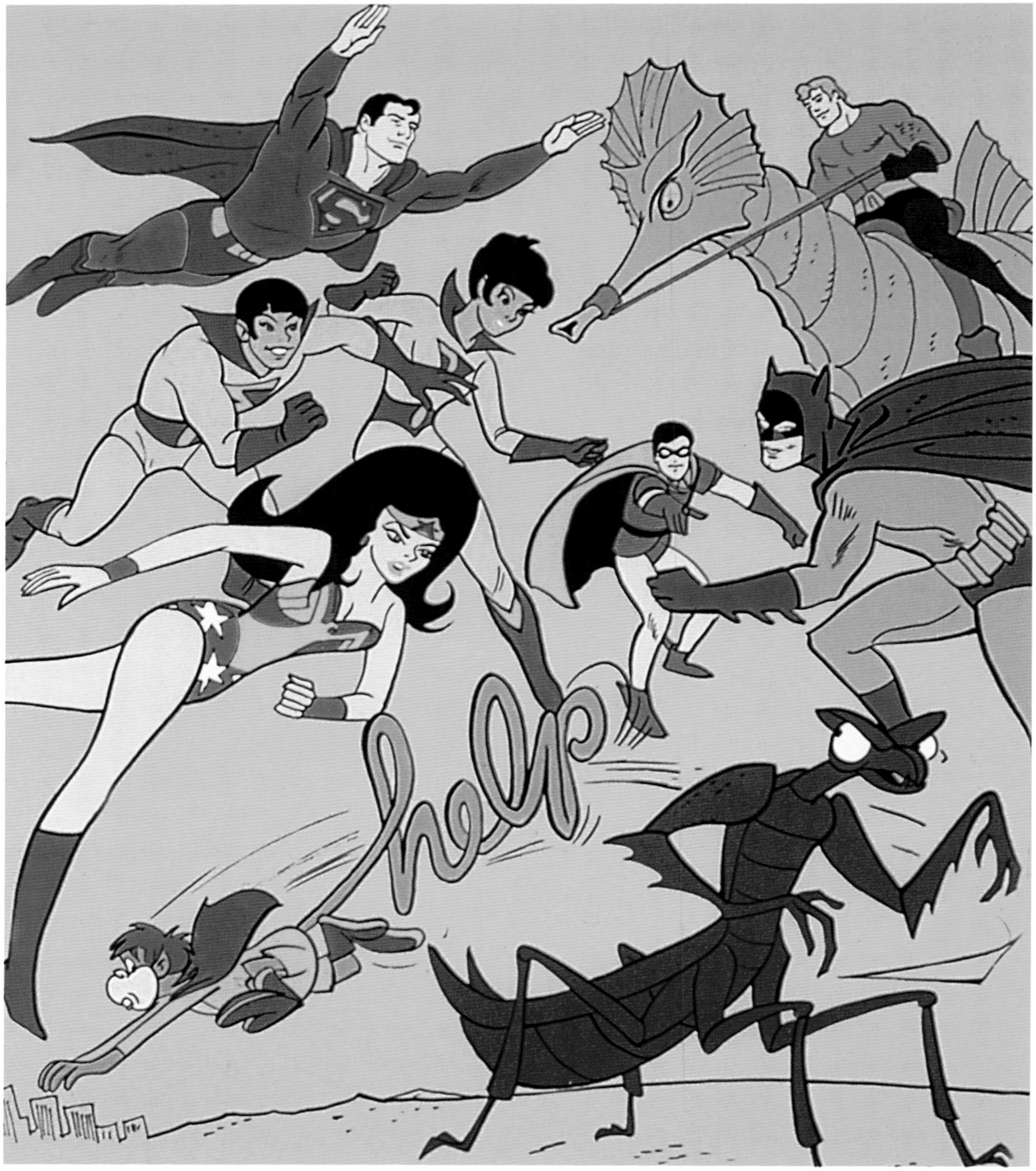
help

to create a new supergroup on Saturday mornings, but they wanted the adventures to be moralistic and nonviolent." Hanna and Barbera therefore tapped cartoonist Alex Toth (*Space Ghost*) to produce a kid-friendly version of the superheroes while keeping the designs sleek and stylized.

Under Toth's direction, most episodes began with a Trouble Alert distress call sent by Colonel Wilcox, the team's government liaison, on the wall-sized computer informing them of some villain's diabolical scheme. For example in the episode "The Balloon People," the Balunians, a family of aliens, landed on Earth after their home world succumbs to pollution. When news of these guests reach the evil genius Noah Tall, he devised a scheme to abduct them for their teleportation secrets. Other super challenges vexing the Super Friends included a malfunctioning super computer called the G.E.E.C. (Goodfellow's Effort-Eliminating Computer) meant to rid mankind of hard work, which inevitably went haywire, a saboteur android Superman bent on destroying a Mars space base, and power pirates seeking to abscond with Earth's energy so they could bring it to their own depleted planet.

PREVIOUS: Super Friends–(left to right) Batman, Robin, Wonder Woman, Aquaman, and Superman–on the move.

ABOVE: The Super Friends work together to win the day.

Heroes. "But, in 1972, a pair of CBS *New Scooby-Doo Movies*, with guest stars Batman and Robin, and two episodes of ABC's *The Brady Kids*, which guest-starred Superman and Wonder Woman, changed the minds of development executives at ABC. Soon the alphabet network commissioned Hanna-Barbera

Though Superman usually led the charge in solving these challenges, as his many powers lent themselves to whatever predicament the team faced, Batman, Wonder Woman, and company always backed him up. Other guest heroes often joined in on the action, including the Flash, Green Arrow, and Plastic Man, a part-time Justice League member capable of stretching his body to superhuman lengths. An assortment of talented actors supplied the character voices, beginning with Ted Knight (Ted Baxter from *The Mary Tyler Moore Show*) as the narrator with the signature line, "Meanwhile, at the Hall of Justice . . .," which became a universal fanboy trope for cutting between storylines.

Danny Dark, the so-called "voice-over king," well-known for supplying lines for Budweiser commercials, Keebler cookies, and StarKist Tuna, provided Superman's voice. Olan Soule, of *The Andy Griffith Show* and *Battlestar Galactica*, voiced Batman, while disc jockey-legend Casey Kasem voiced Robin. Actor Shannon Faron, who played Wonder Woman, described her show experience for Comic Book Resources in 2014. "[Wonder Woman] represented to me, as a child, the strong, capable woman. And not a bully particularly, just a woman who didn't necessarily require the assistance of a man to get through life." Faron particularly saw the importance of a female perspective on the nonviolent show. "Nobody died in these cartoons. People were managed. And Wonder Woman was a representative of that from the female perspective . . . that we needed more of this female aspect in society in order to have a better balance."

TOP: Robin puts his strength to the test.

BOTTOM: Wonder Woman in her invisible plane.

The program didn't suffer from lack of voice talent or creative guidance, but it did end after only one season. However, a wave of live-action superhero TV series, including *The Six Million Dollar Man* (1974), *Wonder Woman* (1975), and *The Amazing Spider-Man* (1977), prompted Hanna-Barbera to reconsider production. In 1977, they brought back

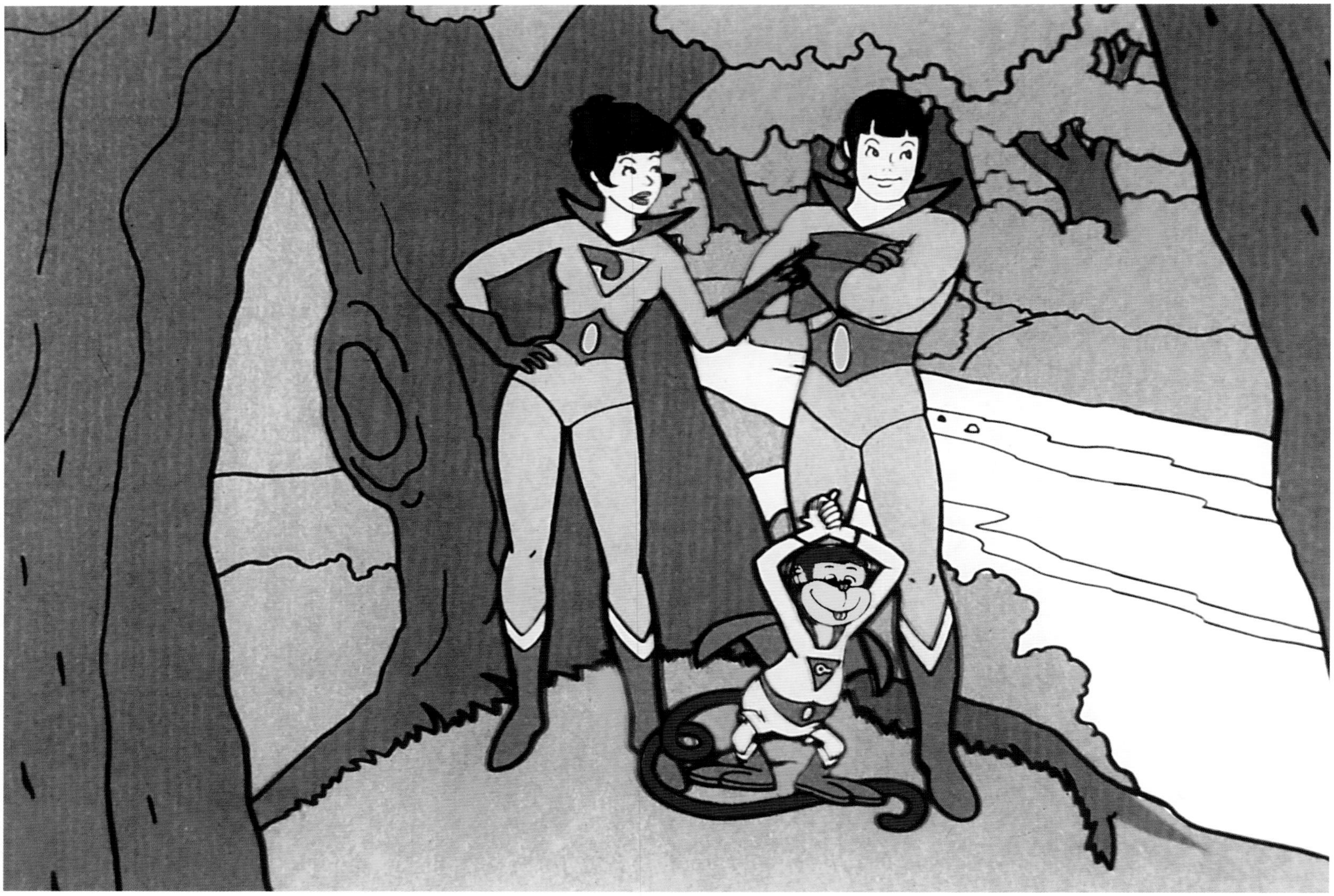

ABOVE: The Wonder Twins were an extraterrestrial twin brother and sister duo who joined the group in 1977 in the *The All New Super Friends Hour.*

the series under the title, *The All-New Super Friends Hour*. The Wonder Twins, Zan and Jayna, along with their pet monkey Gleek, replaced Wendy, Marvin, and Wonder Dog. Unlike their human predecessors, these aliens from Planet Exxor possessed awesome powers. Upon smacking their fists together and chanting, "Wonder Twin powers, activate!" they could transform: Zan could become any form of water and Jayna could morph into any animal. At the same time, more DC Comics heroes appeared in guest spots, including Hawkgirl, Hawkman, Green Lantern, and the Atom. Perhaps as a sign of changing times, multicultural icons, including the Black Vulcan, Apache Chief, and Samurai also came to prominence.

Super Friends transformed once again a year later, in 1978. *Super Friends/Challenge of the Super Friends* were composed of two segments, the latter in particular reached new fandom heights with its introduction of the Legion of Doom—an evil counter organization comprised of well-known supervillains Lex Luthor, Cheetah, The Riddler, Solomon Grundy,

Black Manta, Captain Cold, Giganta, and others. If the good guys hung out at the Hall of Justice, naturally these blackguards called The Hall of Doom home. A mobile headquarters shaped eerily similar to Darth Vader's helmet, it usually stayed docked in a crocodile-infested swamp.

The following decade witnessed a whirlwind of more changes to the show, including titles and formats, while Kenner action figures of the characters flew off shelves. Following on the heels of *The World's Greatest SuperFriends* (1979-80), featuring half-hour episodes with evocative titles, such as "Lex Luthor Strikes Back" and "The Lord of Middle Earth," came the 1980-1982 seasons of *Super Friends*. This iteration consisted of seven-minute shorts and introduced a Hispanic hero, El Dorado, providing additional cultural diversity. *The Best of the Super Friends* (1982-1983) offered reruns from previous seasons before *The Legendary Super Powers Show* (1984-1985) and *The Super Powers Team: Galactic Guardians* (1985-1986) closed out the series.

Clearly, based on the number of reboots and retools of *Super Friends* from Hanna-Barbera over the years, this show defined superheroes for a generation—exposing youngsters to amazing characters they may not have known without reading the grittier comics. *Super Friends* led with humor instead of violence and encouraged cooperation to battle the forces of evil. Most important of all, the show offered something invaluable. For several moments every Saturday morning, it presented an escape from humdrum reality, allowing boys and girls to dream of their own magical powers.

ABOVE: The Super Friends: (clockwise from left) Zan, Aquaman, Wonder Woman, Superman, Batman, Robin, Jayna, and Gleek the monkey.

Super Diversity

The cartoon series introduced a slew of ethnically diverse characters to the Justice League's traditional superhero lineup.

Apache Chief: A Native American superhero who could grow fifty feet tall or larger and had a sixth sense for sniffing out liars and for tracking just about anyone.

El Dorado: A Hispanic hero rumored to be descended from Aztec sorcerers, El Dorado possessed ancient mystical knowledge and had the ability to cast illusions with his eyes and teleport.

Black Vulcan: An African American hero who could transform into a lightning bolt and travel through the sky at the speed of light. He could also shoot electricity from his hands.

Samurai: A Japanese superhero with the ability to command the winds. His real name was Toshio Eto and he was once a history professor. One day Toshio was struck by a beam of light from New Gods, a humanoid race from the Planet New Genesis seeking to develop superheroes to defend against Darkseid, the evil ruler of the planet Apokolips.

YEARS ON AIR

1976-1980

NETWORK

CBS

**NUMBER OF
EPISODES**

36

**CHARACTERS AND
VOICE ACTORS**

Tarzan: Robert Ridgely
Queen Nemone: Joan Gerber
Phobeg: Ted Cassidy
Fana the Huntress: Linda Gary
N'Kima: Lou Scheimer

Tarzan, Lord of the Jungle

"The jungle: here I was born, and here my parents died when I was but an infant," Tarzan narrated at the opening of each episode. "I would have soon perished, too, had I not been found by a kindly she-ape named Kala, who adopted me as her own and taught me the ways of the wild."

Through *Tarzan, Lord of the Jungle*, children in 1976 learned the ways of the wild every Saturday morning. This Tarzan, however, differed from earlier versions, particularly from the simplistic brute played by Johnny Weissmuller in the 1932 movie, *Tarzan, the Ape Man*. In that film, the words "Jane" and "Tarzan" were the extent of Tarzan's vocabulary.

The cartoon version of the character, voiced by the legendary Robert Ridgely, who was known for *Strawberry Shortcake* and *The New Adventures of Flash Gordon*, spoke eloquent English, evoking an air of highborn nobility and English cultivation.

Similarly, the show's visuals, based on the work of comic-strip artist Burne Hogarth, also evoked sophistication. The use of old-fashioned animation and hand-drawn artwork brought the untamed wild to life. Meanwhile, Tarzan's movements appeared fluid instead of jerky, befitting his intellect and refinement. Filmation producer Lou Scheimer described the show's animation approach in the book *Lou*

OPPOSITE: Tarzan with his friends the lion, Jad-bal-ja; the monkey, N'Kima; and the elephant, Tantor.

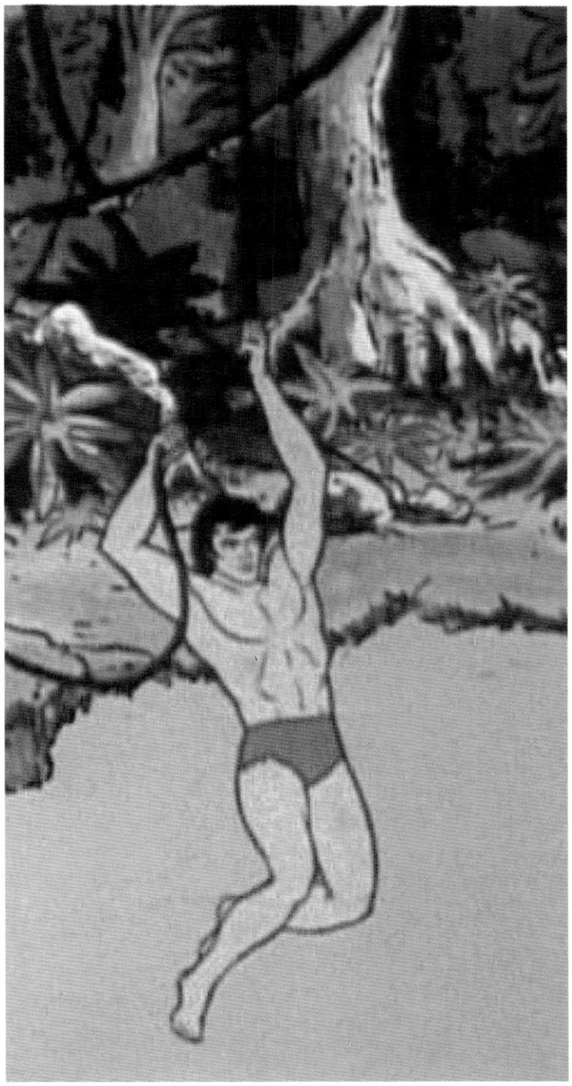

LEFT: Tarzan swings through the jungle with ease in every episode.

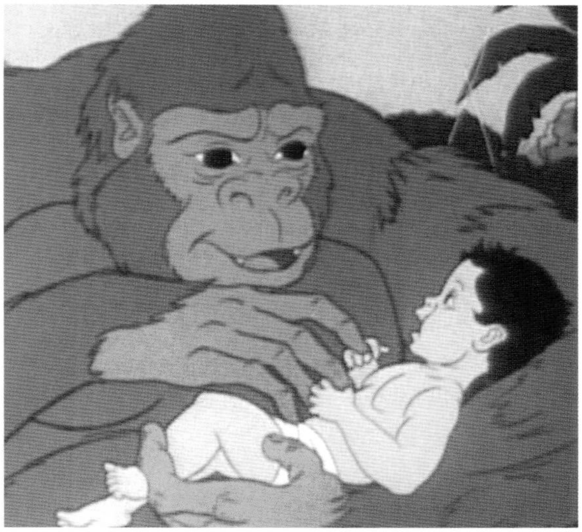

TOP RIGHT: Kala, the ape mother who adopted baby Tarzan and raised him.

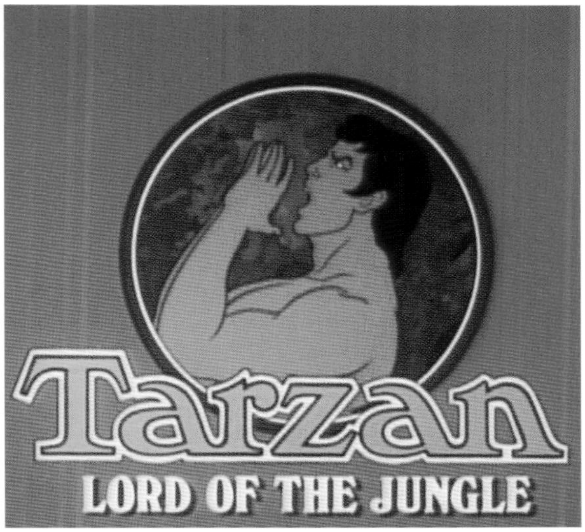
Tarzan
LORD OF THE JUNGLE

BOTTOM RIGHT: Promotional image for Tarzan, Lord of the Jungle.

Scheimer: Creating the Filmation Generation: "We wanted the anatomy to be very realistic, and this included muscular definition and even details such as painting in the eyes completely instead of having them be just the dots used on many adventure series." Scheimer's team shot live-action footage of a model doing the same movements Tarzan would perform in the show: running, jumping, swinging from vines. They then rotoscoped the content over the live-action sequences to create stock imagery. This technique, combined with the usage of facial close ups, enabled artists to make the series appear infinitely more lifelike.

More than the aesthetic, *Tarzan, Lord of the Jungle* stood apart from its cartoon contemporaries and earlier adaptations due to its faithfulness to novelist Edgar Rice Burroughs's source material. To understand how the Saturday morning cartoon Tarzan came to be a thoughtful hero, it's worth recalling the character's original creator, who penned numerous science-fiction novels including the *John Carter* series and *The People That Time*

TOP: A captured Tarzan is inspected by his alien abductor in the episode "Tarzan and the Strange Visitors."

BOTTOM: Tarzan faces his robot doppelganger in the episode "Tarzan's Rival."

Forgot. Though sometimes dismissed as pulp, Burroughs's work had a major impact on twentieth-century authors, including Ray Bradbury, who dubbed him "the most influential writer in the history of the world." Likewise, Rudyard Kipling wrote this about Burroughs in his autobiography: "My *Jungle Books* begat zoos of them. But the genius of all the genii was one who wrote a series called, *Tarzan of the Apes.*"

Scheimer and coproducer Norm Prescott hewed closely to Burroughs's original Tarzan, but they also took the show in new and interesting directions. In the episode, "Tarzan and the Strange Visitors," aliens try to abduct Tarzan as a specimen for their zoo. Robots make appearances too, such as in the episode, "Tarzan's Rival," where a scientist fashions an automaton Tarzan doppelganger to frame him for stealing the Jewels of Opar. Even zanier adventures saw Tarzan grapple with bizarre foes, such as giant spiders and mole people. Tarzan also encountered descendants of Atlantis, the Vikings, and primitives worshipping the woolly mammoth as God. Yet, no matter how far-out story lines became, Scheimer stuck to his original conception of Tarzan's personality. "The most important part was to do a show with a hero who was really sort of a normal adult. He couldn't fly, he couldn't do all the superhero stuff, but he had that capacity to work with animals, and was raised by an animal."

Tarzan's allegiance to his animal friends constituted a substantial part of the story lines. Due to the 1970s Broadcast Standards and Practices, Tarzan rarely battled beasts, nor did he carry a knife or beat up opponents because censors and parents' groups would have objected. Instead, he used his smarts to quell conflict. Aided by his monkey side-kick, N'Kima, Tarzan faced down evil, calling upon jungle pals, such as the lion Jad-bal-ja and the elephant Tantor, to fight for freedom. Whenever in trouble, he could also rely on his trusty yell to really bring the thunder. Interestingly enough, Danton Burroughs, grandson of Edgar Burroughs, supplied this yell, not Ridgely. "The funny part is that Danton lived down a hill and across the street from me," said Scheimer. "I could hear him doing those damn yells every morning; it used to drive me nuts sometimes because you could hear it wafting up over the hill." In another departure from the films, Jane doesn't appear in the cartoon except for one episode in the final season. According to Scheimer, they wrote her in after being requested by the Burroughs estate to resecure the rights to her character, which hadn't been used in visual media since the 1950s.

Tarzan, Lord of the Jungle modernized Burroughs's books in other ways. After swinging on his vine solo in season one, Tarzan teamed up with Batman as half of *The Batman/Tarzan Adventure Hour* the next year. Next, the series became *Tarzan and the Super 7* as part of a ninety-minute content block from 1978-1980, featuring other adventure shows, including *The Freedom Force* and *Jason of Star Command*. Other *Tarzan* iterations followed, including the live-action series *Tarzan* (1991-1994) starring Wolf Larson as a blond environmentalist, and *Tarzan: the Epic Adventures* (1996-1997).

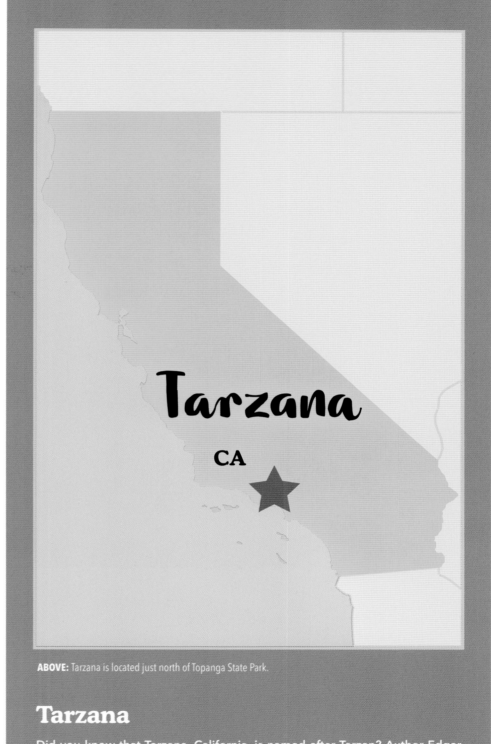

ABOVE: Tarzana is located just north of Topanga State Park.

Tarzana

Did you know that Tarzana, California, is named after Tarzan? Author Edgar Rice Burroughs paid $125,000 for Mil Flores, a 540-acre LA country estate in 1919 he renamed Tarzana after his popular book series. Eventually, a town sprang up around it. Today, Tarzana is home to close to 40,000 Los Angelenos.

LEFT: Tarzan often traveled atop his friend the elephant, Tantor.

RIGHT: Tarzan's faithful friend, the monkey N'Kima, helped him out of many conflicts.

In 2001, Disney introduced *The Legend of Tarzan* series based on their 1999 cartoon film.

It's no surprise the character of Tarzan has figured prominently in various entertainment forms since Burroughs created him in 1912. In his book *Tarzan, Jungle King of Popular Culture*, David Lemmo writes, "The Ape-Man entered popular culture just before the print medium began losing ground to radio, movies, and comics, and the Ape-Man became the first multimedia superstar and seminal superhero of 20th century America."

Clearly, Tarzan tapped into something primal and deep, especially the cartoon version. Kids in the 1970s looked up to him because though he was "Lord of the Jungle," he didn't flaunt his powers—and he always used his strength for good. In story after story, boys and girls witnessed Tarzan master the wild *and* coexist with nature. Though the jungle contained danger, and lost cities were fraught with peril, Tarzan lived up to his legend by being something different from other 1970s cartoon characters—a thoughtful man of action.

Kenner's SSP Smash-Up Derby Set

The Kenner toy company may now be—defunct, having been bought first by Tonka in 1987 and then by the Hasbro company in the mid-1990s—but in its prime in the 1970s, Kenner made some amazing toys, including the original *Star Wars* action figures. The SSP Smash-Up Derby set was released in 1977 and included cars that literally broke apart when they crashed. The commercial, backed by country strumming and catchy lyrics, featured real demolition derby footage along with clips of their derby cars crashing and fly into pieces to the delight of rampaging kids everywhere.

Crash bang, crack 'em up!
Put 'em back again!
Crash bang, smash 'em up!
It's crash-up time, my friend!"

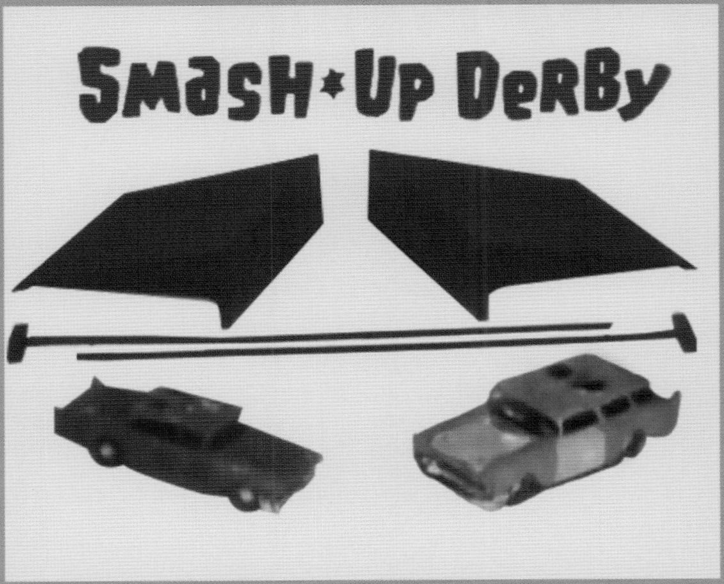
SMASH★UP DERBY

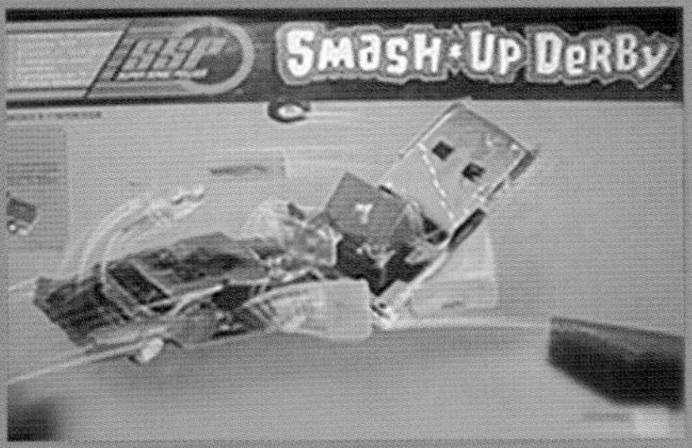
SSP
SMASH·UP DERBY

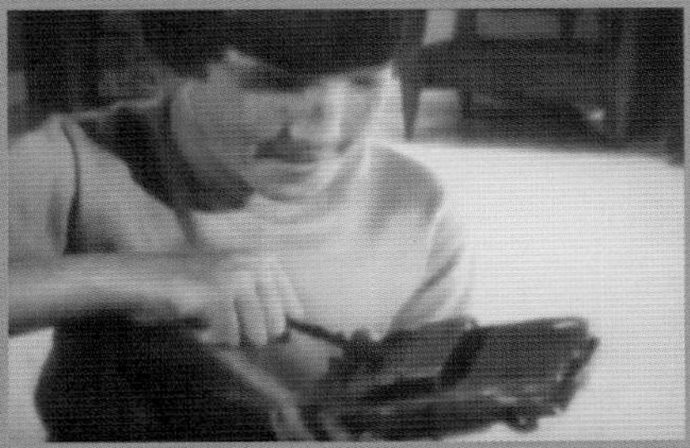

ABOVE: The Smash-Up Derby set came with two break apart cars, two ramps, and two pull cords to make the cars race and crash together.

Battle of the Planets

YEARS ON AIR

1978–1980

NETWORK

First Run Syndication

NUMBER OF EPISODES

85

CHARACTERS AND VOICE ACTORS

Mark: Casey Kasem
Jason: Ronnie Schell
7-Zark-7: Alan Young
Zoltar/The Spirit/Cronos:
Keye Luke
Mala Latroz: (officially unstated)
Tiny Harper/Security Chief
Anderson: Alan Dinehart Jr.
Princess/Susan: Janet Waldo
Commander Gorok:
Alan Oppenheimer
Announcer: William Woodson

A long time ago in a country far, far away, cartoonist Tatsuo Yoshido and Tatsunoko Productions created a Japanese anime program, *Science Ninja Team Gatchaman* in 1972. Five years later, the blockbuster *Star Wars* changed cinema—and the world—forever. Only a month prior, savvy television executive Sandy Frank happened to be at the MIP-TV Conference in Cannes. Here he caught episodes of Yoshido's sci-fi program about five young ninjas in bird suits waging intergalactic war against Berg Katse, a mutant hermaphrodite. No slouch when it came to developing great ideas, Frank sensed growing interest in

science-fiction concepts, even ones with *Gatchaman*'s out-there premise. He therefore seized the property and retitled it *Battle of the Planets* in an attempt to position himself in George Lucas's profitable wake.

Frank soon set about westernizing the series to appeal to American boys and girls gaga over droids and spaceships. With executive producer Jameson Brewer running the series, Sandy Frank Entertainment tackled *Gatchaman*'s adaptation. However, this involved more than just redubbing Japanese dialogue to English. In order to acquiesce to strict network restrictions regarding violence and nudity in children's programming, they had to cut scenes and rewrite narratives while keeping as much of the visuals intact as they could—no easy task. According to battleoftheplanets.info, a fan site created by Jason Hofius, coauthor of *G-Force: Animated: The Official Battle of the Planets Guidebook*, Tatsunoko Productions sent poorly translated scripts and loads of original film footage requiring massive amounts of editing.

Brewer dispatched six team members to watch the Japanese content on a Moviola editing machine, jotting down what happened scene by scene. "When they were through with that, now I would have a script to look at and I could study it in script form," said Brewer. "Then I would rearrange the script into a story line I invented." He gave these scenes to his team to pen new dialogue, however, this proved tricky since the new words needed to precisely sync up with the existing animation. "I had to time each of those speeches down to the split second." In order to bridge the gap between cut *Gatchaman* scenes, and to provide helpful exposition, Brewer and company devised another *Star Wars*-inspired solution. They used studio Gallerie International to insert a new character into the cartoon, a robot named 7-Zark-7. Resembling R2-D2 with a touch of C-3PO's wit, 7-Zark-7 offered comic relief while gluing together incongruent story lines.

7-Zark-7's introduction wasn't the only change to the *Gatchaman* original characters. The writers rechristened the primary bad guy Berg Katse to be Zoltar, while also eliminating references to transgender characteristics existing in the Japanese

version. *Gatchaman*'s Berg Katse possessed male and female aspects, but the American creators played down any androgyny, instead introducing Berg Katse's female personalities as separate characters, including Zoltar's sister, Mala Latroz (whose surname is an anagram of Zoltar). Previously

OPPOSITE: A promotional image for the show featuring (left to right) Princess, Mark, Jason, and 7-ZARK-7.

ABOVE: G-Force team member Mark stands strong.

TOP: A model sheet for 7-Zark-7 from January 23, 1978.

BOTTOM: Mark and 7-Zark-7 make plans aboard the team's ship, Phoenix, in this animation setup cel.

OPPOSITE: A promotional image featuring (left to right) Keyop, Tiny, Jason, Princess, and Mark.

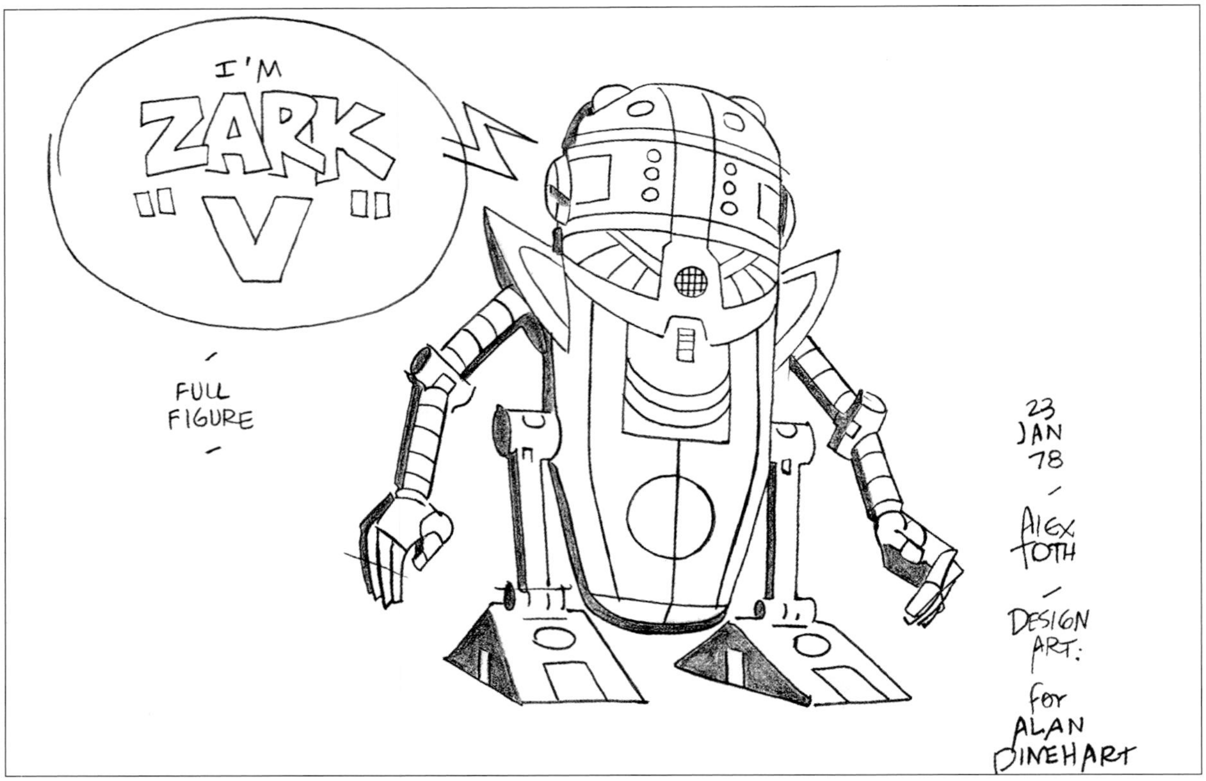
I'M
ZARK
"V"
FULL FIGURE
23 JAN 78
ALEX TOTH
DESIGN ART: FOR ALAN DINEHART

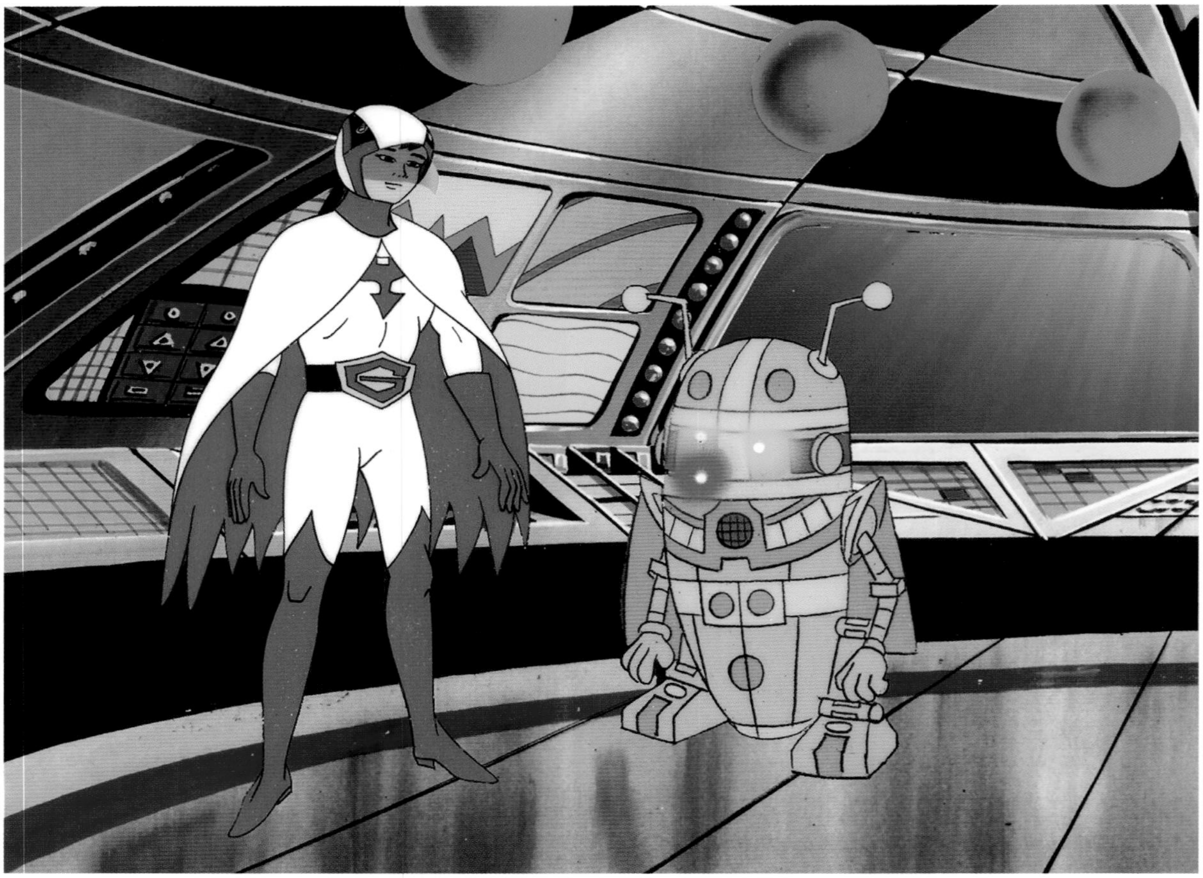

known as the Science Ninja Team, the show's heroes became the G-Force in the *Battle of the Planets* version, receiving new American names: Mark, Jason, Princess, Keyop, and Tiny.

Alan Dinehart Jr., the director, who also voiced Tiny Harper and Security Chief Anderson, selected the cast with great care. "He chose seasoned actors with whom he had worked through the years at Hanna-Barbera that could play the teenaged heroes with conviction," remembered Ronnie Schell, who voiced Jason. Schell had little trouble getting into character. "I have a youthful voice anyway, so I didn't really have to change any of my diction or my timbre or my range. So I just more or less did my own voice, and luckily, it fit the Jason character. I tend to get excited too, like he did." Schell recalls the working environment as being very fun in spite of the show's serious story lines. "It was very loose because the director, Alan, always came in with a series of jokes. And between takes he'd tell jokes."

The sense of comradery between cast and crew dovetailed nicely with the series' creative aspi-

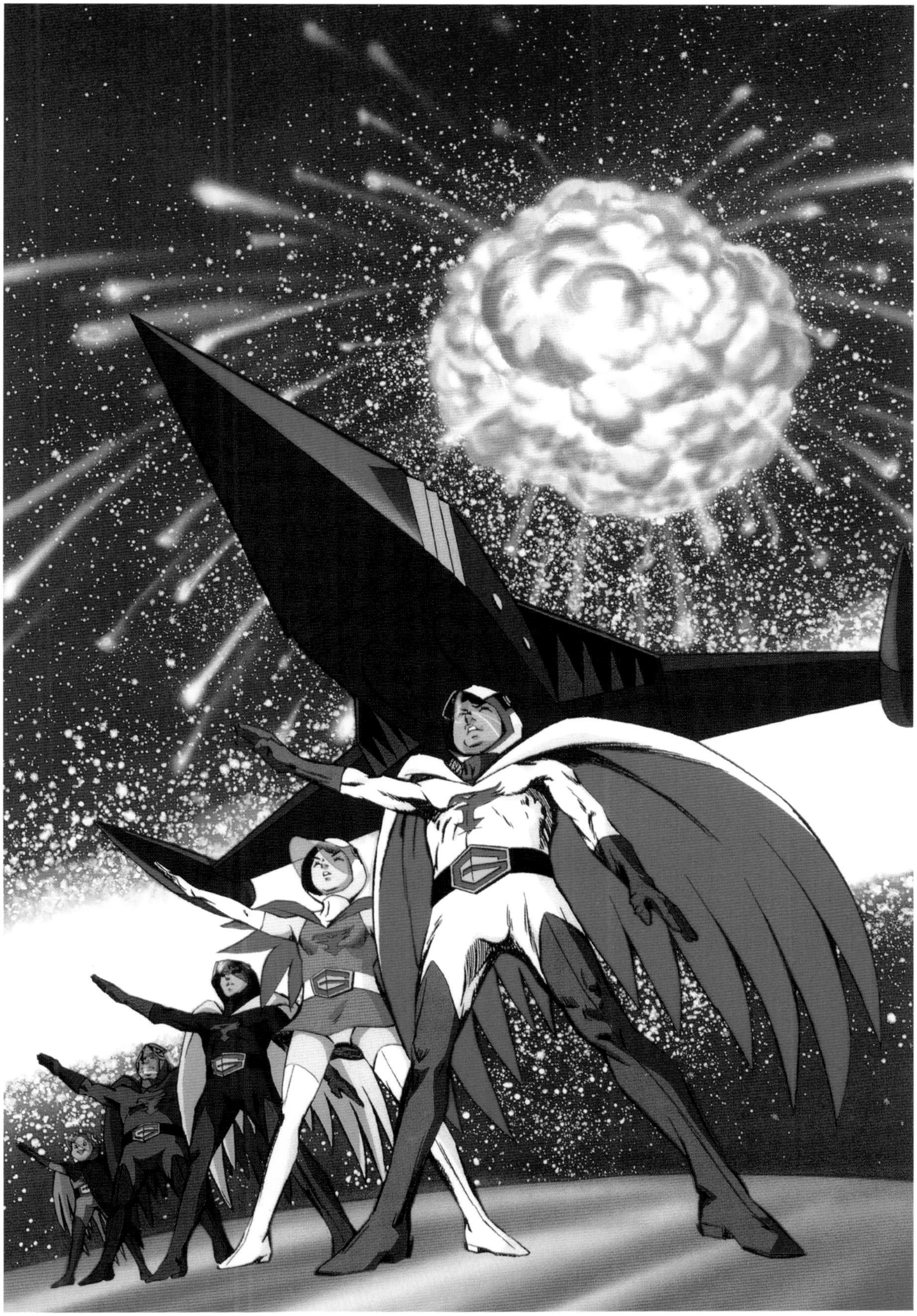

TOP: A cutaway of Pheonix, the G-Force team's ship.

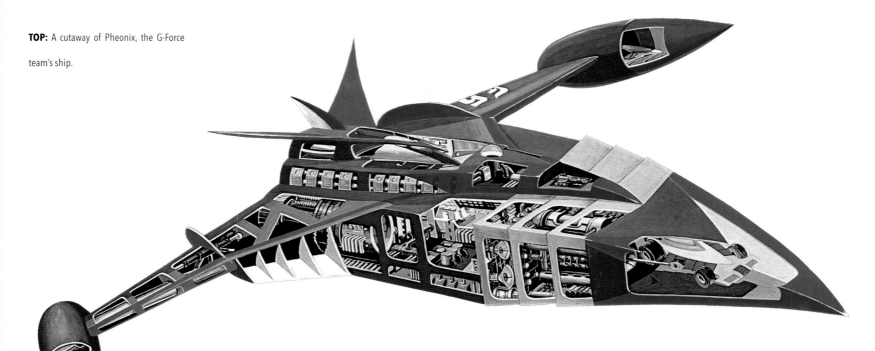

rations. Even though the show was inspired by elements of *Star Wars*, *Battle of the Planets* carved out its own imaginative premise. Set in the year 2020, a group of war orphans led by Mark oppose Zoltar's ruthless campaign to capture new worlds and galaxies. From their headquarters at Center Neptune, located beneath the sea, G-Force relied on their mothership Phoenix, housing smaller vehicles with secret weapons and capabilities to counter alien attacks from Planet Spectra. For instance, Keyop's Space Bubble doubled as a submarine as well as an all-terrain vehicle.

Not only did the G-Force possess kung-fu moves, TBX missiles, and wing suits functioning like personal parachutes gliding them to safety, they possessed complex psychic powers enabling them to defeat their foes. Since the original show emphasized environmentalism and the perils of overdevelopment, the theme remained as an undercurrent through the series. Episodes, such as "Super Space Spies," focused on how the decaying Spectra Planet tried to pollute Earth's water supply, and in "Invasion of the Locusts," Spectra unleashed a plague of insects to devour Earth's food supplies.

In perhaps a final nod to its *Star Wars* influence, Sandy Frank Entertainment amped up merchandising one year before the series ended in 1980. Released by Western Publishing and sold under Whitman and Gold Key labels, *Battle of the Planets* comics emerged. A coloring book aimed at younger kids followed, along with a frame-tray puzzle and magic slate. In addition to a Milton Bradley board game, lunch boxes appeared, as well as a video game by Mikro-Gen for a now defunct UK computer system called Sinclair ZX Spectrum. The object of the game? Stop Spectra from colonizing other planets, naturally. Then in 1986, *Gatchaman* was revamped for US audiences as *G-Force: Guardians of Space*. In collaboration with Turner Broadcasting, Sandy Frank Entertainment reissued

What's in a name?

As part of the conversion from the Japanese show *Gatchaman* to the American *Battle of the Planets*, the characters were renamed.

Here's how they translated.

Gatchaman	*Battle of the Planets*
Ken Washio	*Mark*
Joe Asakura	*Jason*
Jun	*Princess*
Jinpei	*Keyop*
Dr. Kozaburo Nambu	*Chief Anderson*
Ryu Nakanishi	*Tiny Harper*
Red Impulse	*Colonel Cronus*
Sosai X	*Great Spirit or Luminous One*
Berg Katse	*Zoltar*
Planet Selecto	*Planet Spectra/The Science*
Ninja Team	*G-Force*

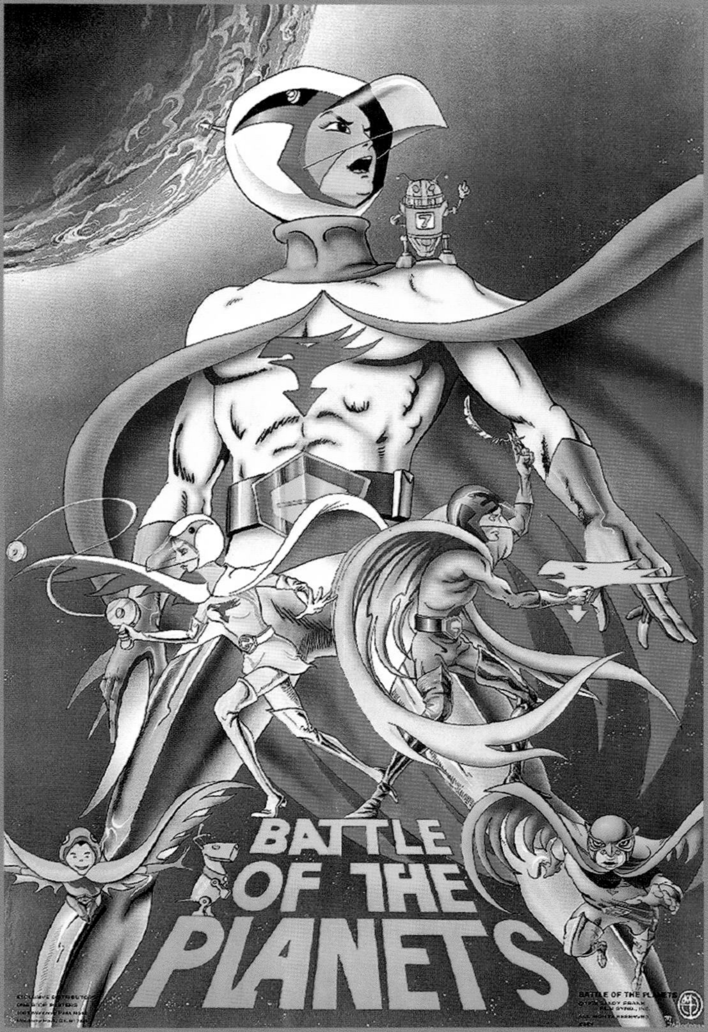
BATTLE OF THE PLANETS

ABOVE: A promotional poster for the cartoon.

their series as a more faithful version to the original Japanese conception.

Despite the fact that censorship protocols hamstrung *Battle of the Planets* from being as provocative as its source material, American kids still connected with the show. At the close of the 1970s when *Star Wars* made box-office history, boys and girls hungered for their own dose of science fiction straight from the TV, and *Battle of the Planets* delivered. Owing to Brewer's ingenuity, coupled with Dinehart's capable direction, the show's characters came alive as fully formed individuals with feelings and motivations. Driven by revenge and their own demons, they went to war against formidable opponents with real stakes. *Battle of the Planets* gave us surprises and thrills, adventures and rushes, becoming a bulwark of 1970s Saturday morning cartooning. Or as the narrator said in the series' opening, "Always five, acting as one. Dedicated! Inseparable! Invincible!"

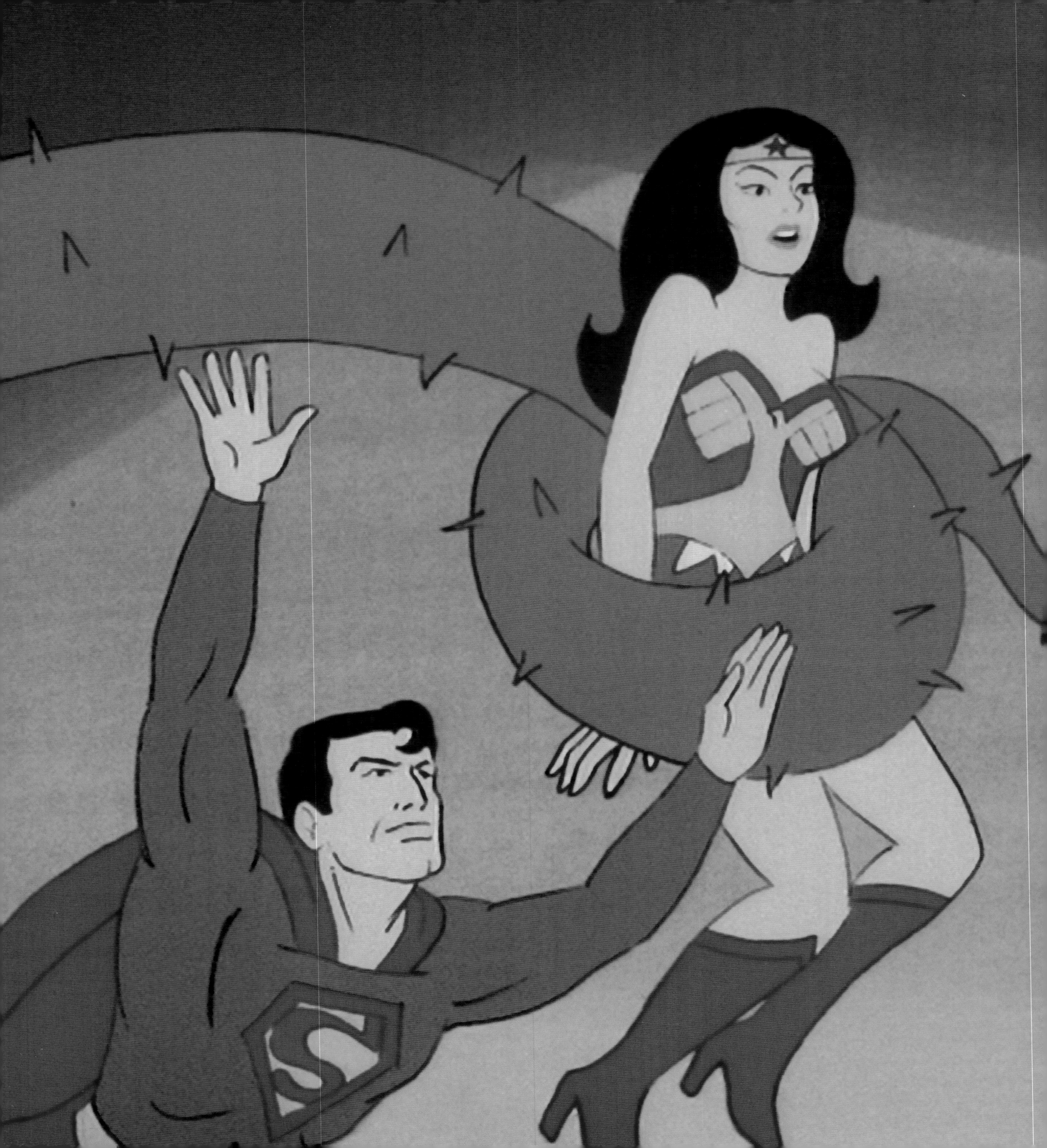

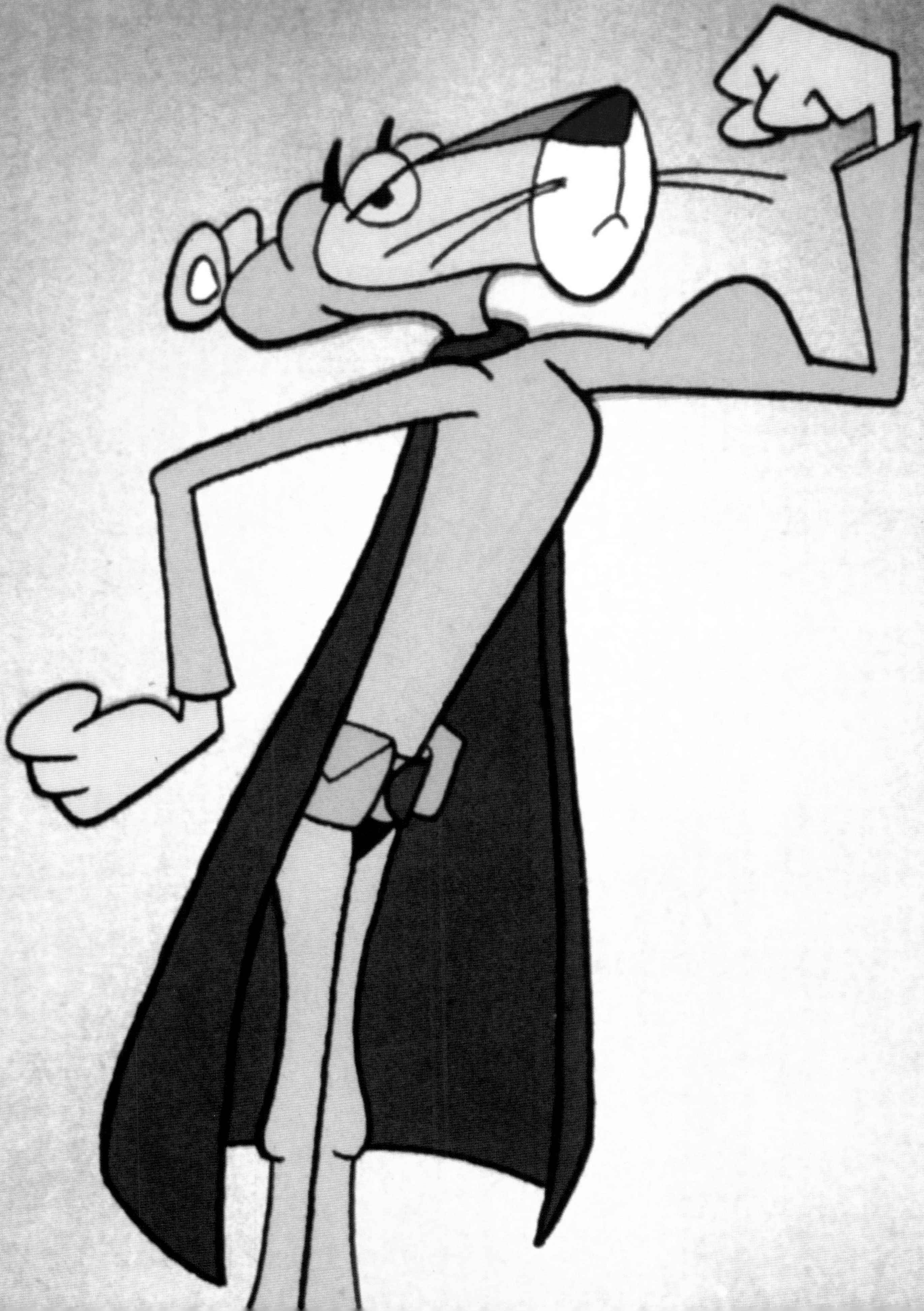

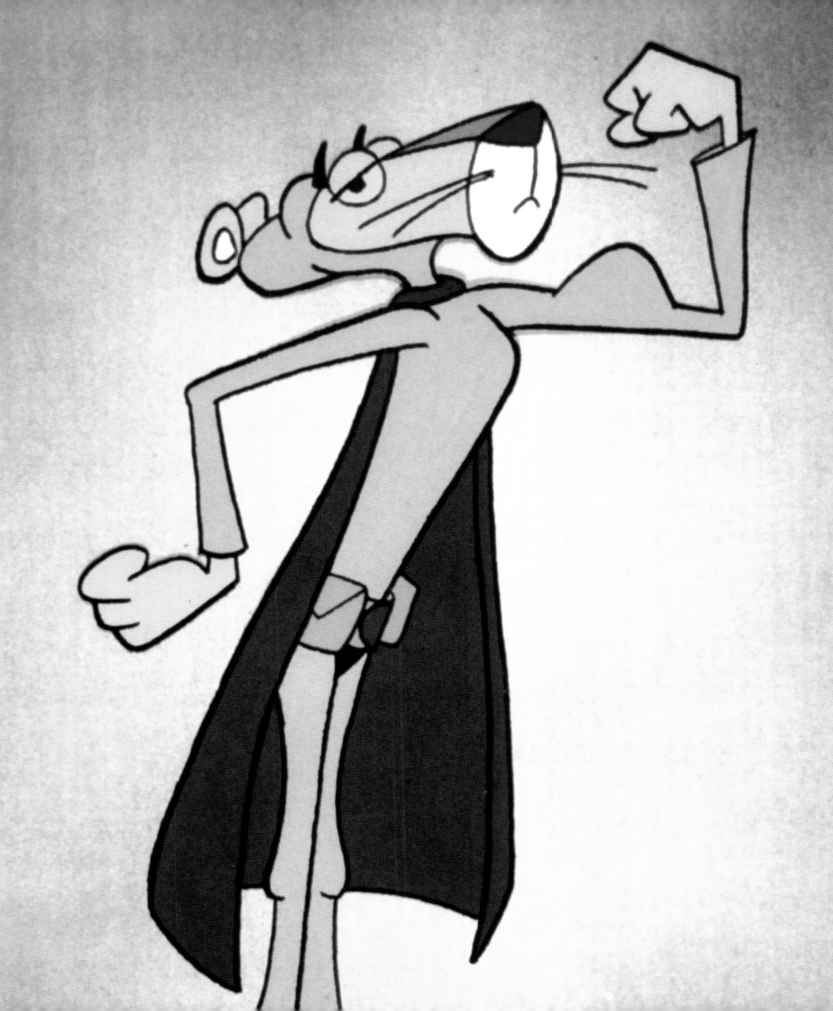

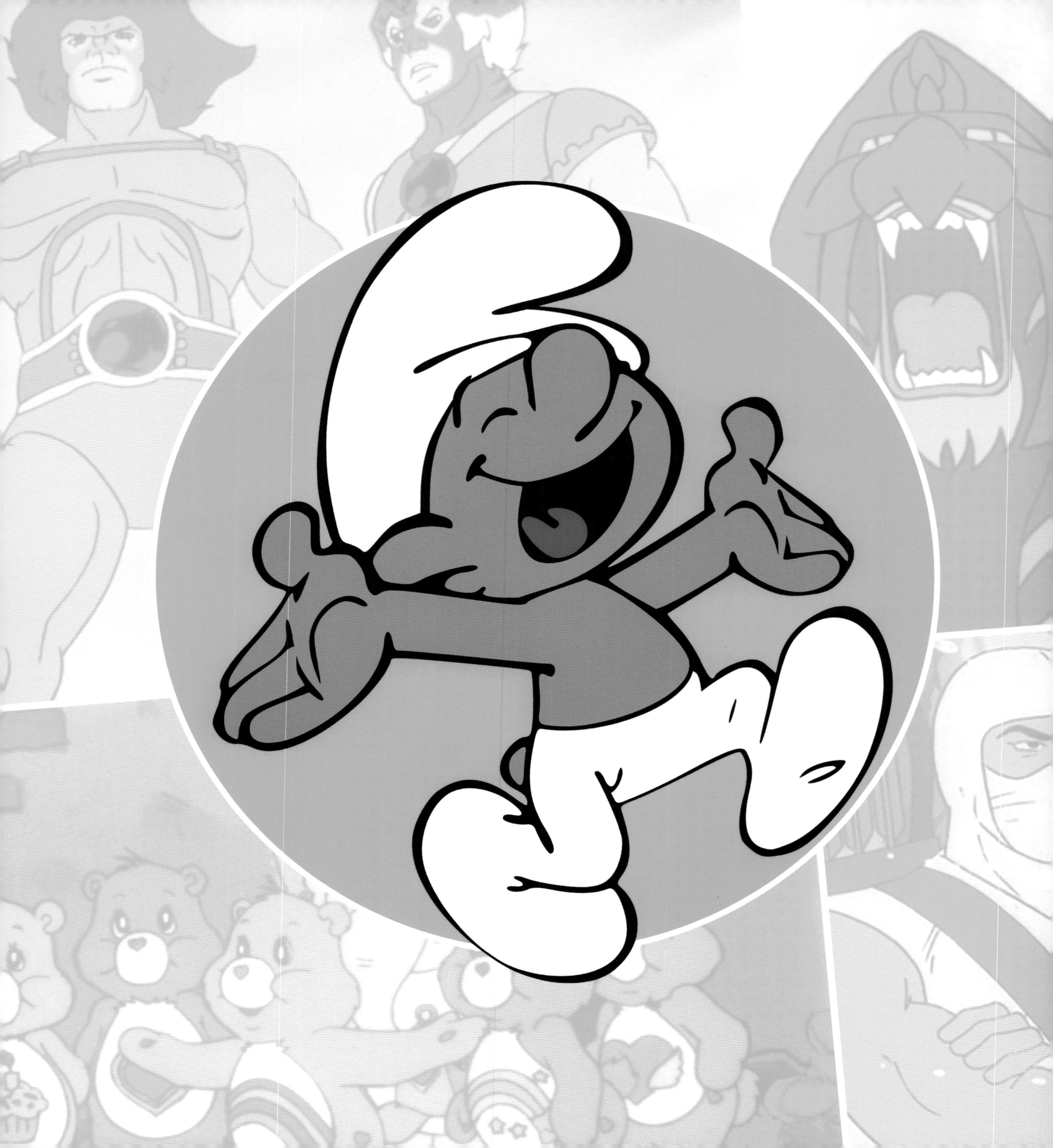

1980s

This decade witnessed an explosion of imaginative cartoons, many of which were based on popular toys, such as such as *ThunderCats* and *Transformers*. In addition, production values increased with an emphasis on more complex storytelling and richly defined characters.

OPPOSITE: *The Smurfs* spread infectious happiness throughout the 1980s, airing 256 episodes.

The Smurfs

YEARS ON AIR

1981–1989

NETWORK

NBC

NUMBER OF EPISODES

256

CHARACTERS AND VOICE ACTORS

Papa Smurf/Azrael: Don Messick
Hefty Smurf/Poet Smurf: Frank Welker
Smurfette: Lucille Bliss
Brainy Smurf: Danny Goldman
Gargamel: Paul Winchell
Handy Smurf: Michael Bell
Jokey Smurf: June Foray
Vanity Smurf: Alan Oppenheimer

For kids growing up in the '80s, *The Smurfs* was *the* quintessential Saturday morning show. And that's saying a lot. *The Smurfs* checked all of kids' cartoon boxes. Bizarrely imaginative? Check. Addictive to watch? Check. Clever toy tie-in? Double check. Just like the opening words to its theme song, "La-la-la-la-la-la," the show was deceptively simple. Belgian cartoonist Pierre Culliford (pen name: Peyo) first created *The Smurfs* as part of a larger comic strip, *Johan & Peewit,* presenting the tales of Johan, a brave young page to the king, and Peewit, his comic

relief sidekick. "My father was first and foremost a storyteller, before being a comic artist," said Peyo's daughter Veronique Culliford in a 2013 interview with Animated Views. "He was always very specific in his way of writing. He created stories for children that could be interesting and entertaining for adults, too."

Though the Smurfs began as minor characters in the comics, they soon proved to be the bigger hit. Beginning in the late 1950s, Peyo invented over a hundred characters, such as Jokey Smurf, the village prankster. Between 1961 and 1967, he released ten

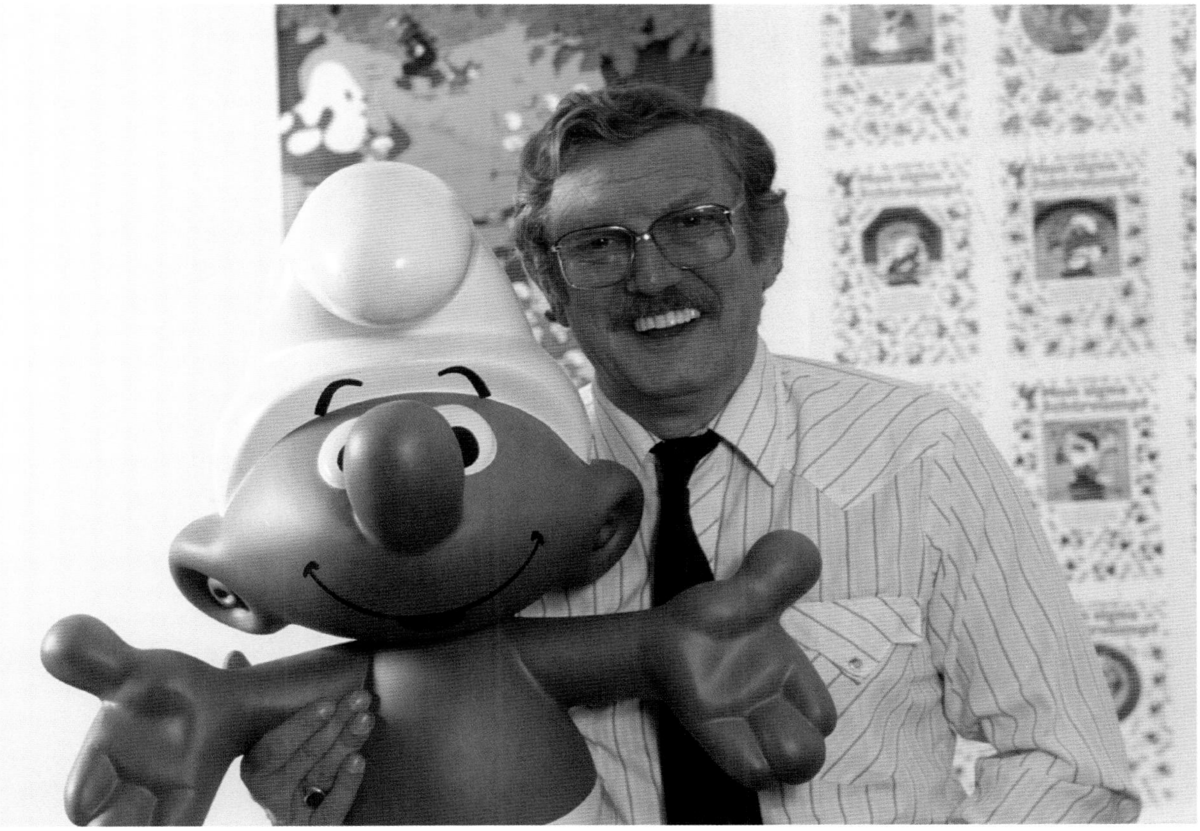

OPPOSITE: Papa Smurf, Smurfette, and the Smurf gang, circa 1984.

TOP: Pierre "Peyo" Culliford, creator of *The Smurfs,* poses with a toy figurine at an exhibition in Bruxelles, Belgium, 1984.

animated shorts, as well as an eighty-seven-minute Belgian film, *Les Aventures des Schtroumpfs* (1965). American media entrepreneur Stuart R. Ross happened to catch these shorts. Foreseeing their massive appeal, he acquired the character rights, launching Smurf toys. According to executive producer Joe Barbera, NBC was considering ending its Saturday morning schedule altogether when executive Fred Silverman noticed his young daughter playing with a Smurf toy and believed there could be potential in creating a cartoon series. "It was a little blue creature with white diapers on it or something like that. So we got interested and involved in it."

In 1981, *The Smurfs* joined NBC's lineup, produced by Hanna-Barbera Productions, in an association with SEPP International. Peyo served as script supervisor and creator, adapting his comic to the screen. "As we have said, my father had always been an animation fan, and he was delighted to have his characters go from paper to television," said the younger Culliford. "He was very excited by this adventure." However, according to Barbera, internal conflicts complicated the production. One NBC executive despised *The Smurfs* so vehemently that Barbera had to fly to New York every year just to convince NBC's head of programming Brandon Tartikoff not to take the show off the air. In addition, some members of the NBC brass "wanted to make 'em all different colors." Barbera pushed back, managing to keep the creatures blue. In her interview, Culliford also provided the background for the

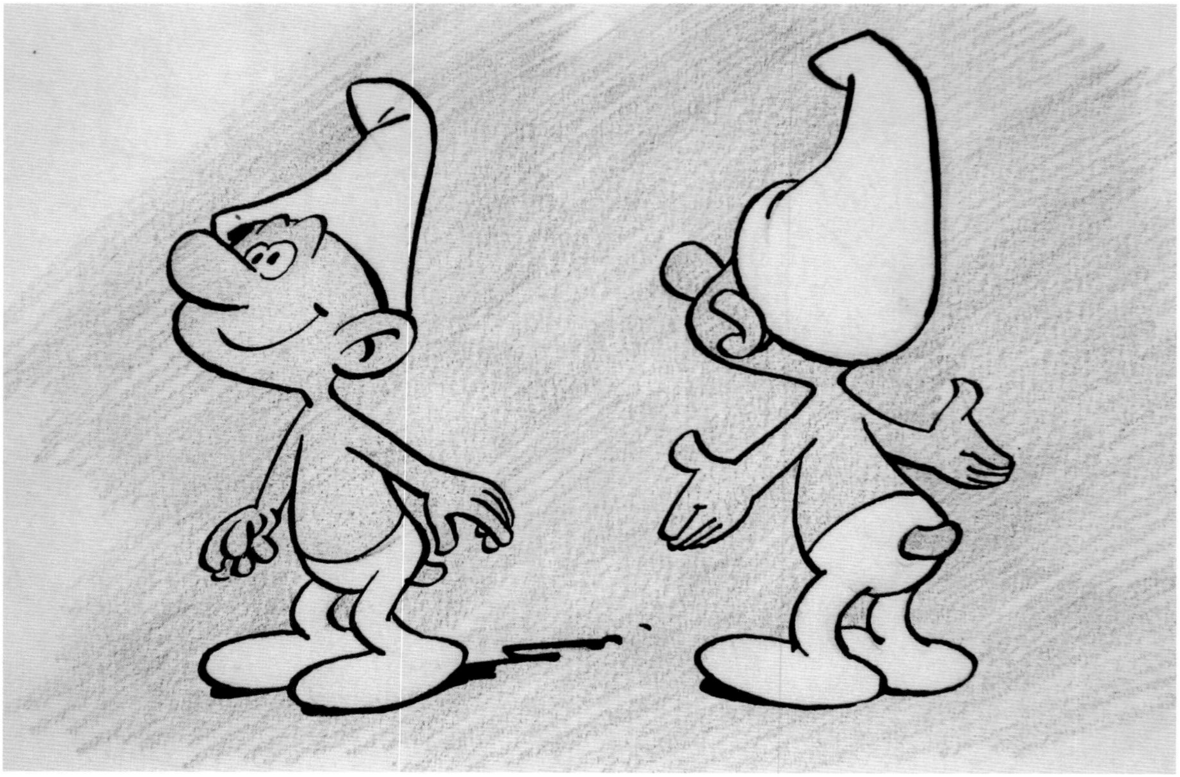

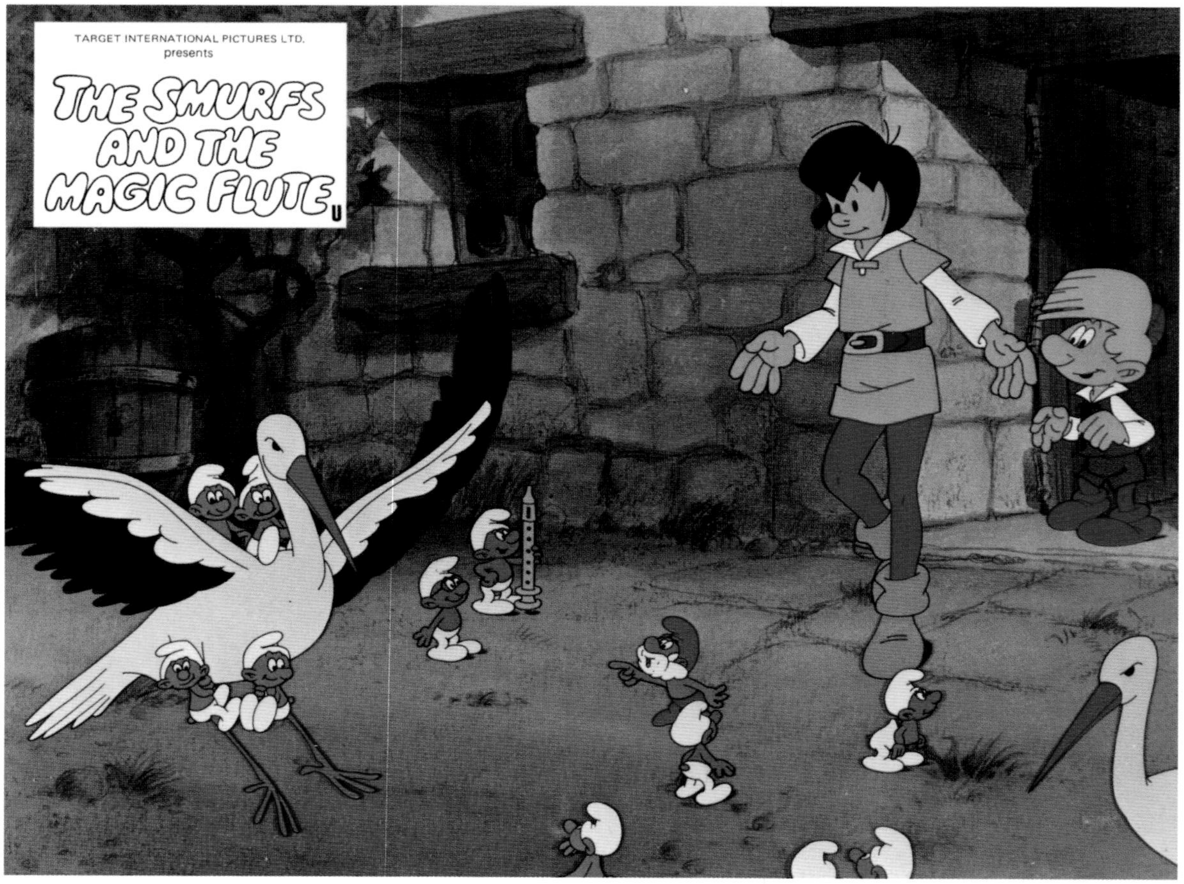
TARGET INTERNATIONAL PICTURES LTD.
presents
THE SMURFS
AND THE
MAGIC FLUTE
U

Smurfs' iconic hue. "My mother, who has always been the colorist of my father's albums, chose the blue. She hesitated between different colors. It couldn't be a human color since they're not humans. Red was too aggressive. Green and brown would blend with the colors of the trees—you wouldn't have been able to see them! So what about blue?"

In due time, the production and creative team settled on both the look and feel for their new series as well as the story lines. While the young page Johan and his sidekick Peewit would make occasional appearances, the show mostly focused on the tiny blue creatures. "No more than three apples tall," the Smurfs lived in a mushroom village within a magical forest requiring stork flight for long-distance travel. Led by Papa Smurf, designated by his red hat and pants, the characters possessed names suggesting their personalities. There was Brainy Smurf, Grouchy Smurf, Vanity Smurf, Lazy Smurf, as well as countless others. The Smurfs all worked together for the common good, sharing the fruits of their labor. The biggest threat to their way of life came from Gargamel, an

OPPOSITE TOP: This sketch of a Smurf was displayed in an exhibition titled "Pierre Culliford, PEYO, The Life and Work of a Master Storyteller" at the Artcurial's auction in Paris in 2011. It showcased over 150 original works, archived material, and personal items never before seen in public.

OPPOSITE BOTTOM: Characters Johan and Peewit from the original comic series appeared in several *Smurfs* episodes.

TOP: The Smurfs show off their smurfy musical talents in this frame, circa 1970.

evil wizard who desired nothing more than to capture his blue Lilliputian neighbors, to boil them, eat them, and/or transform them into gold. The Smurfs also had to contend with Gargamel's nefarious and slightly more intelligent cat, Azrael.

Perhaps because *The Smurfs* began as a comic, and not the outgrowth of a toy like so many other 1980s cartoon series, the show's complex mythology allowed it to produce a whopping 256 episodes over its nine seasons. Many episodes stand out with Smurf-tastic names such as, "All That Glimmers Isn't Smurf," "Spelunking Smurfs," "Smurf-Colored Glasses," "Now You Smurf 'Em, Now You Don't," and of course, "Bewitched, Bothered, and Besmurfed." Episodes explored many themes, including time travel, outer space, and magic. One even showcased elements of zombie culture. In "Purple Smurfs," Papa Smurf must race against time to prevent a *Smurfocalypse* after Lazy Smurf is bitten by a purple fly. And in 1986, the antidrug episode, "The Lure of the Orb" premiered, in which Poet Smurf demonstrates the pitfalls of addiction.

NBC's winning storytelling formula: minimal violence, exciting adventures in mystical realms,

ABOVE: The Smurfs and their nemeses: Gargamel and Azrael.

OPPOSITE: The leader and wisest of all the Smurfs, Papa Smurf.

touches of humor, and a sprinkling of morality, became a recipe for success. "*The Smurfs* became one of NBC's giant hits of the '80s—in a way, the network's Saturday morning equivalent of *The Cosby Show* in prime time," wrote Verne Gay in a 1992 *LA Times* article. The critics loved it, too. Nominated multiple times for Daytime Emmy® awards, it won the Outstanding Children's Entertainment Series from 1982-1983, as well as the Humanitas Prize for Children's Animation in 1987.

Based on the show's popularity, heaps of merchandise flooded the market, including models,

games, figurines, and later, video games. There was even a short-lived breakfast cereal that led to the Smurfberry-Crunch-Blue-Poop Crisis. For a time, edible blue dye used in the sweetened wheat ingredients sent frightened moms to pediatricians across the country concerned by the unhealthy color of their children's excrement.

Even before the 3-D live-action/computer-animated films of the 2000s, *The Smurfs*' craze was so widespread, the word "smurf" penetrated language. It could be used as a noun, verb, adjective, or adverb depending on context. A person could say, "It's such a smurfy afternoon. Let's go to the park and smurf."

The Smurfs lasted so many years, there seemed to be no end to the wealth of creative plotlines and inspired characters, such as Grandpa Smurf, the permanently juvenile Smurflings, and Lord Balthazar, Gargamel's godfather, who turned out to be even crueler than Gargamel. Beyond the legendary actors who inhabited the main characters, a wealth of celebrities lent their voices to the show, including Jonathan Winters, Phil Hartman, Edie McClurg, George Takei, and Ed Begley Jr. To many youngsters,

ABOVE: There ware many ways to use the word "smurf." This image shows a group of Smurfs smurfing around to show Smurfette their smruftastic abilities.

Origin of the Word

Where did the word 'Smurf' come from? Peyo jokingly coined "Schtroumpf," later translated to "Smurf," while dining with fellow cartoonist Andre Franquin when the latter couldn't remember the French word for salt.

The Smurfs epitomized Saturday morning programming. Sweet, yet thought-provoking, whimsical and magical, they couldn't help singing along with their little blue friends: *La-la-la-la-la-la.*

YEARS ON AIR

1983–1990

NETWORK

NBC

NUMBER OF EPISODES

102

CHARACTERS AND VOICE ACTORS

Alvin/Simon/Dave Seville/
Grandpa Seville:
Ross Bagdasarian Jr.
Theodore/Brittany/Jeanette/
Eleanor: Janice Karman
Beatrice Miller: Dody Goodman

Alvin and the Chipmunks

Who doesn't remember Dave Seville blowing his top, screaming "ALVINNN!!!" whenever the lead singer of the world's most adorable musical group did something outrageous? As every child knows, there is nothing funnier than an adult losing his cool. From week to week, the incorrigible Alvin made it an art form to drive his adopted dad up the wall—in between rocking out to pop-culture ditties with his brothers.

Before 98 Degrees, before the Jonas Brothers, even before New Kids on the Block, there were the Chipmunks. The band consisted of Alvin, the mischievous, girl-crazy star; Simon, the bespectacled, logical one who responded to praise with the word "naturally"; and Theodore, the chubbiest of the trio, but the cuddliest and sweetest. As the youngest of the bunch, Theodore could sometimes be seen with his teddy bear, and was both innocent and gullible . . . and a big fan of food.

Warmth, sweetness, and crumbs permeated the Seville household as kind-hearted songwriter Dave raised the Chipmunks like typical human boys in his suburban home. Treating them like regular kids, he expected them to go to school while simultaneously fostering their musical careers. Though the brothers usually ended up in some sort of a predicament instigated by Alvin's shenanigans, the show continually demonstrated their love for each other as a family. Even though Alvin was the catalyst for all kinds of trouble, fans adored him so much that in 2002 *TV Guide* placed him in the "50 Greatest Cartoon Characters."

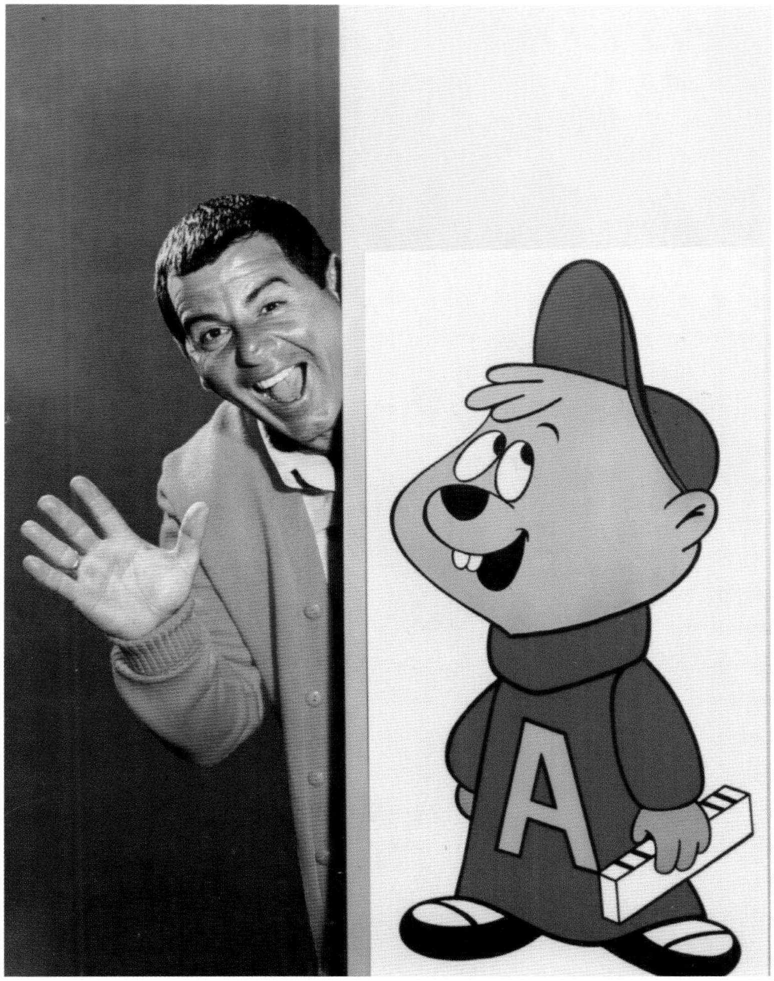
A

OPPOSITE: The singing chipmunks–(left to right) Theodore, Alvin, and Simon–prove they are the stars of the show.

TOP: Creator of *Alvin and the Chipmunks*, Ross Bagdasarian Sr., waves to his invention, crica 1970.

Back in the 1950s, songwriter and producer Ross Bagdasarian, whose stage name happened to be Dave Seville, landed on the ingenious idea to cash in on how a sped-up record player would make your voice sound like you'd just sucked down a helium balloon. Reportedly, it was his children who suggested he create the Chipmunk characters. "I remember [my dad] would always bring my brother and sister and I into his den and play, whether it was 'Witch Doctor' or 'The Chipmunk Song' or whatever," said Ross Jr. "And we loved it when Alvin started talking back to our dad. We just fell in love with not just the song, but the audacity of that little character because we didn't really talk back to my dad that much. So we thought Alvin really had a lot of spunk that we admired."

At the time, Bagdasarian performed all four voices: the Chipmunks, and David Seville. He named his Chipmunks after Liberty Records executives: Si Waronker, Ted Keep, and Al Bennett. Debuting "The Chipmunk Song (Christmas Don't Be Late)" in 1958, the Chipmunks emerged as recording stars with the

ABOVE: The three chipmunks tend to the ailment of their fish friend.

irrepressible Alvin stealing the show and, of course, Dave screaming at him to behave. Soon after, more hits topped the charts, such as "Witch Doctor" (*"Oo-ee, oo-ah-ah, ting-tang, walla-walla, bing-bang!"*), which led Bagdasarian and his three Chipmunk handpuppets to appear on *The Ed Sullivan Show*. In 1961, CBS then presented the first animated Chipmunk TV series on prime time as *The Alvin Show*. Unfortunately, it didn't catch on and was cancelled after a season.

When Bagdasarian died in 1972, his son, Ross Jr. carried the mantle. Though he fulfilled his dad's desire for him to get a law degree, Ross had other aspirations. With the help of his wife, actress Janice Karman, who also loved the Chipmunk characters growing up, Ross Jr. took the show to NBC in 1983. Former Hanna-Barbera writers Joe Ruby and Ken Spears of Ruby-Spears provided the animation and writing while improving the original designs with cuter, rounder images. This time around, Ross Jr. and Janice performed the primary voices. Janice voiced Theodore while Ross Jr. supplied Alvin, Simon, and Dave.

The show quickly became one of the top-rated Saturday morning cartoons at the time. Beyond better animation, the characters of the 1980s series were more richly developed. Simon and Theodore emerged as more individualistic personalities as opposed to simply being foils to Alvin's mischief. Janice Karman also ingeniously created the Chipettes, which included Brittany, Jeanette, and Eleanor. They matched the boys in looks and identities as well as enhancing the storytelling. Australian orphans, the Chipettes escaped their evil warden, Ms. Grudge, moving to the US where they landed in the care of Miss Miller, the Chipmunks' babysitter. With the help of the Chipmunks, they formed their own girl band. Though there wasn't a recurring villain on the show, Uncle Harry came close, a possible con artist who may or may not have been an actual relative.

Aside from the characters and storytelling, the other huge draw was the music. In addition to producing their own original songs, the Chipmunks covered or "munk'd" several hits from the time, including Michael Jackson's "Beat It," Billy Joel's "Uptown Girl," the Bangles' "Walk Like an Egyptian," Kenny Loggins's "Footloose," George Thorogood's "Bad to the Bone," Cyndi Lauper's "Girls Just Want to Have Fun," and Aretha Franklin's "Respect." To fill the

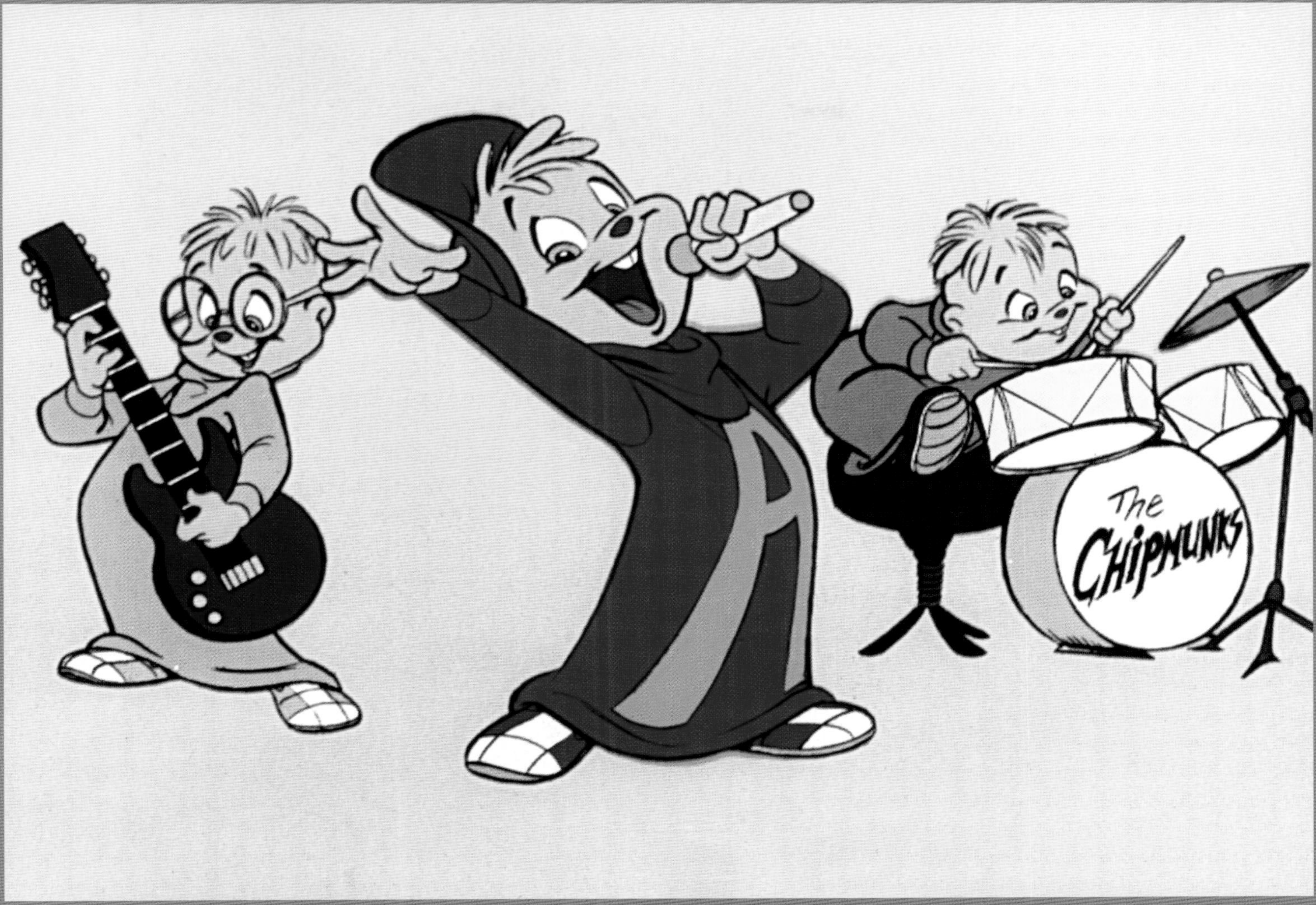
The
CHIPMUNKS

ABOVE: Alvin rocks out center stage with Simon on guitar and Theodore on drums.

Munk'ed

Throughout the '80s, the Chipmunks kept their furry fingers on the pulse of pop culture. Here are a few of the episodes in which they spoofed 1980s era shows.

"Chipmunkmania": A mockumentary look at the history of the Chipmunks' career.

"Dreamlighting": A spoof on *Moonlighting* in which Brittany dreams she is Cybill Shepherd's character, Maddie Hayes.

"Alvie's Angels": Where Alvin becomes "Charlie" with the Chipettes as his "Angels."

"The C-Team": Channelling *The A-Team*, the Chipmunks team up with Mr. T to get their watch back from bullies.

"Urban Chipmunk": The Chipmunks enter a contest to sing with country legend, Dolly Parton.

"Teevee or Not Teevee": The Chipmunks try to get on the "Johnny Letterman Show."

BOTTOM: The lovable and childlike Chipmunks outshined many of their contemporaries to become a pop-culture force.

insatiable demand from fans for Chipmunk music, Bagdasarian and Karman released the album *Songs from Our TV Shows* in 1984, including the show's opening theme song, "We're the Chipmunks."

Reflecting the fact that the Chipettes had become an integral part of the show, and Alvin was no longer the focus, the Saturday morning series was renamed *The Chipmunks* to include both groups of Chipmunks—boys and girls—in 1988 with DIC Entertainment overseeing production. The show's content also spun off in new directions, including their first big-screen movie, *The Chipmunk Adventure* in 1987, in which the Chipmunks and the Chipettes compete against each other in an around-the-world race.

At the dawn of the '90s, in an attempt to stay relevant, the show underwent one final makeover. Now called *The Chipmunks Go to the Movies*, each episode of the 1990 season spoofed a different Hollywood film, such as *Honey, I Shrunk the Kids* and *Gremlins*. Ultimately, the new format didn't resonate as well with audiences and the show was cancelled. Chipmunkmania remained a force to be reckoned with, however. Decades after the cartoon ended, a new generation was introduced to the resilient Chipmunks when they were rebooted as a 3-D animated feature-film franchise in 2007, proving once and for all you can't keep a good Chipmunk down.

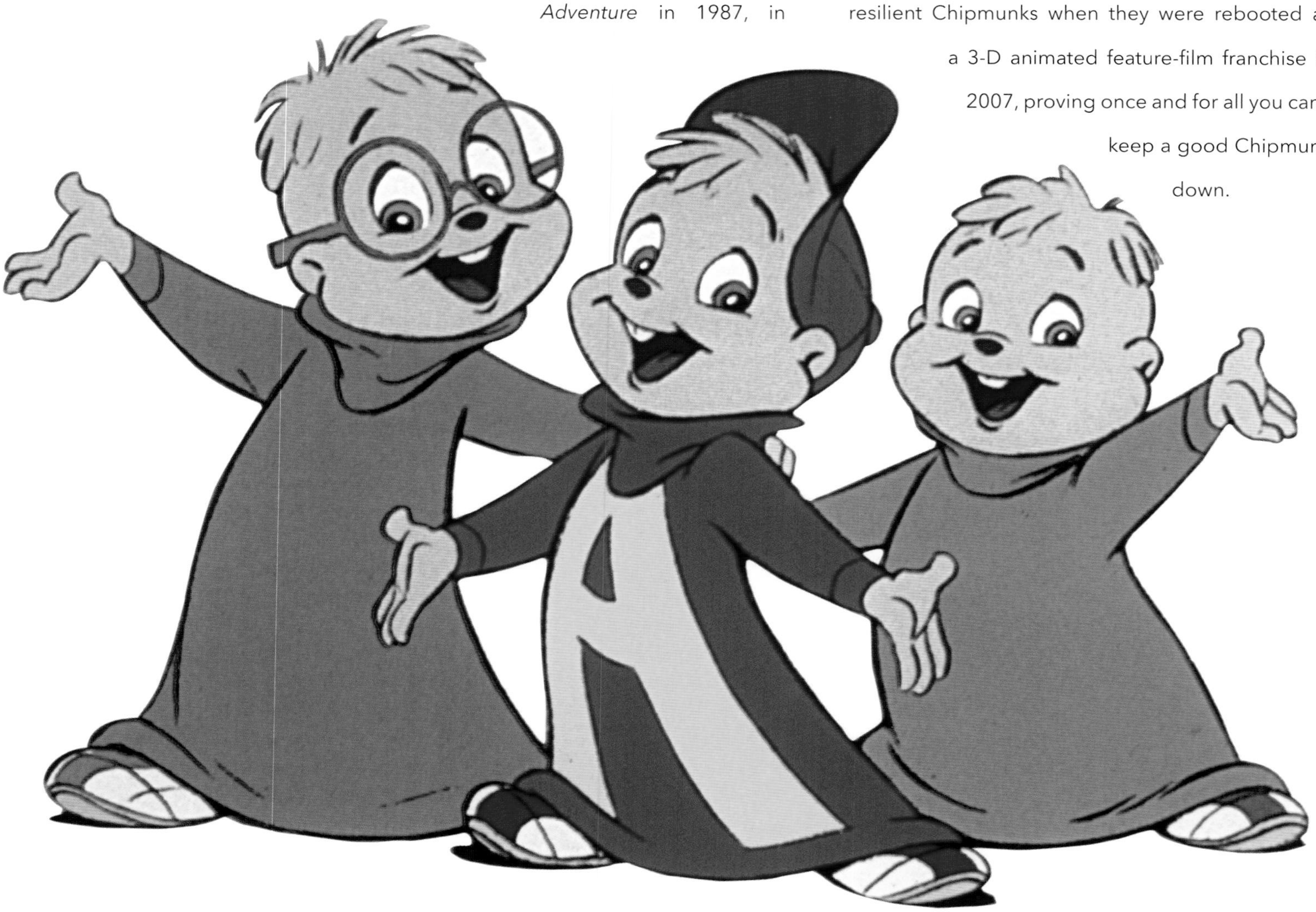

Encyclopedia Britannica

Remember that commercial starring a dweeby kid in the jean jacket and white sneakers whose parents bought everything he needed: a computer, compact disc player, and a video camera? The one thing they didn't supply him? An *Encyclopedia Britannica* to help him with his report on outer space.

The kid's name was Donavan Freberg. In 1988, his father, Stan Freberg, a legendary advertising creative director, put together a series of ads starring Donavan as the kid who had every tool to succeed in life—except a robust encyclopedia set. Of course, nowadays, any kid can gather all of the info they want for free via the internet, but at the time, *Encyclopedia Britannica* was an academic lifesaver.

It turns out the ad campaign was a lifesaver for the company, too. Freberg's commercials aired for five years, continuing into the '90s, becoming the most successful campaign in *Encyclopedia Britannica's* two-hundred-year history.

Britannica
MICROPÆDIA Ready Reference
1
A-ak Bayes
2
Bayeu Ceanothus
11
Solovyov Truck
12
Trudeau Zywiec
Britannica
INDEX
A-K
Britannica
INDEX
L-Z

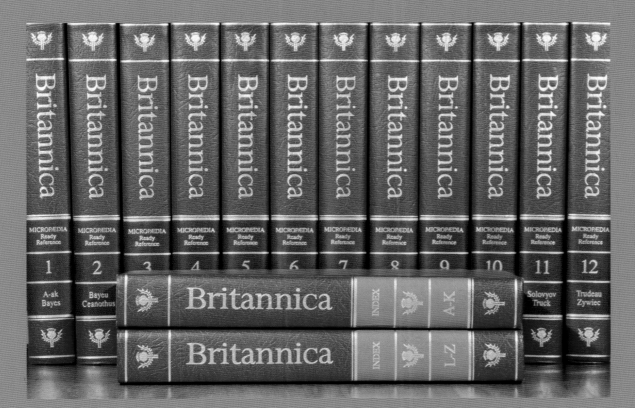

ABOVE: The fifteenth edition of the encyclopedia was published in 1985 and introduced the two volume index to accompany the set.

YEARS ON AIR

1983–1985

NETWORK

Syndication

NUMBER OF EPISODES

130

CHARACTERS AND VOICE ACTORS

He-Man: John Erwin
Battle Cat/Skeletor/Man-At-Arms: Alan Oppenheimer
Teela: Linda Gary
Orko: Lou Scheimer

He-Man and the Masters of the Universe

Most every kid of a certain age can remember chanting the phrase: "By the power of Grayskull!" at some point in their childhood. This line was the spell He-Man said to activate his transformation sequence. Whenever He-Man's alter ego Prince Adam drew his Power Sword and spoke these words, his pink vest and formfitting white shirt vanished, replaced by his battle-harness chest piece and caveman-style undies, morphing him into He-Man, the most powerful man in the universe. "I have the power!" he would yell, finishing his spell.

Before that phrase ever existed, He-Man was a muscular, slightly caveman-looking action figure. The brainchild of Mattel designer Roger Sweet, the

He-Man action figure debuted in 1982. Around this time, Filmation Associates developed a backstory to the action figure, that they took to ABC. The network turned down the idea, but the series still debuted the following year, making it the first syndicated cartoon to be based on a toy.

In the series, He-Man lived a double life as Prince Adam, son of King Randor and Queen Marlena, who rule the mystical planet Eternia. The Sorceress of Castle Grayskull bestowed Prince Adam with unimaginable strength to defend the fortress's secrets from the blue-skinned sorcerer Skeletor and his nefarious minions: Evil-Lyn, Beast Man, Tri-Klops, Merman, and Trap Jaw. Not to be outdone, He-Man was backed by the Heroic Warriors, which included Teela, Man-At-Arms, Fisto, Ram Man, and of course, Cringer, Prince Adam's lazy, wimpy cat that transformed into the mighty Battle Cat.

OPPOSITE: He-Man atop Battle Cat ready to face another battle.

TOP: He-Man action figure, circa 1988.

Fantasy often met science fiction in the story lines. Laser beams and hovercraft merged with magic and medieval mythology, augmented by action and adventure. "This was coming off of the '70s, which was the most regulated era of children's television, where no violence was allowed," explained *He-Man* writer David Wise. "And what had happened in the '70s was that all that violence and adventure and everything was basically knocked out of children's television and it became very pat, very puerile. There was no *Jonny Quest*, there were no superheroes to speak of." Similar to *G.I. Joe*, *He-Man* featured actual violence, including scenes of He-Man hitting opponents, such as the time he grappled with Faker, his evil clone in the episode, "The Shaping Staff."

Despite being decried by parents' groups for featuring hypermuscular creatures, He-Man often used wrestling moves instead of punching his opponents or slaying them with his sword. Other concerns arose from those who disapproved of utilizing

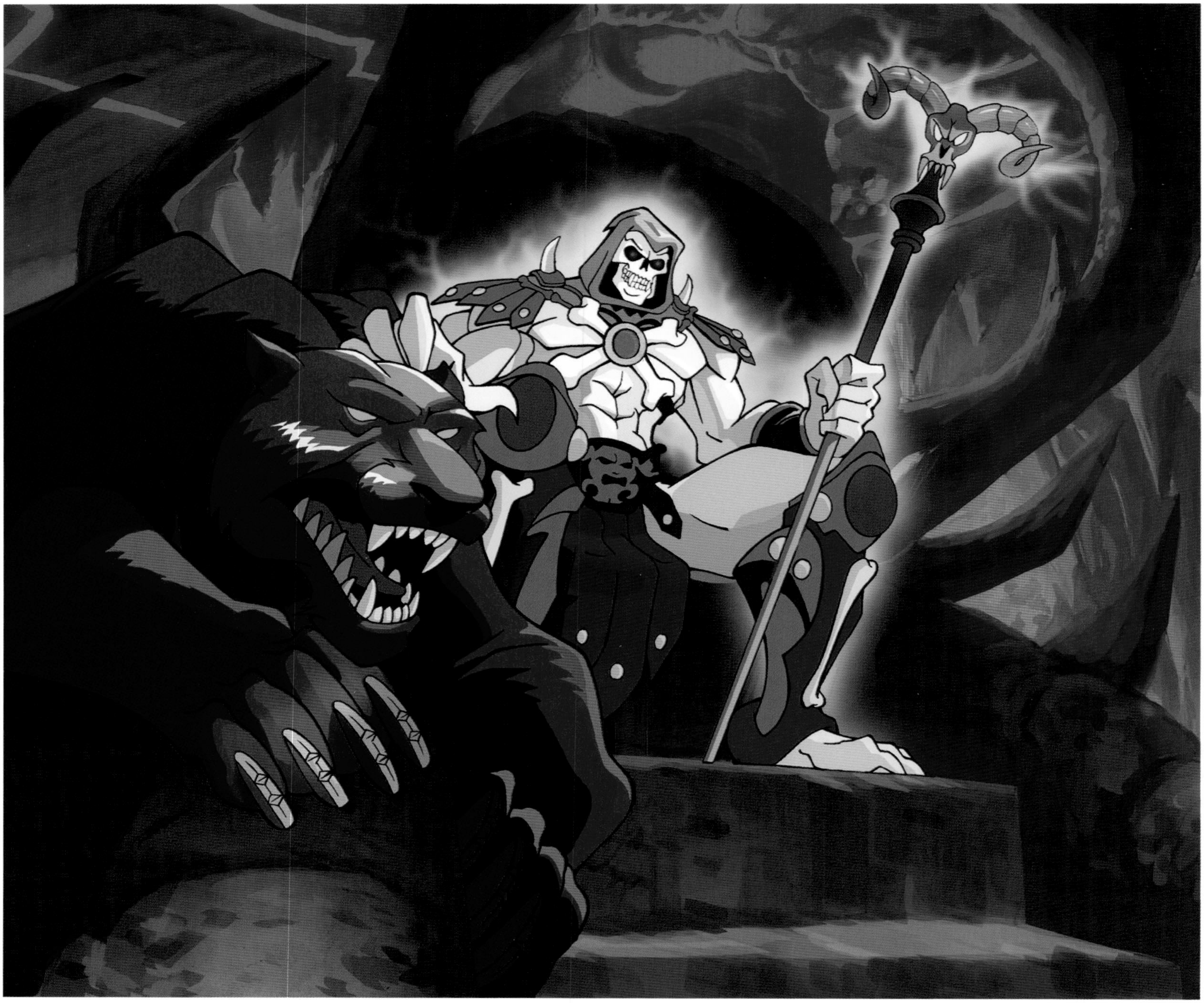

TOP LEFT: Skeletor and Panthor, He-Man's arch enemy.

a cartoon to advertise action figures. In spite of such misgivings, there was real heart to the stories. More than mere fun, episodes featured a sense of justice beyond spectacle. "What differentiated it from others of its genre and why it has resonated for so long and so deeply, was that it was about a family of characters that really cared about each other, and it had a moral tone. It had a lesson and a message that underlined all the action," said Robby Lyndon, another *He-Man* writer.

He-Man's rich imagination, coupled with its positive social messaging, led to its wide spread acceptance in pop culture. "It was probably the first show that was that successful in the history of animation," said *He-Man*'s executive producer Lou Scheimer. By 1984, it had spread to 120 US stations, appearing in more than thirty countries.

As the show caught on with audiences, toy sales soared. Racking up hundreds of millions of dollars, waves of action figures were released alongside other merchandise, including children's books, comics, and read-along records/cassette tapes. In addition to the 1987 live-action movie, *Masters of the Universe*, starring Dolph Lundgren, *He-Man*'s success spawned *She-Ra: Princess of Power,* a girls' spin-off series. This featured Prince Adam's twin, Princess Adora, who wielded her own magnificent Sword of Protection upon transforming into her alter ego.

He-Man's continuing fan loyalty would not have endured if it were not for the show's compassionate, thoughtful stories and fully realized characters. For many youngsters, He-Man was a role model. He taught them how to face life's challenges with integrity. In spite of his outsized muscles and heavy-duty weaponry, He-Man fought with love in his heart alongside his friends. Watching him battle evil with courage, driving back Skeletor to Snake Mountain every Saturday morning, helped shape many children's own moral compasses. Not only was He-Man a tough guy, He-Man was a good guy.

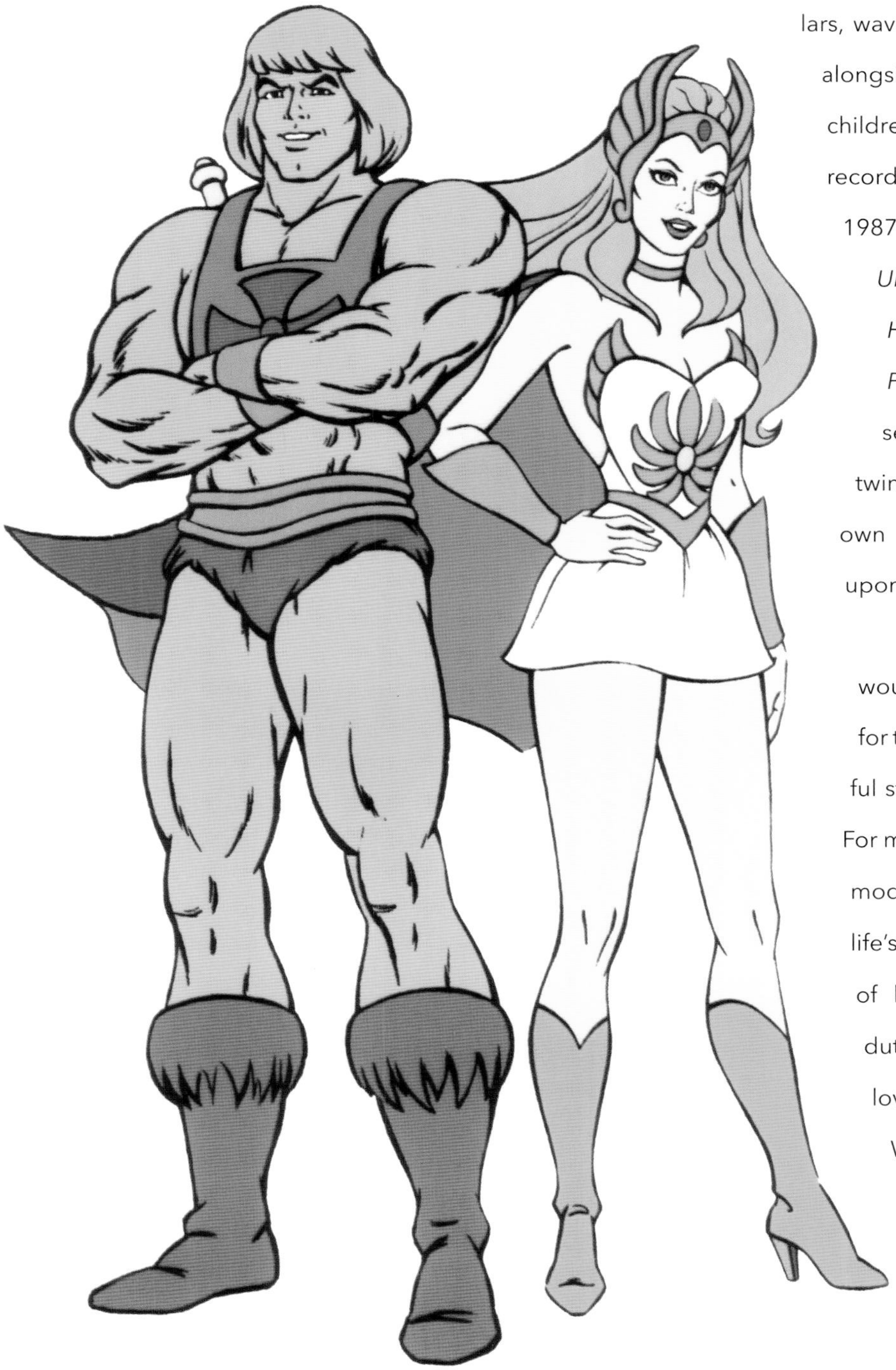

TOP: He-Man and She-Ra present a united front.

ABOVE: Prince Adam, Orko, and Cringer weigh their options

Special Powers Galore!

Unimaginable powers were core to the *He-Man* stories. He-Man and his Heroic Warriors possessed some amazing abilities, as did the foes they faced. A few of the most unique were:

- **Tri-Klops:** He wore a rotating visor helmet supplying him with three artificial eyes: one for distant vision, one for night sight and one that had the power, or Gammavision, to glimpse through objects or a round them.

- **Man-E-Faces:** Endowed with a large blue helmet featuring a screenlike opening, his face alternated between human, robot, and monster as his identity shifted for changing circumstances.

- **Trap Jaw:** Once described as a "wizard of weapons" by Skeletor, Trap Jaw was a cyborg with a crushing steel jaw. A member of the Evil Warriors, he sported a robotic arm capable of housing an array of deadly weapons, including a lasertron, sword blade, claw, hook, flamethrower, grapple, and freeze ray.

Jim Henson's Muppet Babies

Borne out of a dream sequence from the 1984 film *The Muppets Take Manhattan* in which the puppet ensemble pictured themselves as babies, Jim Henson had a vision for a cartoon that would encourage children's innate creativity. *Muppet Babies'* voice director, story editor, and head writer Hank Saroyan explained Henson's idea for the show this way: "He wanted children to believe that anything is possible. That's the only thing that's going to save this planet— the power of imagination." Or, as the show's own theme song lyrics said, *"Just close your eyes and make believe/And you can be anywhere . . ."*

Jim Henson's Muppet creations first took off in the mid '50s, beginning with Kermit on the TV show *Sam and Friends*, airing on WRC-TV in Washington, DC. Marrying the words, "marionette" and "puppet," what made Henson's puppetry so innovative was how he set up camera shots to efface the puppet operators. Not only that, he designed puppets capable of displaying a wide range of emotions. In 1969, the Children's Television Workshop brought on Henson and his team to work full time on PBS's *Sesame Street*, a recently created kids' series aimed at helping children prepare for school.

In the mid 1970s, Henson debuted *The Muppet Show*, a family-oriented variety TV series starring Kermit the Frog as the showrunner tasked with wrangling his cast of Muppets. *The Muppet Show*

YEARS ON AIR

1984–1991

NETWORK

CBS

NUMBER OF EPISODES

107

CHARACTERS AND VOICE ACTORS

Baby Kermit: Frank Welker
Baby Piggy: Laurie O'Brien
Baby Gonzo: Russi Taylor
Baby Fozzie/Baby Scooter:
Greg Berg
Rowlf: Katie Leigh
Baby Animal:
Dave Coulier/Howie Mandel
Baby Skeeter:
Frank Welker/Howie Mandel
Baby Bunsen Honeydew:
Dave Coulier/Howie Mandel
Nanny: Barbara Billingsley

PREVIOUS PAGE: The Muppet Babies (left to right): Piggy, Animal, Kermit, Scooter, Gonzo, Rowlf, Skeeter, and Bean Bunny.

TOP: Fozzie, Piggy, Gonzo, and Animal go on a quest for Piggy's lost library book in the episode "Nice to have Gnome You."

lasted five seasons and led to the extremely popular Muppet movies. But Henson saw a way to expand his Muppet universe even farther and appeal to younger children by creating *Muppet Babies*, a show about exploring childhood imagination. And what better way to establish a safe space for unbridled creativity than to set the program in a nursery?

Henson used a different cast for his cartoon featuring smaller and cuddlier versions of the beloved characters including Kermit, Miss Piggy, Fozzie, Rowlf, Gonzo, Animal, Skeeter, and Scooter. In the series, they happily roamed in their pajamas, bonnets, and diapers. Free to create their own worlds, they navigated the types of problems their kid audience might face, such as attending their first day of school or visiting the dentist.

Magical realism permeated the story lines, reflecting Henson's desire to blend reality with the more fantastical and playful elements of childhood. Live-action footage from film and TV would unpredictably merge with animation. Gonzo would open the closet door and inexplicably live-action dinosaurs would appear. Miss Piggy would be dining at a fancy restaurant and suddenly glimpse Princess Diana. At one point, Darth Vader (Nanny Vader) even made a cameo as their new babysitter "for the next million light-years" at which point Fozzie pleaded with him not to sell them to "Jabba the Slob."

Though the Muppets were babies, or more appropriately toddlers, the show never talked down to kids. If anything, it possessed a knowing sensibility encouraging curiosity. *Muppet Babies* particularly excelled in spoofing movies. In the episode "Back to the Nursery", the gang goes back in time to replace Nanny's yearbook picture from the '50s, and in "Romancing the Weirdo" the Muppets pay homage to the action-comedy *Romancing the Stone* with Gonzo supplying the story line on an old-fashioned typewriter under his pen name, F. Scott Gonzo.

Besides imagination, humor and idealism permeated the show. Recurring jokes included Piggy crushing on Kermit; Fozzie being paranoid about having tomatoes thrown at him; Gonzo obsessing over Camilla, his stuffed chicken; and Beaker being shrunk, zapped, turned invisible, and blown up as the

hapless assistant to Baby Bunsen Honeydew. Balancing that humor were the musical numbers sung in every episode, such as "Being Small Isn't Bad at All," "Dream for Your Inspiration," and "The Future Is Counting on You," which was about the next generation caring for the earth.

TOP: Rowlf and Kermit gather materials to build their own theme park in the episode "Eight Flags Over the Nursery."

The success of blending these themes and Henson's reputation for developing substantive material for youngsters drew many top performers to participate in the series. Besides Barbara Billingsley, other major actors lent their voices to *Muppet Babies*, including Dave Coulier (*Full House*) and comedian Howie Mandel. Notable guests also appeared in cameos, such as Whoopi Goldberg, Ed McMahon, and John Ritter. In "Comic Capers," Skeeter accidentally shoots a stream of spider webbing at the cartoonist Stan Lee's head. Even *Magnum P.I.*'s Tom Selleck showed up for the episode "What Do You Want to Be When You Grow Up" as a smitten fan of Piggy.

Nominated for a string of Daytime Emmy® Awards throughout the decade, the show won "Outstanding Animated Program" in 1987 and 1988. Before long, McDonald's came knocking to cash in on the hit. Throughout the mid '80s, the fast-food franchise offered *Muppet Babies* toys as prizes in their Happy Meals. Marvel Comics published a monthly comic book based on the series that lasted from 1985 until 1989, spanning twenty-six issues. Meanwhile, Parker Brothers/Columbia Records put out two *Muppet Babies* LP records featuring extended versions of the popular songs. It's therefore no surprise a reboot of *Muppet Babies* debuted on Disney Junior in 2018.

The original show tapped into something elemental and precious. Each week, the Muppet tikes explored the vastness of their own world and worries with Nanny acting as the voice of reason, soothing the Muppets' fears as they navigated the thin line between reality and fantasy. Never heavy-handed, but with a light and zany touch, the show delved into crucial themes, such as the importance of friendship, kindness, and self-esteem. Blending animation, live action, and puppetry, *Muppet Babies* served up heaps of joy with a touch of adult humor.

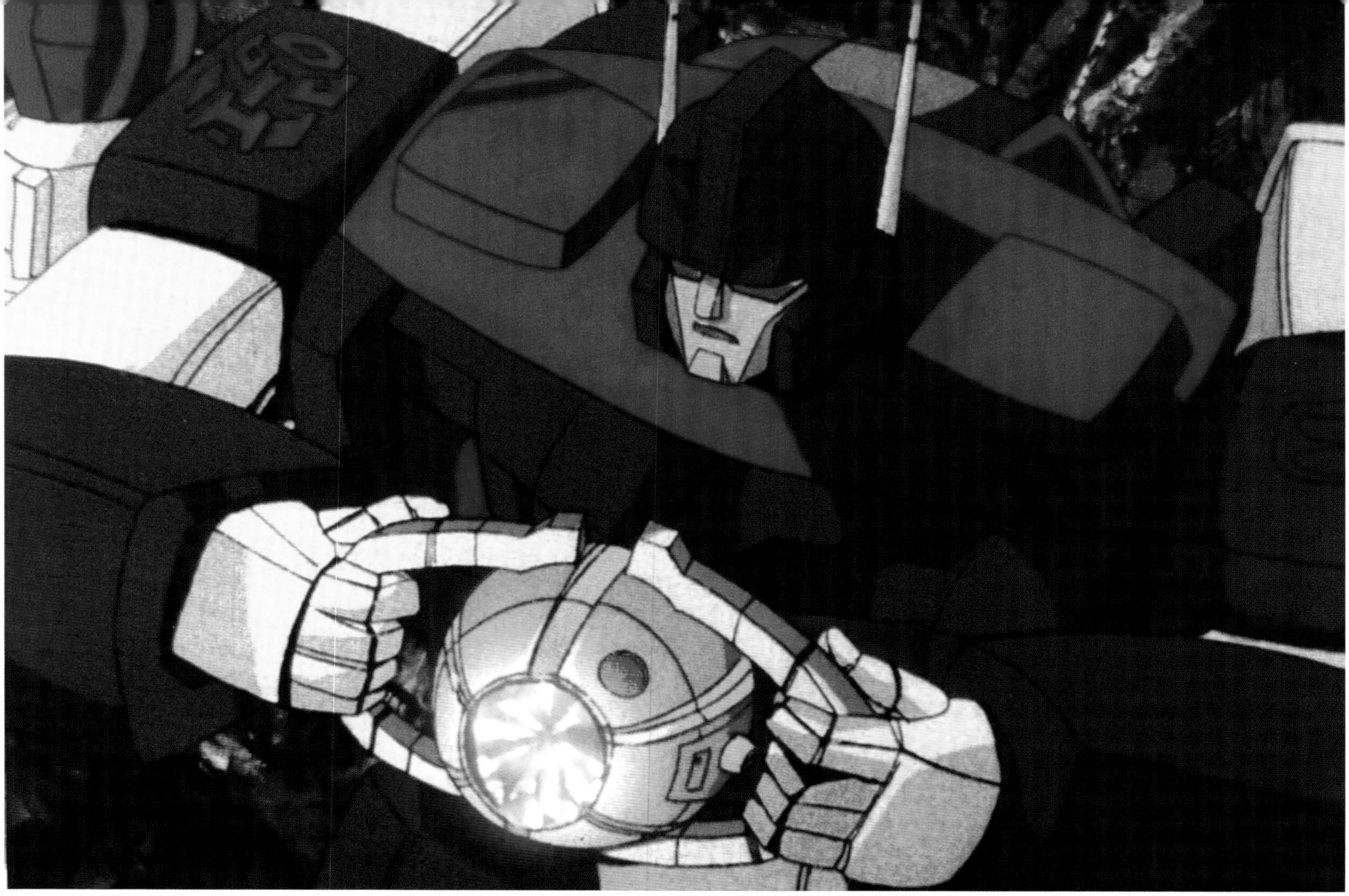

YEARS ON AIR

1984–1987

NETWORK

Syndication

NUMBER OF EPISODES

98

CHARACTERS AND VOICE ACTORS

Optimus Prime/Ironhide: Peter Cullen
Bumblebee: Dan Gilvezan
Cliffjumper: Casey Kasem
Sideswipe: Michael Bell
Megatron: Frank Welker
Starscream: Christopher Collins
Spike Witwicky/Shockwave: Corey Burton

The Transformers

By 1984, the Reagan administration, through the appointment of Mark S. Fowler as FCC commissioner, had removed many of the restrictions regarding promotional content placement within children's TV programming. Championing the "invisible hand" of market forces, as well as kids' ability to discriminate between entertainment and advertising, Fowler cleared the path for new product-based television programming. Rebranded from Takara Tomy, a Japanese entertainment company, *Transformers* first appeared as Diaclone and Microman toys. Then in 1984, America's Hasbro acquired the franchise, retitling the toy line. According to TFormers, Transformers Daily News Source for Transformers . . ., "When Hasbro, Inc. introduced the TRANSFORMERS brand to the U.S. in 1984, it revolutionized a category it had invented some twenty years earlier—action figures."

Witnessing the popularity of the *G.I. Joe: A Real American Hero* toy line among boys, the merchandising team at Hasbro hired writers Jim Shooter and Dennis O'Neil to dream up a rich backstory

OPPOSITE: Optimus Prime struggles to keep the matrix from the Decepticons, in the movie *Transformers*, 1986.

TOP: Hot Rod leaps out of trouble, in the movie, *Transformers*, 1986.

for their toys. With the help of Shooter and O'Neil's creativity, Hasbro didn't just retool the Diaclone and Mircroman robots, they reconceived their identities. The automatons became sentient beings, as opposed to controlled mechs piloted by humans. Utilizing Japanese animation from Toei and AKOM in South Korea, Marvel Productions produced the show as a never-ending war, pitting good robot aliens called the Autobots against bad robot aliens called the Decepticons. *Transformers* began airing in September 1984, and ran for three seasons as a Saturday morning cartoon.

Sure, *Transformers* began as mere merchandising—where a new character served as the focus of

THE TRANSFORMERS
HEROIC AUTOBOT
MORE THAN MEETS THE EYE!
TRANSFORMS FROM SUPER JET TO ROBOT AND BACK!
AUTOBOT AIR GUARDIAN JETFIRE

THE TRANSFORMERS
HEROIC AUTOBOT
MORE THAN MEETS THE EYE!
TRANSFORMS FROM RACE CAR TO ROBOT AND BACK!
TRANSFORMERS
AUTOBOT WARRIOR TRACKS
AGES: 5 & UP INCLUDES SNAP-ON WEAPONS & ACCESSORIES
5956/5766 ASST.

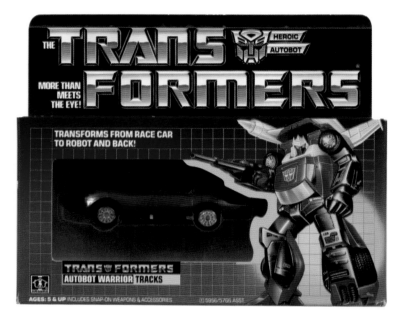

ABOVE LEFT: The Hasbro Transformers Series 2 Jetfire action figure, circa 1985.

ABOVE RIGHT: The Hasbro Transformers Series 2 Tracks action figure, circa 1985.

an episode often to make children aware of its toy counterpart—but it was the richly conceived characters and the thrilling story lines that gave the show staying power. The show's creators put tremendous thought and energy into establishing a complex world in which self-aware machines morphed into various forms, such as cars, helicopters, a microscope, an aircraft carrier, a triceratops, a laser cannon, a Japanese rhinoceros beetle, and even a 1984 radio-cassette deck.

As it stated in the show's theme song, "Autobots wage[d] their battle to destroy the evil forces of . . . the Decepticons." The battles and struggles that played out each week were all part of a larger war that raged between the two groups who fled their home planet of Cybertron after the Decepticons depleted it of energy. At the center of this drama loomed Optimus Prime intoning his signature phrase, "Autobots, transform and roll out!" Commanding an army of heroes with names like Bumblebee, Cliffjumper, and Sideswipe, Optimus Prime didn't just seek to protect his faction from the Decepticons, he aimed to protect all of Earth's inhabitants from the same fate as Cybertron. While seeking to find an alternative energy source, he and his Autobots had to continually hide their identity, posing as "robots in disguise."

Though Optimus Prime was the show's beloved lead, the creators made a bold decision regarding his fate. After two successful seasons, *Transformers: The Movie* was released in 1986 and offed the main hero. Set in the future world of 2005, and featuring the voice talents of Leonard Nimoy, Eric Idle, and Orson Welles, the movie was written so it could be split into four twenty-two-minute segments for television broadcast. Ron Friedman, the outspoken screenwriter, said Hasbro wanted to terminate Optimus Prime to make room for the next group of toys, but he had his misgivings. "To remove Optimus Prime, to physically remove Daddy from the family,

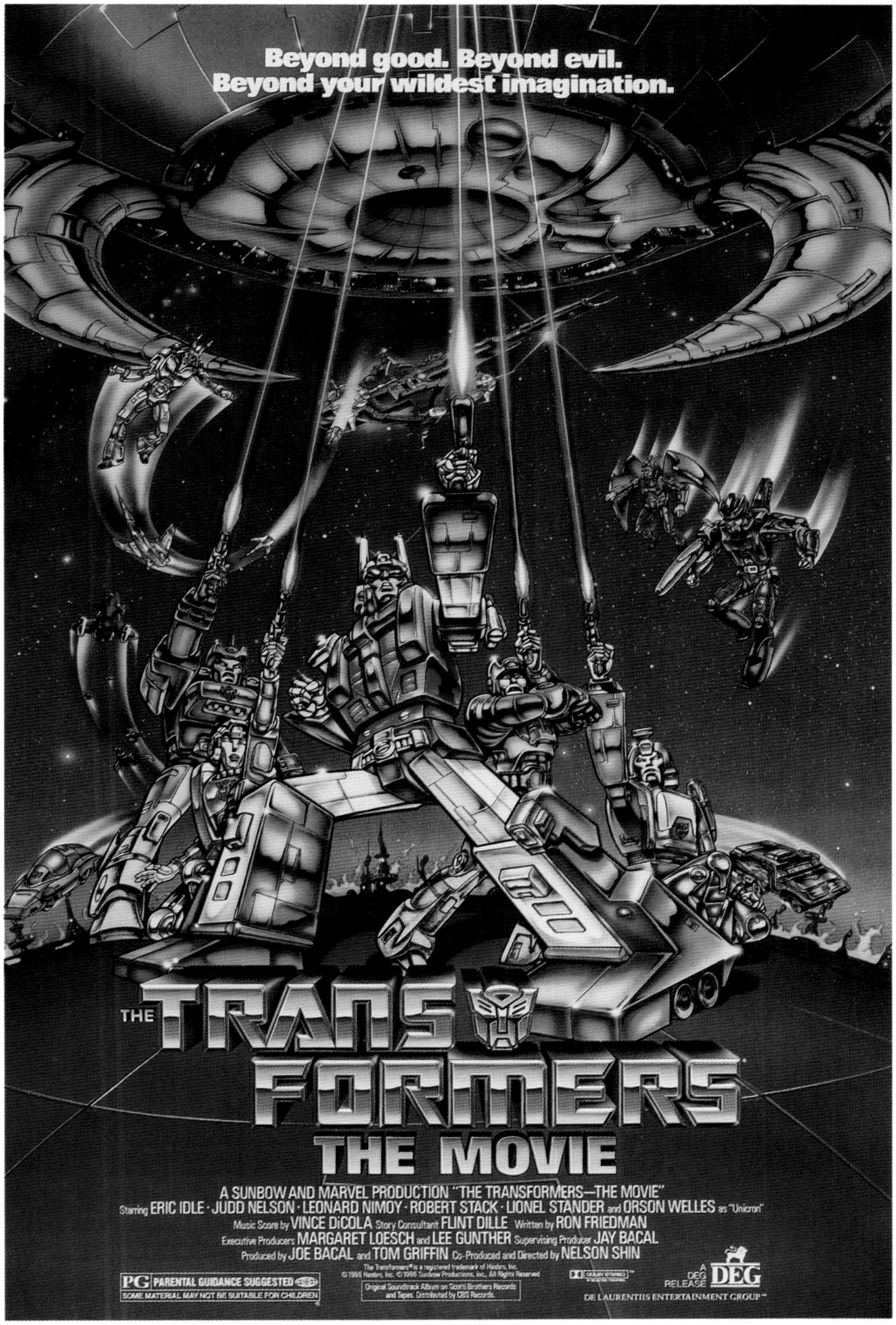
Beyond good. Beyond evil.
Beyond your wildest imagination.
THE TRANSFORMERS
THE MOVIE
A SUNBOW AND MARVEL PRODUCTION "THE TRANSFORMERS—THE MOVIE"
Starring ERIC IDLE · JUDD NELSON · LEONARD NIMOY · ROBERT STACK · LIONEL STANDER and ORSON WELLES as "Unicron"
Music Score by VINCE DiCOLA Story Consultant FLINT DILLE Written by RON FRIEDMAN
Executive Producers MARGARET LOESCH and LEE GUNTHER Supervising Producer JAY BACAL
Produced by JOE BACAL and TOM GRIFFIN Co-Produced and Directed by NELSON SHIN
PG PARENTAL GUIDANCE SUGGESTED
SOME MATERIAL MAY NOT BE SUITABLE FOR CHILDREN
A DEG RELEASE DEG
DE LAURENTIIS ENTERTAINMENT GROUP

that wasn't going to work. I told Hasbro and their lieutenants they would have to bring him back but they said no and had 'great things planned.' In other words, they were going to create new, more expensive toys." Ultimately, Friedman lost the argument and wrote the story so that Optimus Prime succumbed from wounds suffered in his battle against Megatron.

It should have come to no one's surprise that children were devastated by the loss of their hero. In fact, fan complaints and public outcry was so intense that Optimus Prime was resurrected in a two-part story, "The Return of Optimus Prime," replacing the original season three finale in 1987. However, Optimus Prime would go on to be killed more than a dozen times in future iterations of the franchise for various reasons, only to come back from the dead.

In addition to the show's detailed and compelling story lines, the thrilling action sequences featuring fast cars, flying planes, dinosaurs, spaceships, aliens, and blasters captivated kids. *Transformers* completely reimagined the role of robots by giving them double lives and making them sentient aliens from another planet. To bring this innovative story to life, Hasbro tapped superior voice actors, such as Frank Welker as Megatron, who was also known for his work as Fred on *Scooby-Doo, Where are You!* and Kermit on *Muppet Babies*; Christopher Collins as Starscream, who was also the voice of Cobra Commander on *G.I. Joe*; and the well-known disc jockey Casey Kasem as Cliffjumper.

With the talent and innovation the creative team brought to the show, it's no mystery why *Transformers* has come to dominate pop culture, spawning comic books, additional animation series, toys, and video games, as well as a live-action blockbuster movie franchise earning billions of dollars. Originating from

ABOVE: Original movie poster for *Transformers: The Movie.*

ABOVE: The Optimus Prime toy: left disguised as a truck; right, the Autobot leader in all his Transformer glory.

Robots in Disguise

Central to the *Transformers'* universe was their ability to transform. Watching the characters morph on-screen into their alter egos gave the series added excitment. Here are some of the characters' classic dual identities:

Bumblebee	1979 VW Beetle
Cliffjumper	1979 Porsche 924
Prowl's Alternate Mode	1979 Nissan 280ZX police car
Optimus Prime	1984 Freightliner semi
Sideswipe	1974 Lamborghini Countach LP500S

a simple import toy line, *Transformers* has become a media franchise juggernaut, and it all began with the characters and story lines appearing between 1984 and 1993—designated *Generation One*—that started it all. As Peter Cullen, voice of Optimus Prime, noted when he first became involved with the show: "All

of us auditioning went one by one for a series of days, until we all got together and had it explained to us what it was all about and saw more detailed pictures. I knew early on that we were involved with something that was totally revolutionary in the children's entertainment world. And of course, it was."

The Care Bears

Arriving on Saturday mornings amidst clouds, rainbows, and saccharine goodness, *The Care Bears* kept watch over little boys and girls from their home in Care-a-Lot, a magical cloudland, and would venture to Earth in their Cloudmobile to offer support when a child was feeling down. To be sure, *The Care Bears* weren't just huggable bears, they acted as soldiers of love, fixing their formidable "Care Bear Stare" on opponents, such as Professor Coldheart, who wished to freeze people's feelings.

Clearly, much care went into creating the characters and their Care Bear Kingdom. The decades-spanning franchise arrived fresh on the heels of American Greetings Cards' (AGC) success with *Strawberry Shortcake* in 1979. AGC, the world's largest greeting cards producer, played their cards close to the chest. In fact, they were so secretive with *Strawberry Shortcake*, they called her "Project I" until the concept went to market. Greeting cards followed, then a doll, then a series of animated TV specials, such as *The World of Shortcake,* introducing her friends named after desserts, such as Huckleberry Pie, Blueberry Muffin, Raspberry Tart, and her cat, Custard. AGC created the title character,

YEARS ON AIR

1985-1988

NETWORK

Syndication, ABC

NUMBER OF EPISODES

60

CHARACTERS AND VOICE ACTORS

Tenderheart Bear:
Billie Mae Richards
Birthday Bear: Jayne Eastwood
Wish Bear: Janet Laine-Green
Grumpy Bear: Bob Dermer
Professor Coldheart:
Les Lye/Len Carlson
Cheer Bear: Tracey Moore
Treat Heart Pig: Luba Goy

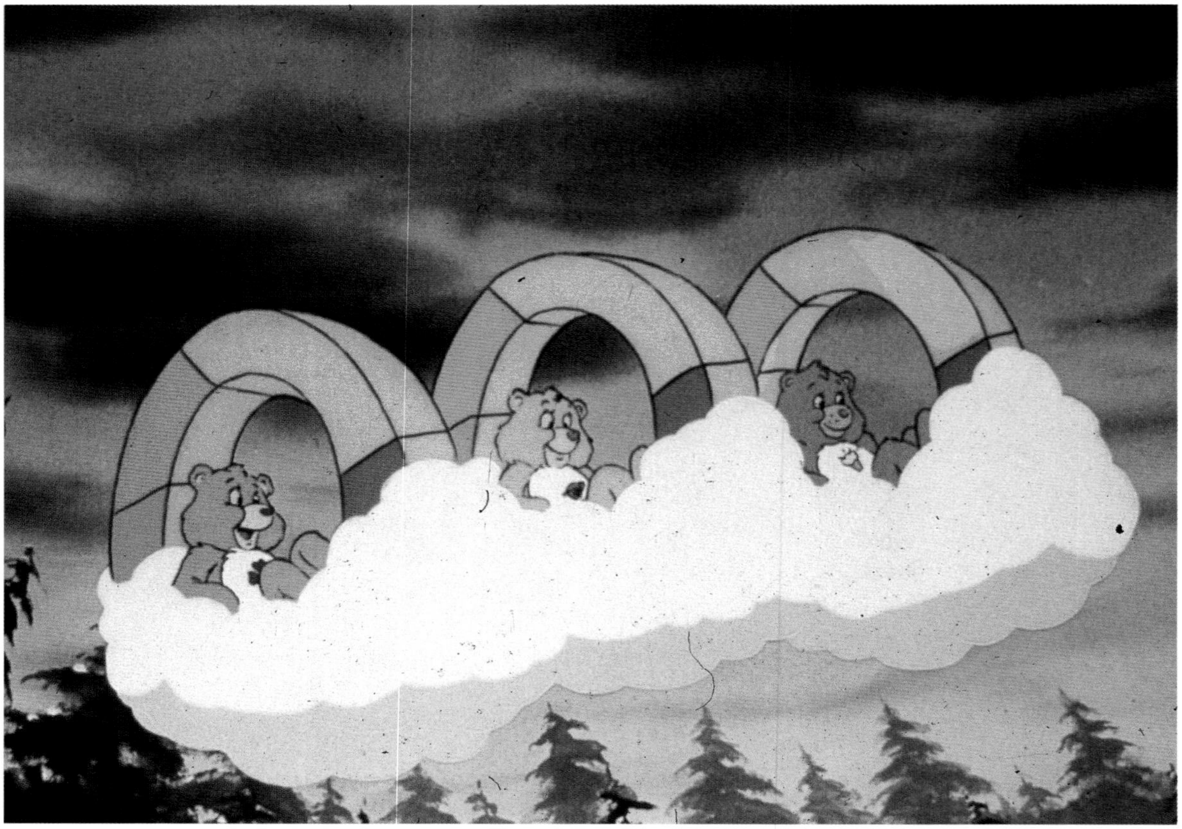

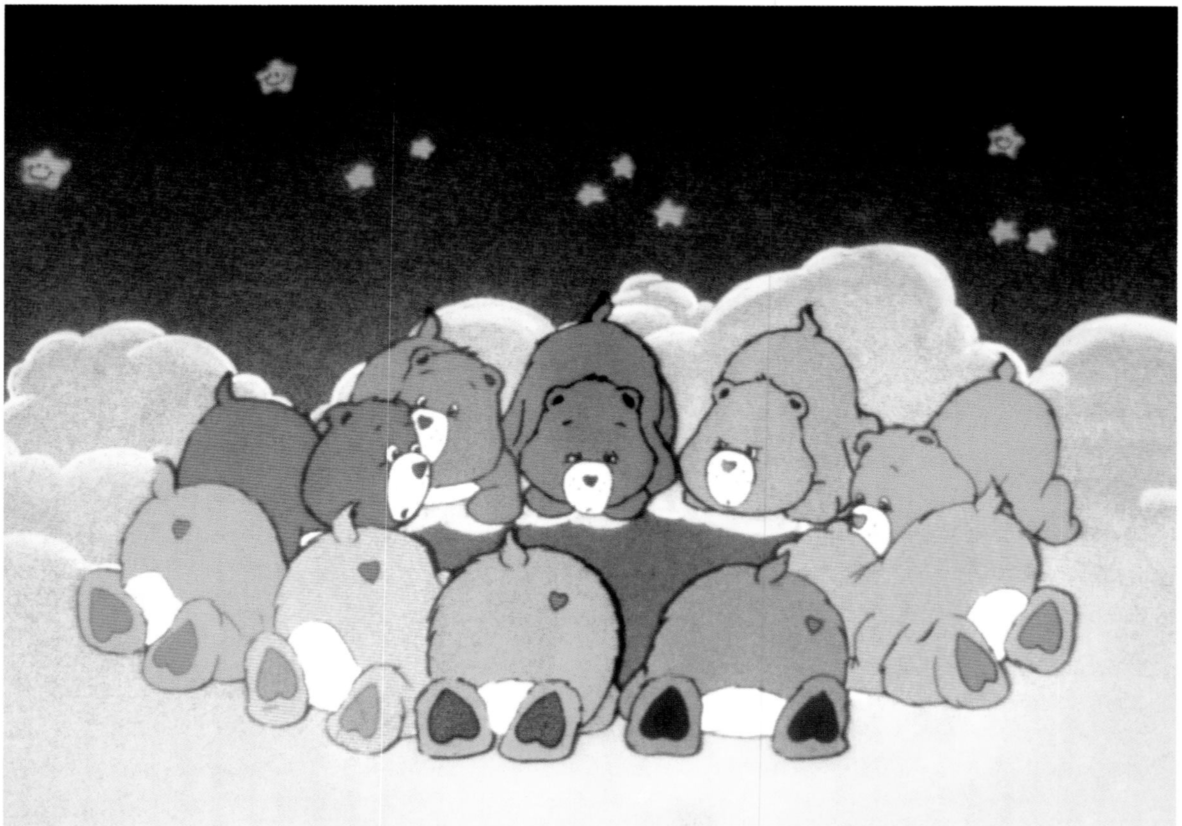

but Kenner produced and sponsored the special. Evidently, AGC's precautions paid off. By the early 1980s, *Strawberry Shortcake* merchandise, from lunch boxes to dolls, was flying off retail shelves. Repeating their covert approach, AGC kept *Care Bears* under wraps with the label "Project II" during development.

Once again under the leadership of copresidents Jack Chojnacki and Ralph Shaffer, AGC teamed up with toy partner Kenner, maker of the *Star Wars* action figures, to develop another concept for children with AGC providing much of the conceptual direction. "I'm sitting here looking at a simple pencil sketch of a bear and thinking, 'What in the hell am I going to do with the bears?'" said Shaffer in a 2017 *Cleveland Magazine* interview. "Something in my head just took those graphics and flopped them over on the bear's stomach. I drew that heart on that bear. Boom! The clouds opened up and the sun shined."

The company also tapped cartoonist Dave Polter and illustrator Elena Kucharik to bring their vision of heartwarming teddy bears to life. "Their appeal went up and down the age range," added Shaffer. "They look really young, but at the same time, you could have them say almost anything. You could have them be funny. Bears are the ultimate anthropomorphic character."

Confident in their new lovable creations, the development team continued to hone the characters. "We had nine bears, each a different color, representing nine different emotions—Bedtime Bear, Birthday Bear, Cheer Bear, Friend Bear, Funshine Bear, Good Luck Bear, Love-a-Lot Bear, Tenderheart Bear, and Wish Bear," said Shaffer. "[But] as I'm sitting there, looking at all these saccharine honey-sweet teddy bears, I said, 'We need a relief in this bunch. Let's do a counter bear to all this sweetness. Let's do a Grumpy Bear.'" Shaffer's instinct was spot-on. Balancing out the cast, this irritable bear became a fan favorite and has appeared as a main character in nearly every iteration of the franchise.

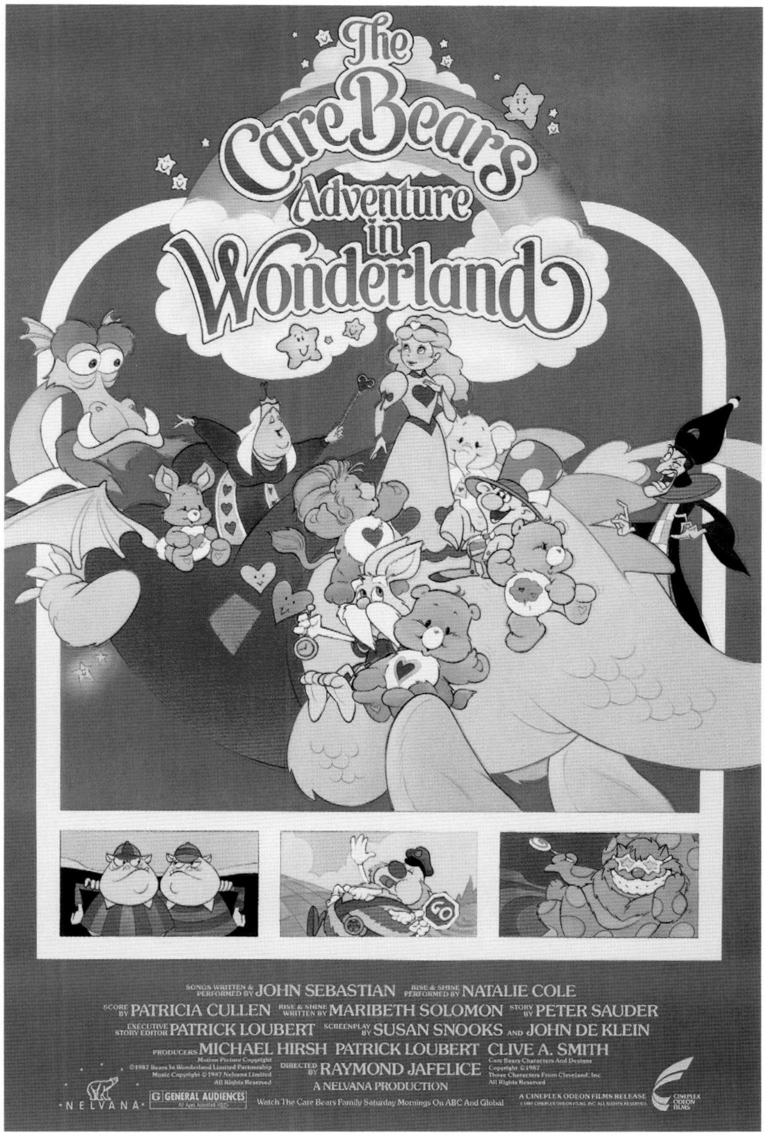

The Care Bears Adventure in Wonderland
SONGS WRITTEN & PERFORMED BY JOHN SEBASTIAN RISE & SHINE PERFORMED BY NATALIE COLE
SCORE BY PATRICIA CULLEN RISE & SHINE WRITTEN BY MARIBETH SOLOMON STORY BY PETER SAUDER
EXECUTIVE STORY EDITOR PATRICK LOUBERT SCREENPLAY BY SUSAN SNOOKS AND JOHN DE KLEIN
PRODUCERS MICHAEL HIRSH PATRICK LOUBERT CLIVE A. SMITH
DIRECTED BY RAYMOND JAFELICE
A NELVANA PRODUCTION
NELVANA
G GENERAL AUDIENCES
Watch The Care Bears Family Saturday Mornings On ABC And Global
A CINEPLEX ODEON FILMS RELEASE
CINEPLEX ODEON FILMS

Once the personalities were in place, Kenner began toy production, partnering with Parker Brothers for a line of plush bears that they launched at the New York City Toy Fair in 1983. The toys were a hit, and AGC knew they had something special. Their television special, *The Land Without Feelings*, premiered the same year. Another special, *The Care Bears Battle the Freeze Machine*, followed, as well as a miniseries distributed by Lexington Broadcast Services Company.

Capitalizing on the franchise's growing popularity, Canadian animation studio Nelvana produced *The Care Bears Movie*. Earning nearly $35 million worldwide in 1985, it starred Mickey Rooney as the voice of Mr. Cherrywood and told the story of how the Bears

PREVIOUS: The Care Bears greet a child in need (left to right): Gentle Heart Lamb, Birthday Bear, Tenderheart Bear, Cheer Bear, Lotsa Heart Elephant, Wish Bear, and Swift Heart Rabbit.

OPPOSITE TOP: Three Care Bears fly through the night sky.

OPPOSITE BOTTOM: The Care Bears peer down at Earth.

TOP: Movie poster for *The Care Bears Adventure in Wonderland*, 1987.

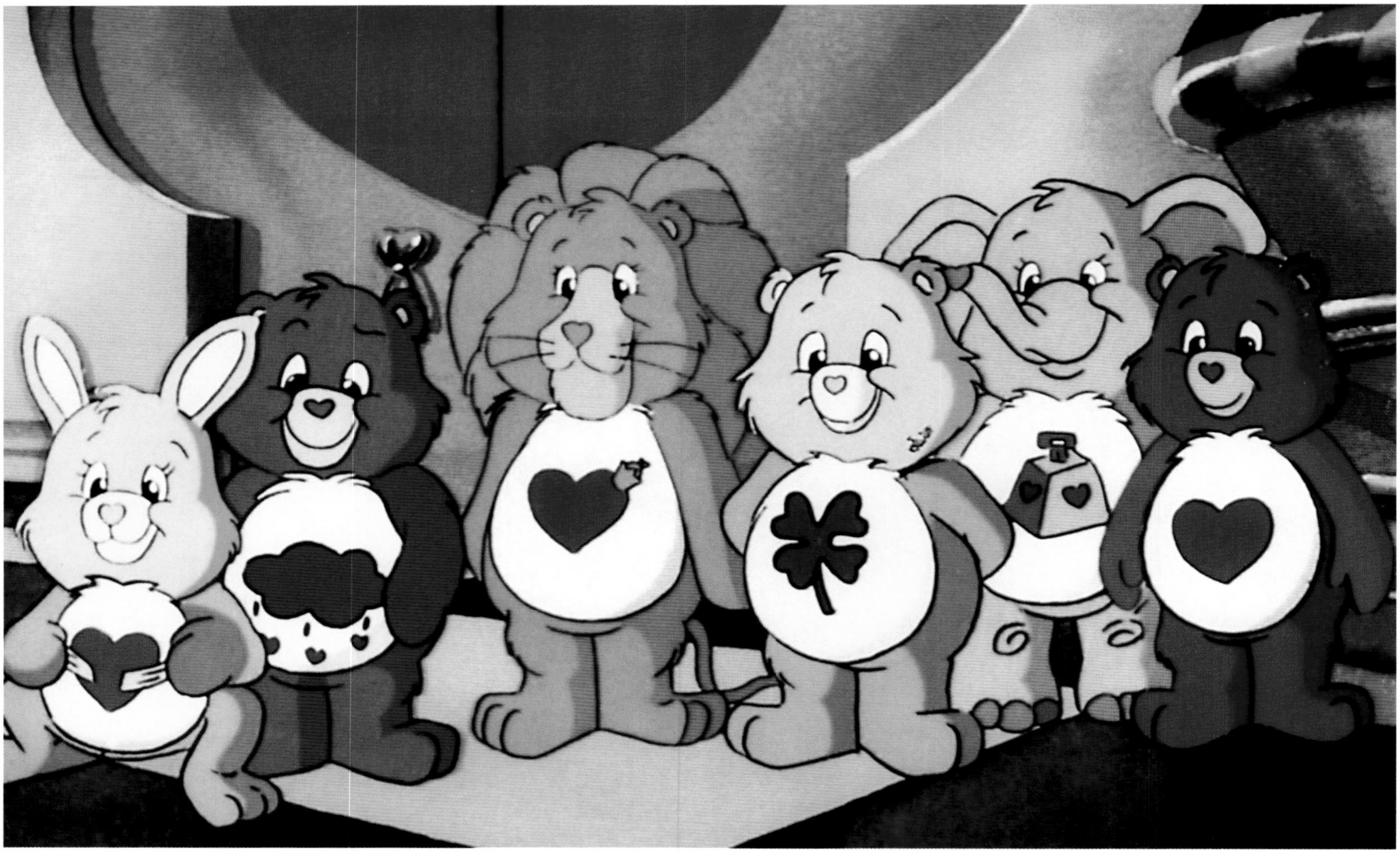

ABOVE: The Care Bears stand proud in *The Care Bears Adventure in Wonderland* movie, 1987: (left to right) Swift Heart Rabbit, Grumpy Bear, Brave Heart Lion, Good Luck Bear, Lotsa Heart Elephant, and Tenderheart Bear.

restored a young brother and sister's trust in people after the death of their parents. Music legends John Sebastian and Carole King contributed their talents to songs, like "Nobody Cares Like a Bear" and "Home Is in Your Heart." In an article appearing in the April 18, 1985 edition of the *Cincinnati Enquirer*, Sebastian admitted to "not being intimately familiar with the Care Bears" before his movie involvement but appreciating their value. "I think their central theme—being candid about your feelings, sharing your feelings—is a very positive message for children."

Like the television specials and toys, the movie connected with audiences, securing the Golden Reel Award, Canada's prize for largest annual box office gross. The same year, the animated series began in syndication with production by DiC Enterprises and LBS Communications. Beyond intervening to help whenever the bears' Caring Meter alerted them a child was in trouble, recurring episode themes focused on No Heart utilizing his lackey Beastly to steal the bears or wreak havoc in Care-a-Lot. Moral lessons grounded the narrative. In the episode "The Best Way to Make Friends," Treat Heart Pig, Cheer Bear, Bright Heart Raccoon, and Champ Bear work together to discover how to win friends. Though the bears put different ideas forward—Champ Bear thought you needed to prove how strong you are and Bright Heart Raccoon thought you needed to make others think you are smart—they all come to the same conclusion: it's better to be yourself.

Combining sweetness with adorable cuteness, *The Care Bears* won over young fans as the ultimate emotional pick-me-up. Additional feature-length movies appeared, including *Care Bears Movie II: A New Generation* (1986) and *The Care Bear Adventure in Wonderland* (1987). Though the first iteration of the TV series ended in the late 1980s, the franchise was rebooted with revamped toys featuring illuminated bellies and updated colors in the 2000s, along with the computer-animated films *Care Bears: Journey to Joke-a-Lot* (2004) and *The Care Bears Big Wish Movie* (2005). A new version of the TV animated series was also created in 2011 called *Care Bears: Welcome to Care-a-Lot* and in 2015, Netflix produced the show *Care Bear and Cousins*.

Remaining intergenerationally relevant, the Care Bears in all of their many iterations have stood the test of time, even acquiring a kind of hipster cache among Gen Xers. "They have retro appeal. *Care Bears* and *Strawberry Shortcake* became the cool things to wear," said cartoonist Dave Polter. "They had a huge second life that is still ongoing." Former AGC CEO Morry Weiss explained the characters' ongoing appeal, no matter the era. "Certain things kind of take you back and slow you down. If you look at everything—from the spectacular illustrations to the stories to the design—we probably did this better than anyone else in the world."

ABOVE: The Care Bears lock in a Care Bear stare during the *Care Bears Movie II: A New Generation*, 1986.

The Care Bear Stare

Drawing on their strong emotions, The Care Bears used the energy force from their tummies to expel powerful energy, producing a light ray. Jam-packed with hearts and stars, this glittery beam, also known as "magic", could blast an enemy, such as Beastly, and subdue him. However, because they are the Care Bears, after all, the stare never produced any lasting or lethal damage.

Cabbage Patch Kids

The world collectively lost its mind in the 1980s over Cabbage Patch Kids, a line of adorable stitched dolls. People camped outside toy stores overnight to be the first inside when they opened. Fights broke out in malls between customers eager to snatch up the toys. When stores ran out of the dolls before the holidays in 1983, it led to a crisis. Riots erupted, one of which caused a woman to break her leg after a crowd of more than a thousand people stormed the store.

Some of the Cabbage Patch charm may be attributed to their personalization. Each came with a unique birth certificate and adoption papers. Though Xavier Roberts is credited as the inventor, controversy surrounds the dolls' origins. No matter the truth of the Cabbage Patch Kids' beginnings, the dolls were a massive hit. According to *Time*, more than two and a half million dolls sold the first year they were introduced by Coleco.

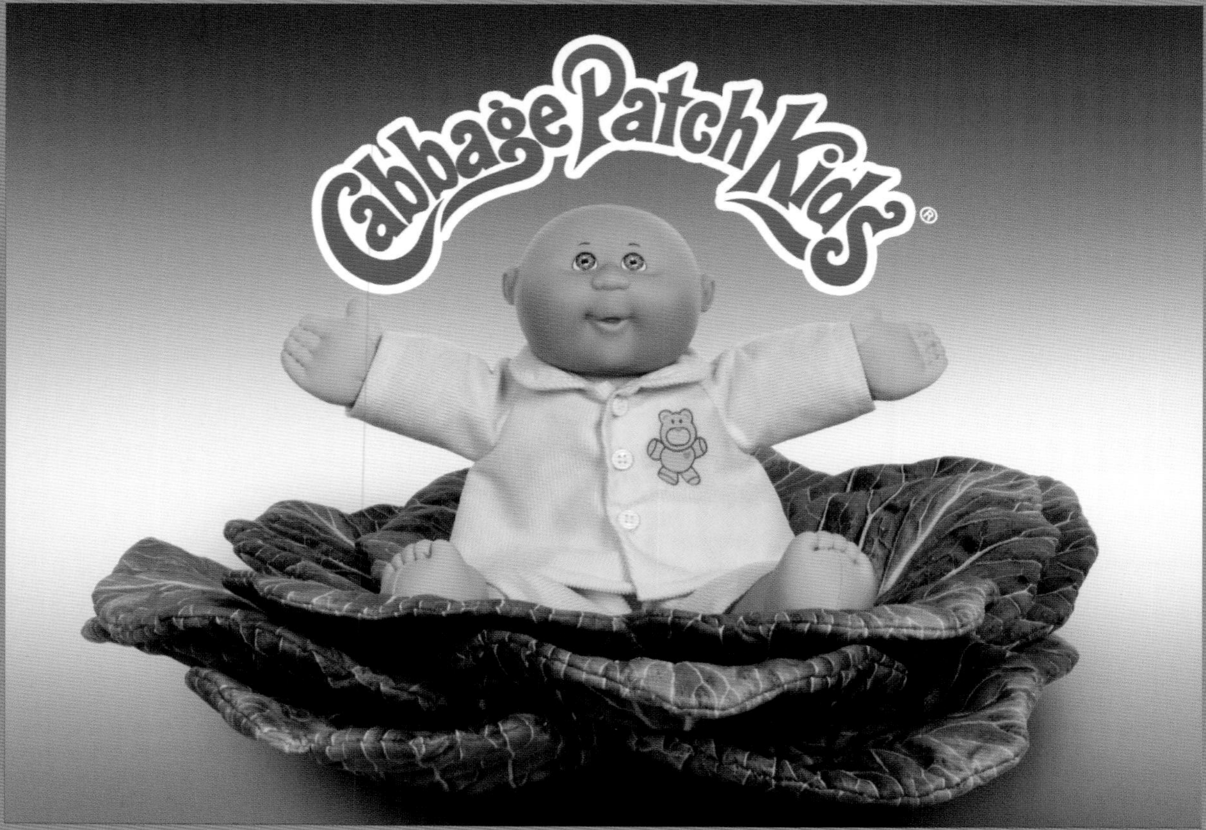
Cabbage Patch Kids®

ABOVE: Each Cabbage Patch doll came with a name and adoption papers.

G.I. Joe:
A Real American Hero

Perhaps it is fitting that a show about army soldiers had to battle against layers of scrutiny and censorship. While the series featured intense action scenes with tanks, guns, and explosions, no human was killed on-screen. Yet it was perceived as too violent, and many parents simply said no to *G.I. Joe*.

Required to adhere to the FCC's programming regulations, the *G.I. Joe: A Real American Hero* characters used laser guns—red for the G.I.

Joe Team and blue for their Cobra enemy—rather than real guns. Presumably to stave off heat from parental groups, the show's coproducers, Marvel and Sunbow Productions, also featured a public service announcement at the close of each episode. Endorsed by the National Child Safety Council, these messages offered boys and girls tips such as "avoid giving strangers your address" and "running away isn't the answer." Each message then ended

YEARS ON AIR

1985-1986

NETWORK

Syndication

NUMBER OF EPISODES

95

CHARACTERS AND VOICE ACTORS

Narrator/Duke: Michael Bell
Cobra Commander:
Christopher Collins
Destro: Arthur Burghardt
Shipwreck: Neil Ross
Torch: Frank Welker
Scarlett: B.J. Ward
Serpentor: Dick Gautier
Cover Girl: Libby Aubrey
Sgt. Slaughter: Robert Remus

PREVIOUS: G.I. Joe (center) and Sergeant Slaughter (left) discuss their next move.

BOTTOM: Cobra members take action in the episode "Arise, Serpentor, Arise!"

OPPOSITE TOP: Members of the G.I. Joe Team in action from the episode "The Further Adventures of G.I. Joe."

OPPOSITE BELOW: Serpentor, an elite Cobra soldier, sits on a throne in the episode "Arise Serpentor, Arise!"

with characters such as Wild Bill saying "Now you know . . . And knowing is half the battle."

In addition to content concerns, some parents took issue with the fact that like its Saturday morning compatriots, *He-Man* and *Transformers*, the show began as a toy line with episodes built around its three-and-three-quarter-inch action figures with names like Breaker, Grunt, and Zap. Marvel cartoonist Larry Hama, who wrote the comic book series based on the Hasbro toy line, is credited with developing the show's characters along with Dwight Jon Zimmerman. "There was a big meeting at Hasbro to discuss the project," Hama said in an interview for *Comics Interview* #37. "It was attended by Jim

Shooter, Tom DeFalco, Archie Goodwin, myself, and, I believe, Nelson Yomtov. Basically, [Hasbro] had decided to switch from having a large single figure of Joe with a lot of accessories to smaller action figures. The big, really major difference was they wanted to give all of the guys characters and backgrounds."

The 1960s version of G.I. Joe America's Movable Fighting Man was twelve inches tall. But *G.I. Joe's* history goes even further back to the Second World War. A publication, first produced by cartoonist and WWII army veteran Dave Breger in 1942, was called *Private Breger* and appeared in *Yank, the Army Weekly*. Breger soon changed the title of his series to *G.I. Joe* based on the military term "Government Issue." The name caught on quickly, becoming a common designation for the American foot soldier in popular culture.

Just as there were different evolutions of the G.I. Joe toy lines, the cartoon program also grew in stages. The 1985 version was the second iteration of the children's cartoon. Prior to this, Hasbro created the 1982 G.I. Joe: A Real American Hero toy line, in tandem with Marvel comics, before producing *The M.A.S.S Device*, a five-part miniseries in 1983, which centered on a teleportation machine and introduced the

conflict between the G.I. Joe Team, an elite counterterrorist unit, and the terrible Cobra Organization. This series led to a second five-part miniseries in 1984, entitled *The Revenge of Cobra* where the G.I. Joe Team members attempted to thwart Cobra's Weather Dominator, a device that weaponized the climate. Ron Friedman, the same screenwriter behind 1986's *The Transformers: The Movie,* penned the scripts for both miniseries before creating the full-blown show in 1985.

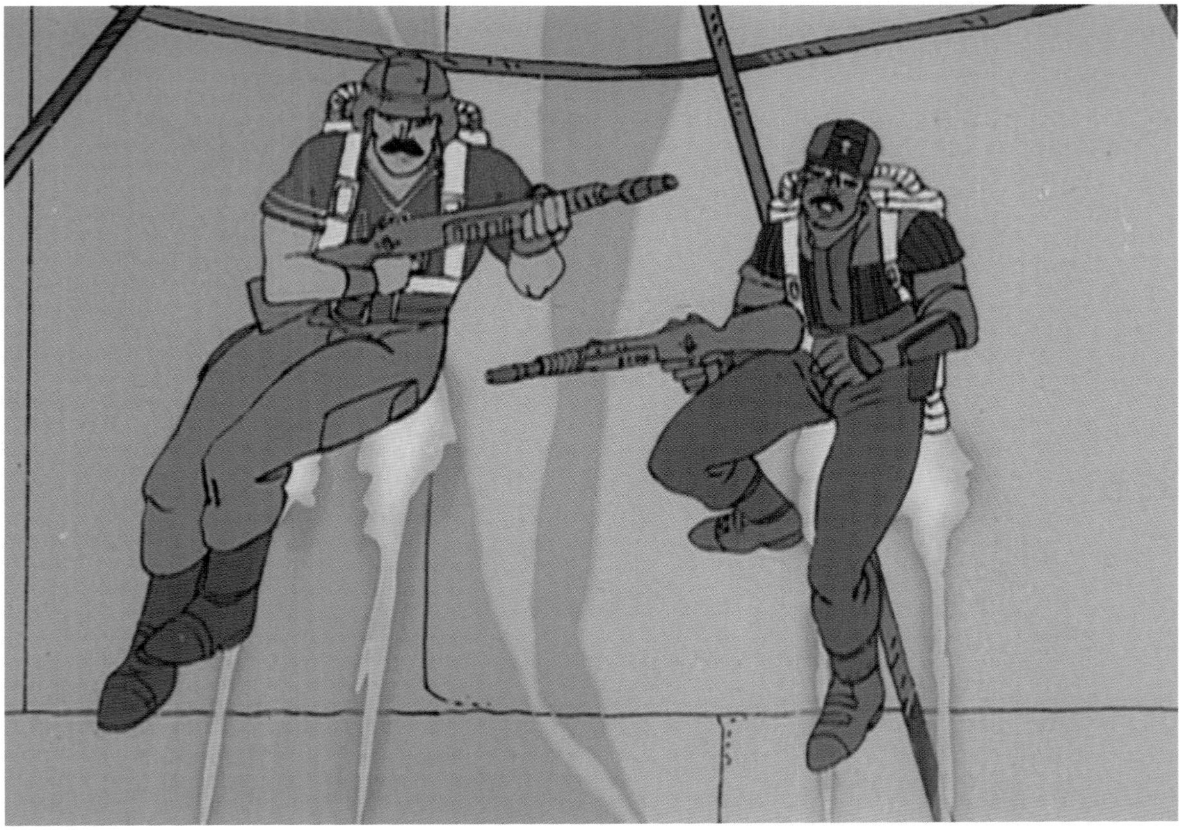

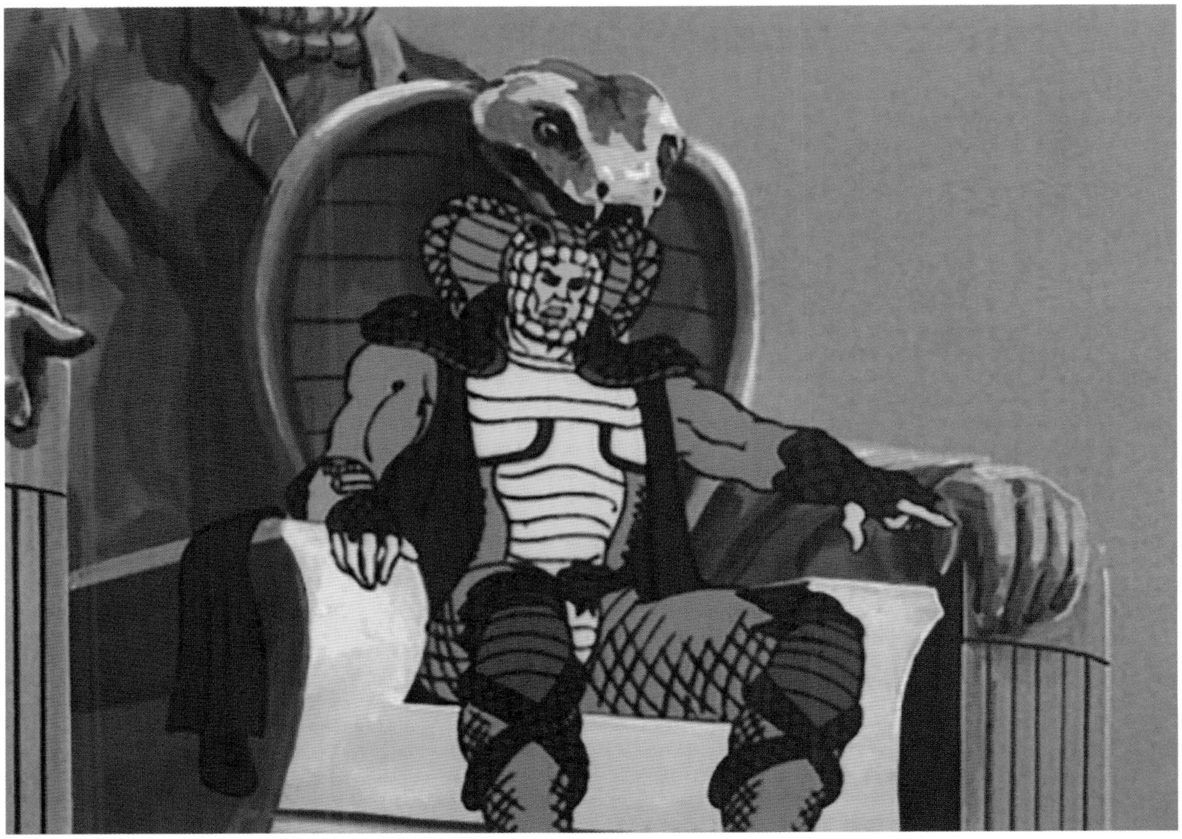

Similar to the concept behind the miniseries, *G.I. Joe* featured mostly stand-alone episodes in which the G.I. Joe Team worked together to stop the machinations of the dastardly Cobra Commander. Or, as narrator Jackson Beck said in the title sequence, "G.I. Joe is the code name for America's daring, highly-trained, Special Mission force. Its purpose: to defend human freedom against Cobra, a ruthless terrorist organization determined to rule the world."

A typical plot involved the G.I. Joe Team heroically thwarting a Cobra misdeed. In "Operation Mind Menace," Cobra kidnapped

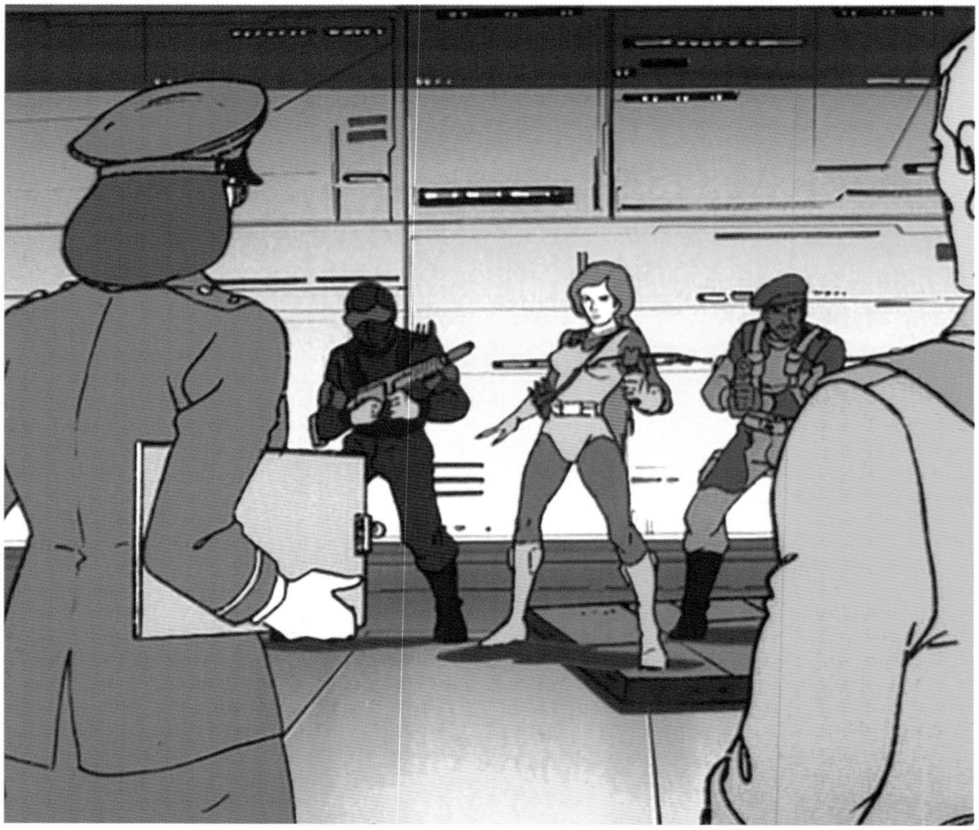

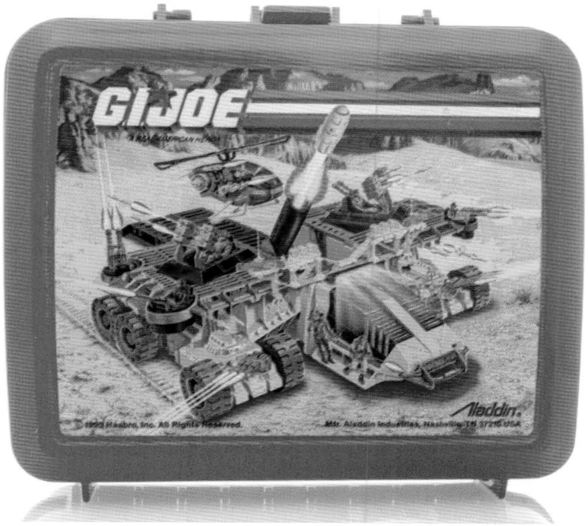
GI JOE
Aladdin

TOP: Cover Girl takes action in the episode "The Cobra Strikes."

BOTTOM: G.I. Joe lunch box, circa 1990.

skydiving hero Airborne's kid brother after learning he possessed psionic, or paranormal, abilities. In "Excalibur," Cobra Commander's ninja bodyguard Storm Shadow obtained King Arthur's Excalibur sword.

G.I. Joe story lines sometimes blurred the line between fantasy, science fiction, and reality. For instance, Long before Michael Crichton wrote *Jurassic Park*, the *G.I. Joe* episode "Primordial Plot" featured Cobra snatching a scientist with the ability to clone dinosaurs, which he had brought to life on a hidden island. And in a nod to *The Philadelphia Experiment*, the two-part episode "Worlds Without End" saw the G.I. Joe Team and Cobra fighting to get a hold of a device capable of transforming matter into any substance, landing them in alternate world.

With creative input from Hama and Zimmerman, *G.I. Joe*'s myriad cast of more than a hundred characters enriched the story lines. Characters, such as Duke, Hawk, Cobra Commander, Storm Shadow, and Snakes Eyes, filled out the show's ranks. "Snake Eyes was purposely made very mysterious," explained Hama. "He's completely covered from head to toe. Nobody knows what he looks like . . . He is your blank slate, and he becomes a universal blank slate for projection of fantasy for anybody, because he is so unspecific. But he is specific in his personality traits: his sincerity, his will, his loyalty." And so as to not exclude the girls, the show introduced characters like Cover Girl, who prior to enlisting as a member of the G.I. Joe Team enjoyed a career as a fashion model. Fed up with objectification, she first joined the squad as a driver of the Wolverine Missile Tank.

By the time the second and final season rolled around, the series featured a collection of new characters, most notably a new villain, Serpentor, the Cobra Emperor. In the 1986 episode,

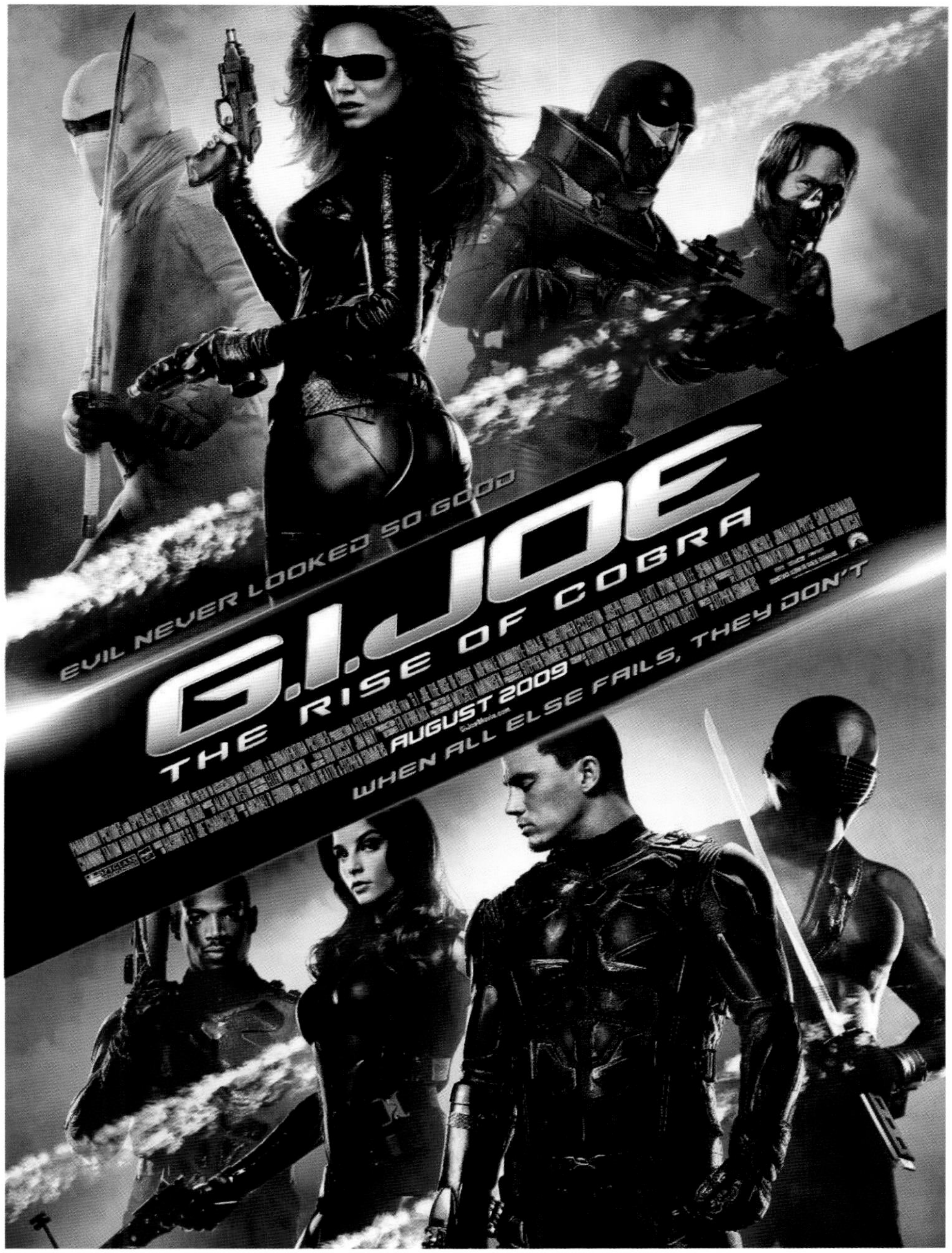
EVIL NEVER LOOKED SO GOOD
G.I. JOE
THE RISE OF COBRA
AUGUST 2009
WHEN ALL ELSE FAILS, THEY DON'T

ABOVE: Promotional poster of the live-action movie *G.I. Joe: The Rise of Cobra*, 2009.

"Arise, Serpentor, Arise!" Cobra scientist Doctor Mindbender uses DNA from history's nastiest conquerors to genetically engineer the villain to end all villains. Though the series concluded in 1986, *G.I. Joe: The Movie* was released a year later in 1987, with another miniseries following in 1989. Twenty years later, the live-action film, *G.I Joe: The Rise of Cobra* (2009) was released.

Despite its appeal among kids during the series' run, the 1985 holiday season witnessed a parental movement against military-themed toys. In particular, the International War Toys Boycott staged a pretend funeral against the action figures. Story editor Buzz Dixon noted in a 1986 *Comics Interview*, "There has always been a tie-in between animation and merchandising, or between everything and merchandising. I think, to say you can't do it because it's for children, or you can't do it because you're going to be manipulating the children. This is baloney. If you have a good product, a product that is interesting to the child and the child wants it, then the child will go for it. If they don't want it, you can't shove it down their throats." Dixon's theory seemed vindicated by the National Coalition on Television Violence. According to this organization, sales of war toys increased by 350 percent between 1982 and 1985, accounting for $842 million in sales each year.

Based on these statistics and the show's high ratings, the success of *G.I. Joe*'s programming can't be denied. Its popularity not only propelled the beloved toy line into a money making machine for Hasbro, it also spawned multiple iterations of its characters through miniseries, crossover shows, video games, and big-budget live-action movies. Despite the many controversies *G.I. Joe* sparked, the cartoon connected with kids who were eager to reimagine the cartoon stories with their own toy versions of Duke, Baroness, Destro, Scarlett, Leatherneck, and Beach Head. So, now you know *G.I. Joe*. And knowing is half the battle.

ABOVE LEFT: Screenwriter Ron Friedman.

ABOVE RIGHT: G.I. Joe Team members, including Cover Girl, race into action in the episode "The Cobra Strikes."

Creating "A Real American Hero"

Screenwriter Ron Friedman drafted the stories and personalities that shaped the G.I Joes into something more than just small plastic figures.

"I was brilliant enough to make sure I grew up when the Golden Age of comic books started: *Batman*, *Superman*, *The Sub-Mariner*, *Plastic Man*, *Captain Marvel* were literally hot off the presses, and I was ready for them . . . I quickly developed a hunger for action-adventure, science-fiction, mystery, historical novels so I was ready for all those comic books, and Big Little Books, and movie serials—and movies, all kinds of movies—the works!

"I always loved stories in which the protagonists seemed to share the same worldview, the same sense of responsibility, the same sense of deciding what needed to be done, and then doing it no matter what—like a loving family acting in harmony with affec-tion for one another, accepting of differences. So, I always tried to depict important characters in family groupings . . . I gave the good guys a warm sense of humor. The Joes could kid one another and the bad guys—Cobras didn't kid, they insulted, defamed, plotted against one another, and castigated each other relentlessly and ruthlessly. But the touchstone was—and is—FAMILY.

"I was given shrink-wrapped little action figures of both Joe and Cobra characters and planes, tanks, etc. On the cardboard backs of the wrappings were brief—I mean brief—character biogra-phies, i.e., Snake Eyes, blind and mute with martial-arts mastery, etc. To help in the process, I vocally modeled and recorded many new Joe characters to ensure the right actors would be cast, and their voice qualities would help 'sell' their individuality. For Shipwreck, I did a Jack Nicholson impression, which appeared in a miniseries, and later in the daily stripping series. In short, I was given great plastic toys into whom I blew the breath of life . . .

ABOVE: Cobra members stand united in "The Further Adventures of G.I. Joe."

"With so many characters to 'service,' that is, provide with 'face time' on screen, and action sequences geared to their special abilities, I knew my story lines would have to provide opportunities to 'pair characters up' in small teams: two, maybe three, or occasionally four, or more Joes or Cobras on a specific, limited assignment or mission that was part of the larger, all involving (a) story, that is the central conflict pitting Joes against Cobras. Consequently, I created the 'Quest Format,' which enabled me to do what I just described, and keep the story pot boiling on high heat throughout . . . satisfying action-packed, storytelling sequences that pleased an enormous worldwide audience of tens of millions by giving an exciting, even thrilling victory to the good guys. I am proud of that accomplishment.

"I never tried to let [fans] down. I always wished to entertain—to make it clear why what was good was always better than what was bad. I wanted [you] to know that [you] must never, never, never give up on yourselves."

Disney's Adventures of the Gummi Bears

YEARS ON AIR

1985–1991

NETWORK

NBC, ABC

NUMBER OF EPISODES

65

CHARACTERS AND VOICE ACTORS

Gruffi Gummi: Bill Scott
Zummi Gummi: Paul Winchell
Grammi Gummi: June Foray
Cavin: Christian Jacobs
Cubbi Gummy: Noelle North
Tummi Gummi: Lorenzo Music
Sunni Gummi: Katie Leigh
Duke Igthorn: Michael Rye

To folks from a different generation, "gummy bears" might mean brightly colored, chewy candies. But to kids who grew up in the '80s, the *Gummi Bears* were the lost members of an ancient race possessing wisdom, advanced technological know-how, and magical lore. Yes, the show was based on the candy, but that is where the similarities ended. Disney CEO Michael Eisner conceived of *Disney's*

Adventures of the Gummi Bears after his son requested the candies one day.

As Jymn Magon, who would be promoted to cocreator and story editor for the show, explained, "I've told this story numerous times and I still can't believe it happened this way. When Michael Eisner took over the company, he asked to meet with a bunch of 'creative types' in his new TV animation department . . . A bunch of us (six or eight, I think) met at Eisner's Beverly Hills home on a Sunday morning . . . Michael mentioned that his kids had eaten this great new candy at summer camp–Gummy Bears. Then, he turned to me–a total unknown, and said, 'Make me a show about that.'"

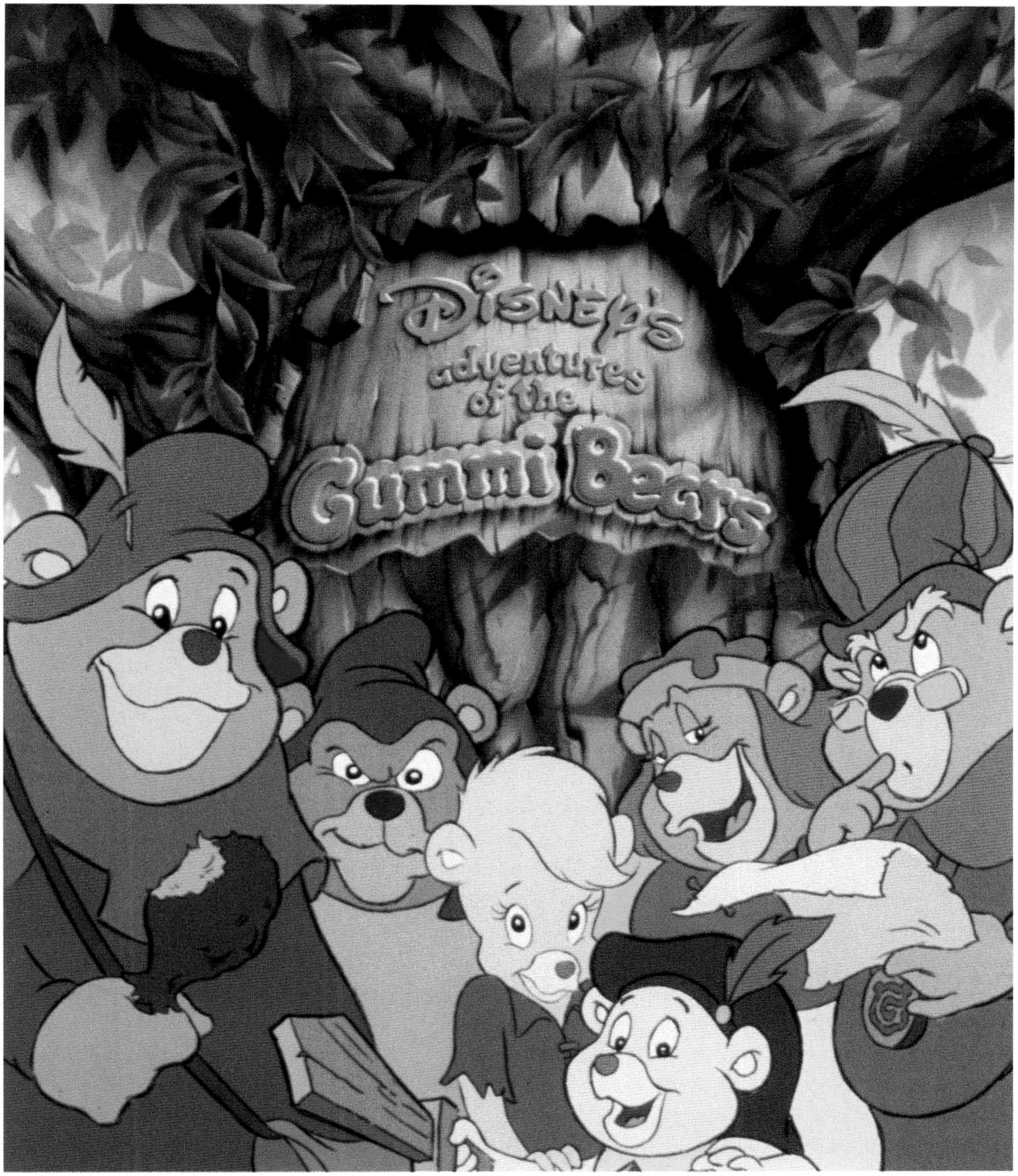
Disney's
adventures
of the
Gummi Bears

When Art Vitello, Jymn Magon and the rest of the production team at Walt Disney Television Animation first went to work executing Eisner's vision, it didn't turn out so well. The initial concept featured a villain named Licorice Whip and sidekick Scummi Gummi. "Who the heck makes a show about characters that get eaten?" Magon wondered. Deciding to scrap the "Candy Land" idea, he drew fresh inspiration from J.R.R. Tolkien, inventing the hollow-tree-living Gummies, such as Gruffi Gummi, the old-fashioned patriarch; Sunni Gummi, the preteen who dreams of being a princess; and Gusto Gummi, the iconoclast artist. ". . . We started thinking of the classic Disney movies, like *Snow White and the Seven Dwarfs* and *Sleeping Beauty*," explains Magon. "These [tales] were set in a European, medieval fantasy world. That seemed like a safe route to go (because we had never made

OPPOSITE: Sunni, Zummi, and Chummi take flight to escape the Carpies in the episode "A Gummi in a Gilded Cage."

TOP: Promotional image for *Disney's Adventures of the Gummi Bears.*

a TV show before) and so castles and knights crept into the development."

Magon's idea to pursue a Tolkienesque narrative worked. When *Gummi Bears* first appeared in the fall of 1985, the series resonated with viewers drawn to its medieval narrative. In the show, the Gummies had fled their home after humans, jealous of their magical skills, forced them into exile. For years, no one believed Gummies even existed. Then one day, a boy named Cavin, owning a Gummi Medallion from his grandfather, stumbled into Gummi Glen, the Gummies' underground colony in the kingdom of Dunywn. Housing just seven Gummies, these bears made up the last members of a once vast tribe that lived on Earth. Though a human, Cavin put the Gummies at ease and they offered him Gummiberry juice, their secret potion that made drinkers "bounce here and there and everywhere." To the Gummies' surprise, Cavin's medallion unlocked the *Great Book of Gummi*, revealing forgotten knowledge. With the help of Cavin and some other good-natured humans, the Gummies embarked on a quest to regain their lost heritage while combating their nemesis, Duke Igthorn, a renegade noble, and his evil ogre army.

This rich Gummi mythology, combined with the show's high entertainment value, propelled *Gummi Bears* into a global success. Though it may be hard to remember a time when Disney wasn't as massive a media company as it is today, *Gummi Bears* was one of Disney's initial forays into serialized animated television. The risk paid off handsomely. The program was renewed for more episodes over the next six consecutive seasons; *Gummi Bears* also spurred a Sunday morning comic strip, which ran from 1986 through 1989.

Almost as memorable as the show itself was its theme song. Written by Michael and Patty Silversher and performed by Joseph Williams, son of composer John Williams, the theme song's catchy tune and lyrics stuck in children's heads:

High adventure that's beyond compare
They are the Gummi Bears
They are the Gummi Bears!

Gummi Bears mania didn't stop with the music, either. The show's popularity led Disney to briefly rename one of their Disneyland rides the "Motorboat Cruise to Gummi Glen," from March to November, 1991.

The longevity of the show wasn't for lack of competition. Saturday morning cartoon programming in 1985 was awash with other anthropomorphic bear shows, including *The Berenstain Bears* and *Care Bears*. *Disney's Wuzzles*, a concurrently released cartoon program, also about adorable animal creatures, only lasted a mere thirteen episodes, meanwhile *Gummi Bears* managed to maintain a significant pawhold on its position on Saturday morning.

Gummi Bears churned out new story lines, generating more fans as its influence spread with merchandising, such as read-along books, color and activity books, plush toys, figures, stamps, stickers, clothing, bouncers, and cereal prizes. The show's commercial success would pave the way for Disney's eventual and successful afternoon time slot, featuring hit '90s fare like *DuckTales*, *TaleSpin*, and *Gargoyles*. In fact *Gargoyles* cocreator Greg Weisman said, "We set out very consciously to create a show like *Gummi Bears* with that kind of rich backstory and mythology to it . . . So we did a couple things right off the bat with that in mind. One was, instead of cute little multicolored bears, we did cute little multicolored gargoyles!"

Whether it was the *Gummi*'s lengthy run or its impact on other shows, much of the cartoon's success is owed to its creative direction, its fairy-tale whimsicalness, and elaborate world building. It also didn't hurt that voice actors Bill Scott and June Foray of *Rocky and Bullwinkle* fame lent their voices for the characters of Gruffi and Grammi. In spite of its simple candy origins, Magon and his team fulfilled Eisner's dream to generate a show with heart and depth. "I don't remember there being an edict from on high stating, 'You'd better not screw this up!'" explained Magon. "But we all knew we were stepping into an arena that was dominated by studios like Hanna-Barbera, Filmation, and such. As it turned out, we ended up raising the bar for what Saturday morning shows looked like."

ABOVE: The Gummi Bears in Gummi Glen.

The Secret of Gummiberry Juice

The mysterious Gummiberry Juice gave the Gummies their ability to bounce, and it was also what led to the downfall in their relations with humans. The secret to the potion was revealed in the episode "The Secret of the Juice," in which Grammi Gummi teaches Sunni Gummi the treasured recipe. It called for six handfuls of red berries, four orange berries, three purple berries, four blue berries, three green berries, and one yellow berry. Then all the berries were mixed with a three-step stir: First to the right, then to the left. Last they had to "bang the pot to banish the bubbles." Now, get bouncin'.

ThunderCats

YEARS ON AIR

1985–1989

NETWORK

Syndication

NUMBER OF EPISODES

130

CHARACTERS AND VOICE ACTORS

Lion-O: Larry Kenney
Panthro: Earle Hyman
Jaga: Earl Hammond
Cheetara/Wilykat: Lynne Lipton
Snarf: Bob McFadden
Tygra/Bengali:
Peter Newman
Lynx-O: Doug Preis
Mum-Ra: Earl Hammond

Thunder, thunder, thunder, ThunderCats, ho!

Of all the '80s Saturday morning cartoons, *ThunderCats* may have been the weirdest, most out-there premise for a show. The concept sprang from the mind of Tobin "Ted" Wolf, a toy inventor with several patents, including an early form of a portable record player. Janice Wolf, Tobin's daughter, recalls fleshing out his humanoid cat people idea together. "We sat around the table creating the characters . . . It was a morality play with superheroes." With his characters somewhat developed, Ted Wolf then took his concept to friend Stan Weston, president of Leisure Concepts, Inc. Weston liked it enough to bring it to Rankin-Bass Animated Entertainment, who went on to distribute the series. Though written, produced, and voice acted in the US, Japanese studio Pacific Animation Corporation created the stunning illustrations.

Being animated halfway across the world meant the visual style differed from most other Saturday morning cartoons. "The style of animation was beautifully Japanese; it was anime," said supervising producer Lee Dannacher. "It was even before American audiences fell in love with anime." Ryan Lambie, deputy editor for Den of Geek, believes the introduction to *ThunderCats* is "one of the greatest pieces of animation ever produced. A level of care and pure love has gone into this seventy-second scene that only becomes clear when you start to look at individual frames. If you don't believe me, head to YouTube and watch the opening again at the slowest possible speed. Only then can you start to see some of the stunning moments that only appear on the screen for a fraction of a second."

Again, the visuals had a distinct Japanese style, but the dramatic narrative and characters were dominated by western-style storytelling. "*ThunderCats* was done with an American comic book sensibility," said animation historian Jerry Beck. "And it really comes through with the kind of stories and imagination on that show."

That imaginative concept focused on a posse of muscular humanoids with feline traits, who were forced to flee their home planet Thundera after the ancient devil priest Mumm-Ra destroyed it. In transit, their ship was attacked by the Mutants of Plun-Darr

OPPOSITE: ThunderCats work as a team: (left to right) Panthro, Lion-O, Tygra, Cheetara.

TOP: Cheetara wields her staff.

BOTTOM: Lion-O brandishes his Sword of Omens.

TOP: Panthro shows off his powerful strength, lifting S-S-Slithe over his head as Lion-O (far left) and Wilykit and Wilykat (far right) look on.

in an attempt to seize the mystical and mighty Sword of Omens. This sword contained the Eye of Thundera, the source of the ThunderCats' power. The ship's journey was so long the crew slept in capsules over "ten galacto years" of space flight. Upon landing and erecting their "cat's lair" headquarters, the Mutants, in tandem with the evil Mumm-Ra, descend on the ThunderCats to once again trying to steal the Eye of Thundera. Thereafter, the ThunderCats must battle these wicked forces so as not to lose control of Third Earth.

If the plot sounds bizarre and complex, the characters were equally unusual. When the ThunderCat leader Lion-O first went into suspended animation, he was twelve years old. When he awoke eons later, his chamber had slowed, rather than stopped his aging, making him an impulsive child in the body of a man. The more rational and stronger Panthro—voiced by Earle Hyman, best known as Grandfather Russell Huxtable from *The Cosby Show*—often had to help Lion-O make important decisions. The rest of the group consisted of Tygra, a male tiger-based character, who possessed the ability to create illusions with his mind and had a whip that could turn him invisible; Cheetara, a female leader who was extremely fast and could shoot telekinetic bursts

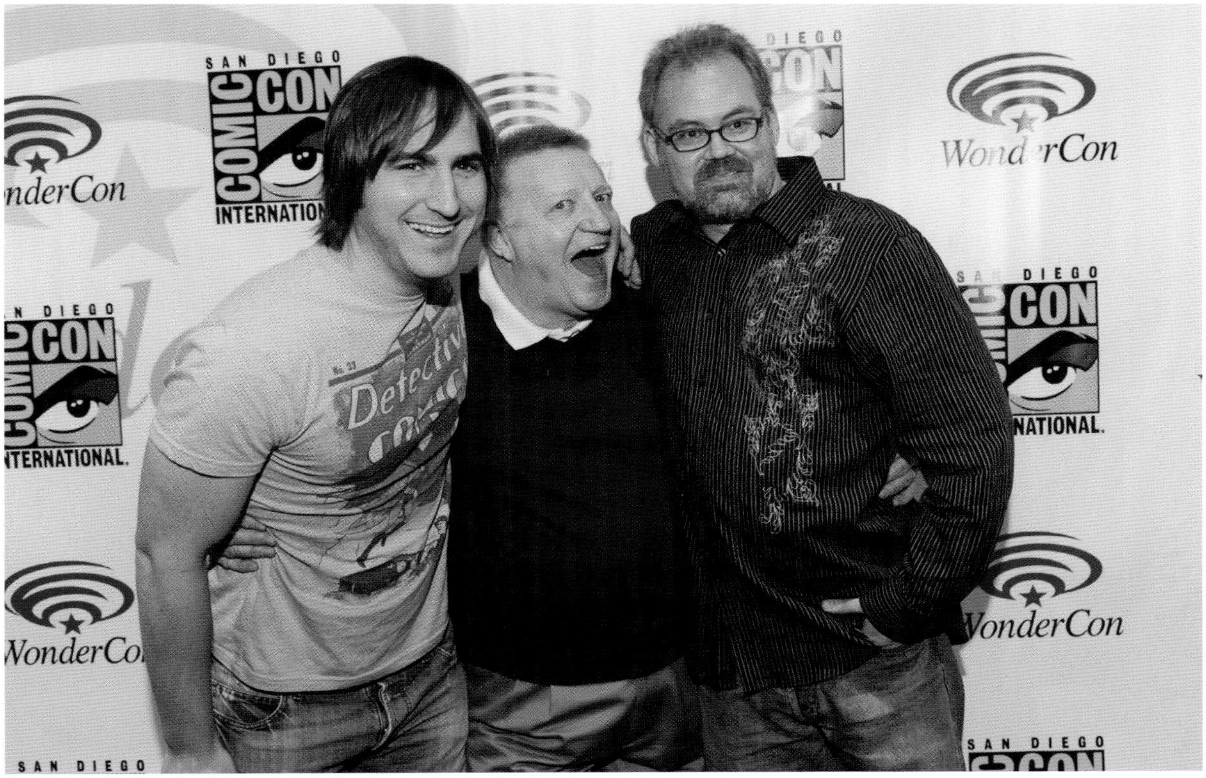
SAN DIEGO
COMIC CON
INTERNATIONAL.
WonderCon

TOP: *ThunderCats* executive producers Michael Jelenic (left) and Ethan Spaulding (right) and cast member Larry Kenney (center) pose together at Wondercon, 2011.

of energy; Bengali, a blue-and-white striped blacksmith; the mischievous twins Wilykat and Wilykit; and Lynx-O, who was blind but also the wisest of them all.

In addition to the considerable amount of care put into crafting the entirely original backstory and characters, a great deal of attention was spent crafting its positive social messaging. Executive producer Arthur Rankin Jr. utilized child psychologist Robert Kusis, PhD, to blend morals into the narratives. Kuisis was tasked with reviewing each script to prevent the introduction of harmful content and to ensure each episode possessed positive messaging. Lynne Lipton, who voiced Cheetara, said, "I think one of the amazing things was the beauty of the art. The richness of the cartoon. . . . It had an innocence and a wholesome message. There were good guys and bad guys . . . It [was] all of the things that send that message—that have a moral value to it."

Over the span of four years, *ThunderCats* produced a whopping 130 episodes. In fact, the series influenced the cultural zeitgeist so profoundly by 1987 that according to the Social Security Administration, dozens of parents were naming their daughters Cheetara. *ThunderCats* left the Saturday morning cartoons lineup in 1989, but its legacy prompted Cartoon Network to reboot the show in 2011 with development by Warner Bros. When creator Ted Wolf passed away in Honolulu, Hawaii, in 1999, cards poured in from fans around the world. Even today, there are still many websites filled with fans eagerly discussing the beloved show. In a sea of cartoon ingenuity, *ThunderCats* reigns supreme as a one-of-its-kind delight.

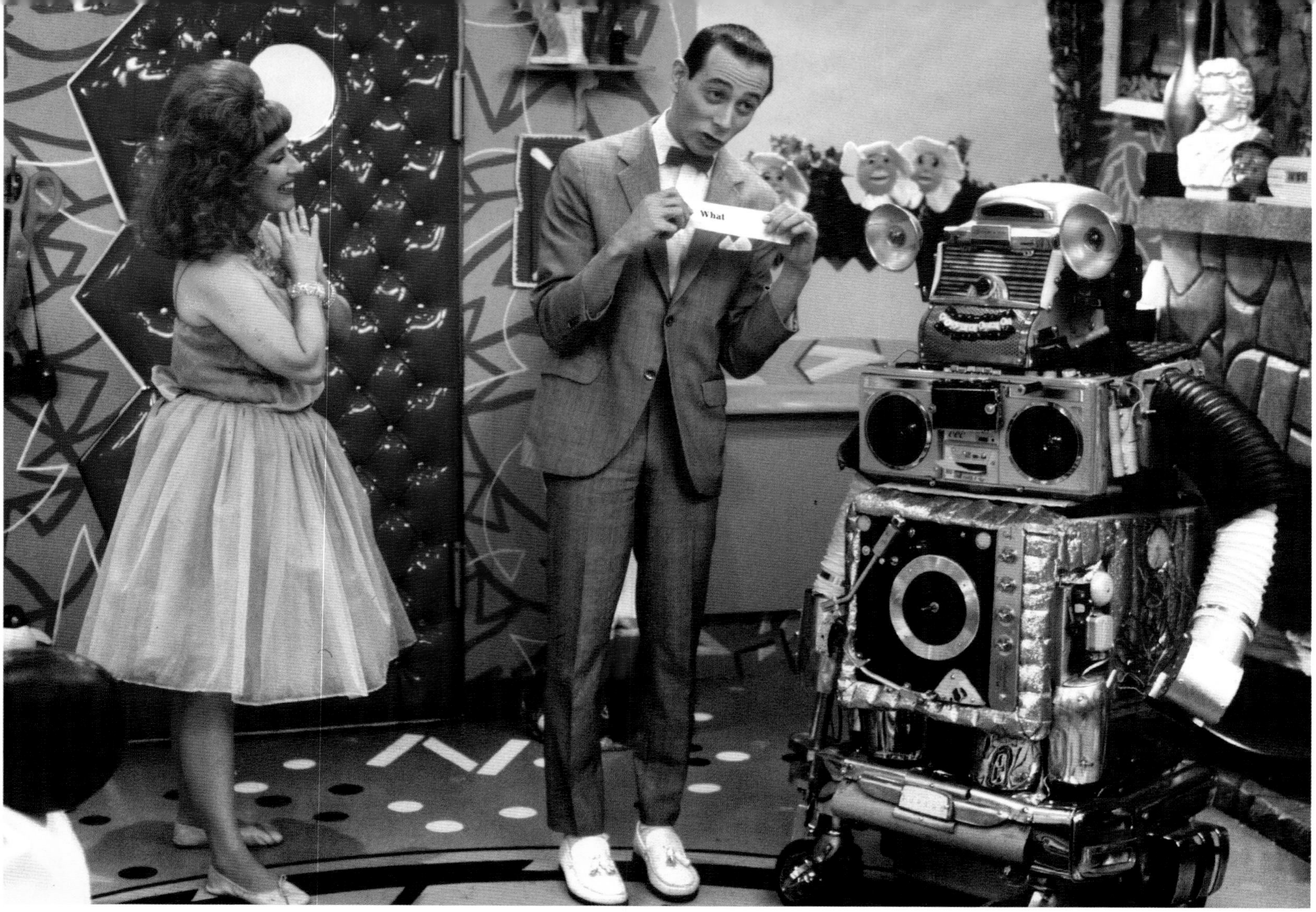
What

YEARS ON AIR

1986–1990

NETWORK

CBS

NUMBER OF EPISODES

46

CHARACTERS AND VOICE ACTORS

Pee-wee Herman: Paul Reubens
Globey: George McGrath
Cowboy Curtis:
Laurence Fishburne
Chairry: Alison Mork
Jambi: John Paragon
Captain Carl: Phil Hartman
Conky: Kevin Carlson

Pee-wee's Playhouse

It's hard to convey the sheer force of Pee-wee hysteria in the '80s. The character of Pee-wee Herman, played by Paul Reubens, catapulted into national consciousness as a wholly original personality in the movie *Pee-wee's Big Adventure* (1985). Defying expectations and earning cult-classic status, the bow-tie wearing, slim-suited Pee-wee hovered somewhere between man and child, normal and off-the-wall crazy. In a move that only perpetuated hysteria, Reubens furthered the notion of his alter ego's existence by listing Pee-wee Herman as playing "himself" in the show's credits.

If Pee-wee is difficult to pin down, his inventive show was equally hard to fit into any box—or recognizable universe. "In the playhouse, anthropomorphized food cavorted inside Pee-wee's refrigerator, the armchair gave out hugs, and even the windows and floors were puppets with plenty to say," noted Jonah Weaver in an article he wrote for the *New York Times Magazine*. Along the same lines, in a 1987

Rolling Stone article, T. Gertler wrote, "His playhouse, which might be the collision of *The Cabinet of Dr. Caligari* with a raspberry-and-lime Jell-O mold constructed by Disney technicians recovering from Taiwan flu, is crammed wall to wall with toys and tchotchkes reminiscent of every flea market, swap meet, garage sale and New Wave gallery between SoHo and Sausalito."

OPPOSITE: Cast members Paul Reubens as Pee-wee Herman and Lynne Marie Stewart as Miss Yvonne receive the Word of the Day from Conky 2000, the robot, 1986.

TOP: Pee-wee gets ready to take a spin around the clubhouse.

Perhaps the best way to break down the series is to call it a kind of vaudeville/variety show that incorporated elements of storytelling, music, puppetry, and animation. The show's quirky nature and surreal characters championed individuality. "I'm just trying to illustrate that it's okay to be different—not that it's good, not that it's bad, but that it's all right," said Reubens. "I'm trying to tell kids to have a good time and to encourage them to be creative and to question things. I think to be an individual is a difficult thing."

Reubens began crafting the highly individualistic character in 1977, as a part of the Groundlings improv group. "The name came from a kid I knew who was kind of off-the-wall," explained Reubens. "The name 'Pee-wee' came from a little harmonica I had that said 'Pee-wee' on it. I loved the idea of a nickname, because it sounded so real to me. 'Pee-wee Herman' sounds like a name that is so odd, how would you make that up?"

TOP: At the end of the every episode, Pee-wee Herman blasted out of his house wearing this awesome helmet.

After honing his alter ego with the Groundlings, Reubens achieved some success in Hollywood with the "Pee-wee Herman Show," an LA theater piece that went on to become an HBO special. This led to a series of live performances on the college club circuit and *Late Night with David Letterman*. But Reubens got his biggest break of all with his movie, *Pee-wee's Big Adventure*. Though it cost around $6 million to produce, it earned approximately $45 million domestically, opening the door for him to launch his Howdy-Doody–type variety show on CBS.

According to Gertler, CBS was willing to grant Reubens everything he wanted so long as he agreed to three things: "(1) Pee-wee should not stick pencils in potatoes; (2) Pee-wee should not emerge from the bathroom with a trail of toilet paper sticking to his shoe; (3) Pee-wee should not say, in the context of a certain presumably innocent scene, "I'll show you mine if you'll show me yours." Ever the iconoclast, Reubens did all three things over the course of the series.

Upon assuming full creative control from the network, Reubens set out to make his dream show.

He recruited talent from his Groundlings improv days, casting Laurence Fishburne as Cowboy Curtis, Phil Hartman as Captain Carl, Lynne Marie Stewart as Miss Yvonne, John Paragon as Jambi, and S. Epatha Merkerson as Reba. Soon after, taping began in a converted loft on Broadway for the exorbitant budget of $325,000 an episode. To put that number in context, most Saturday morning cartoons cost $250,000 per episode. "Why shouldn't Saturday-morning children's programs be just as expensive as the things we watch at night?" said Reubens, who reportedly funded the show out of his personal bank account whenever production costs ran over.

Though both kids and adults could appreciate different aspects of the elaborately produced series, it didn't take off right away. According to Gertler, "At first, ratings for the show, while respectable, didn't match critics' and wide receivers' enthusiasm." However, once *Pee-wee's Playhouse* moved to an earlier time slot, it picked up steam. "[By then] the *Playhouse* had established itself among the top Saturday-morning shows in households with children aged two to eleven—the target group for kid-vid advertisers pushing toys and glucose."

Perhaps audiences of all ages gravitated to the show because Pee-wee's mannerisms seemed downright cartoonish. Episodes such as "Pajama Party," veered into bizarre, hilarious territory. After proclaiming his love for fruit salad, Pee-wee's friends ask him, "If you love it so much, why don't you marry it?" Pee-wee being Pee-wee, he did just that, arranging a

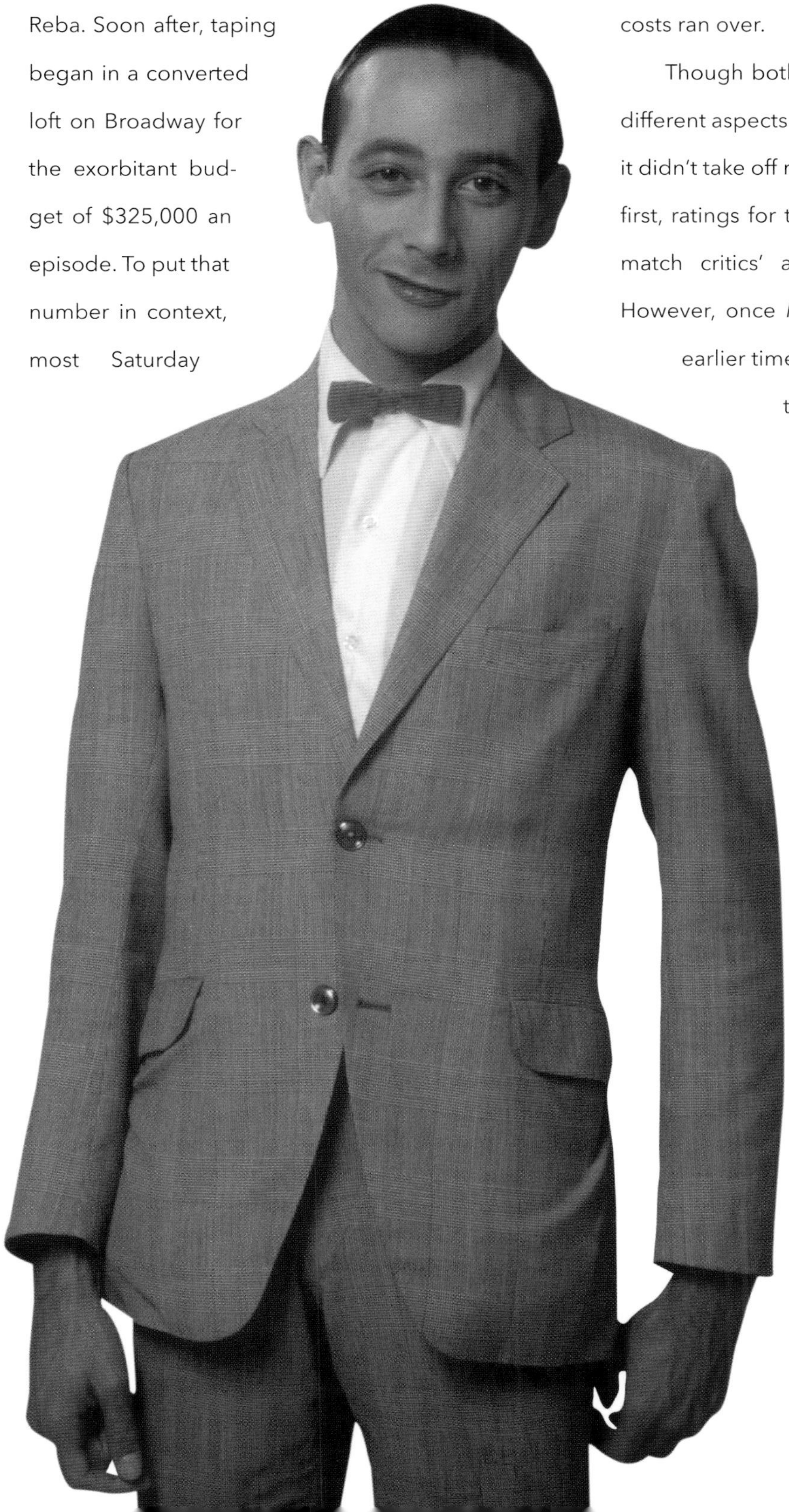

LEFT: Pee-wee Herman in his signature suit and red bow tie, circa 1980.

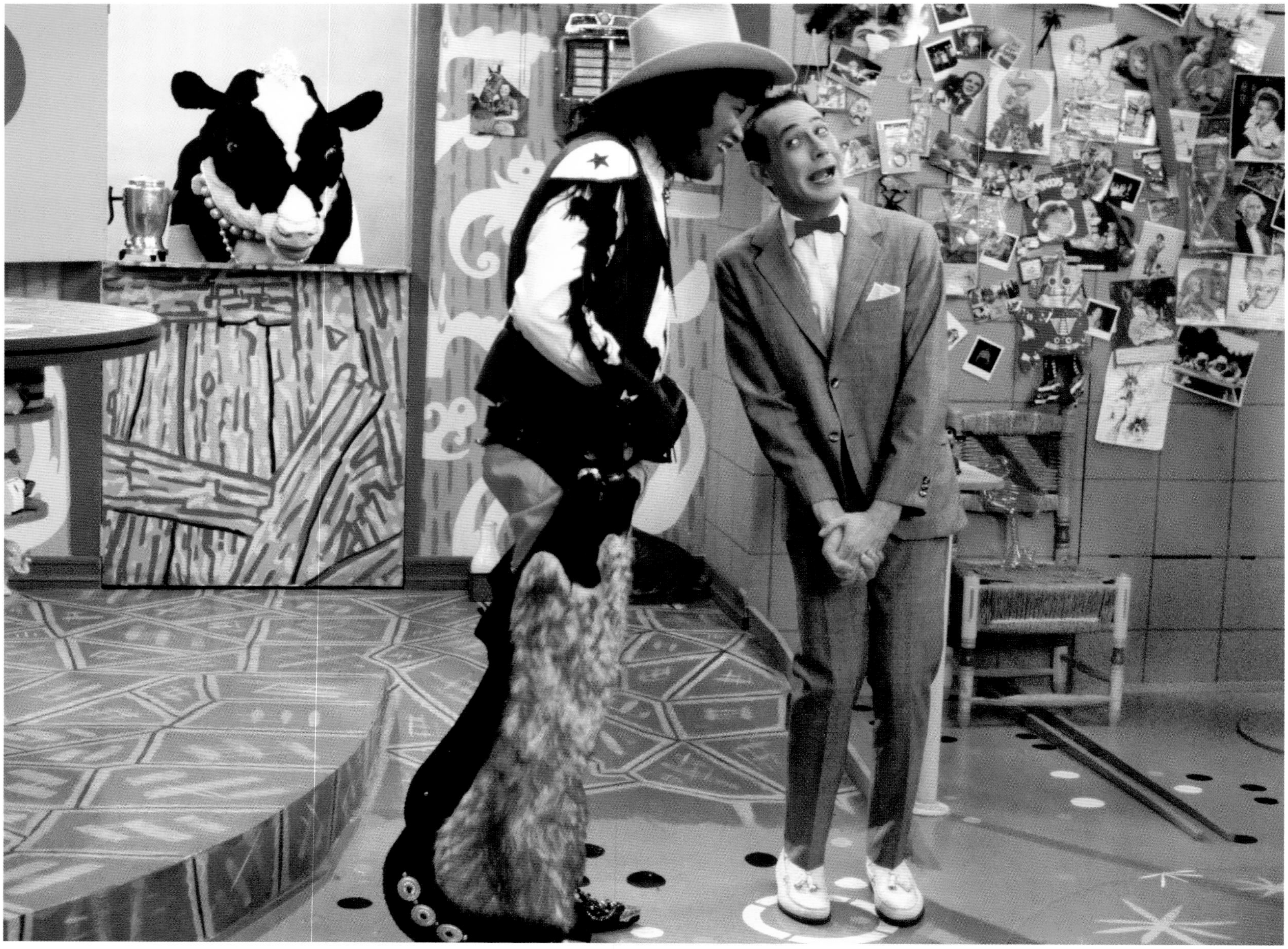

ABOVE: Paul Rubens as Pee-wee Herman with Laurence Fishburne as Cowboy Curtis, 1986.

OPPOSITE: Pee-wee takes a call in the Picture Phone booth.

wedding ceremony in which he tied the knot with his veil-wearing fruit-salad bowl. Outlandish tom-foolery, coupled with elements of adult humor, provided something for everyone. Over its five seasons, the show won fifteen Emmy® Awards and *TV Guide* ranked *Pee-wee's Playhouse* as no. 10 of the *Top Cult Shows Ever* in 2004 and number twelve in 2007. The show's stop-animation segment, "The Penny Cartoons," also provided the inspiration for the 2005 Oscar-winning film, *Wallace & Gromit: The Curse of the Were-Rabbit*.

Receiving such acclaim, it's no wonder the series made a significant impact on the cultural zeitgeist. Credited with helping to launch the careers of Hartman and Fishburne, *Pee-wee's Playhouse* also offered a training ground for production assistants John Singleton, director of *Boyz n the Hood*, and Rob Zombie, heavy metal rocker and filmmaker.

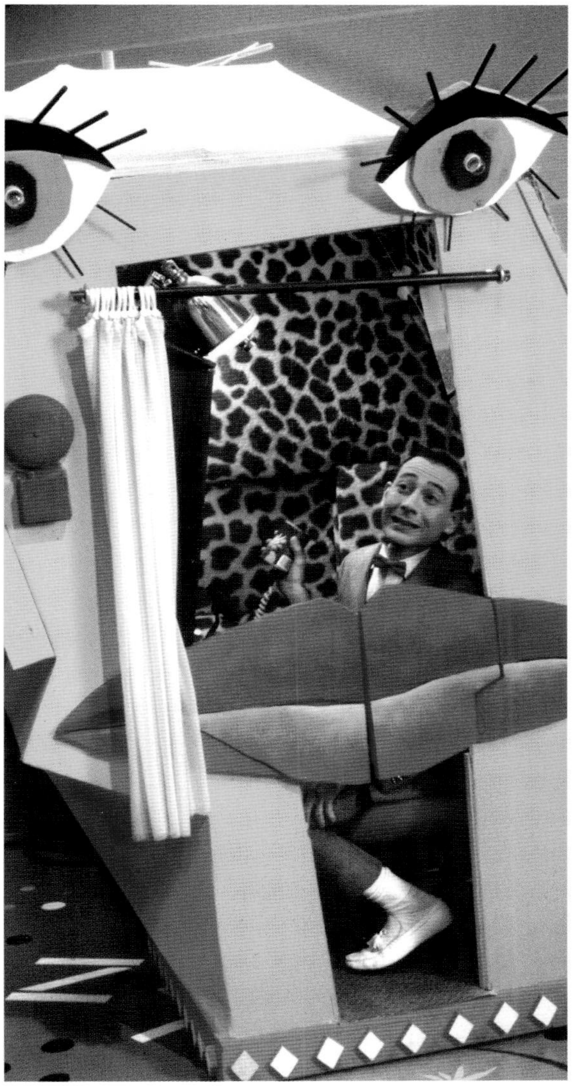

For a while, Pee-wee mania was unstoppable. People everywhere were imitating and quoting Pee-wee—*"I know you are, but what am I?"* The season three all-star *Christmas Special* drew celebrity appearances from the likes of Dinah Shore, Joan Rivers, Oprah, Whoopi Goldberg, Little Richard, Cher, Grace Jones, and many others. Meanwhile, Pee-wee-related merchandise flourished, with offerings from bedsheets and lunch boxes to Topps trading cards and the coveted Pee-wee doll, which sold more than a million units.

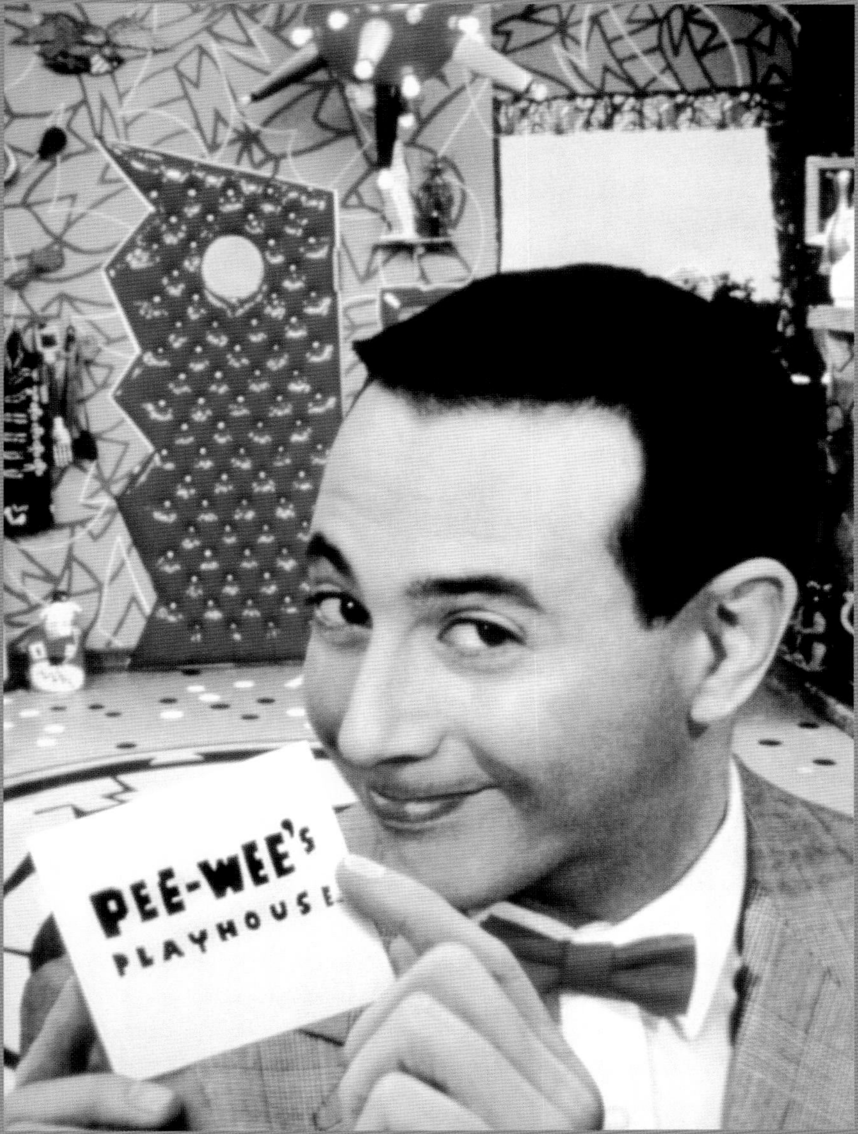
PEE-WEE'S
PLAYHOUSE

ABOVE: Paul Ruben poses on set in this promotional image for *Pee-wee's Playhouse*.

The Quotable Pee-wee Herman

No doubt about it. Pee-wee Herman had a plethora of famous lines that permeated pop culture. Here are some zingers:

I know you are, but what am I?

That's my name. Don't wear it out.

Why don't you take a picture? It'll last longer.

I meant do that.

Connect the dots, la la la la. Connect the dots, la la la la.

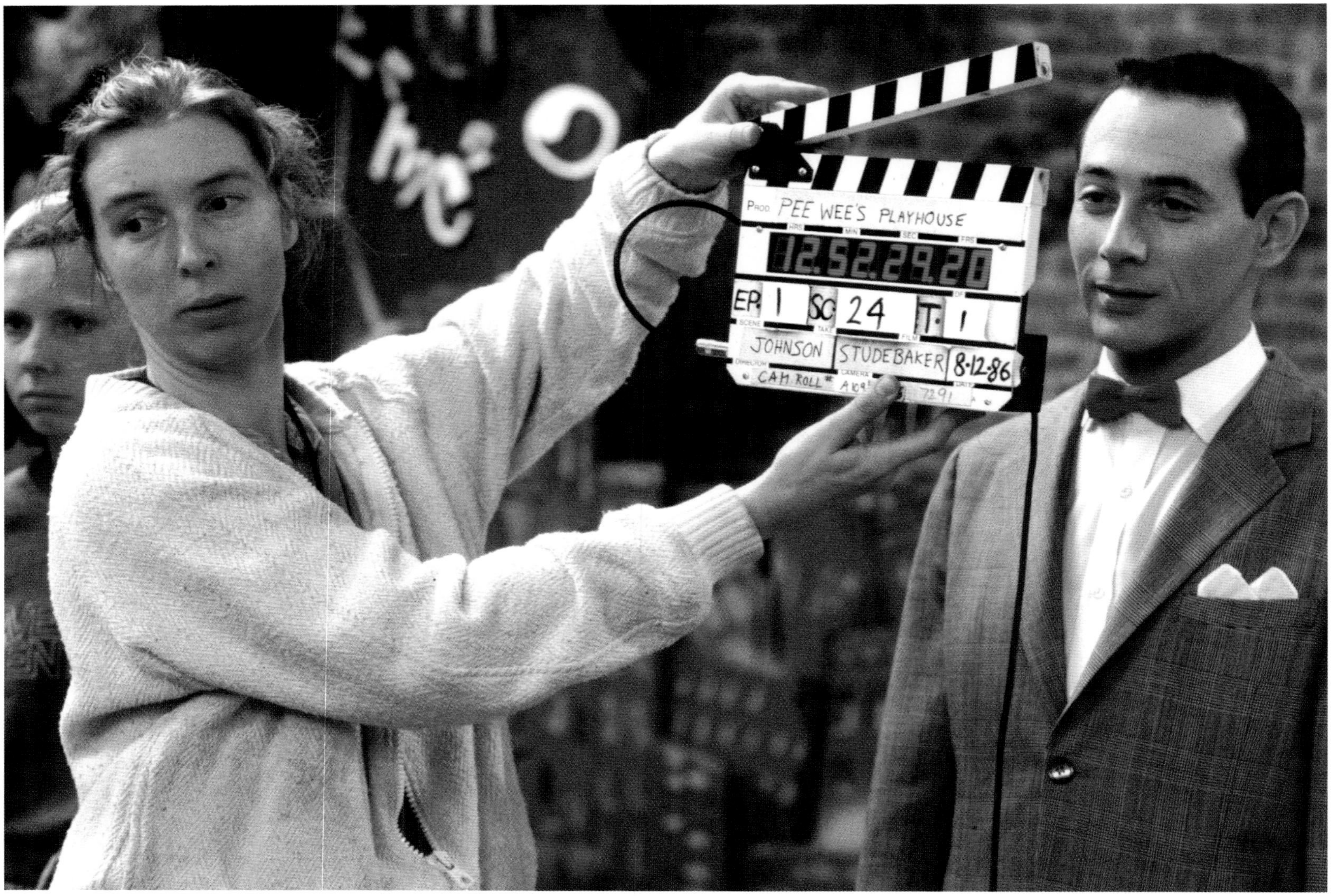
PEE WEE'S PLAYHOUSE
12.52.29.20
EP. 1 SC 24 T. 1
JOHNSON
STUDEBAKER
8-12-86
CAM ROLL

ABOVE: Paul Reubens gets ready for 'Action!' in 1986.

Years after the series ended, Pee-wee's influence is still alive. Director Judd Apatow was greatly impacted by Pee-wee as a young man—so much so that in 2016, Apatow produced *Pee-wee's Big Holiday*, featuring an older Reubens reprising his role in a film about taking a journey through the eyes of a grown-up kid. "When I was younger, I didn't put my finger on why I liked Pee-wee so much—it just made me laugh," said Apatow. "But looking back, it's a group of strange people who are having a great time and being really nice to each other, and as a slightly weird kid I must have understood that. I liked watching someone so different whom the audience loved. The idea that unique people were getting applause, that the crowd was going crazy for Pee-wee, made me feel you didn't have to be the football-team quarterback."

Reubens achieved his goal of truly celebrating individually. Pee-wee made kids' wishes come true with the weirdest show possible. Or as Jambi might say, "*Mekka Lekka Hi, Mekka Hiney Ho.*"

Teddy Ruxpin

"Hi, my name is Teddy Ruxpin. Can you and I be friends?" said the stuffed animal at a show-and-tell to a classroom of children in the 1980s commercial.

Working in animatronics for Sid & Marty Krofft Entertainment proved to be the ideal training ground for inventor Ken Forsse, who went on to create 1985 and 1986's best-selling toy: the storytelling bear. Utilizing cassette-tape-player technology, and voiced by Phil Baron of *Welcome to Pooh Corner* fame, Teddy Ruxpin could giggle, yawn, and ask questions. He would later appear in his own TV show, *The Adventures of Teddy Ruxpin*.

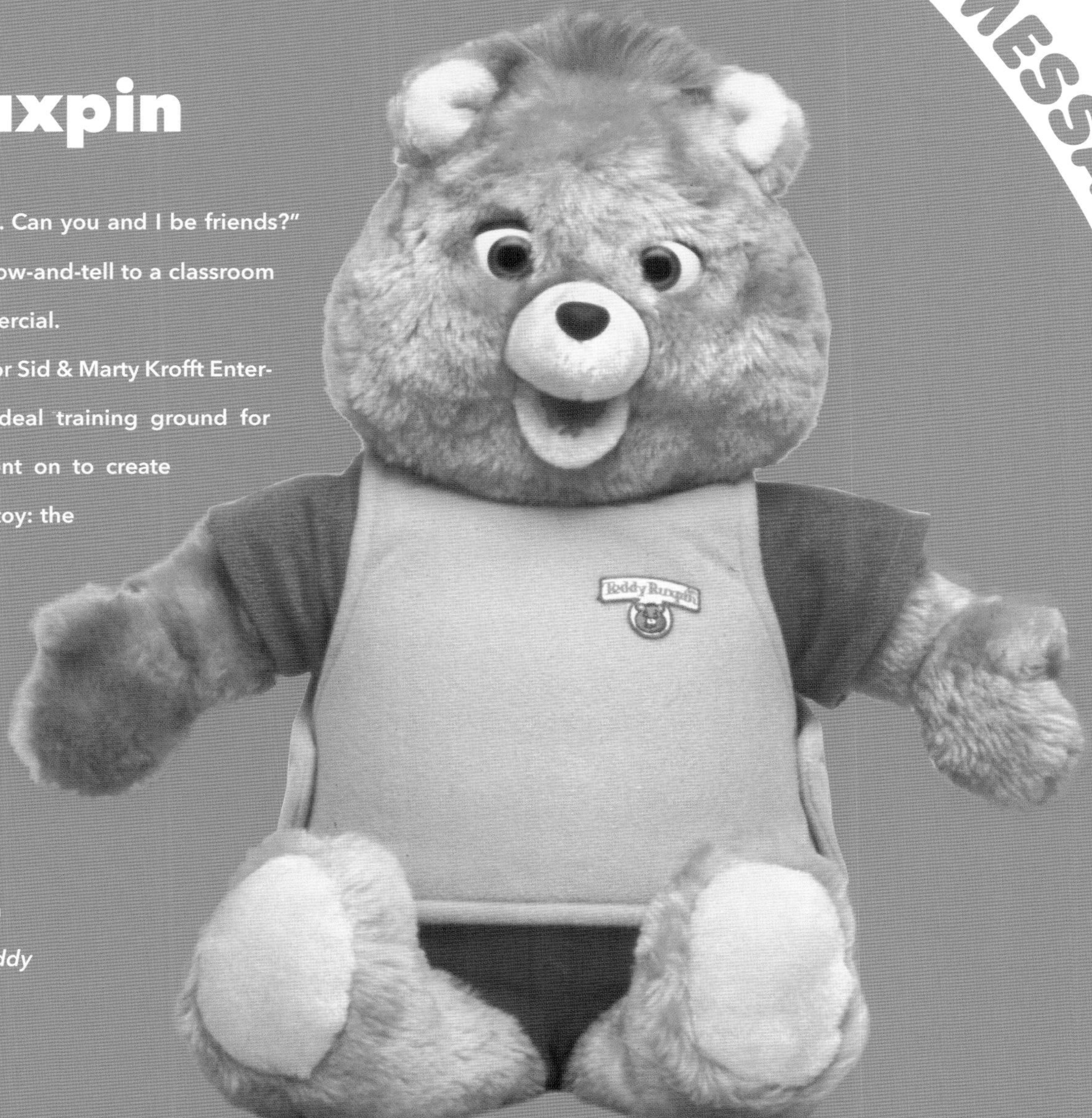
Teddy Ruxpin

RIGHT: The Teddy Ruxpin bear was first released in September 1985.

Garfield and Friends

YEARS ON AIR

1988-1994

NETWORK

CBS

NUMBER OF EPISODES

121 (363 segments)

CHARACTERS AND VOICE ACTORS

Garfield: Lorenzo Music
Jon Arbuckle: Thom Huge
Odie: Gregg Berger
Nermal: Desirée Goyette
Bo: Frank Welker
Wade Duck: Howard Morris
Lanolin: Julie Payne

America's favorite overweight feline curmudgeon, Garfield mastered the subtle art of not giving a crap. Debuting as a comic strip in 1978 through United Feature Syndicate, his presence expanded from forty newspapers to two thousand within a decade. Why? Garfield did and said what he pleased. "We learned early on that Garfield would say what we don't have the courage to say," said cartoonist and creator Jim Davis. "More often than not, when people laugh at the *Garfield* strip and laugh at Garfield, it's because

they're saying, 'Isn't that true?' They see a little bit of themselves in it, and once, I think, if I can get a reader to see a little bit of themselves, see their own lives in the feature, then that helps develop affection and it resonates with the reader."

Unapologetic and hilarious, the *Garfield* comic quickly became a fan favorite. In fact, it presently holds the Guinness World Record for "longest widely syndicated comic strip." At the beginning of what would become its incredibly lengthy run, the

comic caught the attention of CBS producer Lee Mendelson, who in 1980 approached Davis about creating a TV special. "The special on the comics was very well received," said Davis. "Back then, there were only three networks! It was a really big deal when CBS called back. We thought that we'd arrived."

Following Davis's association with CBS, a heap of TV specials aired, including *Here Comes Garfield* (1982), which was nominated for a Primetime Emmy® Award for Outstanding Animated Program; *Garfield on the Town* (1983); *Garfield in Paradise* (1986),

which was also nominated for the same Emmy®; and *Garfield's Halloween Adventure* (1985), which did win the Emmy®. Initially produced by Film Roman, and in association with United Feature Syndicate and Paws, Inc., the Saturday morning cartoon series launched in 1988 with Davis as creator.

Developed as three mini-episodes per show: the "A story" concerned the adventures of Garfield; the "B story" focused on *U.S. Acres*, a lesser-known Davis comic strip about a group of talking farm animals; and Quickies, which were thirty- to forty-five-second gags, rounded

OPPOSITE: Garfield prepares to feast on a classic food creation.

ABOVE: Jim Davis, creator of Garfield, poses with his feline friend.

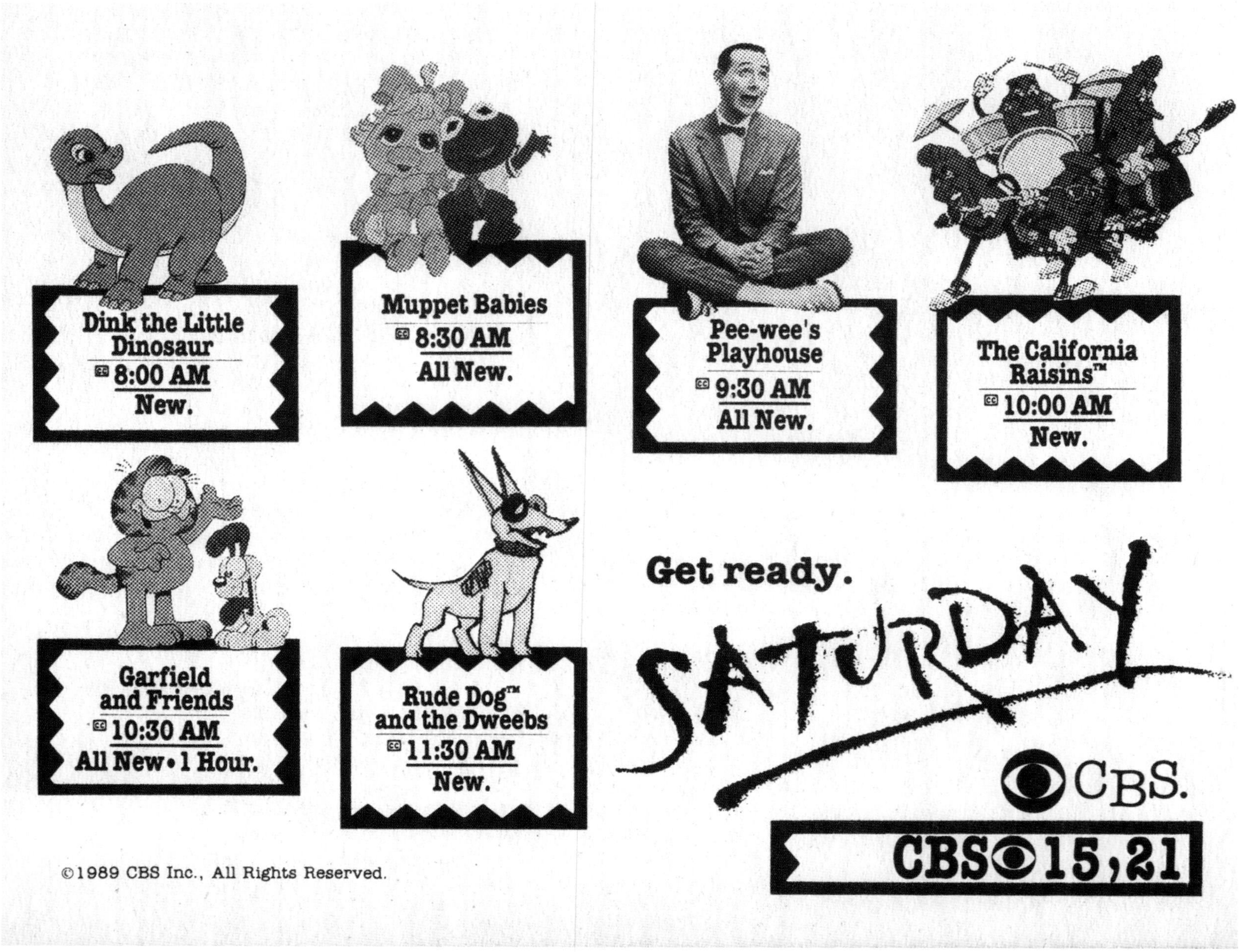
Dink the Little Dinosaur
8:00 AM
New.
Muppet Babies
8:30 AM
All New.
Pee-wee's Playhouse
9:30 AM
All New.
The California Raisins™
10:00 AM
New.
Garfield and Friends
10:30 AM
All New • 1 Hour.
Rude Dog™ and the Dweebs
11:30 AM
New.
Get ready.
SATURDAY
CBS.
CBS 15,21
©1989 CBS Inc., All Rights Reserved.

ABOVE: A 1989 advertisement from *TV Guide* for the CBS Saturday Morning Cartoon lineup, which included *Garfield and Friends*.

OPPOSITE: Garfield flashes a suspicously happy smile.

out the program. "But, because it has to be one story for twenty-two minutes, I wanted to do something where something was put at risk," explained Davis. "Not necessarily by [Garfield's] life or anything like that. But the wellbeing, the health, the family—we wanted something put at risk and then resolved. I wanted to take twenty-two minutes to make them laugh, to make them cry, to make them think somewhere in there so people feel like they spent a half hour well."

Expanding on gags from the comic strip, the character dynamics stayed much the same as in the cartoon story lines. Fat tabby Garfield lived it up as an unabashed slob whose passions included eating lasagna, sleeping, and ridiculing his nerdy human owner, Jon Arbuckle. Garfield also delighted in tormenting Odie, his less intelligent yellow beagle companion, as well as other pets in the neighborhood. Running gags included Garfield kicking Odie off the kitchen table or trying to ship Nermal, a narcissistic neighbor cat, to Abu Dhabi.

In addition to possessing smart storytelling and funny characters, the series featured formidable voice actors. Lorenzo Music expertly voiced Garfield's dry humor with his slow and distinctive delivery. Music, who also cowrote the TV special, *Garfield on the Town,* would often volunteer at a suicide prevention hotline where callers would sometimes remark he sounded a lot like Garfield. The rest of the cast included the legendary Frank Welker (*Scooby-Doo Where Are You?*, *Inspector Gadget, The Simpsons*), who provided the voice of Bo; Gregg Berger, (*The Littles* and *Super Friends*) voiced Odie. Notable celebrity guests also appeared on the program, including James Earl Jones, Chick Hearn, Don Knotts, and Mark Hamill.

In addition to the show's remarkable voice pool, its material was more than merely fat-cat jokes and Odie torture; the show often parodied classic pop-culture movies and characters, offering something for its adult viewers. For instance, after reading a spy novel in the episode "Double Oh Orson," Orson manifested a James Bond scenario involving himself as a secret agent. He reported to W (Wade) to retrieve a thermonuclear device after a final transmission arrives from Casino De Barnyard. Similarly, a cat trainer made a wager he could train any cat off the street, including Garfield, in "My Fair Feline," paying homage to *My Fair Lady*.

However, despite being nominated for a Kids' Choice Award, Daytime Emmy® Awards, and winning the Young Artist for Best Animation Series in 1989, CBS wanted to cut the budget as the show continued into the mid-1990s. When the production companies, Lee Mendelson Productions and Paws, Inc., who were producing the show at the time, pushed back, both parties agreed to end the series despite its high ratings. "We were there at the crossroads when cable took over network," recalled Davis. "It got very hard to compete later on because cable didn't have the kind of controls we adhered to. We also couldn't match the kind of

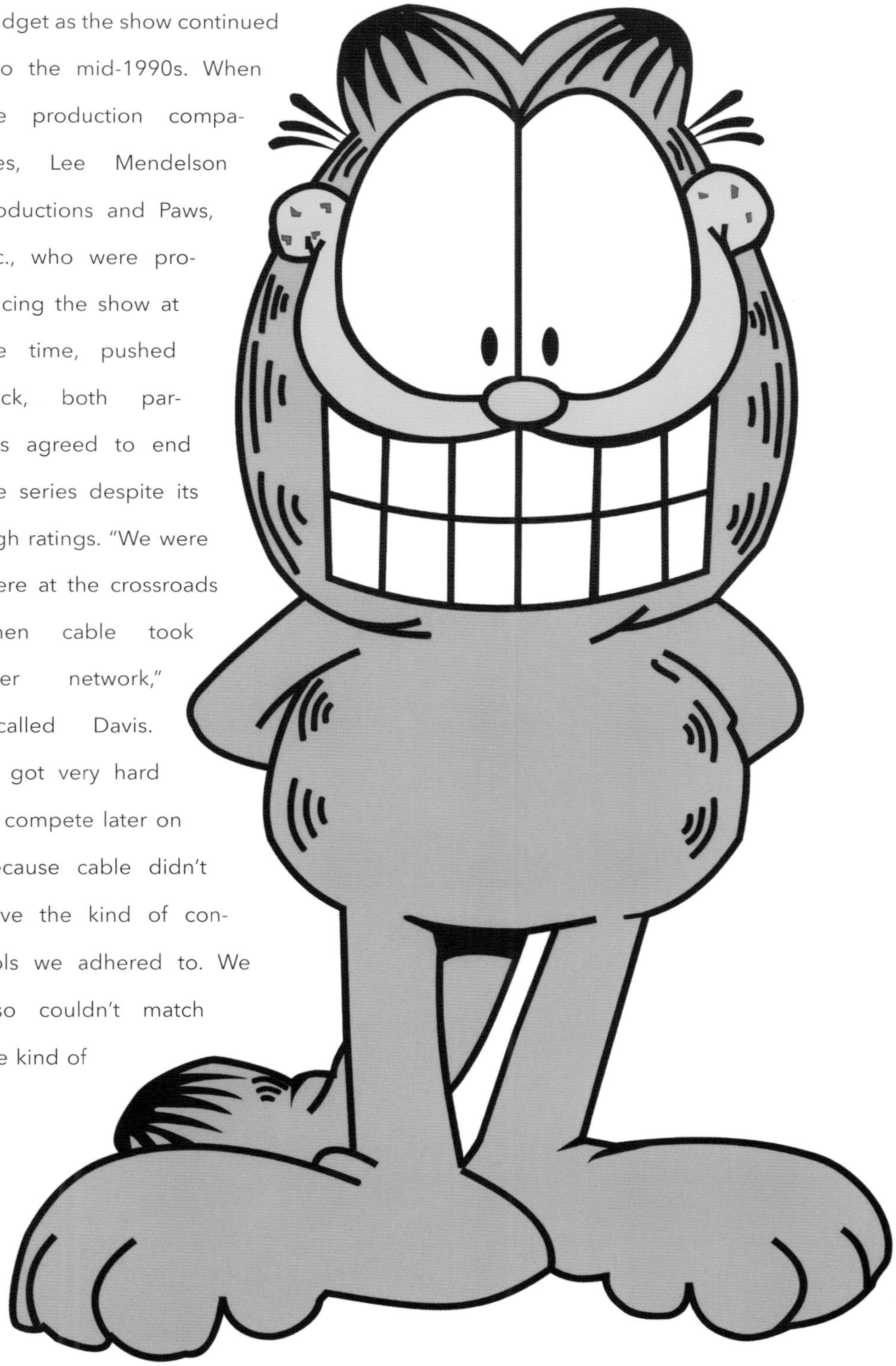

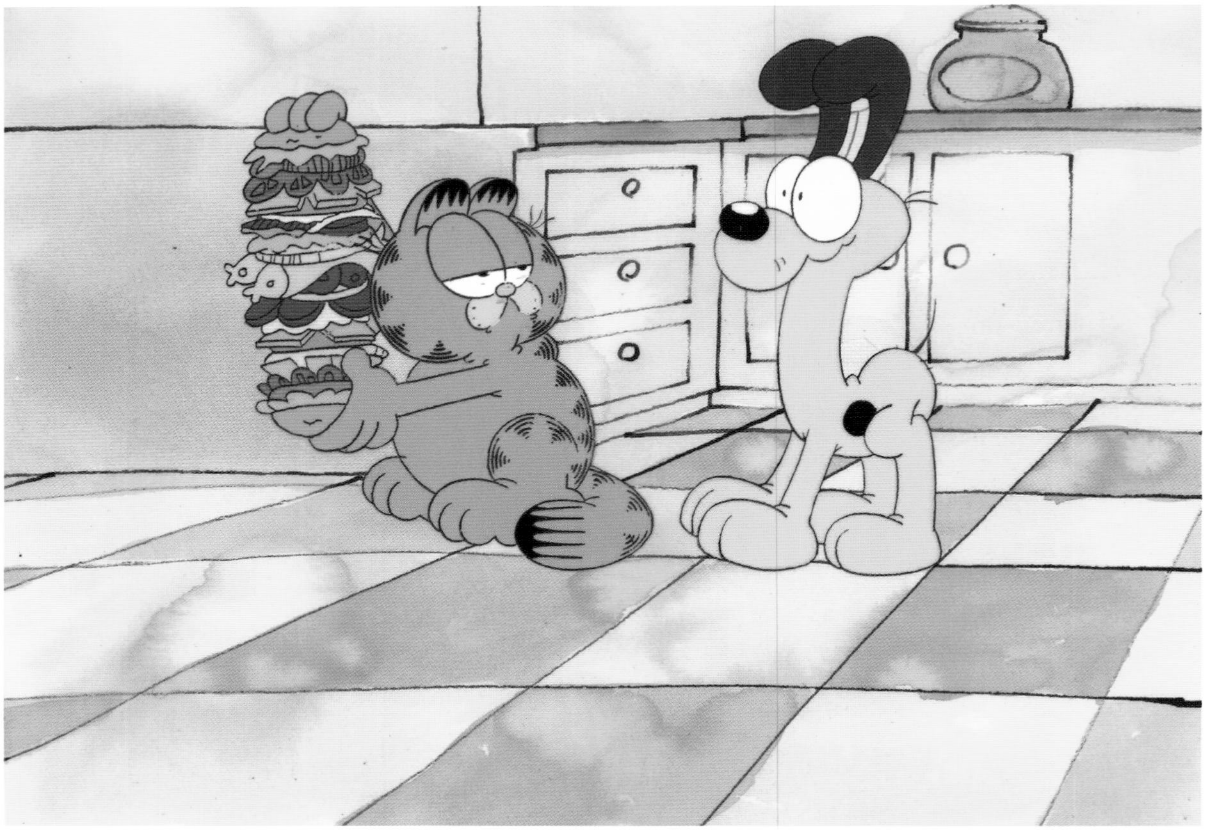

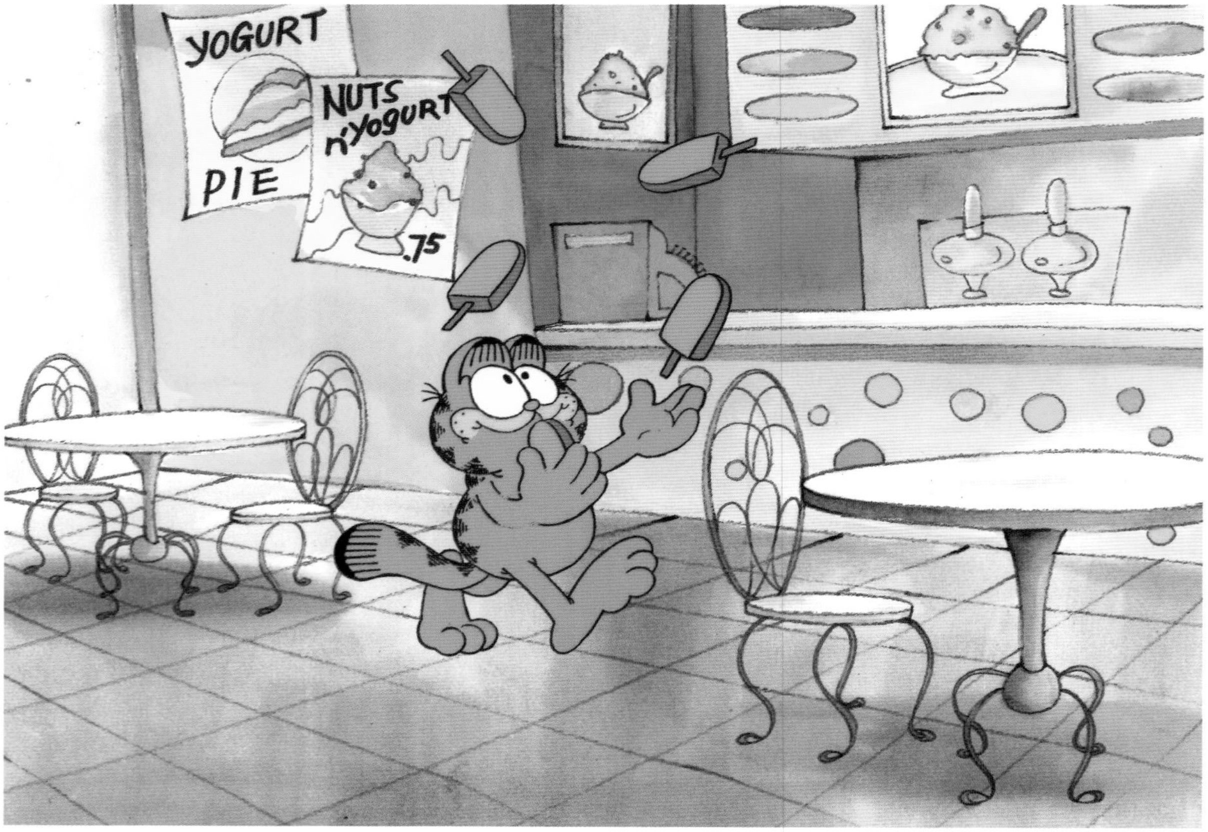
YOGURT
PIE
NUTS n'Yogurt
.75

budgets that the toy companies were working with and offering to the networks to put stuff up for free so it made it very difficult."

As evidenced by the comic strip's enduring lifespan, *Garfield* did not go quietly into the night. International TV syndication deals brought the series to diverse markets, including Latin America, Estonia, Finland, and the UK. Meanwhile, merchandising deals showed no signs of stopping. Over the years, there have been plush toys, diapers, an Atari video game, as well the album *Am I Cool or What*, featuring R&B and contemporary jazz inspired by Garfield. In 2004, the live-action movie *Garfield: The Movie* was released, in which Bill Murray provided the voice of Garfield. It grossed millions of dollars and was followed by several direct-to-video movies as well. Then in 2009, *The Garfield Show*, an updated CGI version of the concept, began on the Cartoon Network, featuring many of the voice actors from the original series.

Through all of these iterations and all of this merchandise,

OPPOSITE TOP AND BOTTOM: Garfield's enormous appetite was a running joke in the series, though everyone knew his favorite food was lasagna.

TOP: Garfield goes cowboy in this animation cel.

BOTTOM: The 2004 live-action *Garfield: The Movie* brought the iconic cat into CGI.

what is the secret to *Garfield*'s ongoing success and continued relevance? In an interview for *Garfield and Friends*, Davis said, "I think Garfield takes our guilt away for being, essentially, lazy slobs. We're constantly hearing: 'Exercise. Reduce cholesterol. Lower your fat intake.' Garfield's out there saying, 'Go ahead. Have that donut!' He's an antihero."

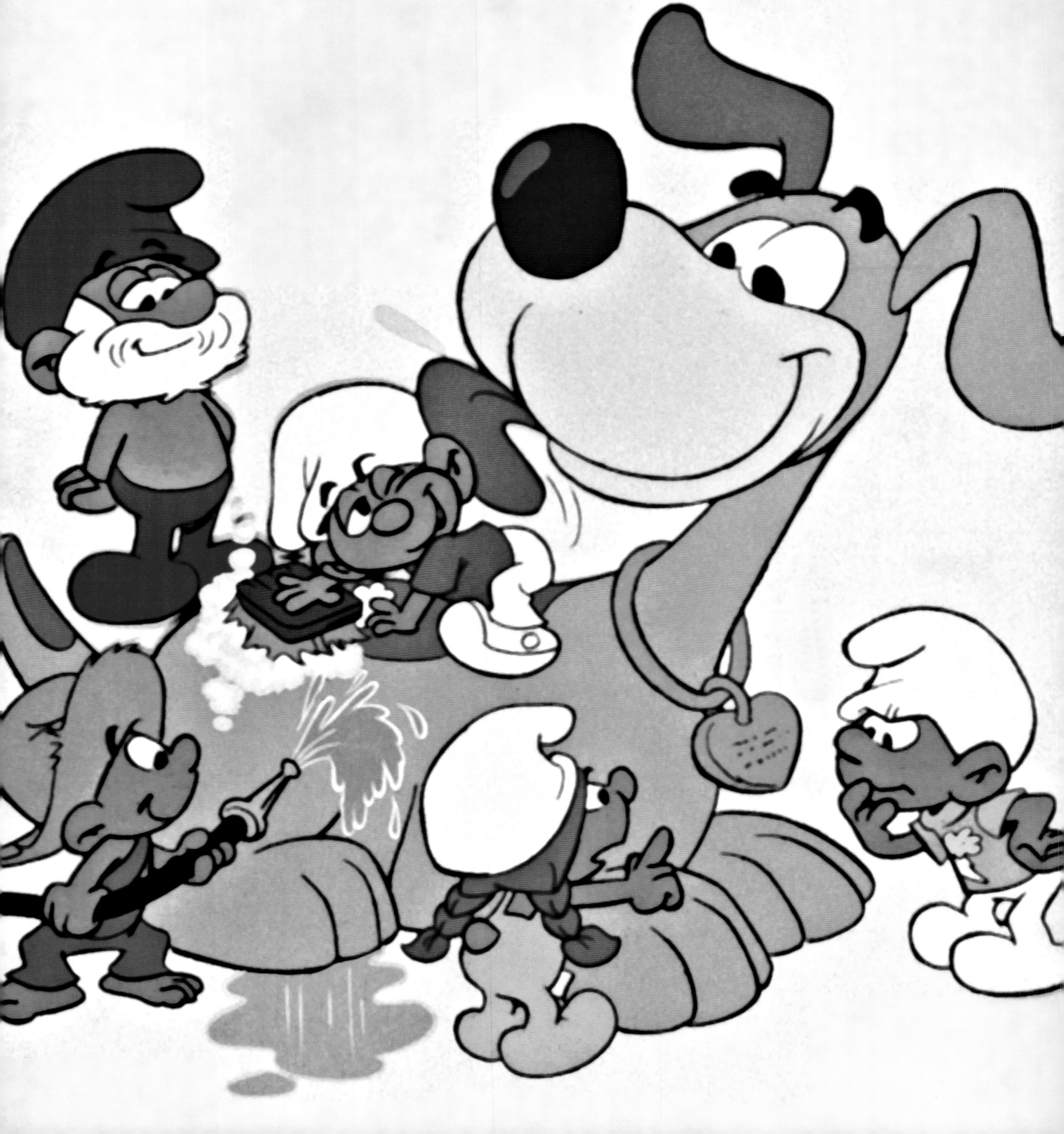

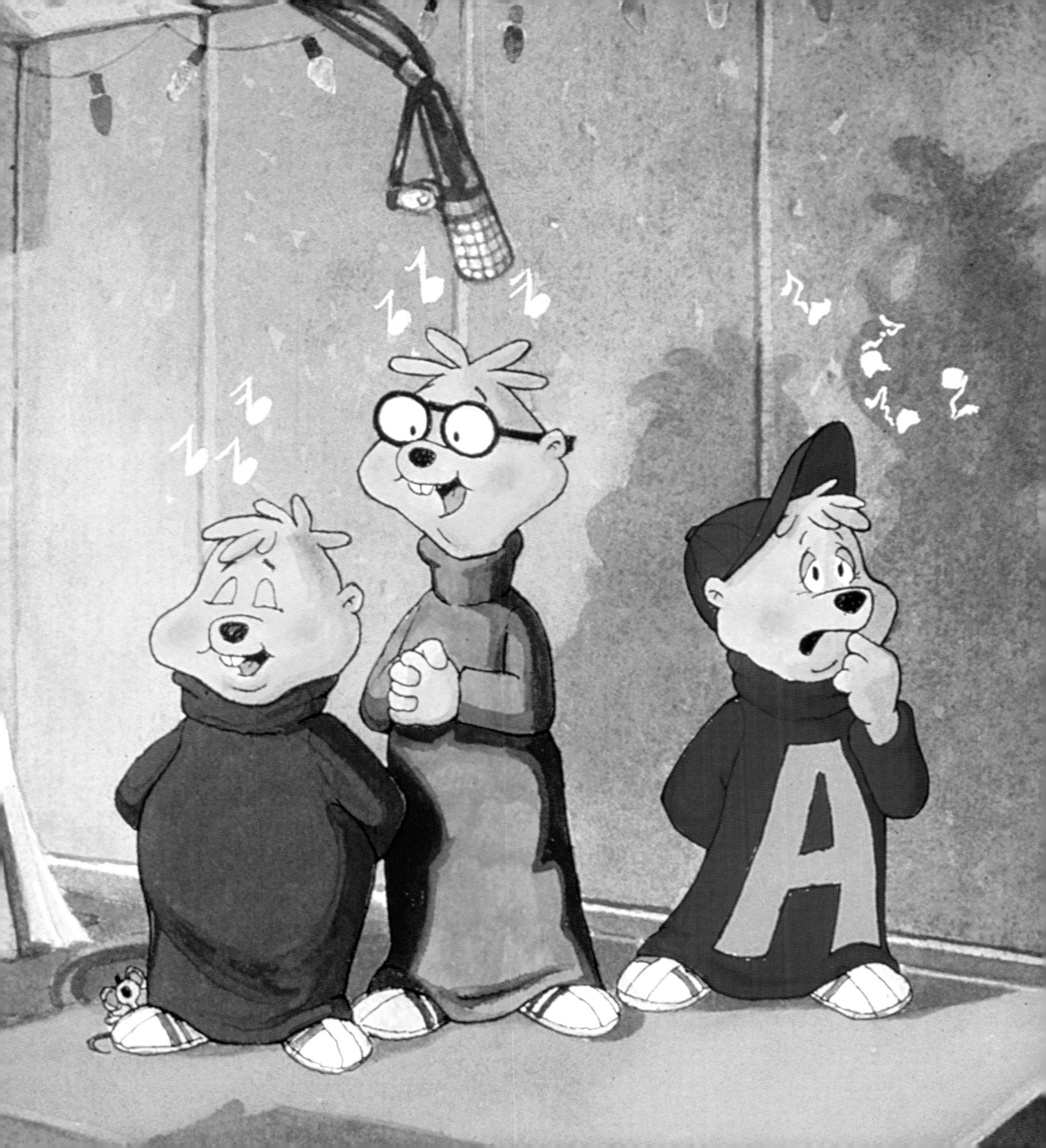

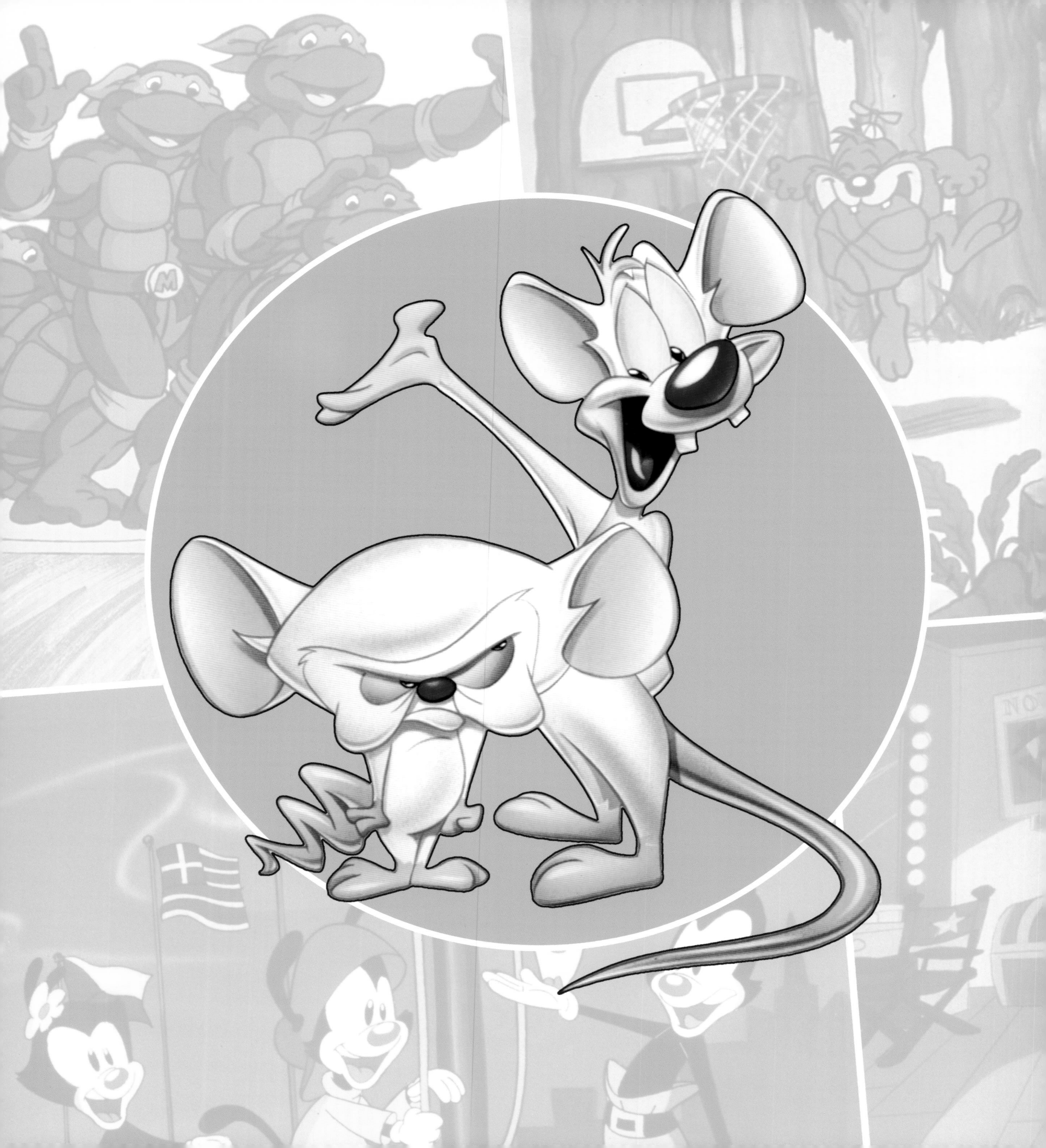

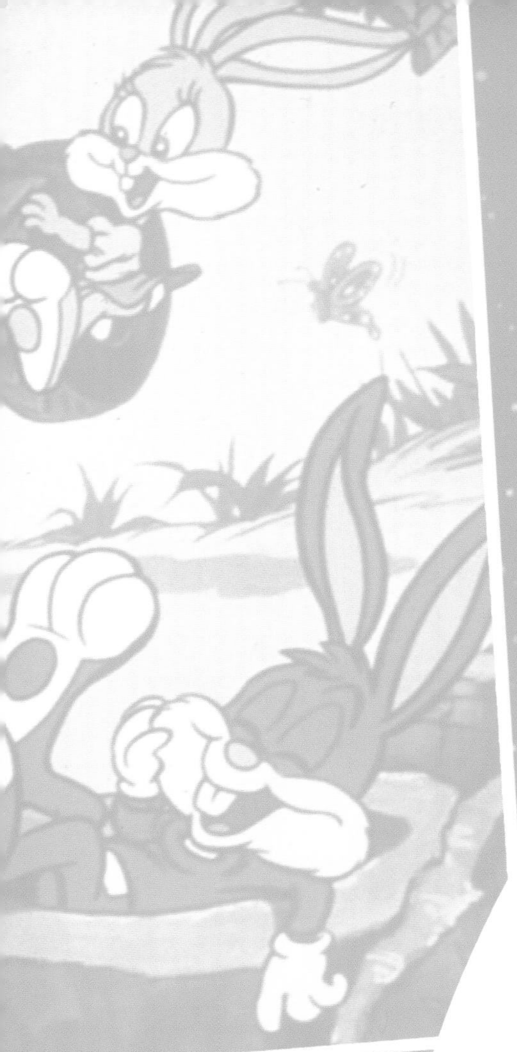

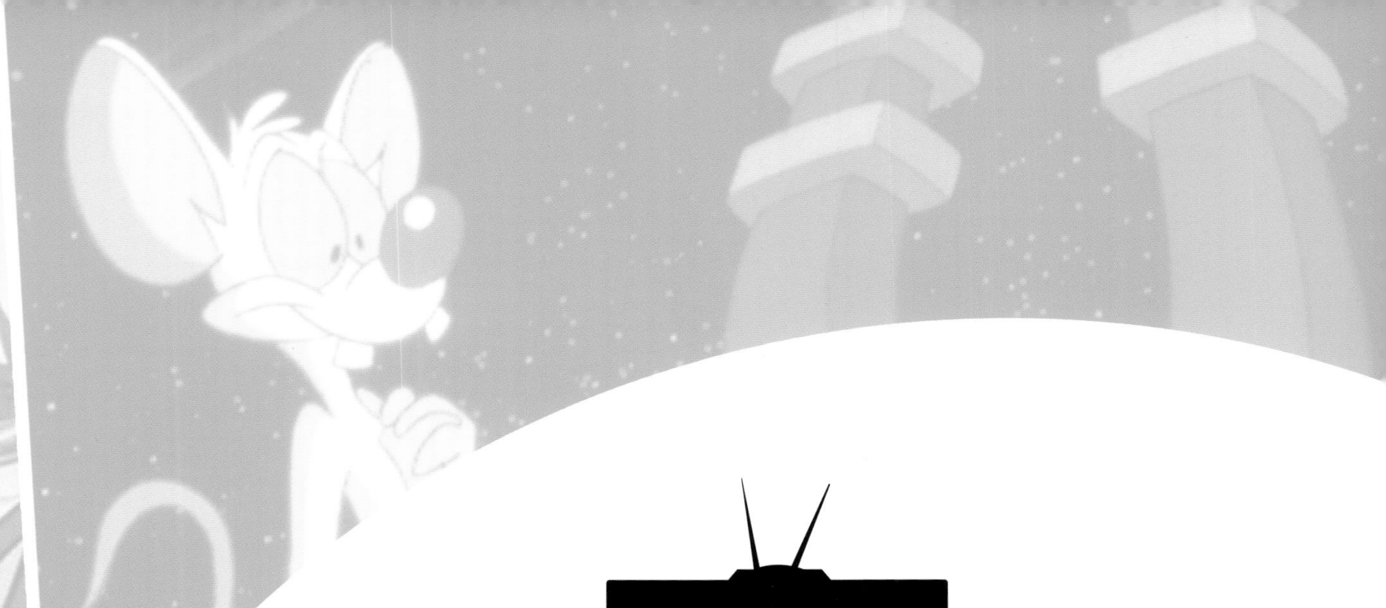

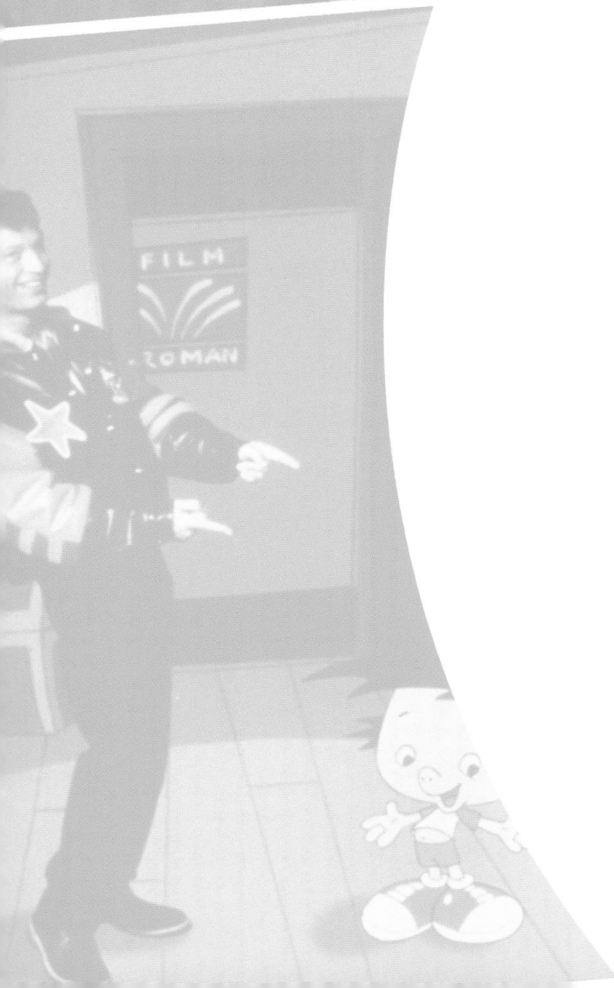
FILM
ROMAN

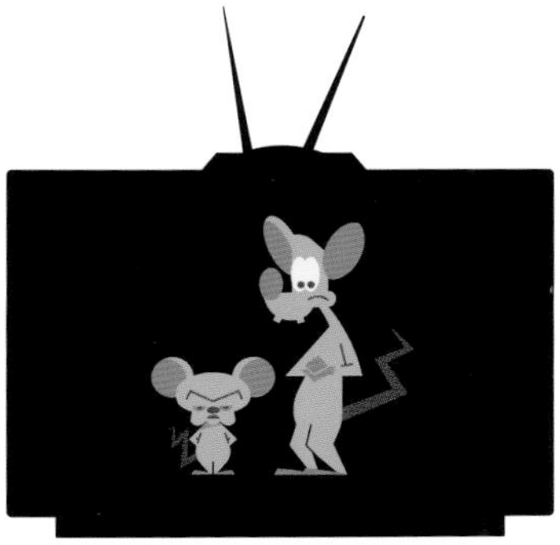

1990s

At the close of the twentieth century, cartoons took a darker and more self-conscious approach to content. Steven Spielberg's production company, Amblin, in association with Warner Bros., sought to revitalize old-fashioned animation in various forms, such as *Tiny Toon Adventures* and *Animaniacs*. In general, cartoon subject matter became more adult-like and less geared toward kids.

OPPOSITE: Pinky and The Brain appeared in two animated shows in the 1990s. They began as characters in *Animaniacs* before they got their own show.

Teenage Mutant Ninja Turtles

YEARS ON AIR

1987–1996

NETWORK

Syndication (1987–1990)
CBS: 1990–1996

NUMBER OF EPISODES

193

CHARACTERS AND VOICE ACTORS

Leonardo: Cam Clarke
Michelangelo:
Townsend Coleman
Donatello:
Barry Gordon/Greg Berg
Raphael:
Rob Paulsen/Thom Pinto/
Hal Rayle/Michael Gough
Splinter: Peter Renaday/
Townsend Coleman
Krang: Pat Fraley
Shredder: Jim Cummings/
Bill Martin
April O'Neil: Renae Jacobs
Casey Jones: Pat Fraley

There are certain phrases or words that can instantly transport you back to childhood. For many, all it takes is the mention of a sublime, four-syllable exclamation evoking pure delight: *Cowabunga*! When spoken by heroes "in a half-shell," *Cowabunga* took on awesome implications. "*Cowabunga, dude! The pizza is here.*" But why did this reptilian quartet appropriate surfer lingo, love slices of pepperoni pie so freakin' much, and have mad fighting skills? For these answers, we must return to *TMNT*'s pioneering days—before the live-action TV series, six feature films, and a galaxy of turtle-related merchandise, when original creators Peter Laird and Kevin Eastman brainstormed the crazy concept.

Recent art school graduates, Eastman and Laird first teamed up in the 1980s to create a young-adult comic based on their mutual appreciation of artist Jack Kirby (*Fantastic Four, The Avengers,* the *Hulk*). "We were sitting around the living room. We'd watched a number of bad TV shows—*T. J. Hooker, The A-Team* and *Love Connection,*" explained Eastman. "We got real punchy, and for some reason I did a sketch of a turtle with a mask. Pete did one, and another. Then I said, 'Wait! Wait!' and drew four turtles, each with a different weapon. I said, 'Why not call them *Ninja Turtles*?' Pete said, 'Why not *Teenage Mutant Ninja Turtles*?'" To their great surprise and joy, Eastman and Laird's comic books, published

OPPOSITE: The Teenage Mutant Ninja Turtles (left to right) Donatello, Leonardo, Raphael, Michelangelo.

TOP: Leonardo leads the charge as the Teenage Mutant Ninja Turtles blast out of a truck.

with borrowed money, connected with fans, leading to a cult following.

Eastman and Laird's genius wasn't just concocting upright, walking superhero turtles—their masterstroke involved packaging, specifically nailing a wholly original head-scratcher of a title. "I think the original *TMNT* comics benefitted from the crazy title," said Laird. "It almost always generated a second look. In fact, one of the most important pieces of promotion in those early days was a story that United Press International (UPI) did on us in 1984—and I don't think they would have given our little independent black-and-white comic any notice if it hadn't been for that title." Eastman and Laird backed their title with a fun, idiosyncratic concept, in which the baby turtles accidentally fell down a sewer drain into radioactive goo, mutating them into anthropomorphic beings.

Splinter, the turtles' master, raised them as his sons and apprenticed them in the ways of martial arts to battle The Shredder, a rival ninja who had killed Splinter's master. The character differed in the cartoon than in the comics. In the comics, Splinter was a human ninja master named Hamato Yoshi who morphs into a rat due to his radiation exposure. In the cartoon, Splinter *was* a rat. Though in both, Splinter named his protégés after Renaissance artists.

In a 2014 interview with ScreenCrush, TV series writer David Wise, who was instrumental in developing the turtle personalities, said, "In the comics, you can't tell one turtle from another. Even when they're speaking, they have no distinctive voices or characterizations." Working in tandem with the

BOTTOM: The four turtles emerge from the sewer with a pizza in this promotional image.

production studio Murakami-Wolf-Swenson, he and cowriter Patti Howeth remedied this fact by differentiating the turtles with various color-coded bandanas and monogrammed belts with their initials—Leonardo: Blue, Raphael: Red, Michelangelo: Yellow, Donatello: Purple.

However, Wise didn't think color-coding went nearly far enough toward establishing the turtles' individuality, so he also assigned them distinct weapons and personality types. "We needed the

martial arts master. That should be the guy with the katana, the Japanese sword. That was Leonardo. That's why Leonardo leads," said Wise. Wise went on to designate Donatello as the nerdy "gadget" guy, assigning him a bō staff as his preferred armament. "You can't do a show with this title and not have humor," recalled Wise when describing the sai-wielding Raphael. "The title is too goofy. Their names are just too out there. Raphael became the audience conduit, the sarcastic wisecracker who sees how silly all of this really is." Recognizing that the turtles required swagger to round out the group, Wise created Michelango.

"[Michelangelo] was the Sid Vicious of the Turtles. Sid Vicious couldn't play or sing but he epitomized punk. Michelangelo epitomizes what the turtles are about."

Not only did Wise and company reimagine the turtles' personalities, first for a 1987 miniseries, then for the CBS Saturday morning cartoon, they also retooled the narrative structure. In particular, they toned down the comic's violence and grittiness, giving it a more kid-friendly atmosphere. In the comics, Splinter trained the turtles to kill The Shredder. However, the TV series expanded the story line to include new threats and foes. Combining forces with Krang, a disembodied alien brain banished from Dimension X, The Shredder attempted to conquer the world with aid from Bebop and Rocksteady (a mutant warthog and rhinoceros respectively), as well as the Foot Clan ninjutsu robot army. "I also knew that the turtles couldn't show their faces much above ground and were stuck in the sewers," explained Wise. "They would need a human compatriot in the city above." To this end, Wise and company formulated a Lois Lane-type confederate in the form of Channel 6 reporter April O'Neil. April, along with allies like Casey Jones, a vigilante wearing a hockey mask to protect his identity, continually rise to the turtle cause, lending human support.

Throughout the series, episodic story lines utilized sardonic humor, action-packed sequences, and elements of surfer culture to appeal to kids who lapped up the fun. "The stories needed to be serious, for-real action adventure stories with real consequences and real problems and just enough grounding in reality," Wise explained. "And the turtles themselves, by the nature of their personalities, would make it funny." For example, in the episode

TOP: The Teenage Mutant Ninja Turtles try to tempt April O'Neil with a slice of pizza.

BOTTOM: *Cowabunga!* Donatello, Michelangelo, Leonardo, and Raphael ride the waves.

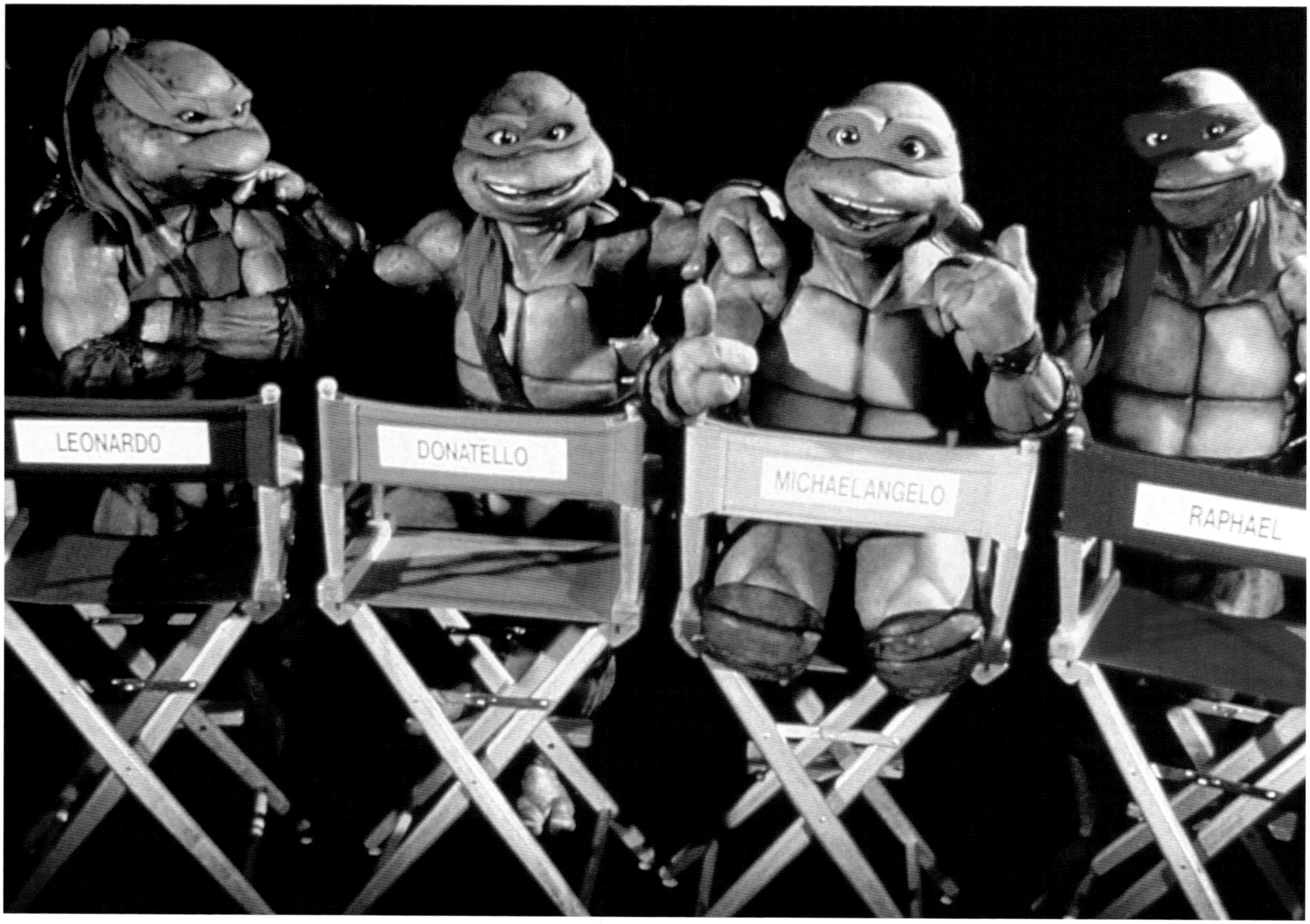
LEONARDO
DONATELLO
MICHAELANGELO
RAPHAEL

ABOVE: Live-action characters pose for a promotion photo, 1990.

OPPOSITE: *TMNT*'s Nintendo video game.

"The Case of the Killer Pizzas," Krang attempted to poison the turtles with meatballs from Dimension X, combining quirky fun with danger and menace.

Launched in October 1988, the show crushed it on Saturday morning television, soon expanding to five days a week as afternoon installments in syndicated markets. A *New York Times* article by Bill Carter gushed about CBS's move to pick up the series once again in 1990 as a sixty-minute block with back-to-back thirty-minute episodes. "The two half hours of *Teen-age Mutant Ninja Turtles* are the two top-rated shows on Saturday morning," wrote Carter. "They also have the strongest ratings among the viewer group most sought by advertisers on Saturday morning: children age two to eleven." Though the series finally concluded in 1996, a host of cartoon reboots emerged with updated illustrations for subsequent generations, paving the way for full-blown live-action blockbusters.

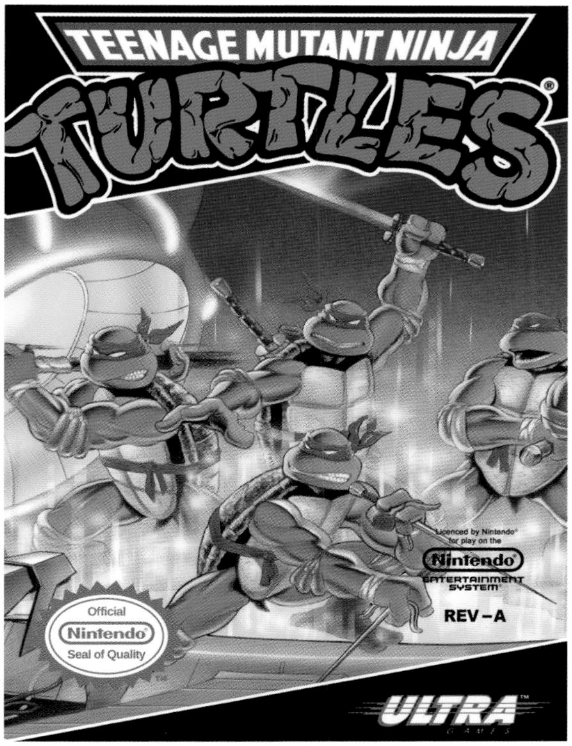
TEENAGE MUTANT NINJA
TURTLES
Licenced by Nintendo for play on the
Nintendo
ENTERTAINMENT SYSTEM
REV–A
Official
Nintendo
Seal of Quality
ULTRA

In addition to various cartoon versions and movies, the ensuing decades have produced innumerable *TMNT* merchandise. Is it any wonder enterprising companies have released a mass of turtle-related products, from action figures and Halloween costumes to beanies, backpacks, boxer shorts, gelatin desserts, video games, lunch boxes, socks, bikes, shot glasses, wallets, and, yes—even condoms? In fact, the *TMNT* franchise shows no signs of stopping. In 2016, the feature-film release of *Teenage Mutant Ninja Turtles: Out of the Shadows* revealed both the comic's initial freshness and the show's emphasis on clever storytelling and playfulness. Still, no matter how many *TMNT* iterations climb out of the primordial ooze, for many children, this Saturday morning cartoon will remain their green go-to. *Cowabunga*, turtle power!

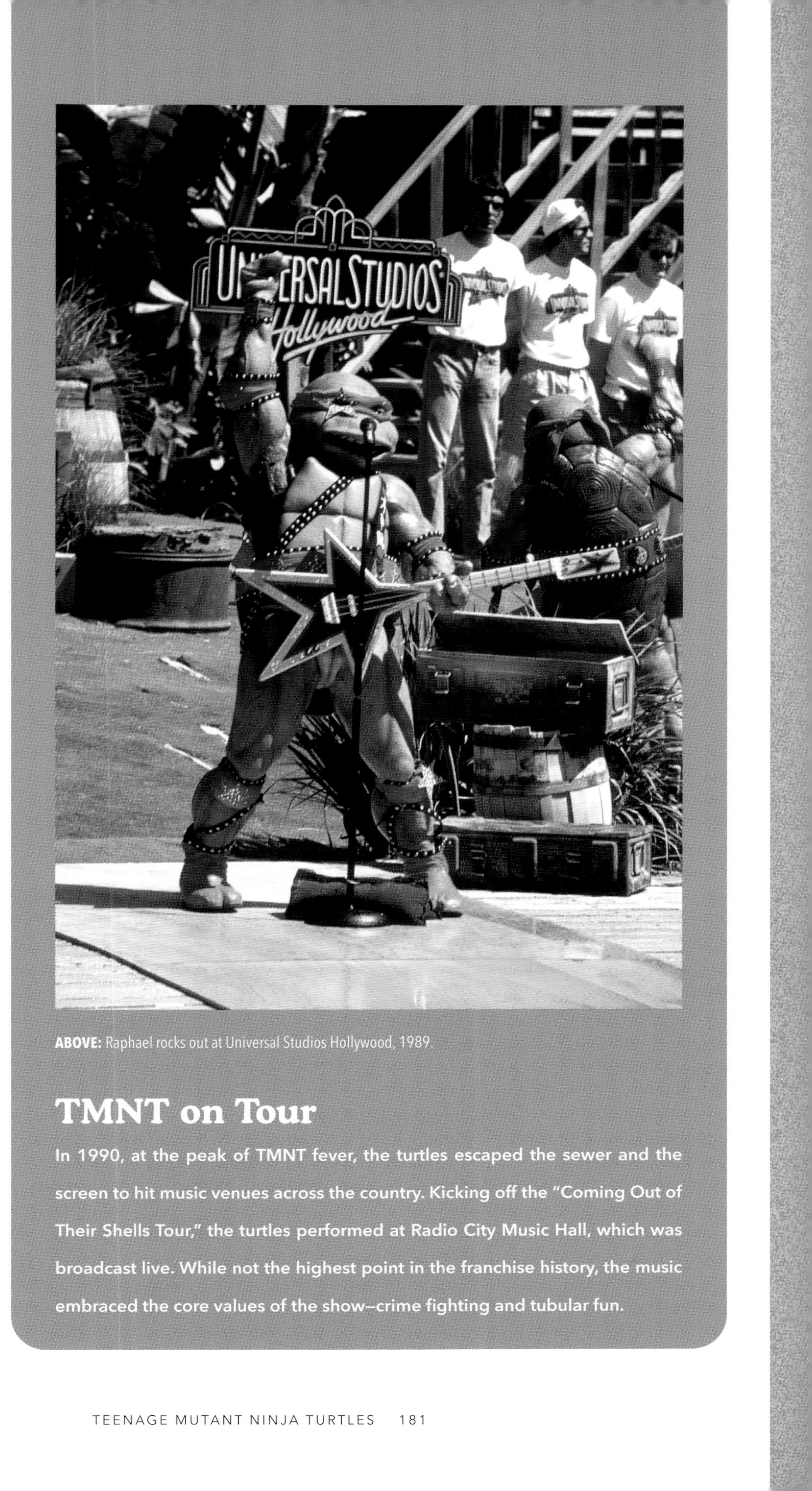
Hollywood

ABOVE: Raphael rocks out at Universal Studios Hollywood, 1989.

TMNT on Tour

In 1990, at the peak of TMNT fever, the turtles escaped the sewer and the screen to hit music venues across the country. Kicking off the "Coming Out of Their Shells Tour," the turtles performed at Radio City Music Hall, which was broadcast live. While not the highest point in the franchise history, the music embraced the core values of the show—crime fighting and tubular fun.

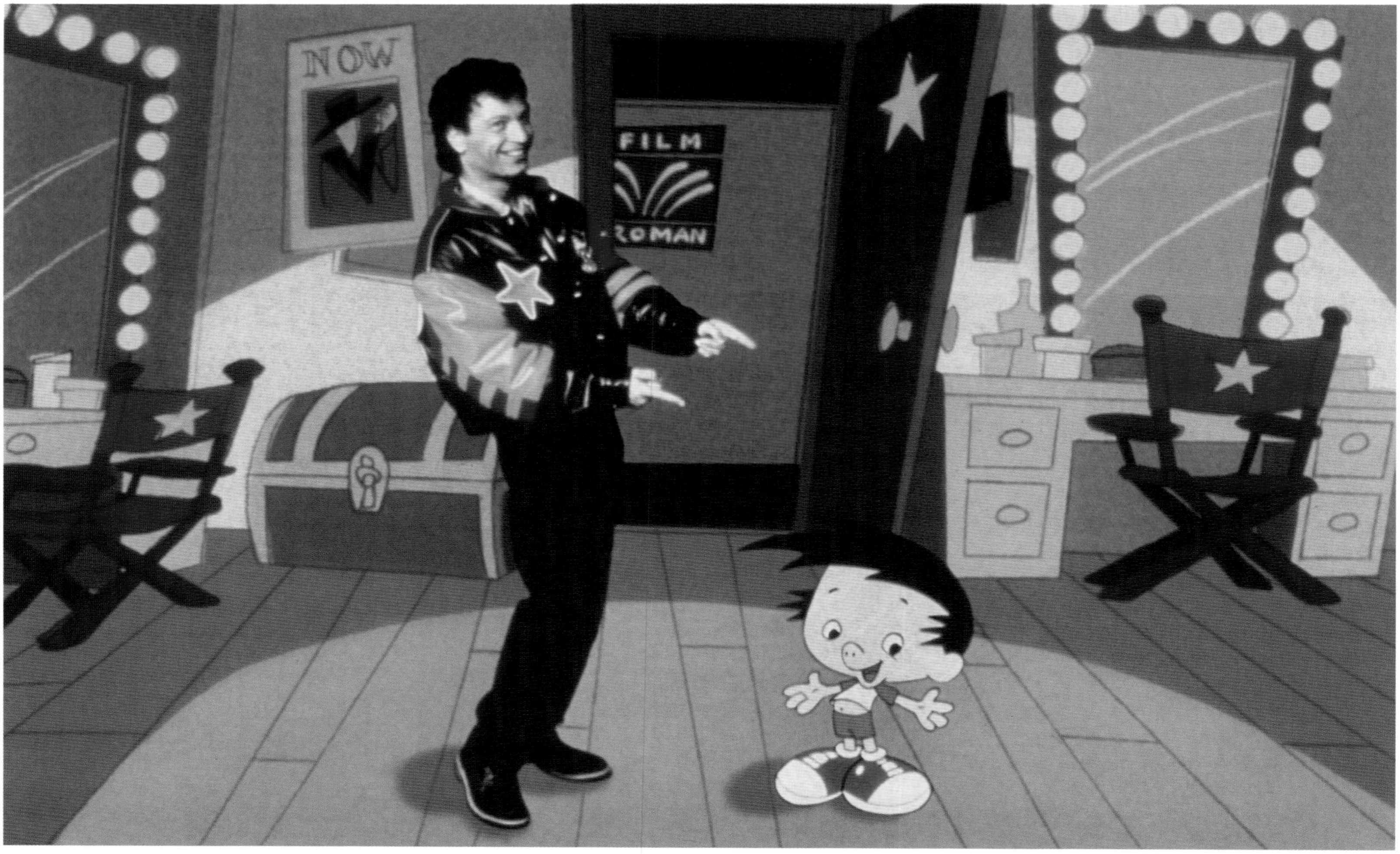
NOW
FILM

YEARS ON AIR

1990–1998

NETWORK

Fox Kids

NUMBER OF EPISODES

81

CHARACTERS AND VOICE ACTORS

Bobby Generic/Howard Generic: Howie Mandel
Martha Generic: Gail Matthius
Derek Generic: Kevin Smets
Kelly Generic: Charity James
Aunt Ruth: Edie McClurg
Roger: Frank Welker
Uncle Ted: Tino Insana

Bobby's World

Navigating everyday life can be hard. Just ask any kid. Not only must they take orders from pesky grown-ups, they must also depend on the same bossy oafs for survival. To cope, many boys and girls retreat to the safety of their own imaginations. That was the premise of *Bobby's World*. Comedian Howie Mandel brought the concept, based on material from his own childhood in Canada, to fruition via the adorable and adorably voiced Robert Adelvice Generic, aka Bobby.

The once curly-headed Mandel first came to prominence in the 1980s, starring in TV shows such as *St. Elsewhere* (1982–1988) and movies such as *Walk Like a Man* (1987). Known for creating iconic, silly voices, Mandel voiced Gizmo in *Gremlins* (1984) as well as multiple characters on *Muppet Babies*.

Before entering show-biz, Mandel once ran a carpet business. One evening, a producer happened to catch his Amateur Night performance at the LA Comedy Store and put him on the game show *Make*

Me Laugh. Over the ensuing years, Mandel developed the character of Bobby in his stand-up act. "I started doing that voice originally in Toronto when I was eleven," said Mandel in a televised routine. "I was at a birthday party. I was choking on a piece of cake. I couldn't breathe, it was halfway down my throat. That's the sound that was coming out of me: 'Help meeeee! I can't breaeeethe!'" Everyone laughed so hard he thought, "If I could just bring myself this close to death each and every night, it could be entertaining."

Though the original comic material was intended for adult audiences, two writer/actor friends, Jim Staahl and Jim Fisher, whom Mandel collaborated with to create the 1982 show *Laugh Trax*, took it to the Fox television division in 1989. Launched as a competitor to the Big Three networks in 1986, the Fox Broadcasting Company had picked up steam by the decade's end with hit shows, like *Married . . . with Children* and *The Simpsons*. The upstart network now wanted a piece of children's programming and debuted *Bobby's World* on Fox Kids in 1990 with Staahl and Fisher as the development team and Mandel at the helm as creator.

Though the brass at Fox didn't exactly consider Mandel's comedy "family entertainment," Mandel and company made the concept work by incorporating cleaner material from Mandel's, Staahl's, and Fisher's respective childhoods. As the series continued, *Bobby's World* also drew real-life inspiration from writers Dianne and Peter Tilden, as well as producer Mitch Schauer. Prior to his involvement with *Bobby's World*, Schauer worked as a storyboard

artist for a number of series, including *Flash Gordon* and *The Smurfs*. However, in a 1990 interview with John Cawley at Cataroo.com, Schauer said, "*Bobby's World* [was] the first time that [I] had control with regards to working with the writers and the story editor . . ."

OPPOSITE: Live-action Howie Mandel poses with animated Bobby.

ABOVE: Howard pushes Bobby in a tree swing.

RIGHT: Bobby sits in Howie Mandel's lap.

OPPOSITE: Jim Staahl, circa 1980.

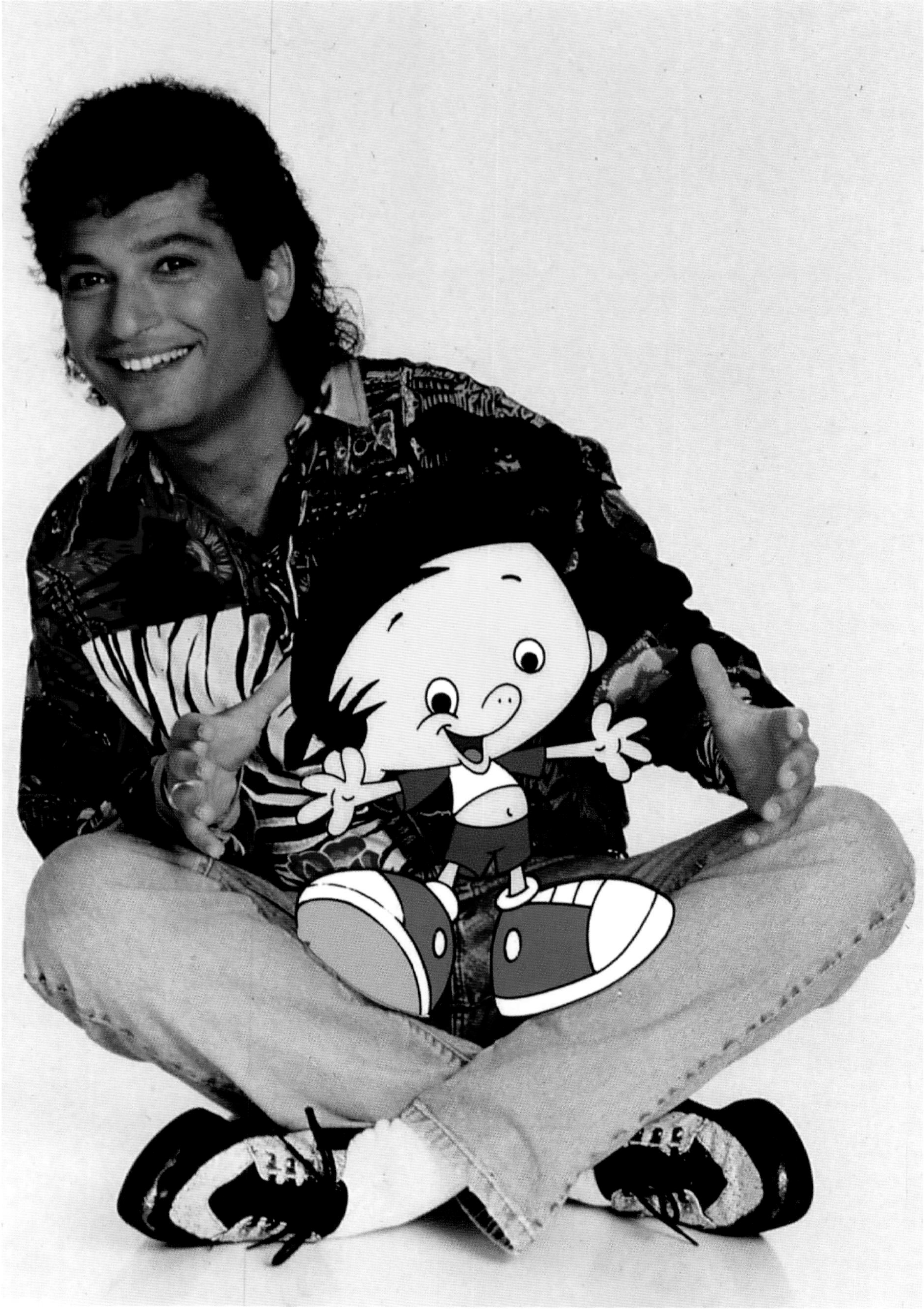

Similar to Schauer, Mandel maintained significant control over the show's development. TV voice legend Frank Welker, who also co-starred on *Laugh Trax* and voiced the dog, Roger, on *Bobby's World*, noted, "Giving birth to a project and keeping artistic control is very appealing. Howie Mandel is one of the few people I know who did it and was very successful." Part of Mandel's duties, besides supplying fodder for story lines, involved appearing in short live-action segments before and after the main story. Breaking the fourth wall, Mandel offered his perspective, interjecting morality to the show's universe while sometimes conversing with an animated Bobby.

Mandel's take on events, whether it was in the live-action sequences, or actual episodes, offered a comedic, yet warm and friendly spin for kids at home maneuvering through their own juvenile dilemmas. Throughout the series, Bobby used his

ABOVE: The Generics (left to right) Webley, Bobby, Derek, Martha, Uncle Ted, Kelly, Howie, and dog Rodger.

The Quotable Generics

The Generics didn't shy from saying what was on their minds, leading to some memorable lines.

Martha Generic: "Fer corn sakes?"

Kelly Generic: "Get real."

Derek Generic: "If you wet the bed, I'll kill you."

Uncle Ted: "Time for noogies."

Uncle Ted and Bobby Generic singing together: "Fish don't stink! Under the water the fish don't stink."

Bobby Generic: "Hush, little baby, don't say a word, mama's gonna buy you a mockingbird. And if that mockingbird don't sing . . . I'm gonna rip off his feathers and tear off his wings!"

BOTTOM: Bobby lost in thought.

big imagination to cope with new and frightening things, like being left home with the babysitter. In the episode "Adventures in Bobby-Sitting," Bobby dealt with his fears about the babysitter by concocting wild fantasies, including a slasher parody of the horror film, *Friday the 13th*. Bobby's lack of life inexperience and tendency to take things literally often led him to misunderstand the world in amusing ways. For instance, when Bobby hears the phrase, "dude ranch," he literally imagines a bunch of dudes hanging out. Similarly, he envisions a "traffic jam" involving little cars spread out on a piece of bread.

Bobby's imaginative hijinks seemed to know no bounds. In the series, he even created his own origin story. Though Bobby had a typical suburban life—attended the Little Red School with girlfriend Jackie, lived with dad Howard, mother Martha, brother Derek, sister Kelly, and later twins Al and Jake—he believed he came from Bobbyland, a place where Bobby once played, flew, and had as much fun as he wanted, until the day an evil queen banished him to a five-bedroom home in Oregon to live with his bullying older siblings who call him "dork."

The fact that the show dealt with real-world issues in a hilarious fashion was a big part of its staying power. Another aspect of the appeal was the cast of supporting characters and voice actors. In addition to Welker's talent, Gail Matthius brought Martha to life with her Minnesota-Norwegian accent, which was based on Matthius's *SNL* character, Roweena, a chain-smoking hairdresser. Charity James also lent her voice as Kelly, who was also based on a *SNL* favorite: Vicky the Valley Girl. Finally, the show's theme song, composed by radio host and American pianist John Tesh, provided a whimsical backdrop to the opening sequences that set the tone for the show.

While many other Saturday morning cartoons disappeared in the 1990s, *Bobby's World* stayed on the air for almost a decade. Its enduring popularity stemmed from the show's capacity to present childhood as a time of wonder and creativity—with dash of a zany and irreverent humor.

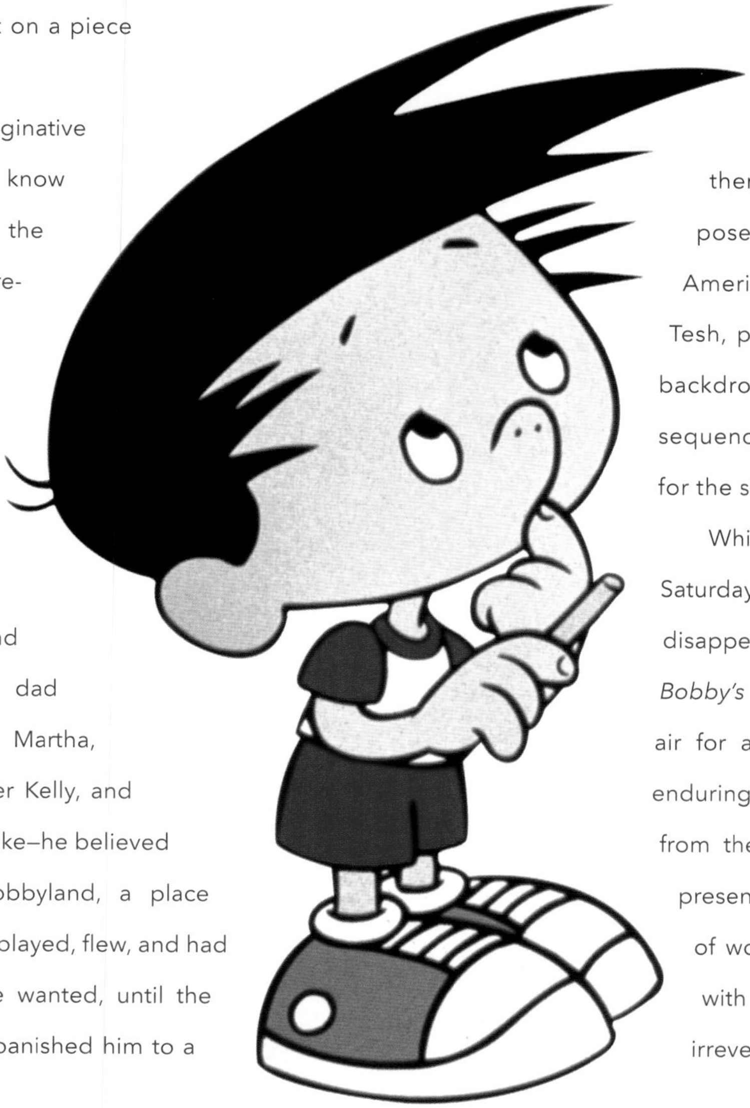

Micro Machine Cars

The typical TV commercial actor can speak approximately 125–150 words per minute. John "Motor-mouth" Moschitta Jr., once credited as the "World's Fastest Talker" by *The Guinness Books of World Records*, delivered his Micro Machines commercials at the pace of nearly 600 words per minute. He always capped off his rapid-fire rant with this catchphrase: "Remember: if it doesn't say Micro Machines, it's not the real thing."

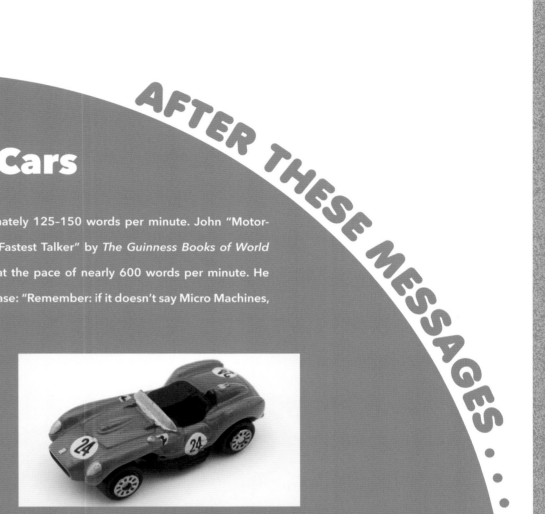

LEFT: John Moschitta Jr., the 'Micro Machines Man,' appeared in over 100 commercials for the toys.

RIGHT TOP: The Ferrari 250 TR Micro Machine.

RIGHT BOTTOM: Micro Machines look tiny, even in the hands of a three-year-old.

YEARS ON AIR

Syndicated: 1990-1992
Fox Kids: 1992-1995

NETWORK

Fox Kids

NUMBER OF EPISODES

100

CHARACTERS AND VOICE ACTORS

Buster Bunny: Charlie Adler
Babs Bunny: Tress MacNeille
Plucky Duck: Joe Alaskey
Furrball: Frank Welker
Hamton J. Pig: Don Messick
Elmyra Duff: Cree Summer
Montana Max: Danny Cooksey
Dizzy Devil: Maurice LaMarche

Tiny Toon Adventures

We're tiny, we're toony.

We're all a little loony.

And in this cartoony, we're invading your TV.

Ask anyone who grew up in the '80s and '90s to name the movie director who most influenced their childhood and you are bound to hear the name Steven Spielberg. After all, Spielberg brought audiences *Jaws, Close Encounters of the Third Kind, E.T., Indiana Jones,* and *Jurassic Park.* Spielberg also produced *Who Framed Roger Rabbit* (1988), combining classic animation with live action. Fresh off the success of that hit, Spielberg used his momentum to bring back the spirit of the old Warner Bros. cartoons from his youth. In an interview with the *LA Times,* Tom Ruegger, creator of *Tiny Toon Adventures,* said Spielberg wanted "to carry on their irreverence, to make Looney Tunes for the '90s."

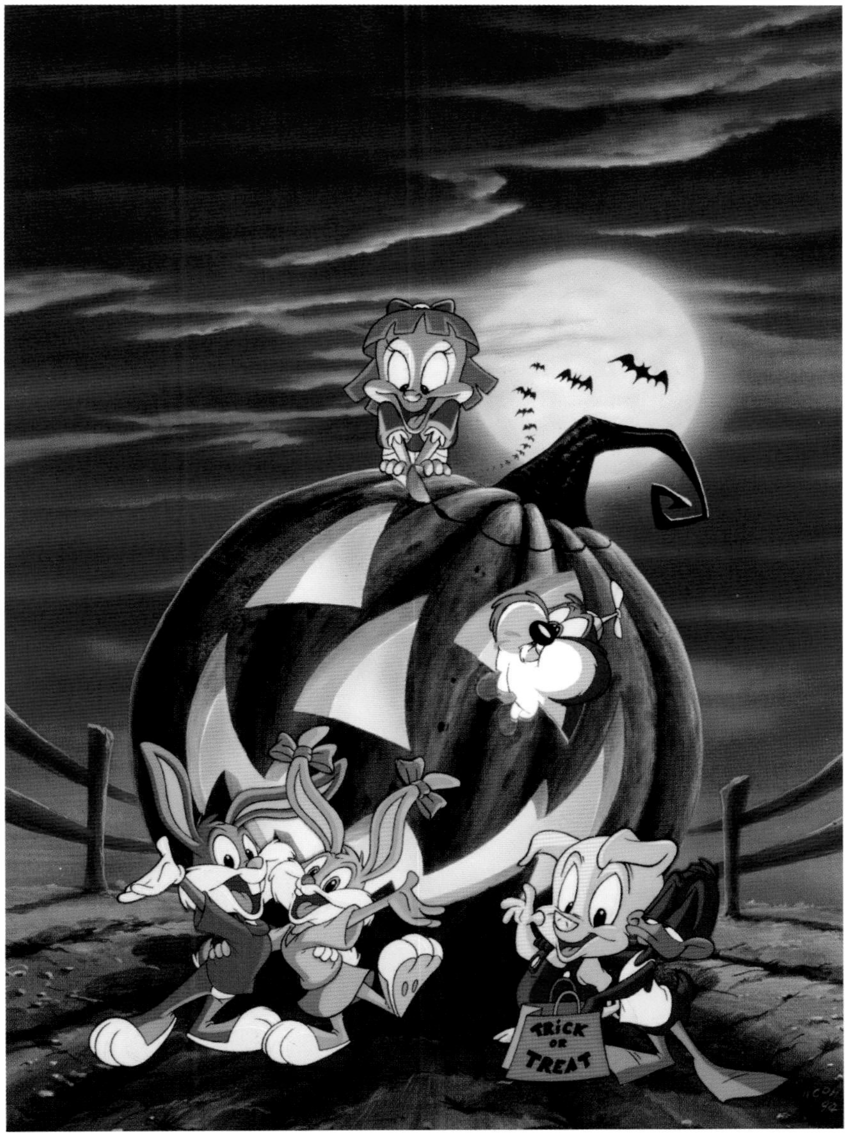
TRICK OR TREAT

OPPOSITE: The Tiny Toon gang: (left to right from the back) Sweetie Bird, Calamity Coyote, Furrball, Little Beeper, Dizzy Devil, Montana Max, Gogo Dodo, Fifi La Fume, Elmyra Duff, Hamton J. Pig, Buster Bunny, Babs Bunny, and Plucky Duck.

TOP: *Tiny Toon Adventures* wishes everyone a Happy Halloween.

Employing his usual modus operandi, Spielberg spared little expense to realize his cartoon dream. Collaborating with Warner Bros., he assembled a one hundred-person production staff to make the series appear more like a film than a TV show, and used a live thirty-piece orchestra to score each episode. "And so I knew already that that was going to be special because, right from the very beginning, Steven was not just a masthead name," said Andrea Romano, the show's casting and voice director. "Steven was reading every storyboard. Steven had story ideas. He came to recording sessions. I actually directed him in a session." According to Joe Rhodes in an *Entertainment Weekly* profile, Spielberg's quality control meant managing "every step of the production process," including characters, scripts, background design, and voice-overs.

The extreme attention to detail was an effort to revitalize classic characters for contemporary audiences. Set in fictional Acme Acres, *Tiny Toon Adventures* focused on the next generation of Looney Tunes characters attending Acme Looniversity, where they learned to be funny from old pros like Bugs Bunny, Daffy Duck, and Porky Pig. The theme song listed many of the new characters in its lyrics: *"They're furry, they're funny. They're Babs and Buster Bunny. Montana Max has money. Elmyra is a pain. There's Hamton and Plucky. Dizzy Devil's ducky. Furrball's unlucky and Go-Go is insane."* Similar to a big brother/big sister dynamic of a fraternity or sorority, the younger cartoon characters latched on to a mentor. Professors

BOTTOM: Babs Bunny and Buster Bunny were the stars of the show.

like Pepé Le Pew offered a curriculum in Smellogy. Meanwhile, Dean Wile E. Coyote instructed pupils in the School of Hard Knocks while colleague Dean Road Runner offered Outwitting Guidance. Knowledge seekers also learned the finer points of getting clobbered on the head by falling anvils. For their efforts, graduates received the Diploma of Lunacy, allowing them to become full-fledged cartoon characters.

Though story lines concerning Acme Looniversity were typical, academics weren't always the main focus. Parodies also figured prominently in the series, including "The Acme Acres Zone," a spoof on *The Twilight Zone*, starring Buster Bunny as Rod Sterling. "Citizen Max" offered homage to *Citizen Kane's* mystery behind the word "rosebud" by having Hamton play a reporter seeking to discover what Montana Max meant when he said, "Acme."

Chock, full of pop culture allusions, episodes like these, along with "Life in the '90s," offered not only sight gags, but satiric jokes for older viewers. "This show really was designed for a kids' audience," explained Jean MacCurdy, former vice president and general manager of Warner Bros. Animation. "But we [were] also

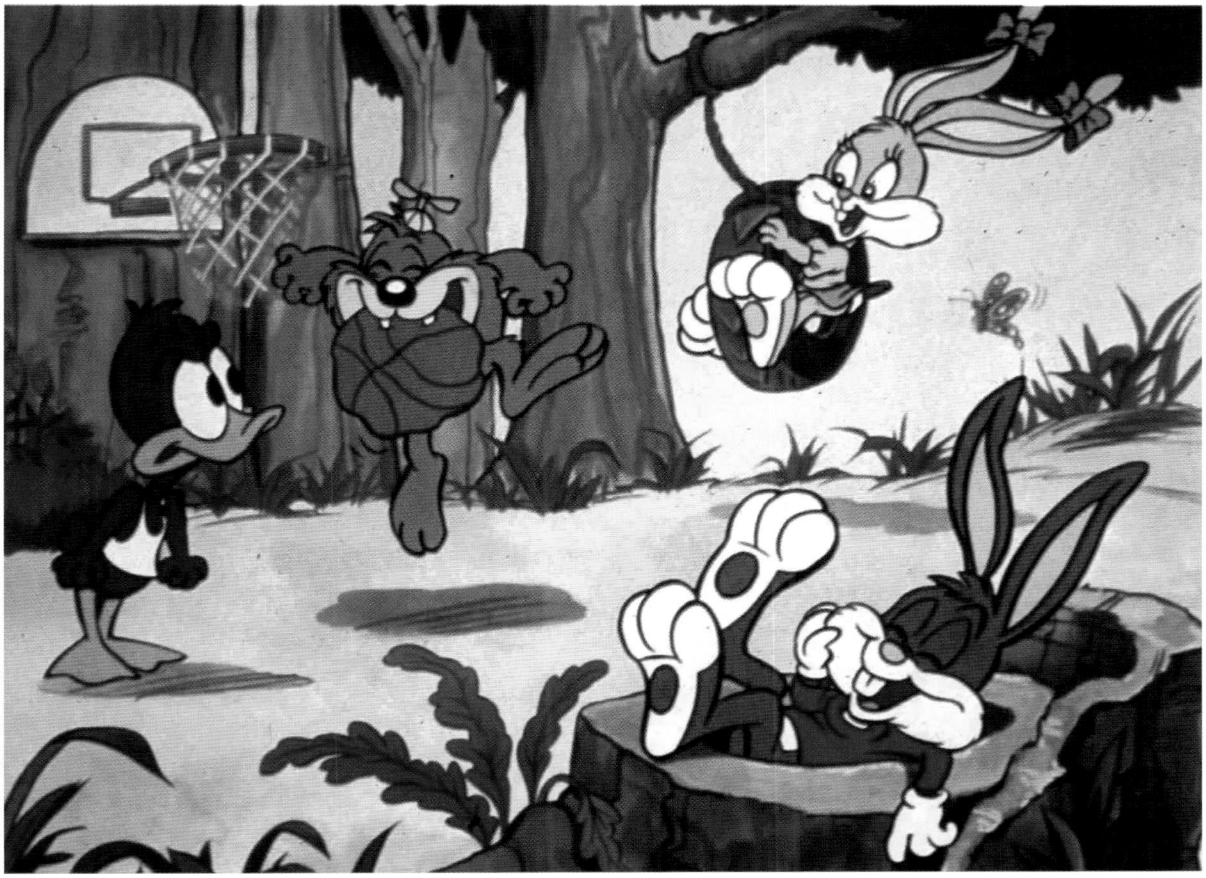

TOP: Plucky, Taz, Babs and Buster enjoys some games and relaxation.

doing something the old guys did. Chuck Jones and Friz Freleng both said that if they could make each other laugh then they felt they were successful. All I know is [we were] making ourselves laugh."

Undoubtedly, Spielberg and his team possessed outsized ambitions for *Tiny Toon Adventures*, both creatively and technically. Though the production tapped voice actor mainstays, like Charlie Adler (*TaleSpin*, *The Real Ghostbusters*) and Don Messick (*Scooby-Doo Where Are You?*, *The Smurfs*), they also screened more than 1,200 voice auditions in less than three months to assemble the robust cast. According to *EW*, each episode required thirty-four weeks to finish, including fourteen weeks of preproduction and fourteen weeks at animation houses in Japan, Korea, Canada, and Taiwan to draw and paint each frame.

All of this preparation and hard work paid off handsomely. First syndicated as an afternoon program in 1990 on 135 stations, *Tiny Toon Adventures* received higher ratings than some of its Disney Afternoon competitors. In 1992, Fox Kids added *Tiny Toon Adventures* to its Saturday morning lineup after it had won numerous Daytime Emmy® Awards in multiple categories, including "Outstanding Animated Program" in 1991. It also earned the Young Artist Award for "Best New Cartoon Series" in 1990 and the Environmental Media Award (EMA) for a "Children's Animated Series" for the 1991 episode "Whales Tales."

ABOVE: Buster, Fifi, and Babs score Plucky on his diving, but Montana Max has the last laugh.

OPPOSITE: Plucky Duck joins Hamton and his family on a trip to Happy World Land in *Tiny Toon Adventures: How I Spent My Summer Vacation* (1992).

In addition to garnering top ratings and critical acclaim, *Tiny Toon Adventures* introduced beloved characters to youngsters who missed out on the Golden Age of cartoons. It reinvigorated Looney Tunes by addressing current events and global issues, like ecology. Though official production ceased in 1992, the show spawned spin-offs, including *The Plucky Ducky Show* and *Pinky and the Brain*. In 1992, the feature-length film *Tiny Toons Adventures: How I Spent My Vacation* debuted as a direct-to-video title. That same year Fox premiered

the prime-time special, *It's a Wonderful Tiny Toons Christmas Special* as a parody of Frank Capra's *It's a Wonderful Life*. Beyond the release of numerous video games on platforms, such as Atari, as well as plush and plastic dolls based on the characters, DC Comics published *Tiny Toons Adventures Magazine* in 1990.

Over the years, Spielberg has often been lauded for infusing portrayals of the past with grandiose charm and nostalgia. Though *Tiny Toon Adventures*, his ode to classic animation, featured beloved characters, the show wasn't sentimental. Due to the creative input of its many talented minds, the series could be both biting and absurd, just like the classic Looney Tunes. As Ruegger said in 1990, "Children's television has always been thought of as this ghetto. But we don't think of ourselves as doing just another show. Right now, at least at *this* company, this is the golden age." Ultimately, *Tiny Toon Adventures* succeeded for the same reason children far and wide have always adored cartoons: they're ridiculous good fun, especially when they do what they've always done best—drop an anvil on someone's head to just make you giggle.

ABOVE: Hamton, Buster, Babs, and Plucky enjoy the beach.

Schooled for an Episode

Middle-schoolers Renee Carter, Sarah Creef, and Amy Crosby were such big fans of the show they penned an original script for an episode entitled, "Buster & Babs Go Hawaiian," which they sent off to the show. "Deluged with mail from thousands of would-be screenwriters, Tinseltown's studios routinely send back such unsolicited offerings without so much as a cursory reading," wrote Mark St. John in a 1991 article for The *Daily Press*. "Luckily for these kids, however, they mistakenly sent their 120-page script for Spielberg's syndicated cartoon show, *Tiny Toon Adventures,* to the Fox broadcasting network's Los Angeles office. There, a conscientious clerk slipped the misdirected story into an official Fox mailing envelope and forwarded it to Spielberg's production company, Amblin Entertainment.

Defying the odds, their script landed in the hands of Steven Spielberg, who flew the girls out to California to punch up the material with the show's writing staff. Not only were they paid well for their work, the trio were caricatured by the animators into a small scene in the episode.

Darkwing Duck

YEARS ON AIR

1991–1993

NETWORK

ABC

NUMBER OF EPISODES

91

CHARACTERS AND VOICE ACTORS

Darkwing Duck: Jim Cummings
Launchpad McQuack:
Terry McGovern
Gosalyn Mallard:
Christine Cavanaugh
Megavolt: Dan Castellaneta

"I told the guys, every episode you have to do at least one catchphrase, and every episode, Darkwing has to say the words, 'Let's get dangerous,'" said *Darkwing Duck* Creator Tad Stones in a 2016 interview with the *Hollywood Reporter*. "If you are going to have a slogan you have to commit to it as a slogan." Stones stayed true to his word. His witty film noir superhero homage lit up the night— or rather Saturday mornings—with snappy dramatic entrances: "I am the terror that flaps in the night,

I am the batteries that are not included." Or "I am the terror that flaps in the night, I am the finger that scrapes the blackboard of your soul."

Combining witty dialogue with spy fiction and comic clichés found in such comics as *The Shadow*, *Green Hornet*, and *Batman*, *Darkwing Duck* brilliantly lampooned the seriousness of a vigilante crime fighter battling sinister forces in the dark. "[*Darkwing Duck*] was really fun because it was totally original," said Stones in an interview for

Animation World Network. "I could make up all the characters and use all those Silver Age comic book clichés on purpose, not because we had run out of story ideas, but because that was the whole point of the show."

In 1989, a *DuckTales* episode, "Double-O-Duck," spoofing James Bond, caught the attention of Disney executive Jeffrey Katzenberg. Katzenberg took the idea for a new series to Stones, a creative manager in charge of developing content. "To clarify, I was assigned the name 'Double-O Duck', a title Jeffrey Katzenberg thought would make for a good show," explains Stones. "The first attempt was a spy parody with little heart. I didn't believe in it at all. Neither did Jeffrey. The difference was that I was ready to wipe my hands of it and move on, [but] Jeffrey wanted me to try again."

At the time, Stones had been engaged in a reboot of the cartoon classic *The Rocky and Bullwinkle Show*. However, when Disney ultimately decided not to pursue the production, Stones decided to turn his attention toward developing the secret-agent duck idea. Though the original *DuckTales* episode starred Launchpad McQuack, Stones wanted Drake Mallard, a vain caped crusader, to be the lead. "Everybody loved the show except for the lawyers who said the rights to the 'Double-O' name belonged to the guys making the *Bond* films. We held a contest to name the duck and Alan Burnett won with the suggestion, 'Darkwing.' I added 'Duck' for silliness and a legend was born."

Saddled with an ego, "the size of a small planet," according to criminal mastermind Taurus Bulba,

and possessing no special skills, Darkwing was not exactly Bruce Wayne. Voiced by Jim Cummings (*Chip 'n' Dale Rescue Rangers*, *The New Adventures of Winnie the Pooh*), the Darkwing hero—once known as "Drake the Dweeb" in high school—bumbled, alliterated, and wore cheap cologne and boxers with tiny hearts. His preferred weapon of choice was a gas gun that expelled itching powder as well as plain, old, regular blue gas—when it worked. Answering to the name Drake Mallard, he pretended to live an average existence at 537 Avian Way to throw off suspicion. Nestled in suburbia, he endured his brainless neighbors, the Muddlefoots, sleeping through most of the day. By night, he donned a cape and mask and targeted bad guys. Not for selfless reasons. This duck was out for fame and notoriety.

Yet, for all his bluster and pretension, Darkwing had a soft side. In the episode, "Darkly Dawns the Dawk, Part 2," he adopted nine-year-old Gosalyn after her only living relative, Professor Waddlemeyer, died at the hands of Bulba's henchmen. According to Stones, when conceiving *Darkwing Duck*, he and his creative team wondered what would happen if Batman had to raise a little girl. "That's what gave the show real heart, the real dynamic. Gosalyn was kind of inspired by my own daughter, who was only about two at the time." Both an egomaniac and a do-gooder, Darkwing had to continually balance his lust for glory against his desire to be a good dad in the series. "I get told at conventions how important that relationship was to people," said Stones. "I've had people near tears saying they had a rough family life and the father-daughter energy of that show

OPPOSITE: (left to right) Gosalyn Mallard, Darkwing Duck, Honker Muddlefoot, and Launchpad McQuack on the go.

BELOW: No one could ever contend Darkwing Duck wasn't a snappy dresser.

was super important to them."

Besides Gosalyn, the fictional city of St. Canard metropolis—a parody of Batman's Gotham City—was populated by other amusing characters. Though Stones maintains there is no continuity between *DuckTales* and *Darkwing Duck*, fans of the former will recall Darkwing's loyal sidekick, Launchpad McQuack, also played a lead-ing role in that series. However, according to

Stones, the *Darkwing Duck* Launchpad McQuack, voiced by Dan Castellaneta (*The Simpsons*), was not the same character from *DuckTales*. "Because Launchpad appeared in *DuckTales* and we used Roboduck as the Superman character, the hero who gets all the glory as opposed to Darkwing, fans try to connect the two realities. They are two different universes in my book. We work in the alternate Duckiverse." In addi-tion to Bulba, a profusion of inspired villains opposed Darkwing, includ-ing Megavolt, Quackerjack, Bushroot, Steelbeak, Tuskerninni, the Liquidator, Splatter Phoenix, Moliarty, and Negaduck, Darkwing's evil doppelganger from an alternate universe.

Produced by The Walt Disney Company, *Darkwing Duck* first appeared on The Disney Channel's syndicated pro-gramming block, The Disney Afternoon, as well as ABC's Saturday morning lineup in 1991. The show went on to earn several interesting distinctions. *Darkwing Duck* was one of the first syndicated American cartoon series broadcast in the former Soviet Union. In both 1992 and

TOP LEFT: Jim Cummings, the voice of Darkwing Duck.

TOP RIGHT: Christine Cavanaugh, the voice of Gosalyn.

BOTTOM LEFT: Dan Castellaneta, the voice of Megavolt.

BOTTOM RIGHT: Tim Curry, the voice of Taurus Bulba.

1993, the show received Emmy® nominations for Outstanding Animated Programming.

Though *Darkwing Duck* ended after three seasons, it lived on in other ways. Multiple video games based on the show appeared on different platforms, including the Nintendo Entertainment System and Game Boy. Disney Comics published a *Darkwing Duck* miniseries in 1991, and

BELOW: In a few episodes, Darkwing Duck worked as a member of the Justice Ducks, a group of fellow crime fighting superheroes. The group included (clockwise from the center top) Stegmutt, Gizmoduck, Darkwing Duck, Neptunia, and Morgana Macawber.

in 2010 Boom! Studios released *The Duck Knight Returns*, parodying the Frank Miller comics and Christopher Nolan's 2008 live-action movie *The Dark Knight*. Rap aficionados may also fondly remember "Kickin' in the Groove," a hip-hop video used to promote *Darkwing Duck*'s premiere with awesome lyrics like: *Whack! Smack! What was that? Darkwing Duck is on the attack!*

For a show based on beloved tropes and comic book conventions, Darkwing Duck proved to be an original synthesis, combining humor, slapstick action, and genuine heart. Week after week, the one and only Darkwing Duck got witty, he got bold, he got daring, he got dangerous . . . but not too dangerous.

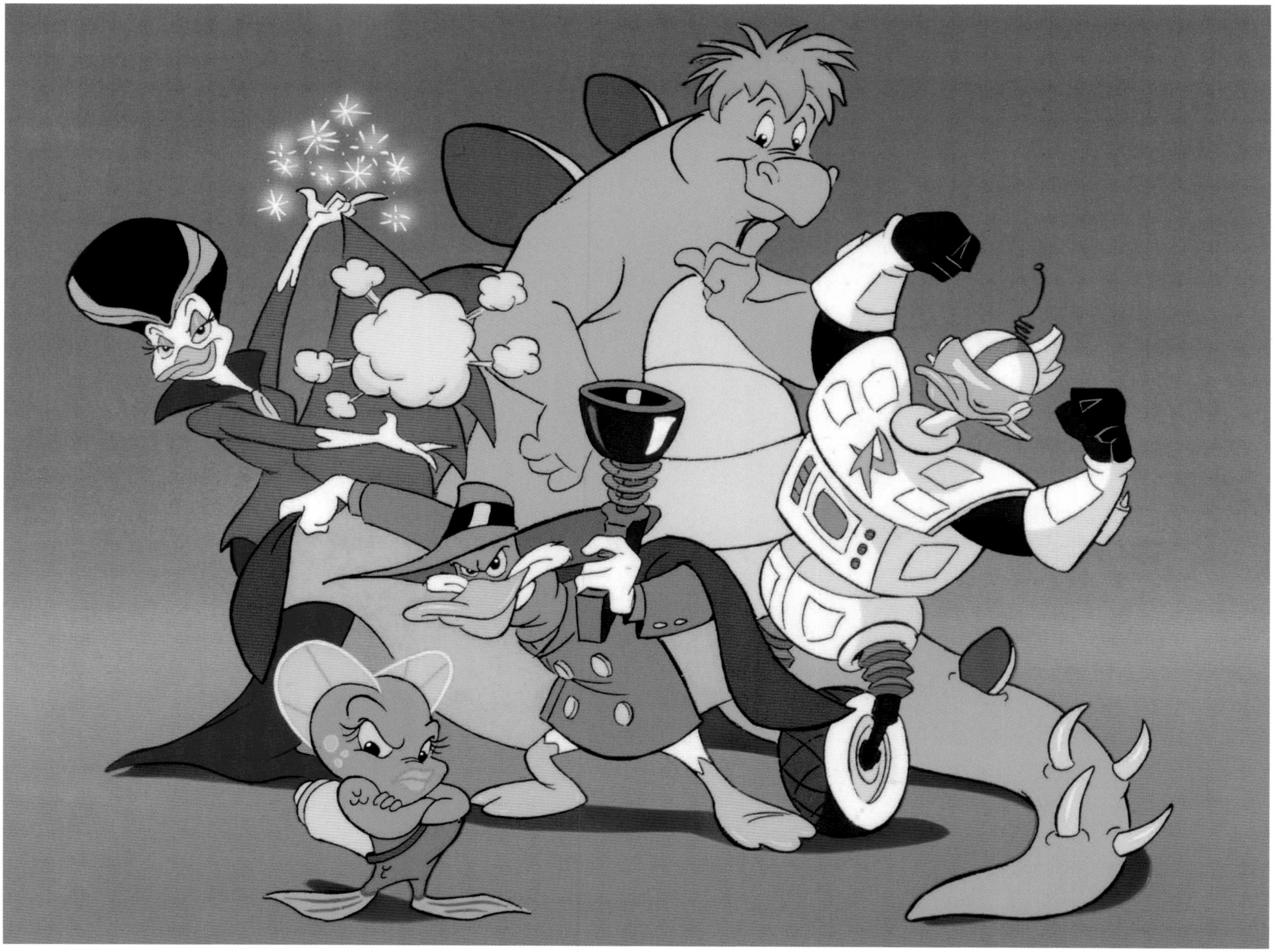

Golden Crisp Cereal

"Can't get enough of that Golden Crisp! It's got the crunch with punch."

In the '90s, boys and girls were served up energy-packed puffed wheat to power up. To make sure they received their "delicious part of a complete breakfast," their pal Sugar Bear faced down formidable nemeses bent on stealing the cereal, such as Blob, Sugar Fox, and greedy Granny Goodwitch, the old lady who hid out in her suburban fortress with high-tech surveillance gear to get her box of golden goodness.

Voiced for decades by actor Gerry Mathews in the crooning manner of Bing Crosby, Sugar Bear had his own smooth style and never got rattled. Much care went into crafting Sugar Bear's personality, going back to the '40s when he began as a mascot for the cereal, then called Sugar Crisp. He was featured in the 1964 Saturday morning cartoon, "Linus the Lion-Hearted," and developed a muscular alter-ego called "Super Bear" in the '80s to fight monsters keen on pilfering the puffs.

Sugar Bear was so cool his theme song appeared in other pop cultural mainstays, such as *The Simpsons* and *The Sopranos* proving Sugar Bear was a sweet dude.

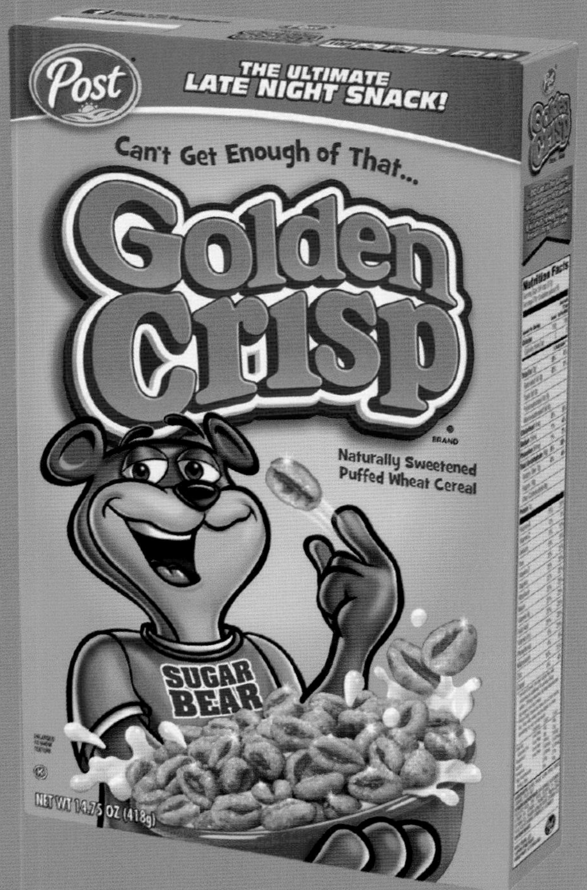
Post
THE ULTIMATE LATE NIGHT SNACK!
Can't Get Enough of That...
Golden Crisp
BRAND
Naturally Sweetened Puffed Wheat Cereal
SUGAR BEAR
NET WT 14.75 OZ (418g)

RIGHT: The Sugar Bear character was central in the kid-friendly commercials and box packaging.

Animaniacs

YEARS ON AIR

1993–1998

NETWORK

Fox Kids, WB

NUMBER OF EPISODES

99

CHARACTERS AND VOICE ACTORS

Yakko: Rob Paulsen
Wakko: Jess Harnell
Dot: Teresa MacNeille
Ralph the Guard: Frank Welker
Slappy Squirrel: Sherri Stoner
The Brain: Maurice LaMarche

Just as Hanna-Barbera Productions dominated Saturday mornings for much of the latter twentieth century, Steven Spielberg had big designs to usurp 1990s cartoon programming. Following his success with *Tiny Toon Adventures*, Spielberg, once again, tapped producer Tom Ruegger and Warner Bros. Animation to generate another irreverently wacky series. At the time, Ruegger had three characters in the works, modeled on the personalities of his three sons. In homage to classic animation, Ruegger conceived of a sibling trio physically resembling Mickey Mouse, with elements of the 1920 through 1930s black-and-white characters Bosko and Honey, as well as Felix the Cat.

The quick-witted siblings exhibited some of the cartoon lunacy found in Merrie Melodies, Looney Tunes, and the more recent *Tiny Toon Adventures*, but, make no mistake—*Animaniacs* was a deeply

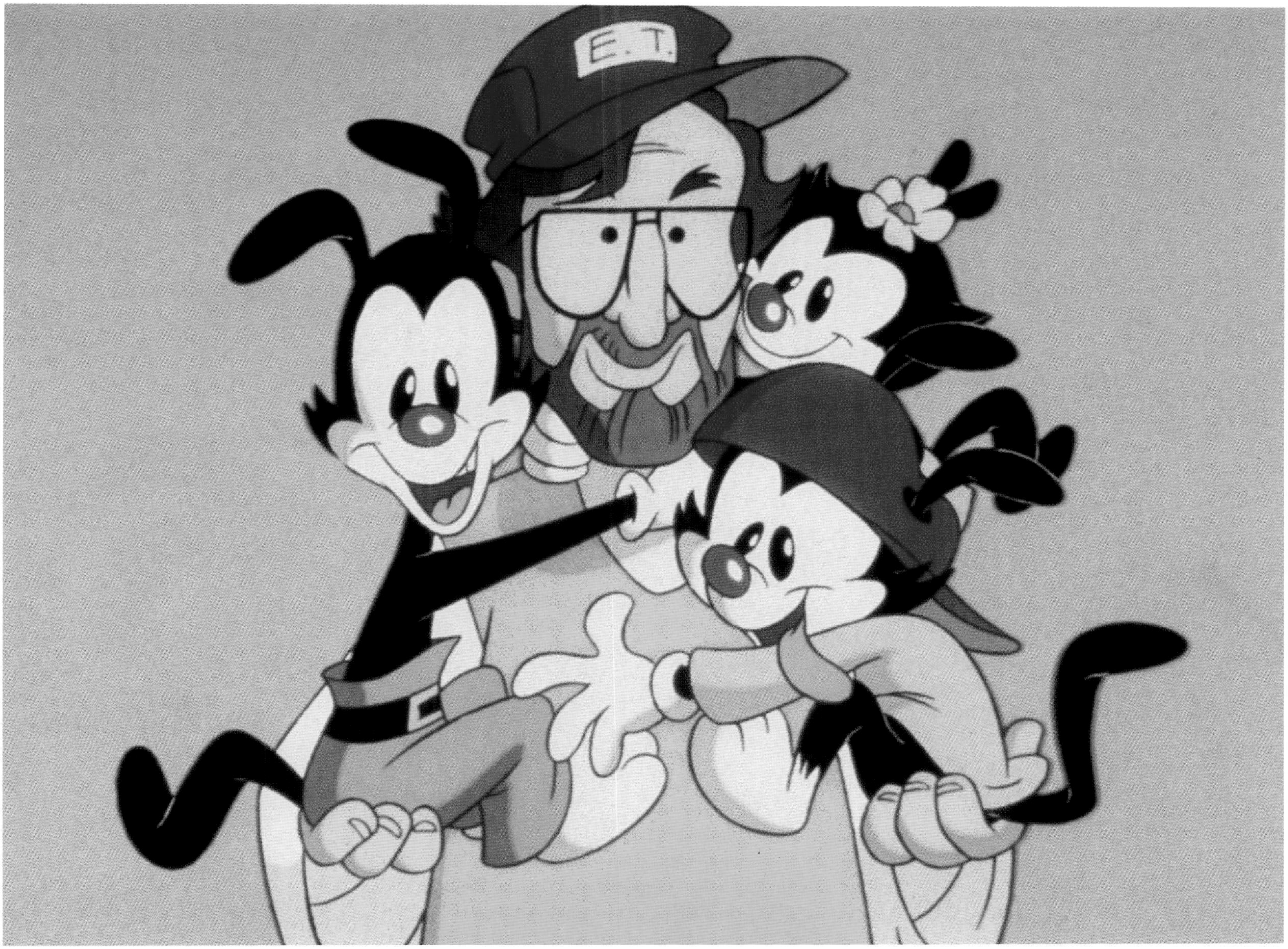

smart program aimed at kids and adults alike. "It's the only children's programming right now that is intelligent, honestly," said Tom Ruegger in a 1993 *Los Angeles Times* article. "Most cartoons today are (characters) chasing each other and hitting each other and making glib comments. Our program deals with ideas that are looked at in humorous ways, dealing with intelligence at major events through history."

Informed by clever writing, *Animaniacs* focused on the Warner siblings, delightfully incorrigible stars from the 1930s, who were locked in the Warner Bros. water tower until their escape in the '90s. This familial trio consisted of Yakko, the oldest who owed some of his comic styling to Groucho Marx of the Marx Brothers, with his motor-mouthed wisecracking. The least intelligent of the group, Wakko, the middle brother, possessed a British

OPPOSITE: Set on the Warner Bros. studio lot, *Animaniacs* starred the Warner siblings: Yakko, Wakko, and Dot.

ABOVE: The Warner siblings give their creator Steven Spielberg a hug.

BOTTOM: Dot being ever so cute (and presumably dreaming of her crush Mel Gibson).

Liverpool accent and liked to chow down. Dot, the spunky little sister, routinely proved she could keep up with the boys. Whenever her brothers encountered an attractive female, they'd wolf whistle, "Hellooo Nurse!" Not to be undone, Dot would say the same thing upon encountering handsome men, including her crush Mel Gibson.

The Warners comprised just a fraction of the cast, however. Because *Animaniacs* functioned as a variety show with brief segments, their costars had plenty of time to indulge in their own hijinks. Similar to *Tiny Toon Adventures*, the theme song aptly introduced the characters in a clever and funny way: *Meet Pinky and the Brain who want to rule the universe, Or meet Ralph and Dr. Scratchansniff, Say hi to Hello Nurse. Goodfeathers flock together; Slappy whacks 'em with her purse. Buttons chases Mindy, while Rita sings a verse.*

In a 1995 interview with *TV Guide*, Spielberg defended his irreverent show against critics who complained of violence from characters like Slappy, the grumpy squirrel who liked to shove dynamite down villains' pants. "It's not the kind of provocative violence that the earlier Warner Bros. cartoons inspired. . . . I think cartoons should make people laugh, but I think they should also make people stop and say, 'Wow, did I hear that in a cartoon?'"

Spielberg's desire to elevate kids' programming to where viewers might wonder about the things they saw or heard led *Animaniacs* to become an unconventional series with a

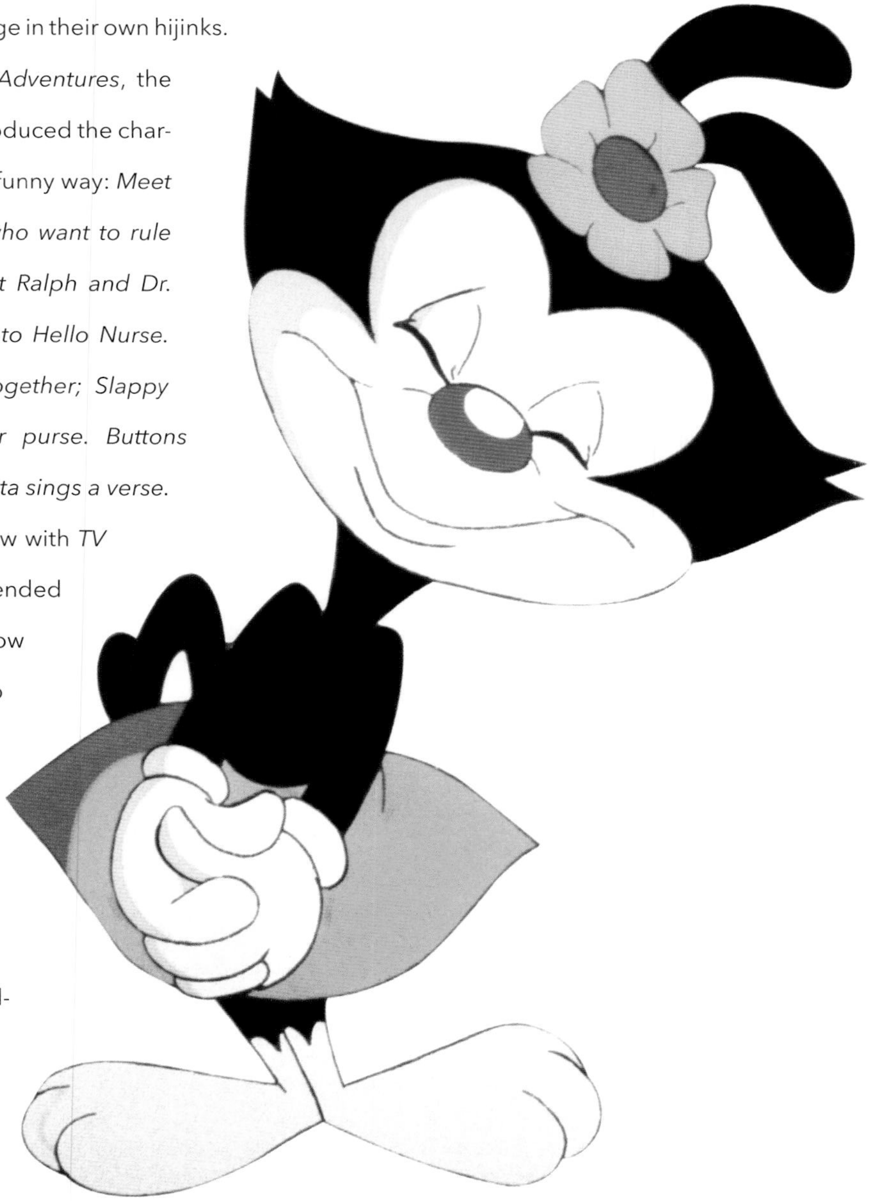

precocious sensibility—one that took on political correctness, popular culture, and, yes, even educated audiences. Preferring not to talk down to kids, *Animaniacs* invited children into the world of grown-ups by parodying the Beatles' movie *A Hard Day's Night*, and R-rated fare like *The Godfather* and *Goodfellas* in the "Goodfeathers" segments. In the episode, "Three Tenors and You're Out," Slappy and Skippy planned to see a Dodgers game but end up at a concert parodying the Three Tenors. The musical skit, *Yakko's World*, offered an ode to the world's countries set to "Mexican Hat Dance." Meanwhile other musical numbers taught boys and girls the difference between time zones and how to remember US presidents—*Jimmy Carter liked camping trips/And Ronald Regan's speeches'* scripts all came from famous movie clips.

Undoubtedly, the music featured in *Animaniacs* provided much of the show's appeal, and to get it right, Spielberg pulled out all the stops. Neil Strauss, writing for the *New York Times*, explained, "Instead of relying on canned synthesizer melodies, as most cartoons have since they moved from the cinema screen to the television set in the 1960s, the team that work[ed] on *Animaniacs* employ[ed] a twenty-piece orchestra, [wrote] elaborate song-and-dance numbers in the styles of everyone from Tom Lehrer to Stephen Sondheim, and use[d] the same piano that has been play[ing] in Warner cartoons since 1928."

Once more Spielberg relied on *Tiny Toon Adventures*' casting and voice director Andrea Romano to get the right voices for the characters.

TOP: Jess Harnell, the voice of Wakko.

CENTER: Rob Paulen, the voice of Yakko.

BOTTOM: Tress MacNeille, the voice of Dot.

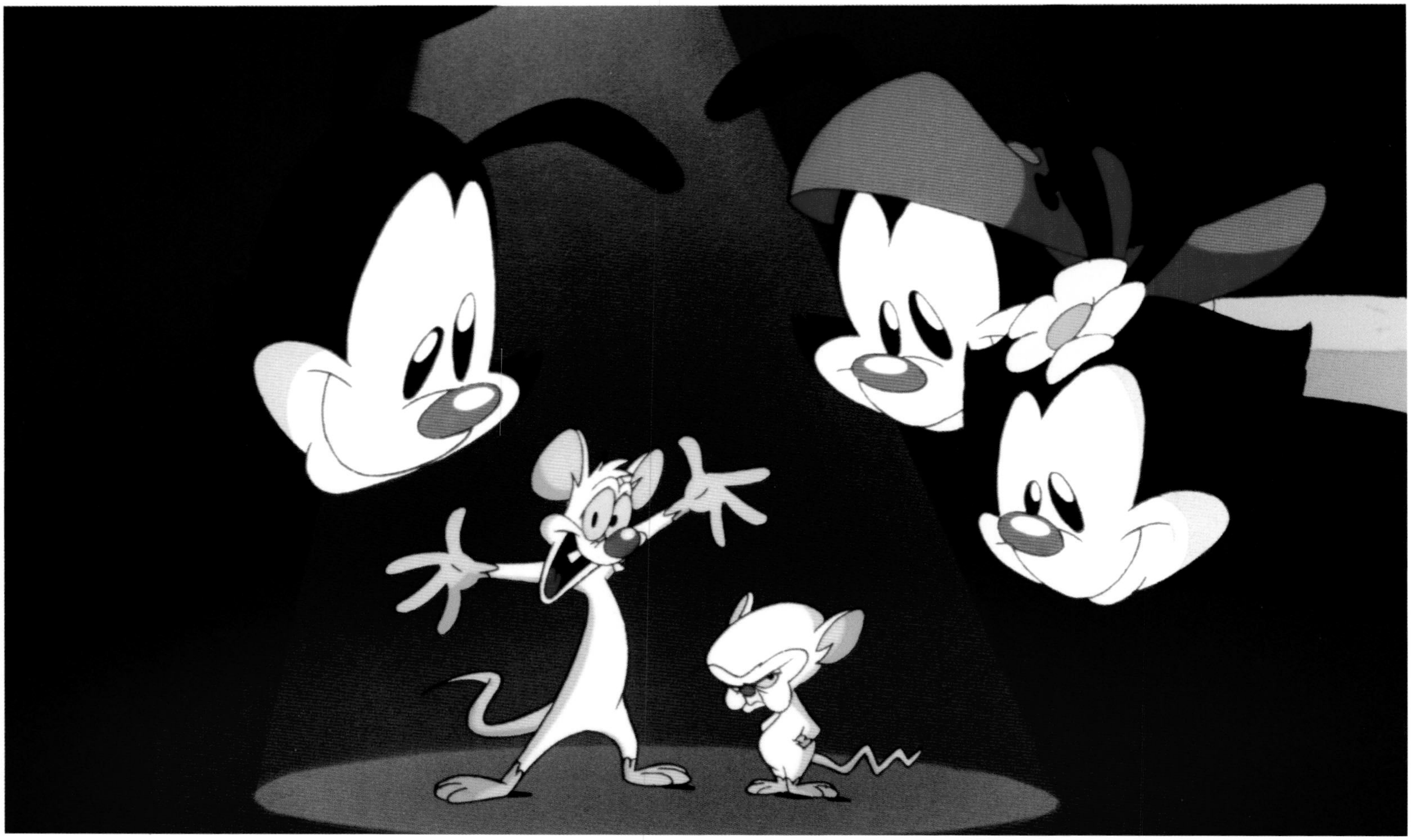

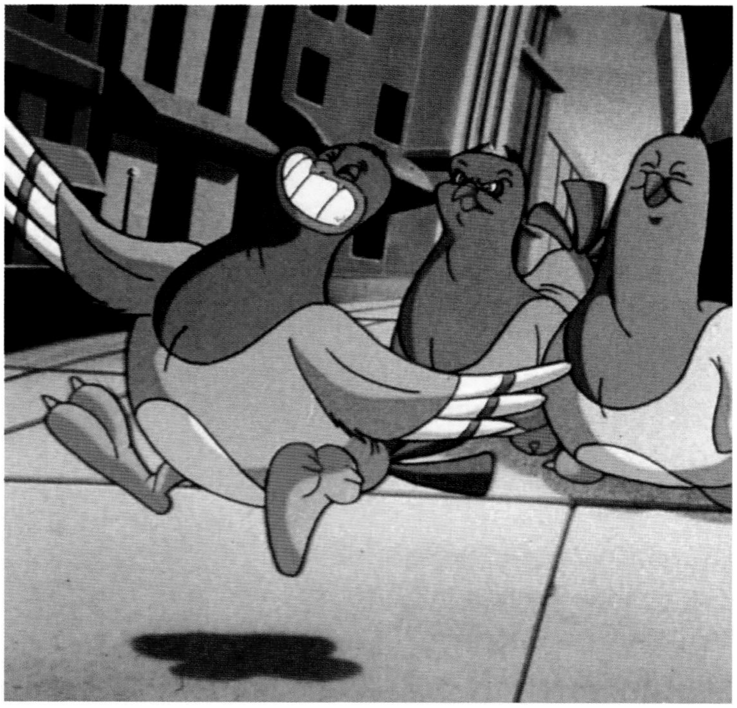

TOP: Yakko, Wakko, and Dot observe Pinky and the Brain.

BOTTOM: Presenting "The Goodfeathers," a parody segment spoofing mafia movies like *The Godfather*.

Romano knew she wanted Rob Paulsen (*Teenage Mutant Ninja Turtles*) for Yakko and Tress MacNeille (*The Simpsons*) for Dot, but had trouble casting Wakko. After screening hundreds of auditions, she brought in Jess Harnell, a relative newbie in animation. After proving himself by doing impressions of all the Beatles, Romano knew they had found Wakko's voice. "Wakko [was] kind of cute and a smart-ass," said Romano. "He's really kind of the silly one, and the Ringo voice that Jess did worked so well for that character."

ABOVE: Yakko gives a lesson in geography.

The Wheel of Morality

Designed to satirize the FCC's insistence on adding moral values and educational requirements to programming, the show's creators hit upon an ingenious idea. Why not set up a revolving wheel to learn the day's lesson?

Typically, Yakko, Wakko, and Dot would be doing something else, when Yakko would suddenly stop and say, "It's that time again!" Then he'd spin the wheel while intoning the rhyme: "Wheel of Morality, turn, turn, turn; tell us the lesson that we should learn." The funny twist was that the moral would turn out to be nonsensical and ridiculous. Some of the "lessons" were:

- "If you can't say something nice, you're probably at the ice capades."

- "Early to rise and early to bed makes a man healthy but socially dead."

- "Possums have pouches like kangaroos."

- "People who live in glass houses should get dressed with the lights out."

- "The answer, my friend, is blowing in the wind, except in New Jersey where what's blowing in the wind smells funny."

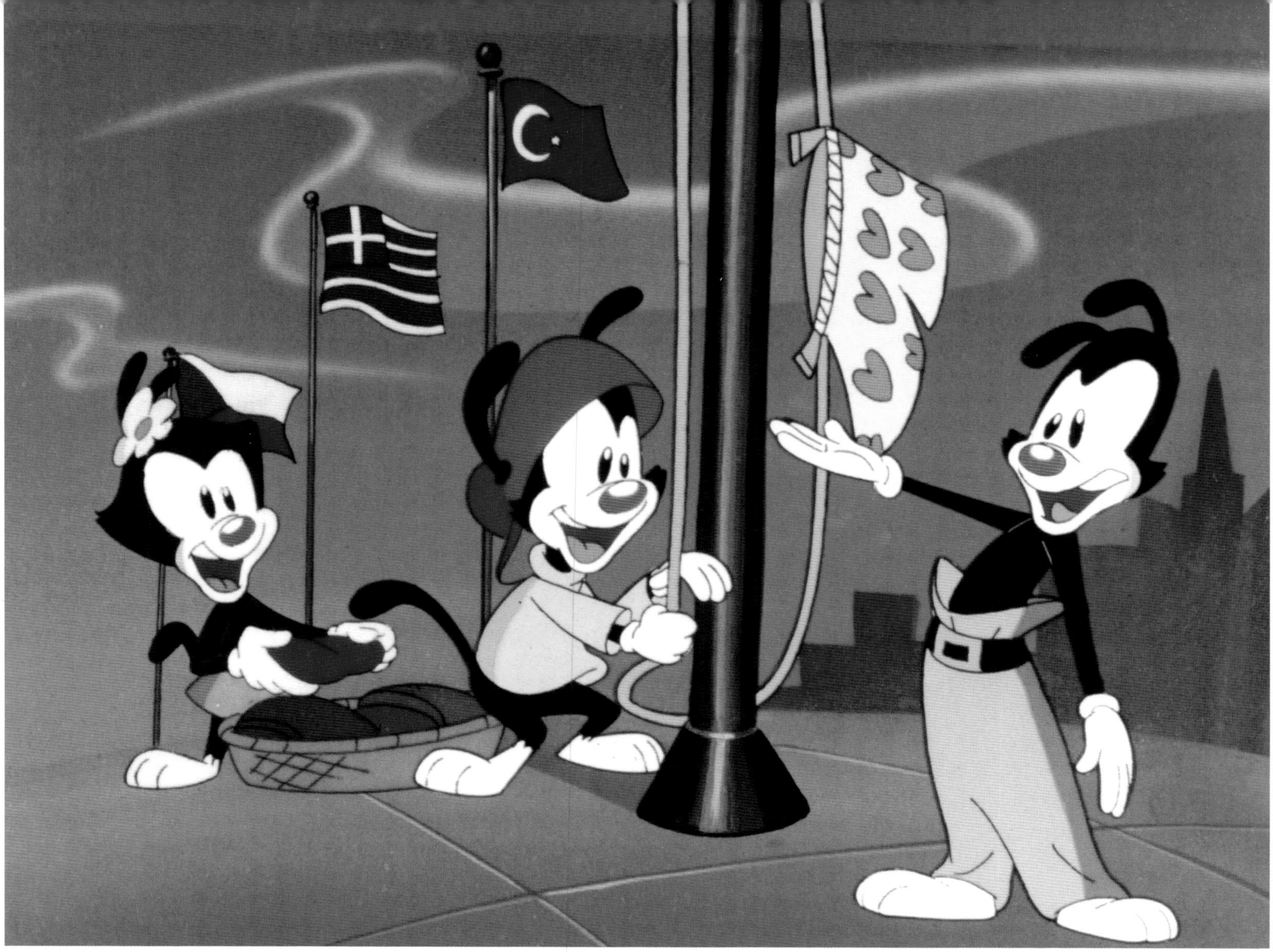

ABOVE: The Animanicas raise their shorts for a salute.

With excellent voice talent, exceptional musical prowess, and clever, yet subversive, screenwriting, *Animaniacs* quickly secured a strong fan base upon airing in 1993 on Fox Kids. According to the *New York Times*, *Animaniacs* held the distinction of being the "second most popular children's series on television (outranked only by *Mighty Morphin Power Rangers*)." Interestingly, the *Times* pointed out, *Animaniacs*' popularity extended to grown-ups. "More than 23 percent of the Saturday morning (9 A.M.) viewers are adults 25 or older." Taking advantage of nascent internet technology, *Animaniacs* aficionados used the web to generate sites discussing the show.

Despite early objections from critics regarding violence, *Animaniacs* became a critical darling, taking home the Peabody Award for its debut season, and it was nominated for two Annie Awards in 1994 for "Best Animated Television Program" and "Best Achievement for Voice Acting" (Frank Welker). It won eight Daytime Emmy® Awards in various categories, including "Outstanding Music Direction and Composition." Beloved characters Pinky and Brain would also go on to launch their own eponymous breakout show in 1995. *Animaniacs* would inspire Genesis, Game Boy, and Xbox video games as well as a DC Comics comic book based on the series, which ran from 1995-2000. *Wakko's Wish*, a direct-to-video feature length movie, also appeared in 1999.

According to Spielberg, the best shows "are those that leave some substance behind in the wake of flamboyant entertainment." Now considered a cult classic for its cheeky innuendo, the series wasn't afraid to push the envelope on social mores, offering naughty, yet good-natured humor most kids' programming wouldn't dare try today. It was a roller coaster ride of a cartoon with quippy, high and low-brow comedy that left you wondering, "Hey! Are they are really allowed to do that?"

AFTER THESE MESSAGES . . .

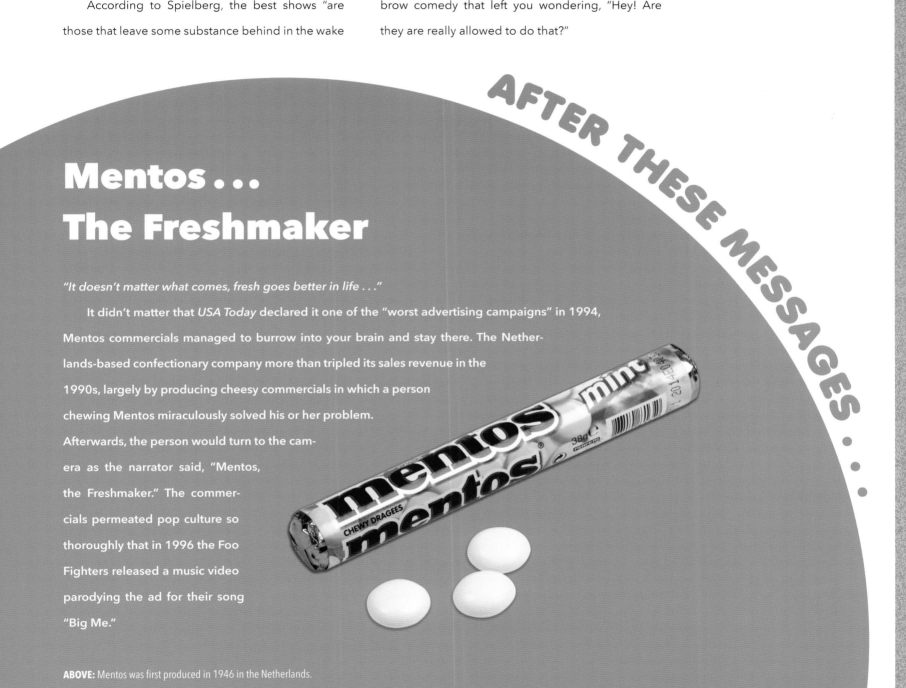

Mentos . . . The Freshmaker

"It doesn't matter what comes, fresh goes better in life . . ."

It didn't matter that *USA Today* declared it one of the "worst advertising campaigns" in 1994, Mentos commercials managed to burrow into your brain and stay there. The Netherlands-based confectionary company more than tripled its sales revenue in the 1990s, largely by producing cheesy commercials in which a person chewing Mentos miraculously solved his or her problem. Afterwards, the person would turn to the camera as the narrator said, "Mentos, the Freshmaker." The commercials permeated pop culture so thoroughly that in 1996 the Foo Fighters released a music video parodying the ad for their song "Big Me."

mentos
mint
CHEWY DRAGEES
mentos
38g

ABOVE: Mentos was first produced in 1946 in the Netherlands.

YEARS ON AIR

1995–1998

NETWORK

The WB

NUMBER OF EPISODES

65

CHARACTERS AND VOICE ACTORS

Pinky: Rob Paulsen
The Brain: Maurice LaMarche
Snowball the Hamster: Roddy McDowall
Billie: Tress MacNeille
Pharfignewton: Frank Welker
Larry: Billy West

Pinky and the Brain

First introduced in the *Animaniacs* episode "Win Big," this rodent duo broke the glass ceiling for lab mice everywhere when they got their own spin-off series. However, even this feat wasn't good enough for the megalomaniac Brain—after all, there was only one thing he desired: global domination. Pinky and Brain began their journey in a cage within the Acme Labs research facility located beneath a suspension bridge in an unidentified American city. The two received their language abilities and extraordinary intelligence—Brain clearly more so than Pinky—as part of a genetic splicing experiment known as the Biological Recombinant Algorithmic Intelligence Nexus or B.R.A.I.N. Ever since, Brain set his sights on international subjugation alongside his hapless accomplice, Pinky.

Created by *Animaniacs* producer Tom Ruegger, the mice were based on the writing team of Tom Minton and Eddie Fitzgerald. According to Maurice LaMarche, the voice of Brain, Ruegger observed the

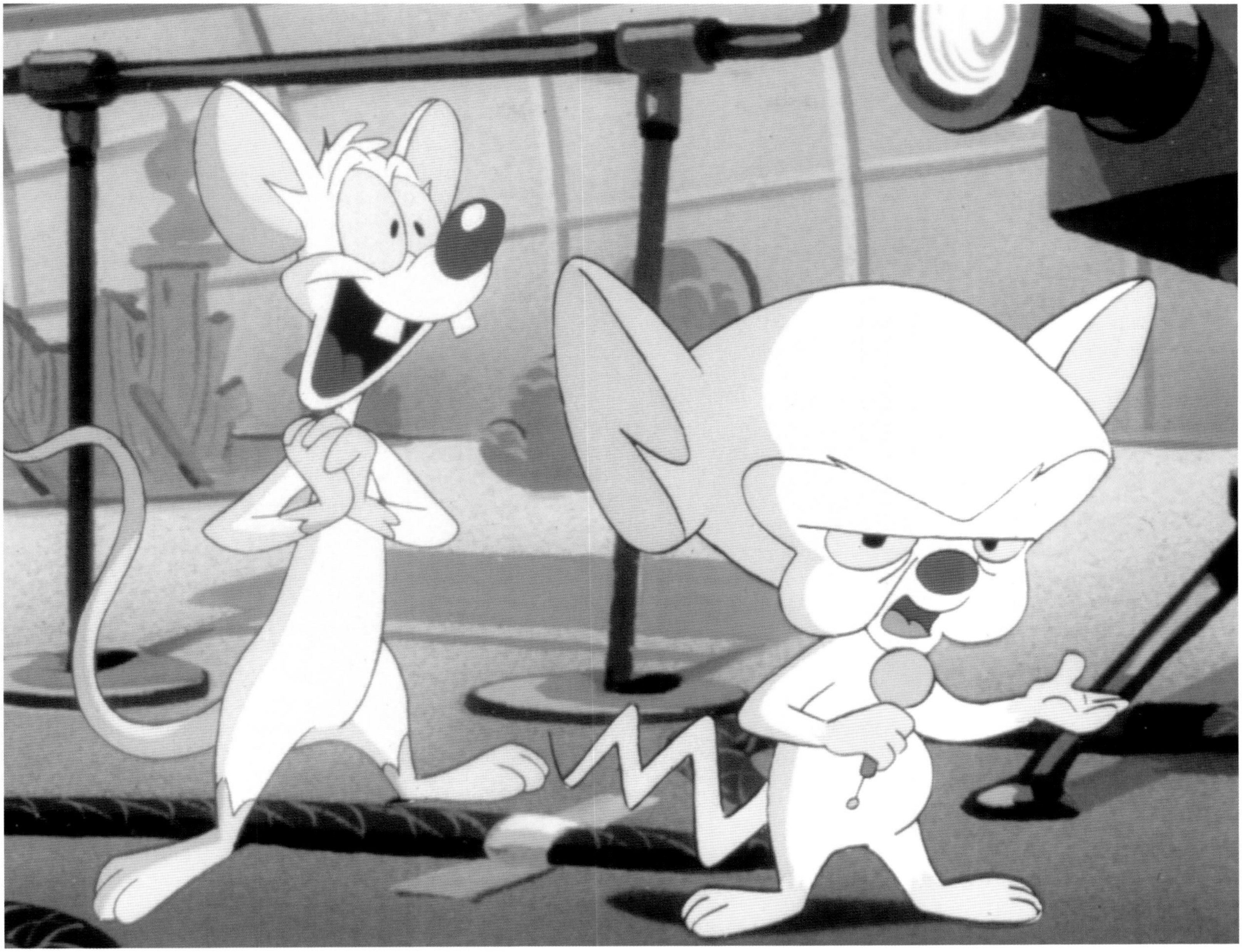

two writers together so much that he asked, "'What if Eddie and Tom tried to take over the world? What if they were lab mice?'" Two years into the *Animaniacs'* run on Fox Kids, *Pinky and the Brain* had amassed a very strong fan base. "*Pinky and the Brain* stood out for its ingenuity and extreme economy," explained Jonah Weiner in the *New York Times*. "The show has only two recurring characters to speak of—the talking lab mice of the title—and precisely one plot set into motion in the opening moments of each installment with the same twenty-three words: 'Gee, Brain, what do you want to do tonight?' 'The same thing we do every night, Pinky. Try to take over the world.'"

Based on its growing popularity, it made sense for Amblin, Spielberg's production company, in

OPPOSITE: Why wouldn't you decide to place a large magnet atop the Earth?

ABOVE: Brain hatches another misguided plan with Pinky's unwavering support.

PINKY
BRAIN 16
CAN TAKE OVER THE WORLD

ABOVE LEFT: Rob Paulsen, voice of Pinky, attends an *Animaniacs* panel in a fitting t-shirt, 2017.

ABOVE RIGHT: Maurice LaMarche, voice of Brain, speaking to a panel audience, 2017.

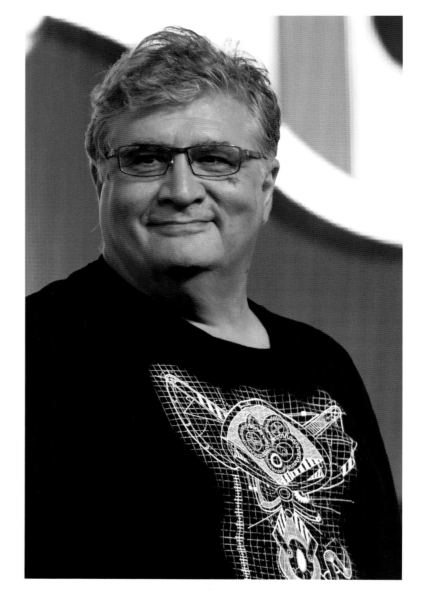

conjunction with Warner Bros., to spin off the series to the WB, a new network, in 1995. Under Ruegger's development, *Pinky and the Brain* expanded from a short skit to a twenty-two-minute program. As a result, Brain's schemes became ever more elaborate—and ludicrous. In the episode "Brainania," Brain created a fictional island nation to fleece America for billions in foreign–aid all so he could construct a humongous clothes dryer for the purposes of generating enough static electricity to enslave humanity. In the *Animaniacs* episode "When Mice Ruled the Earth," Brain concocted an equally absurd plan to steal H.G. Wells's time machine to modify history in his favor.

"By utilizing the invisible forces of nature, we shall make this time machine work, with this. This paper clip will serve as an antenna grabbing neutrinos from the cosmos and providing ignition for this craft. But first, we shall travel back to the primordial era, alter the course of evolution, and then return to the present world not dominated by humans, but by mice, and they will choose me as their leader."

Naturally, the grandiloquent Brain served as the show's narrative engine, driving plotlines with his preposterous plans. Often rude and coldly unemotional, Brain wore a perpetual scowl on his face. LaMarche recalls he was the first and only person to audition for this role. "I saw the model sheet for Brain, with that furrowed brow and dour expression and pudgy cheeks, I thought immediately, 'Oh, this is Orson Welles.' I did Welles with the dialogue and they went, 'Oh my God, that's genius. We didn't think of that!' They cast me on the spot." Though Brain possessed frightfully keen intelligence allowing him to conceive of complex schemes, he often inadvertently foiled his own plans. He bungled little details, such as forgetting that gold is quite heavy in "Opportunity Knox," and therefore impossible for two small mice to lift.

When Brain wasn't derailing his own plots, lovable Pinky was there to undermine them with baffling idiocy. Childlike and curious, Pinky possessed a scatterbrained personality, prone to delivering outlandish non sequiturs any time Brain posed the question: "Are you pondering what I'm pondering?" "I think so, Brain, but if we covered the world in salad dressing wouldn't the asparagus feel left out?"

Pinky also suffered from verbal tics, forcing him to spit out gibberish like "gonk," "poit," "zort," and "troz." Deeply loyal, Pinky also served as the show's moral compass. Rob Paulsen, who voiced Pinky, said, "I hope, it is truly my hope, that Pinky teaches us that having almost unconditional love and support for people in whom you believe is important."

A variety of supporting characters surrounded Pinky and Brain, comprised of other genetically modified animals. Billie, voiced by Tress MacNeille (*Futurama*), was an attractive female mouse with an IQ rivaling Brain's. He was naturally smitten with her but worried she might beat him to the punch of world domination. A racing mare named Pharfignewton supplied the love interest for Pinky. Meanwhile, another mouse named Larry

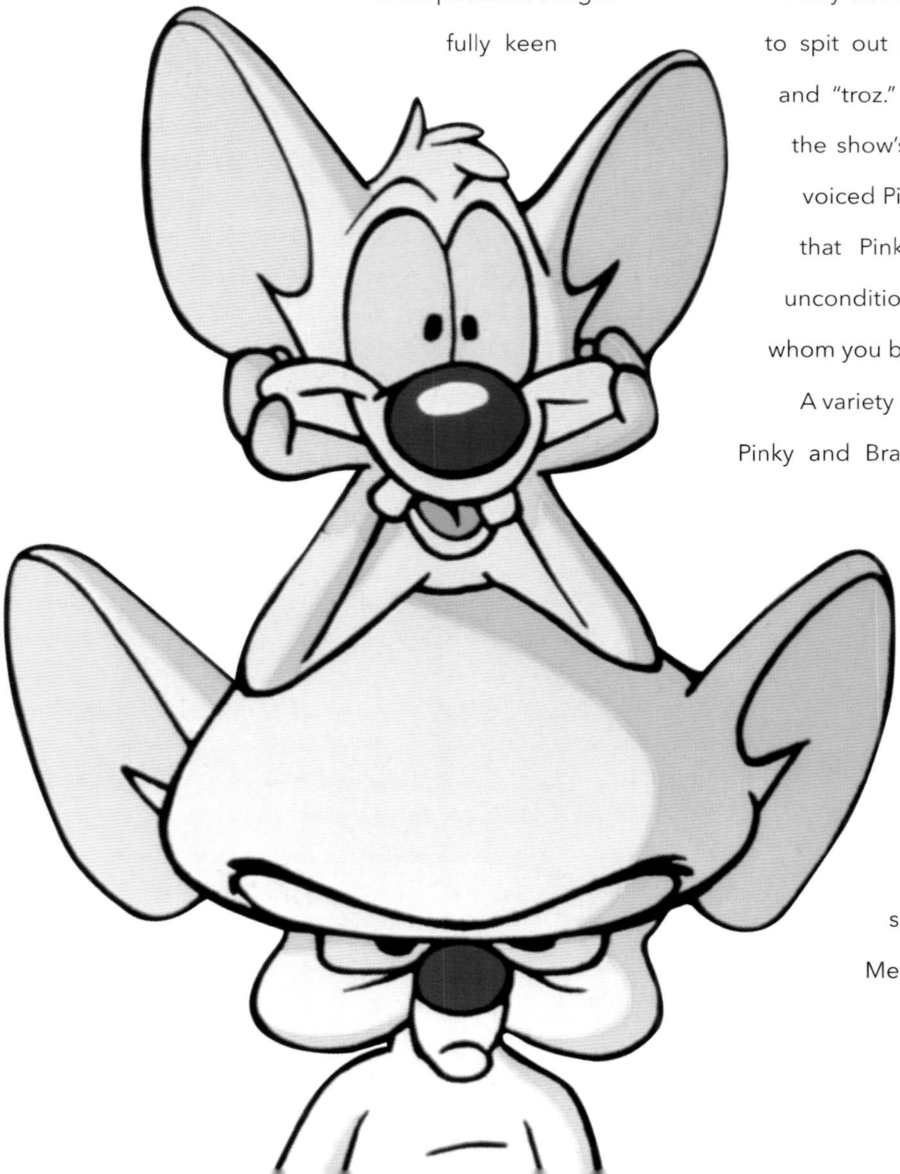

BOTTOM: Pinky and his pal Brain.

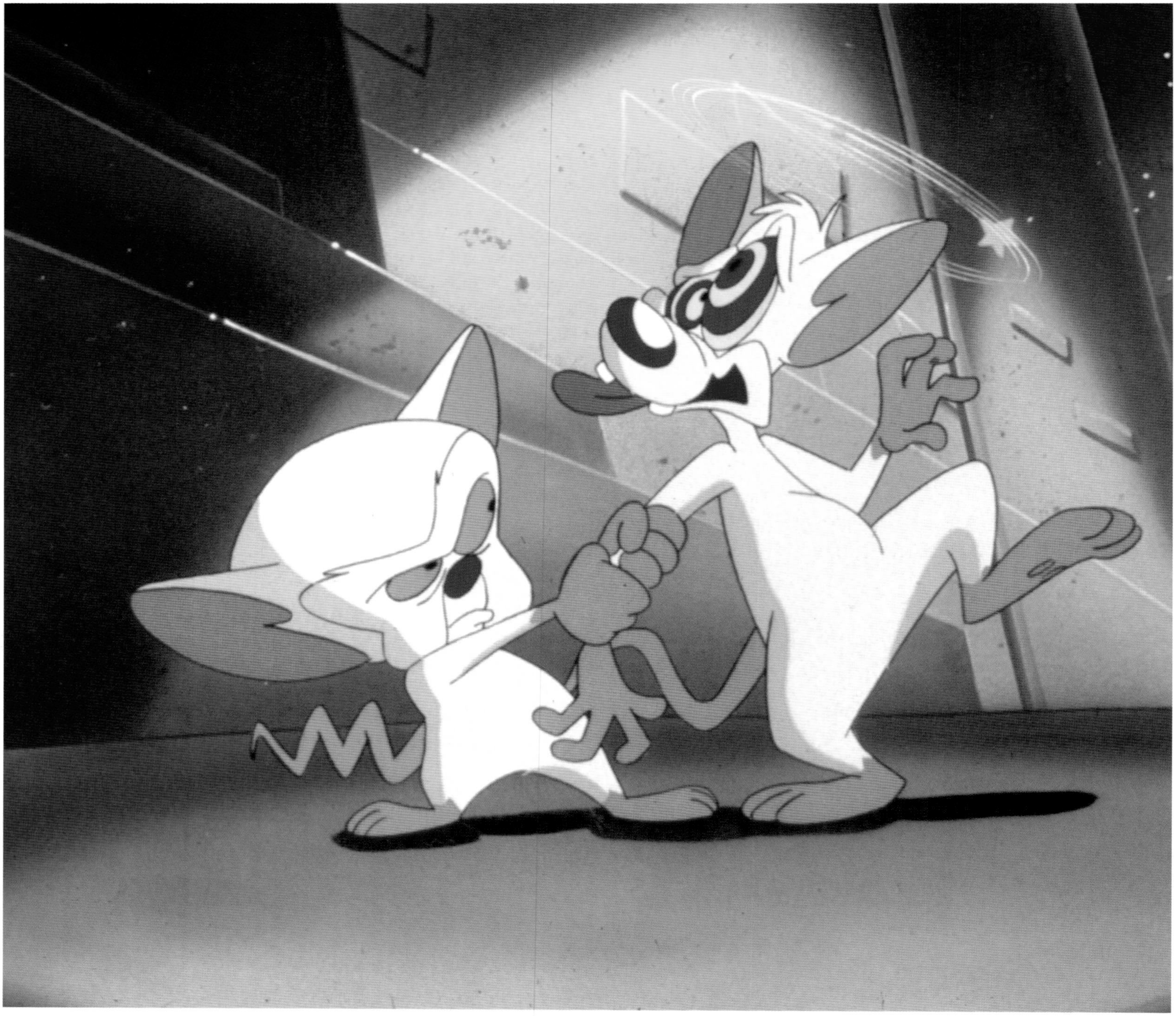

ABOVE: Pinky suffers the effects of another plot gone awry.

was eventually introduced in response to demands from WB executives to expand the number of characters. Modeled after Larry from The Three Stooges, the writers made a joke of hastily inserting him into the credits: *"They're Pinky and the Brain (and Larry), yes Pinky and the Brain (and Larry), one is a genius, the other's insane (and the other one's Larry)."*

Though Brain could theoretically be considered an archvillain based on his unquenchable thirst for power, the character's nemesis was Snowball, a cute hamster with a pronounced egg-shaped cranium who also longed to take over the world. In their 2018 book, *A Celebration of Animation: The 100 Greatest Cartoon Characters in Television History,* Marty Gitlin and Joe Wos, name Pinky and Brain as number fifteen and suggest the duo are not villains. "They are heroes. Brain's motives are purely for the betterment of humanity. As he sees it, he is the only mouse for the job!" Despite all of his foibles and shortcomings, Brain viewed his desired ascendancy as a boon for the planet. "Now, The Brain, although he may have had his subversive reasons for wanting to take over the world, he never hurt anybody," said Paulsen. "It was never about hurting . . . it was about, 'I can help you all, just trust me. I'm a megalomaniac.'"

The series turned out to be the kind of hit show the WB needed in its initial broadcasting foray. Also a critical success, the series won a 1996 Emmy® for "A Pinky and the Brain Christmas," in which the duo tries to trick Santa into delivering hypnotic presents to brainwash the masses. The series went on to spur another spin-off, the ill-fated *Pinky, Elmyra, and the Brain* (1998), which only lasted one season.

Similar to its predecessor, *Animaniacs,* the show's humor skewed toward more adult themes. Even so, it handily won over children with its brilliant ridiculousness. Some jokes sailed over kids' heads, but they could always laugh at Pinky's stupidity and all of the hilarious physical comedy. Are you pondering what we're pondering? We think so, Brain, but first you gotta pick up the phone and ask for the twenty-first-century reboot.

ABOVE: If it were easy, everyone would take over the world. At least once.

Best Laid Plans

Time and again, the hapless duo missed their target for global domination. But not for lack of trying. Brain never seemed to run out of audacious schemes. Here are a few gems:

- Episode—"Bubba Bo Bob Brain": Brain attempts to wrest control of society by becoming a country music performer by the name of Bubba Bo Bob Brain (managed by Pinky, naturally). His plan? Plant a subliminal message in his songs to compel the masses.

- Episode—"Ambulatory Abe": Brain utilizes ventriloquism to convince the people he is the reincarnated soul of Abraham Lincoln.

- Episode—"It's Only a Paper World": Upon creating "Chia Earth," an alternate planet composed of papier-mâché, Brain attempts to lure people into it based on the promise of free T-shirts. Unfortunately, a comet demolishes the real Earth, forcing Brain and Pinky to relocate to their new planet. v

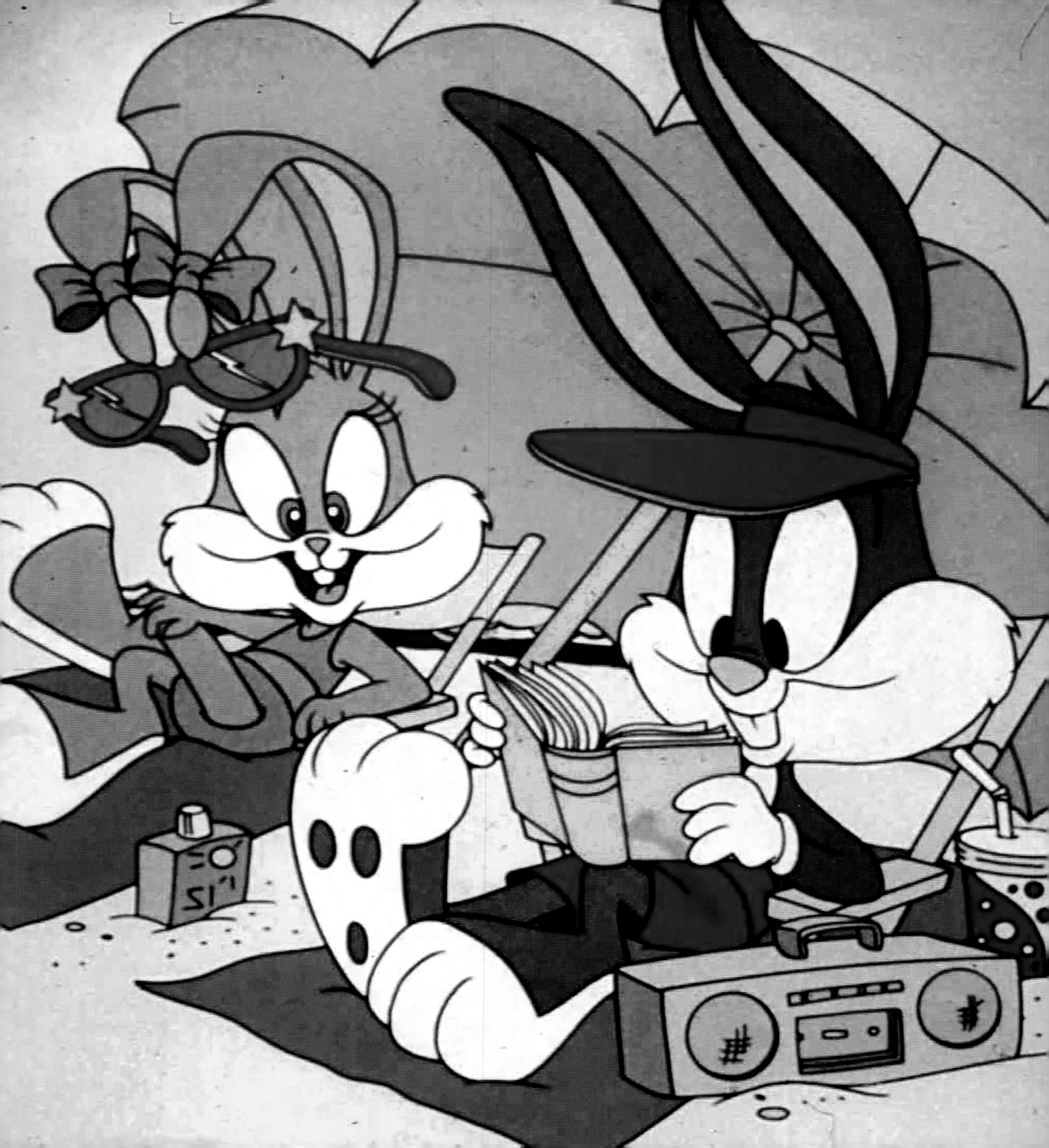

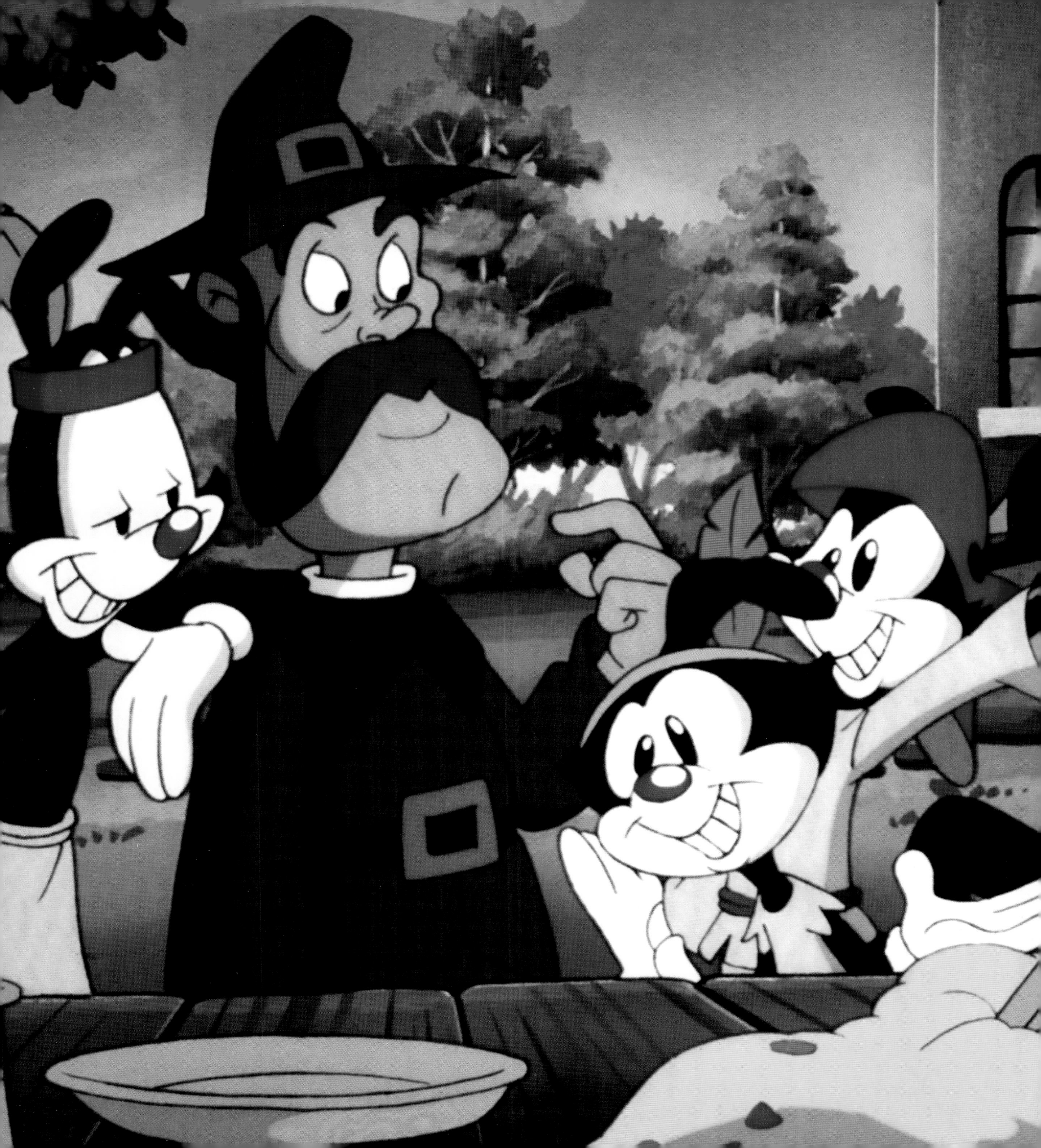

Epilogue

A host of economic and social factors drove the collective Saturday morning cartoon experience to extinction, including the landmark TV mandate of 1996 requiring educational broadcast programs for kids and limiting advertising. Even before this, the big networks had been slowly abandoning their animated lineups.

Before cable dominated the television market, the bulk of households relied on NBC, ABC, and CBS for their viewing options. As the twentieth century drew to a close, however, new cable and satellite channels cropped up. These avoided the purview of the FCC's strict guidelines. They could also get away with a lot of things the networks couldn't, like reduced educational content and more advertising, thus making it more profitable to produce shows. In addition, cable's splintering into specific niches allowed whole channels, such as Cartoon Network, to play nothing but animation all day, every day.

At the same time cable and satellite channels proliferated, competing entertainment options exploded, including the biggest juggernaut of them all: the internet. An array of video game platforms also emerged, shrinking the number of potential viewers. As the internet's reach became more ubiquitous, streaming video via sites such as YouTube allowed anyone to watch anything at any time. By this time, Saturday morning cartoons belonged to a bygone era anyway.

After fifty years, the last animation block officially disappeared from network TV in the fall of 2014. The big three had long since abandoned the model, but the *CW* still held on for a time with its batch of Vortexx cartoons, such as *Sonic X*, *Dragon Ball Z*. Like all good things, Saturday morning cartoons had finally come to an end. However, as author Gladys Hasty Carroll once wrote, "Nothing lasts forever on this earth. But whatever's good comes back every once in a while if you let it."

We hope this book brought some good memories back to you—something worth sharing with all the other kids-at-heart who really miss Kidsday.

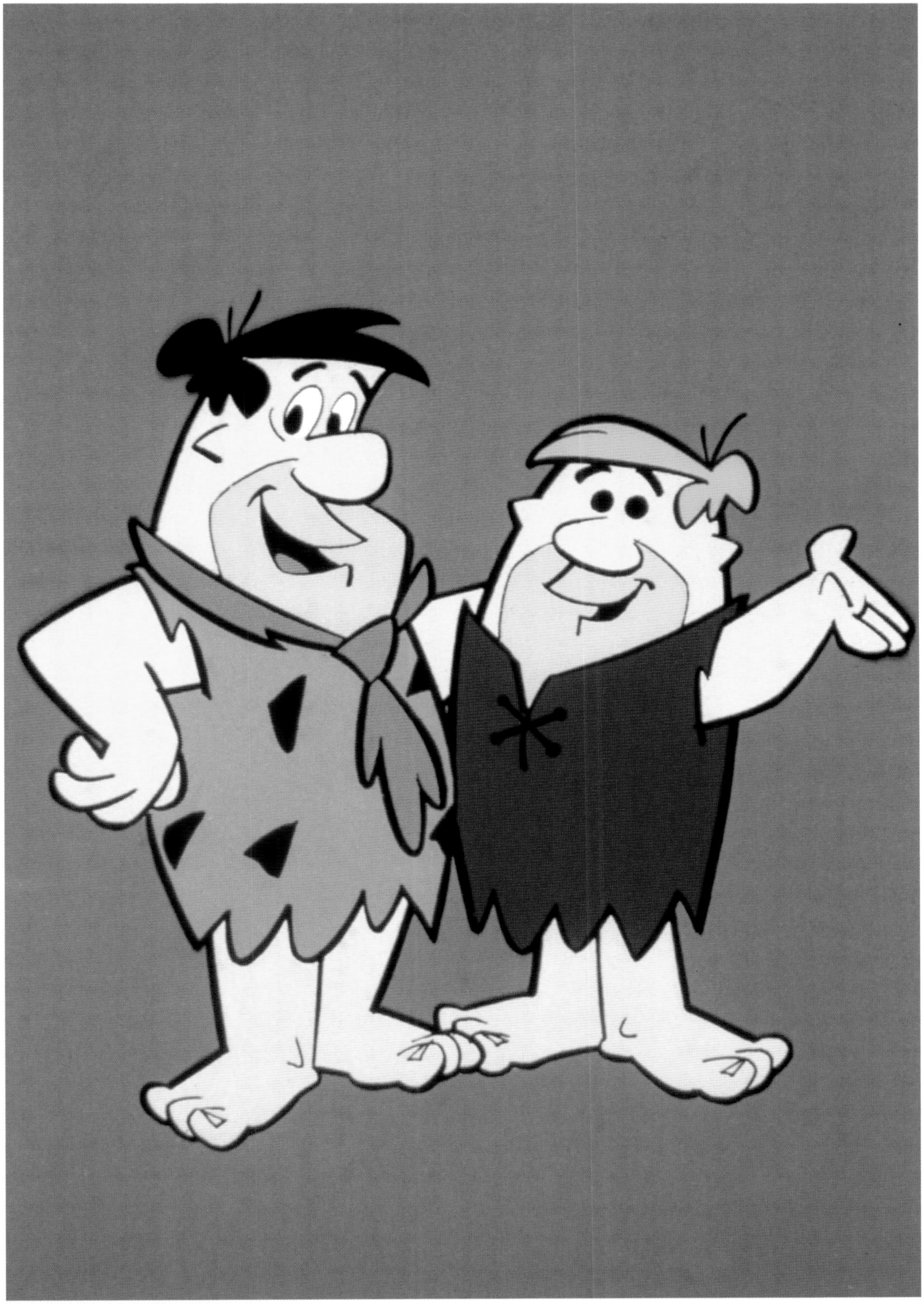

LEFT: Fred Flintstone and Barney Rubble, next door neighbors and fellow members of the Water Buffalo lodge, made a lasting impression on Saturday morning cartoons.

Acknowledgments

First, our profound gratitude goes to our amazing editor and publisher Delia Greve and all of the wonderfully talented folks at Quarto and becker&mayer! for putting this book together.

We are extremely grateful to Howie Mandel for sharing his personal passion for—and his professional experience in—Saturday morning cartoons. And a big thank you goes to Rich Thurber in Howie's office for his invaluable help in coordinating Howie's foreword.

Thank you to Julie Heath, V.P. Clip and Still Licensing and her team at Warner Bros.; Image Permissions Team at Disney Enterprises, Inc., Image Permissions Team at Marvel, Inc.; Marvel Entertainment, Inc., Kathy Carpano, Global Communications, Hasbro, Inc; Swayze at Hasbro Studios; Kim Campbell Beasley and Bob Beasley at Paws, Inc., Jill Bollettieri and Blaise Hill at Post Consumer Brands, LLC. Margaret McLean, Director of Corporate Communications Cabbage Patch Kids.

A considerable amount of research went into this project, so we are grateful to Michael's team members Megan Sandberg and Daniela Hristeva.

Joe Garner

My sincerest gratitude goes to Michael, my collaborator, for his boundless enthusiasm, exceptional talent, and creativity. I had a blast working with him on this book.

A special thank you to my friend and kindred spirit in all things pop culture (especially '70s pop culture) Wally Wingert. An incredibly talented and versatile voice actor, Wally's knowledge of the cartoon world was invaluable.

I remain eternally grateful to my parents, Jim and Betty Garner, for their love and their encouragement to always dream big.

To my son James and daughter Jillian, I am so grateful for their love and support. It fuels me every day.

And to Laura Swanson, for her unwavering encouragement, advice, astute business sense, devoted friendship, and her profound love.

Michael Ashley

This book would not be possible without the unconditional support of my loving, brilliant wife Valerie. Not only has she always encouraged my writing career, she continues to be my dedicated partner, advisor, and of course, #1 proofreader and critic.

I am grateful to my parents for their love and guidance. I would like to thank these close family members and friends who have always been there for me, backing and inspiring me: Janet Brakensiek, Cynthia Seltzer, Nancy Miller, Kevin and Erin Seltzer, Blake and Courtney Hamilton, Donald and Carla Shepherd, Tyler and Ashley Dockins, Charles Borg, Louis Mendiola, Peter and Emmy Schroeder, Aaron Margolis, Evan Howard, Matt Watkins, Christopher Hodson, Bryan Swaim, Charlie Woodward, Chris Frazier, Judy Rawdon, Les Weinberg, Zach Laurie, Lisa Caprelli, Alicia Dunams, Amir Motlagh, Tom Flynn, Jaime Morgans, Larry and Lorna Collins, Milly Trejo, Bryan Clinton, and Willie Talbert.

A big thank you is due to Joe Garner, my esteemed partner and mentor. I am also thankful to these mentors: David Crespy, Ron Friedman, Dave Kost, Behzad Mohit, Paul Wolansky, Barbara Jaworski, and Cindy Cowan.

Last, I would like to thank my little boy Theodore London who reminds me to never stop laughing and enjoy life.

About the Authors

Joe Garner

Joe Garner is a six-time *New York Times* bestselling author. His book, *We Interrupt This Broadcast*, not only hit the *New York Times* bestseller list, it was a *Wall Street Journal*, *USA Today*, and *Publisher's Weekly* bestseller.

Among his other bestsellers are *Now Showing: Unforgettable Moments from the Movies* and his comedy history, *Made You Laugh: The Funniest Moments in Radio, Television, Stand-Up and Movie Comedy*. He documented the greatest moments in NFL history in *100 Yards of Glory*, his fourth collaboration with famed sportscaster Bob Costas. His latest, *Jeff Gordon: His Dream, Drive & Destiny*, the first-ever authorized biography of the racing legend, was Garner's sixth *New York Times* bestseller.

Michael Ashley

A former consultant for Disney, Michael Ashley worked as a reader for Creative Artists Agency's Literary Department. Michael began his writing career as a reporter for the *Columbia Missourian* and has served as a columnist for publications, such as *Newsbase*. The co-author of several books, including *The Six-Figure Writer*, *Fiction in a Weekend*, and *Evolution by God*, he has also ghostwritten two Amazon number one bestsellers.

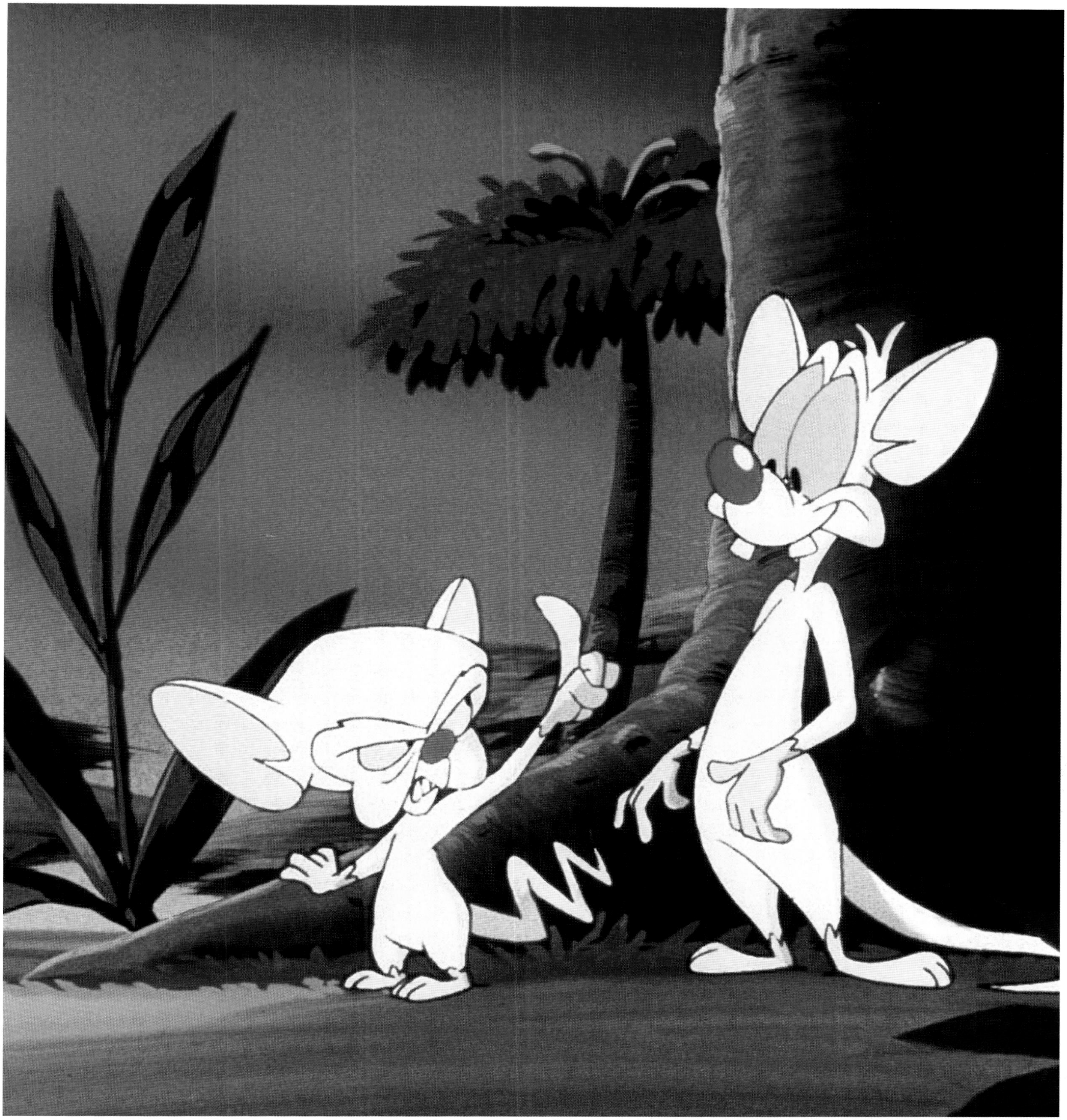

Image Credits

Cover: (Top Left) Courtesy Everett Collection; (Top Center) ©Columbia Pictures/Courtesy Everett Collection; (Top Right) ©Hanna-Barbera/Courtesy Everett Collection; (Middle Left) Courtesy Everett Collection; (Middle Right) ©Hanna-Barbera/Courtesy Everett Collection; (Bottom Left) ©Warner Bros/Courtesy Everett Collection; (Bottom Center) Courtesy Everett Collection; (Bottom Right) Courtesy Everett Collection

Back Cover: carlos cardetas/Alamy Stock Photo

Page 2: (Top Left) ©Twentieth Century Fox/Courtesy Everett Collection; (Top Right) Courtesy of Battle of the Planets.info; (Bottom Left) ©Hanna-Barbera/Courtesy Everett Collection; (Bottom Right) ©Hanna-Barbera/Courtesy Everett Collection

Page 6: Courtesy Everett Collection

Page 9: (Top Left) RGR Collection/Alamy Stock Photo; (Top Right) ©Columbia Pictures/Courtesy Everett Collection; (Bottom) ©Hanna-Barbera/Courtesy Everett Collection

Page 11: ©20th Century Fox/Courtesy Everett Collection

Page 12: Courtesy Howie Mandel

Page 15: Courtesy Everett Collection

Page 16: ©Hanna-Barbera/Courtesy Everett Collection

Page 17: ©Warner Bros/Courtesy Everett Collection

Pages 18 & 19: (Top Left) ©Hanna-Barbera/Courtesy Everett Collection; (Top Center) Courtesy Everett Collection; (Top Right) ©Hanna-Barbera/Courtesy Everett Collection; (Bottom Left) Courtesy Everett Collection; (Bottom Center) Courtesy Everett Collection; (The Jetsons) Warner Bros./Handout

Page 20: Licensed By: Warner Bros. Entertainment Inc. All Rights Reserved.

Page 21: (Top) Boris Spremo/Contributor; (Bottom) Lawrence K. Ho/Contributor

Page 22: Courtesy Everett Collection

Page 23: (Top) RGR Collection/Alamy Stock Photo; (Bottom) Licensed By: Warner Bros. Entertainment Inc. All Rights Reserved.

Page 24: (Left) CSU Archives/Everett Collection; (Right) Archive Photos/Stringer

Page 25: (Left) Bettmann/Contributor; (Right) Richard Watkins/Alamy Stock Photo

Page 26: Licensed By: Warner Bros. Entertainment Inc. All Rights Reserved.

Page 27: Courtesy Everett Collection

Page 28: (Top) Licensed By: Warner Bros. Entertainment Inc. All Rights Reserved.; (Center) Allan Grant/Contributor

Page 29: (Top) Courtesy Everett Collection; (Bottom) Licensed By: Warner Bros. Entertainment Inc. All Rights Reserved.

Page 30: Courtesy Everett Collection

Page 31: ABC Photo Archives/©ABC/Getty Images

Page 32: ©Hanna-Barbera/Courtesy Everett Collection

Page 33: ©Hanna-Barbera/Courtesy Everett Collection

Page 34: Licensed By: Warner Bros. Entertainment Inc. All Rights Reserved.

Page 35: Licensed By: Warner Bros. Entertainment Inc. All Rights Reserved.

Page 36: Courtesy Everett Collection

Page 37: (Top Left) CLEO Photo/Alamy Stock Photo; (Bottom Left) digitalreflections/Shutterstock.com; (Right) MBI/Alamy Stock Photo

Page 38: ©Hanna-Barbera/Courtesy Everett Collection

Page 39: Courtesy Everett Collection

Page 40: Licensed By: Warner Bros. Entertainment Inc. All Rights Reserved.

Page 41: ©Hanna-Barbera/Courtesy Everett Collection

Page 42: AF archive/Alamy Stock Photo

Page 43: Courtesy Everett Collection

Page 44: New York Daily News Archive/Contributor

Page 45: Courtesy Everett Collection

Page 46: Pictorial Press Ltd/Alamy Stock Photo

Page 47: Michael Ochs Archives/Stringer

Page 48: Bobby Bank/Contributor

Page 49: Michael Ochs Archives/Stringer

Page 50: With Permission of Post Consumer Brands, LLC

Page 51: ©Hanna-Barbera/Courtesy Everett Collection

Page 52: ©Hanna-Barbera/Courtesy Everett Collection

Page 53: Frazer Harrison/Staff

Page 54: Courtesy Everett Collection

Page 55: ©Hanna-Barbera/Courtesy Everett Collection

Page 56: Courtesy Everett Collection

Page 57: Courtesy Everett Collection

Page 58: Licensed By: Warner Bros. Entertainment Inc. All Rights Reserved.

Page 59: Courtesy Everett Collection

Pages 60 & 61: (Top Left) Courtesy Everett Collection; (Top Center) Courtesy Everett Collection; (Top Right) Courtesy Everett Collection; (Bottom Left) ©Hanna-Barbera/Courtesy Everett Collection; (Bottom Center) Courtesy Everett Collection; (Scooby Doo) ©Warner Bros/Courtesy Everett Collection

Page 62: Courtesy Everett Collection

Page 63: Courtesy Everett Collection

Page 64: Courtesy Everett Collection

Page 65: Courtesy Everett Collection

Page 66: Courtesy Everett Collection

Page 67: Courtesy Everett Collection

Page 68: Ben Olender/Contributor

Page 69: ©Warner Bros/Courtesy Everett Collection

Page 70: Courtesy Everett Collection

Page 71: ©Hanna-Barbera/Courtesy Everett Collection

Page 72: ©Hanna-Barbera/Courtesy Everett Collection

Page 73: AF archive/Alamy Stock Photo

Page 74: Licensed By: Warner Bros. Entertainment Inc. All Rights Reserved.

Page 75: Michael Ochs Archives/Stringer

Page 76: Licensed By: Warner Bros. Entertainment Inc. All Rights Reserved.

Page 77: ©Hanna-Barbera/Courtesy Everett Collection

Page 78: Cabeca de Marmore/Shutterstock.com

Page 79: Courtesy Everett Collection

Page 80: Courtesy Everett Collection

Page 81: Courtesy Everett Collection

Page 82: Courtesy Everett Collection

Page 83: Courtesy Everett Collection

Page 84: Courtesy Everett Collection

Page 85: Courtesy Everett Collection

Page 86: Courtesy Everett Collection

Page 87: Kari Rene Hall/Contributor

Page 88: (Top) Courtesy Everett Collection; (Bottom) Kari Rene Hall/Contributor

Page 89: Courtesy Everett Collection

Page 90: With Permission of Post Consumer Brands LLC

Page 91: Courtesy Everett Collection

Page 92: Courtesy Everett Collection

Page 93: (Top) Licensed By: Warner Bros. Entertainment Inc. All Rights Reserved.; (Bottom) Courtesy Everett Collection

Page 94: Courtesy Everett Collection

Page 95: Courtesy Everett Collection

Page 102: Courtesy of Battle of the Planets.info

Page 103: Courtesy Everett Collection

Page 104: Courtesy of Battle of the Planets.info

Page 105: Courtesy of Battle of the Planets.info

Page 106: Courtesy of Battle of the Planets.info

Page 107: Courtesy of Battle of the Planets.info

Page 108: Licensed By: Warner Bros. Entertainment Inc. All Rights Reserved.

Page 109: Courtesy Everett Collection

Pages 110 & 111: (Top Left) Courtesy Everett Collection; (Top Center) Courtesy Everett Collection; (Top Right) Mary Evans Picture Library/Everett Collection; (Bottom Left) ©DIC Enterprises/Courtesy Everett Collection; (Bottom Center) G.I. Joe: A Real American Hero/Courtesy of Hasbro Studios LLC; (Smurfs) carlos cardetas/Alamy Stock Photo

Page 112: ©Hanna-Barbera/Courtesy Everett Collection

Page 113: Marc Deville/Contributor

Page 114: (Top) Patrick Kovarik/Staff; (Bottom) Mary Evans Picture Library/Everett Collection

Page 115: GAB Archive/Contributor

Page 116: ©Hanna-Barbera/Courtesy Everett Collection

Page 117: (Left) carlos cardetas/Alamy Stock Photo; (Right) ©Hanna-Barbera/Courtesy Everett Collection

Page 118: Courtesy Everett Collection

Page 119: Michael Ochs Archives

Page 120: Courtesy Everett Collection

Page 121: Courtesy Everett Collection

Page 122: Courtesy Everett Collection

Page 123: DWD-photo/Alamy Stock Photo

Page 124: Courtesy Everett Collection

Page 125: Mirrorpix/Contributor

Page 126: ©Mattel Inc./Courtesy Everett Collection

Page 127: Courtesy Everett Collection

Page 128: Courtesy Everett Collection

Page 129: ©Disney

Page 130: ©Disney

Page 131: ©Disney

Page 132: Mary Evans Picture Library/Everett Collection

Page 133: Mary Evans Picture Library/Everett Collection

Page 134: www.benstoybarn.com/Alamy Stock Photo

Page 135: ©De Laurentiis Group/Courtesy Everett Collection

Page 136: (Left) Chris Willson/Alamy Stock Photo; (Right) Everett Collection, Inc./Alamy Stock Photo

Page 137: ©DIC Enterprises/Courtesy Everett Collection

Page 138: (Top) Mary Evans Picture Library/Everett Collection; (Bottom) ©DIC Enterprises/Courtesy Everett Collection

Page 139: ©Cineplex-Odeon Pictures/Courtesy Everett Collection

Page 140: Courtesy Everett Collection

Page 141: ©Columbia Pictures/Courtesy Everett Collection

Page 142: ©Cabbage Patch Kids

Page 143: Courtesy Everett Collection

Page 144: G.I. Joe: A Real American Hero/Courtesy of Hasbro Studios LLC

Page 145: G.I. Joe: A Real American Hero/Courtesy of Hasbro Studios LLC

Page 146: Keith Homan/Alamy Stock Photo

Page 147: Mary Evans Picture Library/Everett Collection

Page 148: (Left) Courtesy Friedman Family; (Right) G.I. Joe: A Real American Hero/Courtesy of Hasbro Studios LLC

Page 149: G.I. Joe: A Real American Hero/Courtesy of Hasbro Studios LLC

Page 150: ©Disney

Page 151: ©Disney

Page 153: ©Disney

Page 154: Courtesy Everett Collection

Page 155: Courtesy Everett Collection

Page 156: Courtesy Everett Collection

Page 157: Tim Mosenfelder/Contributor

Page 158: John D. Kisch/Separate Cinema Archive/Contributor

Page 159: Courtesy Everett Collection

Page 160: CBS Photo Archive/Contributor

Page 161: Michael Ochs Archives/Stringer

Page 162: John D. Kisch/Separate Cinema Archive/Contributor

Page 163: (Left) John D. Kisch/Separate Cinema Archive/Contributor; (Right) ©CBS/Courtesy Everett Collection

Page 164: John D. Kisch/Separate Cinema Archive/Contributor

Page 165: James Keyser/Contributor

Page 166: ©Paws. Used by Permission.

Page 167: Thomas S. England/Contributor

Page 168: CBS Photo Archive/Contributor

Page 169: carlos cardetas/Alamy Stock Photo

Page 170: ©Paws. Used by Permission.

Page 171: (Top) ©Paws. Used by Permission.; (Bottom) ©20th Century Fox/Courtesy Everett Collection

Page 172: ©Hanna-Barbera/Courtesy Everett Collection

Page 173: ©USA Networks/Courtesy Everett Collection

Page 174 & 175: (Top Left) Courtesy Everett Collection; (Top Center) United Archives GmbH/Alamy Stock Photo; (Top Right) ©Warner Bros/Courtesy Everett Collection; (Bottom Left) ©Warner Bros/Courtesy Everett Collection; (Bottom Center) ©20th Century Fox/Courtesy Everett Collection; (Pinky and the Brain) Courtesy Everett Collection

Page 176: ©Group W. Productions/Courtesy Everett Collection

Page 177: ©Group W. Productions/Courtesy Everett Collection

Page 178: Courtesy Everett Collection

Page 179: (Top) ©Group W. Productions/Courtesy Everett Collection; (Bottom) Courtesy Everett Collection

Page 180: ©New Line Cinema/Courtesy Everett Collection

Page 181: (Left) Game Shots/Alamy Stock Photo; (Right) Paul Harris/Contributor

Page 182: ©20th Century Fox/Courtesy Everett Collection

Page 183: United Archives GmbH/Alamy Stock Photo

Page 184: United Archives GmbH/Alamy Stock Photo

Page 185: (Left) Michael Ochs Archives/Stringer; (Right) ©20th Century Fox/Courtesy Everett Collection

Page 186: ©20th Century Fox/Courtesy Everett Collection

Page 187: (Left) Amy Graves/Contributor; (Top Right) JHPhoto/Alamy Stock Photo; (Bottom Right) Tosca White/Alamy Stock Photo

Page 188: United Archives GmbH/Alamy Stock Photo

Page 189: Licensed by: Warner Bros. Entertainment Inc. All Rights Reserved.

Page 190: United Archives GmbH/Alamy Stock Photo

Page 191: United Archives GmbH/Alamy Stock Photo

Page 192: United Archives GmbH/Alamy Stock Photo

Page 193: Licensed by: Warner Bros. Entertainment Inc. All Rights Reserved.

Page 194: ©Disney

Page 196: ©Disney

Page 197: (Top Left) Michael Germana/Everett Collection; (Top Right) ZUMA Press, Inc./Alamy Stock Photo; (Bottom Left) Stephen Shugerman/Stringer; (Bottom Right) Kurt Krieger - Corbis/Contributor

Page 198: ©Disney

Page 199: With Permission of Post Consumer Brands, LLC

Page 200: ©Warner Bros/Courtesy Everett Collection

Page 201: RGR Collection/Alamy Stock Photo

Page 202: ©Warner Bros/Courtesy Everett Collection

Page 203: (Top) Mathew Imaging/Contributor; (Middle) Craig Barritt/Stringer; (Bottom) Michael Tullberg/Contributor

Page 204: (Top) ©Warner Bros/Courtesy Everett Collection; (Bottom) United Archives GmbH/Alamy Stock Photo

Page 205: ©Warner Bros/Courtesy Everett Collection

Page 206: ©Warner Bros/Courtesy Everett Collection

Page 207: David J. Green/Alamy Stock Photo

Page 208: ©Warner Bros/Courtesy Everett Collection

Page 209: ©Warner Bros/Courtesy Everett Collection

Page 210: Tim Mosenfelder/Contributor

Page 211: ©Warner Bros/Courtesy Everett Collection

Page 212: ©Warner Bros/Courtesy Everett Collection

Page 213: ©Warner Bros/Courtesy Everett Collection

Page 214: United Archives GmbH/Alamy Stock Photo

Page 215: ©Warner Bros/Courtesy Everett Collection

Page 217: Courtesy Everett Collection

Page 218: Courtesy Everett Collection

Page 219: Courtesy Everett Collection

Page 221: AF archive/Alamy Stock Photo

Page 224: ©Hanna-Barbera/Courtesy Everett Collection

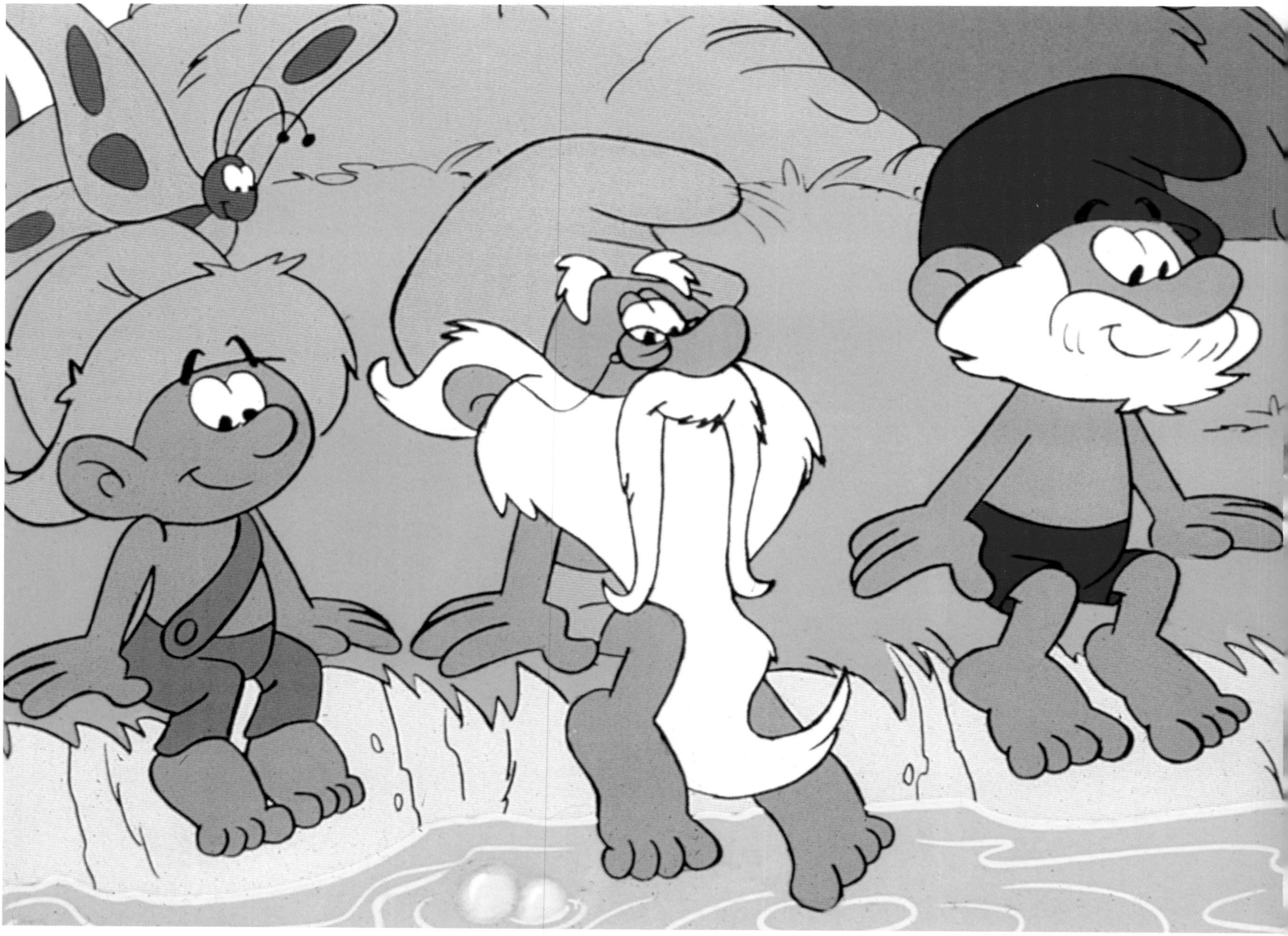